Fundamentals of Social Research Methods
An African Perspective

Fundamentals of Social Research Methods
An African Perspective

Fifth Edition

Claire Bless
Craig Higson-Smith
Sello Levy Sithole

Fundamentals of Social Research Methods: An African Perspective

First edition by C Bless and P Achola
published in Lusaka, Zambia, in 1988

Second edition 1995
Reprinted 1997
Third edition 2000
Fourth edition 2006
Reprinted 2007
Reprinted 2008
Reprinted 2009
Reprinted 2011
Fifth edition 2013
Reprinted February 2013
Reprinted March 2014
Reprinted August 2015
Reprinted June 2016

Juta and Company Ltd
First Floor
Sunclare Building
21 Dreyer Street
Claremont
7708
PO Box 14373, Lansdowne, 7779, Cape Town, South Africa

© 2013 Juta & Company Ltd

ISBN 978-0-70218-683-7

All rights reserved. No part of this publication may be reproduced or transmitted in any
form or by any means, electronic or mechanical, including photocopying, recording, or any
information storage or retrieval system, without prior permission in writing from the publisher.
Subject to any applicable licensing terms and conditions in the case of electronically supplied
publications, a person may engage in fair dealing with a copy of this publication for his or
her personal or private use, or his or her research or private study. See Section 12(1)(a) of the
Copyright Act 98 of 1978.

Project Manager: Martie Oudkerk
Editor: Annette de Villiers
Proofreader: Glynne Newlands
Typesetter: Ink Design
Cover designer: Nicole de Swardt
Indexer: Jenny de Wet
Printed and bound in South Africa by Formeset Print

Typeset in Times New Roman 10.5 pt on 13. 5 pt

The authors and the publisher believe on the strength of due diligence exercised that this work
does not contain any material that is the subject of copyrights held by another person. In the
alternative, they believe that any protected pre-existing material that may be compromised in it
has been used with appropriate authority or has been used in circumstances that make such use
permissible under law.

Contents

Preface x

Note on the authors xiv

CHAPTER 1
The different methods of acquiring knowledge 1

Non-scientific methods of acquiring knowledge 1

The scientific method and its properties 4

Properties of scientific research 8

CHAPTER 2
The scientific method applied to social reality 12

The distinction between natural and social sciences 12

Relationship between facts and theory 13

Quantitative, qualitative and the mixed-method approaches 15

Developing theory from facts 18

Steps in scientific research 20

CHAPTER 3
Research ethics 25

The need for ethics in research 25

Researchers' social responsibility in developing countries 27

What are research ethics? 28

Principles of ethical research 29

Important ethical guidelines 31

A final word about ethics 36

Appendix: Example of an informed consent form 39

CHAPTER 4
Problem conception and background information 41

Sources and identification of research problems 41

Literature review 49

Other background information 53

Chapter 5

The types of research 56
Ways of classifying research 56
Quantitative, qualitative and mixed-methods research 58
Basic and applied research 59
Exploratory, descriptive, correlational and explanatory research 60
Demonstrating causality 63
Research and the internet 68

Chapter 6

Research questions and variables 71
Formulation of the research question 71
Concepts, variables and constants 72
Identification of the variables 73
Conceptual and operational definitions 80
Hypothesis formulation 82

Chapter 7

Participatory and action research 89
Participation in knowledge generation 89
Steps in action research 90
Using action research in developing countries 97

Chapter 8

Research and community development 101
Research and community projects 101
Needs assessment 102
Pilot projects 107
Feasibility studies 109

Chapter 9

Project monitoring and evaluation 113
Project indicators 113
Project monitoring 118
Project evaluation 119

Contents

Chapter 10
Research planning and design 130
What is a research design? 130
The focus of research 132
The unit of analysis 133
The time dimension 135
Types of research design 136
Pre-experimental designs 138
Quasi-experimental designs 142
Experimental designs 146
Developing a research design 153
Summary of sources of bias in research design 154
Relationship between internal and external validity 157

Chapter 11
Sampling 161
The purpose and types of sampling 161
Sampling theory 162
Main sampling concepts 164
Probability sampling for quantitative research 167
Non-probability sampling for quantitative research 172
Other sampling possibilities 173
Sample size: How large should a sample be? 174
Sampling errors and related problems 175
Sampling for qualitative research 175
The importance of good sampling 179

Chapter 12
Data collection: Basic concepts and techniques 183
Facts, data and measurement 183
Relationship between types of research and methods of data collection 184
Scales of measurement 185
Methods of data collection 187
Data collection in practice 202

Chapter 13
Ensuring the quality of data 220
Quantitative research: Reliability and validity of measurements 221
Reliability 222
Validity 229
Balancing reliability and validity 235

vii

Qualitative research: Ensuring trustworthiness 236
Scientific rigour in mixed-methods research 240

CHAPTER 14
Quantitative data analysis and interpretation 245
Part I: Descriptive statistics 245
    Data representation: Frequency distributions and tables 245
    Measures of central tendency 254
    Measures of variability or dispersion 260
Part II: Inferential statistics 264
    Distributions 264
    Hypothesis testing and statistical tests 272
    Parametric tests: Comparing means 283
    Non-parametric tests 295
    Non-parametric tests for independent samples 301
    Non-parametric tests for dependent samples 305
    Correlations and scatter graphs 309
    Regression and time series 318
    Managing missing data 324
    Use and abuse of statistics 324

CHAPTER 15
Qualitative data analysis and interpretation 338
Fundamental themes in qualitative analysis 338
High quality qualitative data 340
Qualitative analysis of unstructured data 341
Qualitative analysis of structured data 347
Coding from theory 351
More advanced forms of qualitative research 352
Final comments on the quality of qualitative analysis 353

CHAPTER 16
Research findings and dissemination 356
Interpreting the findings: Detection of possible errors 356
Drawing conclusions 362
Ways of disseminating findings 363
Organisation of a research report 365
Guidelines for writing 369

Contents

CHAPTER 17
Research management 374
The research world.......374
Science and values.......376
The role of research-funding institutions.......377
Planning and managing a research project.......379
Conclusion: Highest quality research.......383

Bibliography.......385

Glossary.......389

Index.......396

Preface

The first edition of *Fundamentals of Social Research Methods: An African Perspective* was conceived by Claire Bless in Zambia in 1988 in response to a need for an accessible textbook on social research methods in African contexts. It was observed that many African government, non-government and private-sector organisations were starting to attach greater value to social research and the information it provides. As a result, more and more people entering the workplace were expected to be able to design and implement their own problem-centred research projects, and to evaluate the research work of others.

Twenty-five years later many things have changed, and yet the importance of building a larger pool of Africans who are able to conduct social research of the highest quality remains.

The original edition of this book was written as a resource for non-professional researchers and students of research methods. This group included, and still does, university students, government administrators, community activists, business managers, social workers, educationists and any other people interested in conducting social research. It also aims at assisting social scientists who, although familiar with the research process, would like to refresh some aspects of their knowledge. The content finds direct application in a wide variety of fields, including community development, public health, agricultural extension and regional planning, to mention only a few.

Early editions were designed to have a strong African focus, and there are few enough texts on social research methods that take such a perspective and that were aimed at people new to social research. These editions were written and organised in a way that conformed to the syllabi of social science methods courses in many African universities at the time.

Subsequent editions, including the current one, have remained true to these principles. As our continent has entered the 21st century, many exciting challenges confront our societies. These challenges are transforming the requirements of social research and placing new demands upon those responsible for training new research-ers. The reader should be aware that the term 'social sciences' is used here in the widest sense to include all sciences referring to society and social issues. Thus it embraces such disciplines as sociology, economics, political science, education, psychology and social work. Throughout the book, examples are drawn from diverse fields, and from actual research done in Africa.

Preface

The present revision, unlike the previous ones, not only updates the material, but also introduces substantial additions. From a book mainly dealing with quantitative research, it has become a textbook covering aspects of quantitative, qualitative and mixed-method research. The text strives to present, in a clear and concise way, the fundamentals of research methods in the social sciences. In this sense, the various topics are not necessarily covered exhaustively and more advanced social researchers should cover more specialised texts. At the very least, the text is a concise introduction that should be expanded, diversified, further elaborated and deepened by lecture notes and supplementary readings.

Further, it is worth stating that we, the authors, believe that the ultimate aim of social science methodology is to enhance the day-to-day lives and circumstances of people. Thus, we aim to provide the reader with the information and skills needed to conduct a research project. For this reason, the chapters essentially follow the steps of the scientific process. Each chapter begins with a general overview of the content followed by a set of outcome-based guidelines designed to assist both the learner and teacher. Each chapter ends with Key points, summarising the main elements introduced in that chapter, a Checklist allowing the students to ensure that they have understood all new concepts, as well as a few points they should consider for their own research. Finally, some exercises that allow the learners to evaluate their own progress, followed by a short list of additional readings, close the chapter.

Chapter 1 opens with a discussion of the usefulness of the scientific method for acquiring knowledge as opposed to other ways by which human beings understand their environment.

Chapter 2 covers the main characteristics of social science and the intrinsic relationship between facts and theory are discussed. This helps to clarify the core components of all research projects.

Chapter 3 deals with the ethics of social research that must be considered early in the process of research planning. For this reason we have moved this chapter closer to the beginning of the book. This chapter also includes a discussion of the use of science in the developing world.

Chapter 4 focuses on the identification of research problems and the process of literature review. Also discussed are sources of background information, an important part of building a complete understanding of the problem at hand.

Chapter 5 presents various types of research with a focus on the differences between descriptive, exploratory, correlational and explanatory research methods. New in this edition is more material on qualitative and mixed-methods research.

Chapter 6 explains the different types of variables in social research and how variables are defined. This chapter also explores the process by which research questions are developed in qualitative research, and hypotheses are formulated in quantitative research.

Chapter 7 is a new chapter which expands on the importance of participation and action in the research process, especially in the developing world.

Chapter 8 is also a new chapter which expands on the discussion of community needs assessments and their importance in development work.

Chapter 9 is a further new chapter which expands the previous edition's discussion of monitoring and evaluation. New in this edition is a discussion of the selection and measurement of appropriate indicators.

Chapter 10 covers research design, and includes a discussion of the focus of research, the unit of analysis and the time dimension. In addition, this chapter covers the most commonly used pre-experimental, quasi-experimental and experimental research designs. Further material on qualitative research design has been added in this fifth edition.

Chapter 11 provides a detailed account of sampling theory as well as a range of techniques for selecting samples. New in this edition is material on sampling for qualitative research.

Chapter 12 deals with data collection. Various aspects of this process, ranging from scales of measurement to the construction of questionnaires and the facilitation of focus groups, are considered. New in this edition is a discussion of internet-based research and emailed questionnaires.

Chapter 13 is much elaborated in this edition and tackles questions of scientific rigour in research. This chapter explores reliability and validity in quantitative research, as well as trustworthiness in qualitative studies.

Chapter 14 is a wholly new chapter which deals with quantitative data analysis. The section on descriptive statistics covers distributions as well as measures of central tendency and dispersion. The section on inferential statistics includes both parametric and non-parametric tests for independent and dependent samples. Much of this material is drawn from the companion text to previous editions of this book, *Fundamentals of Social Statistics: An African Perspective* by Claire Bless and Ravinder Kathuria.

Chapter 15 is another completely new chapter and this one deals with qualitative data analysis. Processes of coding both structured and unstructured data are discussed.

Chapter 16 presents a discussion of the process of drawing conclusions from the results of a research study and looks at ways in which research findings are disseminated. Particular attention is given to the structure and style of research reports.

Chapter 17 is the final chapter of this edition and has been expanded to include a discussion of research management. This chapter closes the textbook by examining more closely the various role players in the world of social research, and the need for social researchers to maintain the highest levels of quality in all their work.

We would like to thank Dr Paul Achola (Kenya) for his contribution to the original version. Although the two chapters authored by him in the first edition have been completely rewritten, his constructive criticisms expressed at the time of first publication are still relevant. We would also like to thank Professor Ashraf Kagee for his work on the Fourth Edition, and Dr Ravinder Kathuria for her work on *Fundamentals of Social Statistics: An African Perspective*, that has served as resource material for Chapter 14 in this edition. Thank you also to Denis Hutchinson and Alan Goss for their work on the text. Many welcome comments and encouragements have come from other colleagues, among them, Dr K Myambo (Zimbabwe), Dr A Maleche (Botswana), Dr H Lemba and Mr D Mulenga (Zambia), Prof. S E Migot-Adholla (Kenya), Ms H Shale (Lesotho) and Ms Tina Uys (South Africa). Thank you to the Research Office of the University of Limpopo, in particular Dr Jessica Singh.

The authors hope to receive comments for further improvements from readers, especially students.

CLAIRE BLESS
CRAIG HIGSON-SMITH
SELLO LEVY SITHOLE

Note on the authors

Claire Bless studied psychology / genetic epistemology with J Piaget at the University of Geneva, Switzerland. She has lectured and conducted research in universities of several African countries and after 10 years of running diversity and training programmes in South Africa, became director of a College of Educational Technology. She is presently an independent consultant in the fields of human resources, executive and leadership coaching, training and facilitation in diversity management, leadership and conflict resolution, as well as social research.

Craig Higson-Smith studied research psychology at the University of Natal and is currently pursuing a doctorate at the University of the Witwatersrand. He works as a researcher with special interests in the areas of war, civil conflict, peace, community intervention and traumatic stress, and he has published several books, journal articles and chapters in these areas. Higson-Smith currently works as an International Monitoring and Evaluation Advisor with the Center for Victims of Torture, supporting projects in many African countries.

Sello Levy Sithole is associate professor in the Department of Social Work at the University of Limpopo-Turfloop campus. He taught a research methodology undergraduate course for all students in the Social Sciences for several years. At present he offers a research methodology module to undergraduate students in the social work programme. He also supervises undergraduate and postgraduate research projects at the University of Limpopo. He took part in several sponsored projects for the government and other commercial concerns. His interests are in Social Policy and Employee Assistance Programmes.

The different methods of acquiring knowledge

CHAPTER

1

In order for society to progress, new knowledge about the world must constantly be generated. Gaining new knowledge involves a process of formulating specific questions and then finding answers to them, in order to gain a better understanding about ourselves and our environment. Social scientists use systematic rational thought and observation to gain knowledge about human beings and the world they inhabit. However, the scientific approach is not the only way of thinking about the world. The study of ways of knowing about the world is called *epistemology*. In this chapter the major methods of acquiring knowledge, or epistemological approaches, are presented. Some methods are more accurate and reliable than others, and the scientific method has clear advantages. The need to adopt a scientific approach as the most appropriate and reliable method becomes obvious as its properties are described in detail. However, due to the complexity of social reality, other, more adaptable, methods also have to be considered.

CHAPTER OBJECTIVES

Learners who have completed this chapter will be able to:
- Describe in detail the various methods by which human beings acquire knowledge, including the scientific method.
- Compare the scientific method with other means of acquiring knowledge.
- Describe and contrast inductive or probabilistic reasoning, and deductive reasoning.
- Discuss reductionism in social science research.

Non-scientific methods of acquiring knowledge

There are many ways of acquiring knowledge about the world. For children, the first source of knowledge is most often their parents or caregivers. This **method of authority** is not only used by children but very commonly by each of us when we rely on the knowledge and 'wisdom' of prominent and significant people who are recognised as having a better grasp of their environment than ordinary people. Thus the statements of these 'qualified' people are rarely questioned or challenged. On the contrary, the knowledge imparted by them is usually accepted as absolute and a certain amount of trust is placed in these authorities as sources of knowledge. Elderly people in a village, who, because of their age, have had more opportunity to accumulate experience in a society where formal education is minimal, are often placed in this position. Other examples would be kings in feudal societies, heads of churches or, in modern societies, technocrats who are regarded as highly specialised persons in a particular field of knowledge. Which lay patient would question the diagnosis of a cardiologist? And how trustful are we of the skills of the specialist who solves our computer problems?

Such a situation is not without dangers. Once individuals are placed in such a position of authority, they often rely on particular strategies to justify and preserve their position. This may take the form of masking their own ignorance with impressive rituals, using a very specialised way of expression (professional jargon), or by emphasising the uniqueness of their position ('it is true because I, *the minister*, say so'). Very often this method allows individuals to hide the superficiality of their knowledge, its underlying ideology, as well as other weaknesses in their argument.

A variation of this 'method of authority' is the **mystical method**, where the correctness of the knowledge is assumed to reside in a supernatural source. In this case the 'knowledge producers' are regarded as authorities due to their ability to transmit the truth or knowledge imparted to them by supernatural forces. In traditional African societies, traditional healers and diviners occupy a central space in the governance of the people because chiefs depend on them. Even patients depend on the traditional healers and seldom question their wisdom.

Whether a person's authority in knowledge is recognised because of their position or because of their presumed supernatural powers, their credibility is strongly related to the level of education and general knowledge of the audience. This is why growing children realise that their parents do not have the answers to all questions and that they even give dubious explanations at times. In the same way, the authority and mystical modes of acquiring knowledge lose influence when better, alternative explanations can be found. The history of the natural sciences is full of examples of mystical explanations being replaced by scientific ones. Who, for example, would still believe that the earth is flat or that it is the centre of the solar system? Some centuries ago, this was the dogma of the Catholic Church, accepted by all Christians as the truth!

The **intuitive method** is another way of making sense of the world. People sometimes make judgements about the world based on what 'feels' right for them. They may not always be able to explain their feelings in a way that makes sense to other people, but they have great faith in these feelings to help guide them in their lives. For example, a doctor may arrive at a diagnosis for a patient because she has an intuitive feeling about the ailment, and may want to prescribe treatment accordingly. In such a situation the doctor may be tempted not to place too much emphasis on the results of laboratory tests but instead to rely on an intuitive sense of the patient's problem.

The problem with intuitive reasoning is that the criteria that the doctor uses to arrive at diagnostic conclusions and make therapeutic decisions are not plain for everyone else to see. Thus others may not come to similar conclusions in the same situation, as their intuitive feeling may be different. In other words, this method depends on the individual and his or her personal understanding of the issue. The intuitive method is not transparent and cannot be communicated easily to others. As such, decisions and conclusions arrived at by means of the intuitive method are not easily replicable.

CHAPTER 1 The different methods of acquiring knowledge

A variation of the intuitive method is what is referred to as **conventional wisdom**. Conventional wisdom reflects so-called common sense understandings of the world that are commonly accepted as being true. However, the 'common wisdom' statements, being very general, without details on when they are applicable, are often contradictory. For instance, which of the two contradictory statements is true: 'opposites attract' or 'birds of a feather flock together'; or 'out of sight, out of mind' compared to 'absence makes the heart grow fonder'?

There is no systematic way of determining which of these statements is accurate. In contrast, the rationalistic and empirical methods do not attribute special aptitudes to particular persons, but differ only in the importance that they give to reasoning and observation.

The **rationalistic method** is based on human reason. According to this approach, human beings have the ability to think logically (or to reason), and thus to discover laws through purely intellectual processes. The basis of knowledge is correct reasoning which enables one to know what must be true by principle. A good example is pure mathematics where laws and principles are discovered without relying on any reality but on the basis of axioms. Observation of reality, collection of facts and using the five human senses are unnecessary. Although this approach to knowledge has had some success in the natural sciences, it has made little progress in the social sciences.

The opposite of the rationalistic method is the **empirical method**, where facts observed in nature are the foundation of knowledge. Objectivity of observation is emphasised and only what is observable, what can be perceived by our senses, constitutes knowledge. A piece of wood floats on water, while a piece of iron does not float on water. For an extreme empiricist, knowledge stops here, since the reason for the difference cannot be observed. Interpretations of observations and speculation about relationships between facts introduce subjectivity and are therefore seen as distortions of the data. But critics of both the rationalistic and the empirical methods are justified in asking: What are facts without the establishment of a relationship between them, without an explanation for their connection in time and space? Of what use is a theory that is totally divorced from reality? Obviously, these two extreme methods are inadequate for the acquisition of knowledge, although each one has advantages. The scientific method, as described on page 4, is a synthesis of the rationalistic and the empirical methods. It uses rationalism to develop theories about the world and empiricism to test these theories. Science thus involves a continuous interplay of rational thought and empirical observation.

Finally, for the sake of completeness, one should also mention the existence of other methods like the ones used in philosophy, theology or aesthetics. However, the field of investigation and application of these methods is qualitatively different to that of science and thus beyond the scope of this book. The differences will become clear in Chapter 4, which deals with the identification of research questions.

The scientific method and its properties

To illustrate how the scientific method integrates the above-mentioned two methods, the process of knowing must be examined.

The distinction (elucidated further in Chapter 2) between quantitative and qualitative research methods is mainly to address different research aims. For example, the study of the efficiency of a certain training programme is quantitative while the investigation of the attitudes and problems encountered by the participants of that programme is qualitative.

In the case of quantitative research, the first step to knowing is a *description* of the object, relationship or situation. The object of the study must be accurately depicted. Here, evidently, the empirical method of objective observation must be used. Thereafter, an *explanation* or statement of the relationship between the described facts should be expressed, where possible in the form of a law. The explanation is thus the result of a reasoning process using the rationalistic method, and leads to the formulation of a natural or social law ('law' is not used here in a legal sense). The stated explanation should permit a *prediction* of future events under well-defined conditions. In other words, the explanation should allow one to foretell the occurrence of some event. But to ensure that this explanation or law will enable prediction, the correctness of the explanation must be tested. This is achieved by confronting it with reality as perceived by the five human senses, using the empirical approach. Correct explanations leading to the ability to predict events should yield intelligent *intervention*, which enables changes to occur that improve a situation.

> **Example**
>
> The observation and *description* of the adult population of an African country have evidenced a very high level of unemployment. The low level of education and lack of specific technical skills of that population are seen as being a partial *explanation* for this unemployment. Based on these facts, the *predictions* are that, with an increased need for technical skills and without some positive changes, the unemployment rate will increase. As an *intervention*, a strategy is developed for raising the quality of the education system as well as for motivating and channelling the youth towards technical professions.

In the case of qualitative research, most frequently the researcher is concentrating on the observation and recording of the events under study. Since very little is known about the situation under observation, no *a priori* explanations are given and thus no expectations or predictions can be tested. However, it may be expected that some explanations will be found at the end, on the basis of the data collection and analysis.

> **Example**
>
> To use the issue of adult education and unemployment given above, qualitative research focuses on the attitudes and social factors that are affecting the motivation of the adult population towards further education in technical skills. Here the explanations for the lack of motivation for technical skills training may be inferred from the collected data.

CHAPTER 1 The different methods of acquiring knowledge

Science can be defined as the building of knowledge obtained by the use of a particular methodology, the scientific one. The scientific method of acquiring knowledge, also called scientific research, is a systematic investigation of a question, phenomenon or problem using certain principles. All sciences are united not by their different subject matter but by their common method, in the way in which knowledge is acquired. There is a tendency to confuse the content of science with its methodology. Astrology and divination are not non-scientific because of their aims but because of their methods. The identification of a relationship between the course of human destiny and the position of the stars (in astrology) or with the clairvoyance of a diviner may be scientific, if a scientific method is used.

Some issues, such as the existence of God, whether a person is good or bad, or any issue related to moral values, do not allow for scientific investigation. It thus becomes imperative to specify the main characteristics of the scientific method in order to differentiate it from other methods.

Science assumes the following:

1. *The existence of natural and social laws*. Science presumes order and regularity in natural and social events. Without this assumption some of the main aims of scientific research, such as explanation, prediction and the possibility to act, would not be attainable. These laws are assumed to exist independently of the observer and they describe the way phenomena interact or social events occur.

2. *Laws can be discovered by human beings*. Scientific research assumes that, although human beings are part of nature and are themselves subject to its laws, they can discover those laws. We obey biological laws determining the growth of our body, psychological laws determining the development of personality, sociological laws in the organisation of society, as well as economic and political laws. Again, it should be emphasised that these laws are not laws in a legal sense. Instead they are the result of observations of certain regularities, which indicate that natural events proceed according to our expectations based on our understanding of those events. For example, if an infant did not grow but remained the same size for several months, this would be a violation of our expectations and we would rightly conclude that some abnormality is present.

3. *Natural phenomena have natural causes*. No supernatural powers are necessary to grasp the cause of events and no unexplainable supernatural forces are needed to explain the way nature functions. A classical example where this assumption is not met is in the use of religious beliefs to explain physical phenomena. For example, some people may regard thunderstorms or the natural death of a person as an expression of anger of their ancestors, or they may regard a hurricane's damage as God's wrath on a sinful city. Scientific understandings are based on parsimony of ideas. Parsimony requires that explanations for phenomena be based on as few assumptions as possible: that is, that they be as simple as possible. If both a complex and a simple explanation exist for an observation, then the simple one is superior.

4. *New knowledge is accumulated gradually and sequentially*. Numerous examples show how invention of new instruments of investigation and new approaches to studying a problem can lead to new advances in science. The new understandings yielded by these advances often demonstrate the limitations of previous knowledge. Examples of such advances include the invention of the electron microscope in biology, the theory of relativity in physics, and cross-cultural comparisons in social sciences.

5. *Knowledge and truth are founded on evidence*. There are specific and commonly accepted rules that need to be adhered to for something to constitute evidence. Much of the time observations that are made on the basis of the senses constitute evidence. Sophisticated instruments have been developed to observe and measure social phenomena when observations are in danger of being inaccurate or insufficient. In general, whenever a scientific claim is made, it is necessary that the researcher provide evidence to support that claim. In the absence of evidence (or proof that the claim is tenable), the claim remains at the level of conjecture or hypothesis. We will return to the question of evidence in subsequent chapters.

6. *Scientific statements must be distinguished from common-sense statements*. Common sense is often characterised by contradictory statements. 'Absence makes the heart grow fonder' and 'Out of sight, out of mind' are opposing statements of common wisdom. Clearly, both are possible in different situations and neither is appropriate to all situations. Common-sense statements are the result of non-scientific observations in that they do not take into consideration the different variables at stake. The weakness of the approach is that the preconditions for the validity of the statements are not specified due to lack of systematic investigation. This illustration emphasises once more the empirical aspect of science that relies on experience and observation of the real world.

7. *Scientific observation is objective*. Objectivity here means that the result of the observation is independent of a single observer. In other words, it corresponds to the description made by anyone examining the same phenomenon. The more accurate a description is, stating measurable properties, for instance, the greater the objectivity of the observation.

8. *Scientific observation is systematic*. All possibilities are considered one at a time, in a logical order. Natural sciences allow the best illustration of systematic observation. In chemistry, for example, different substances can be mixed two at a time, under the same conditions and in the same proportions, to observe their reaction. On the other hand, when investigating the effects of two different painkillers, it would be confounding to prescribe these two pills to patients with different medical backgrounds or to give the two medicines to the same patient at the same time. What could one conclude with confidence if the ailment disappeared? A researcher who gives the same medicine to people suffering from different ailments in order to test the effect of that medicine is not being scientific. If a patient recovers, the researcher is unable to determine whether the positive

CHAPTER 1 The different methods of acquiring knowledge

result was due to the particular medicine or to the nature of the original illness. Since the method was not systematic, the results are ambiguous.

Similarly, in a social research context, if an educator wants to test whether teaching rural workers crop-harvesting by way of demonstration is superior to a 'chalk-and-talk' method, it is necessary for this to be done systematically. It would be inappropriate to use both methods with all the farmers, and it would be a good idea to make sure that all farmers have the same prior understanding of harvesting. If, for example, at the beginning of the study, the group that receives the demonstration has a greater understanding of harvesting than the group subjected to the 'chalk-and-talk' method, then a fair comparison cannot be made about which method is superior.

Unfortunately, it is not always possible to observe every phenomenon or all of its aspects systematically. Most often some characteristics remain unknown so that the explanation and, as a result, the prediction may not be accurate. In fact, one can only predict that an event will take place if one knows *all* the conditions and circumstances, which cause the event. In the social sciences in particular, one is rarely in possession of all the information leading to the occurrence of a certain phenomenon and so can seldom explain this phenomenon with *certainty*. In these cases, one has to content oneself with a *probability* statement, asserting that if some given conditions are satisfied, the event will occur more often than if some of these conditions are not met. Explanations that concede some uncertainty are called **probabilistic explanations**.

Example

Given precise initial conditions, the trajectory of a falling stone can be predicted with certainty. However, given some initial genetic, physical, socio-economic information about a newborn baby, it is not possible to predict with certainty the personality, intelligence and physical condition of the same child at five years of age. Too many unknown and not measurable factors are involved. One can only predict that, coming from a middle-income family, the child will in all probability enjoy a good education and a good diet, and will generally have good opportunities to develop his or her intellectual potential adequately.

Arguments of the type 'all men are mortal; X is a man; therefore X is mortal' predict a fact with certainty: X will die. There is no doubt about it; the result has been obtained by deduction from the two premises. However, the age X will reach cannot be predicted with certainty. One can only assess that he will probably not reach the age of 100 and that the probability that he will reach the age of 50 is larger than the one of his reaching 70 years. In fact, life insurance companies function on the basis of life expectancies that are probabilities of the time of death obtained through generalisation from many observations.

In short, the object and the method of investigation will determine the type of causation that can be expressed, and thus the type of prediction.

Properties of scientific research

Methods that are accepted today as being appropriate for scientific research have a long and complex history. The details of this history fall outside of the scope of this text. However, it is appropriate to mention some of the most important characteristics of scientific research.

1. Scientific research is *empirical* since the aim is to know and understand reality. Each step is based on observation, be it when collecting the basic facts or when testing an explanation, or assessing the value of a prediction or the result of an intervention. The assumption of scientific research is that reality exists outside of the observer. Scientists attempt to understand the world beyond their personal biases and assumptions about their particular research subject. Quantitative methods use a variety of tools to help scientists be more detached and dispassionate about what they research. Qualitative methods focus on acknowledging, understanding and allowing for the biases in a transparent manner. Whether or not this is attainable is often debated by social scientists.

2. Scientific research is *systematic* and *logical*. Not only must the observation be done systematically, but a certain logical order must also be followed. Logical predictions cannot be made before a description has been given and an explanation of the observed phenomenon found. One cannot prepare a questionnaire to gather all data necessary for a study, before having a clear idea of the type of information required. An analysis of the different variables involved must be undertaken prior to the formulation of the questions to be answered by the respondents.

3. Scientific research is *replicable* and *transmittable*. Since the observation is objective and the explanation logical, anyone placed in exactly the same circumstances can observe the same event and, by reasoning, arrive at the same explanation and prediction. Moreover, it is possible to communicate each step of the research and to transmit the acquired knowledge. The usual way of doing this is to present the research and its results in a report or an article published in a journal. In this sense, science is a very transparent process that invites criticism and skepticism. When scientific ideas are able to withstand such challenges they remain tenable. When evidence is amassed that demonstrates a scientific idea to be false, then that idea must be abandoned.

4. Scientific research is *reductive*. By grasping the main relationships between laws, the complexity of reality is reduced. All details which are not essential or which have little influence on the process under investigation are omitted.

> **CHAPTER 1** The different methods of acquiring knowledge

> **Example**
>
> When the quality of a blanket is being investigated, the material of the blanket must be analysed, since its property of conserving heat depends on whether it is made of cotton or of wool. But the colour of the blanket has little relevance to its thermal function and need not be considered. Thus, only the necessary properties are taken into consideration.

In social sciences, by controlling for many variables, one nearly always reduces the complexity of reality. One presupposes that the variables that have not been taken into consideration have little effect on the issue in which one is interested.

> **Example**
>
> When studying the loan facilities available to women for small-scale agricultural projects, one rarely takes into account the personality of the policy makers or that of the loan recipients. The economic, technical and social factors at stake are so much more important that one would want to gather information on the type of project, the types of crop to be produced, the size of the field and quality of the soil, the availability of fertiliser and labour power, transport and market conditions, perhaps also the age and marital status of the woman, the number of dependants who would help her, and her health condition as far as it might affect her work. But individual characteristics, such as her personality traits, are considered to be of little relevance for the study under consideration. They are discarded in order to maintain a certain level of generality in the study.

Reductionism, or the method of considering only the essential and necessary properties, variables or aspects of a problem, has to be used with great care as it can lead to significant bias in the research process. If the selection of variables to be excluded is based on false assumptions, some important variables may not be taken into consideration. For instance, in the previous example on loan facilities available to women, one could argue that some individual characteristics of these women, such as whether or not they are hard-working, perseverant and highly motivated, might greatly influence the results.

5. A scientific claim, statement or theory must be *falsifiable*. This means that a scientific claim must be stated in such a way that can be demonstrated to be false. For this to be the case the claim must be testable, that is, it must withstand empirical scrutiny. If a 'scientific statement' affirms that the capability to drive a race car at 400 km/h is related to some genetic male characteristic, the event of one single woman driving such a car at the given speed will falsify that statement. In making a prediction, a scientific theory should *not* only tell us what *should* happen but what *should not* happen. If these things that should not happen do in fact happen, then we have a clear indication that the theory is untenable, that is, it is wrong. It must then be rejected for being inconsistent with the evidence or it must be modified to address that inconsistency. So, an effective and useful theory

9

is not one that accounts for every possible event, but one which actually forbids some events from occurring. If these forbidden events do occur, then the theory is no longer credible. Thus, predictions need to be stated in such a way that they are both testable and falsifiable.

Key points

1. The rationalistic method of acquiring knowledge is based on the reasoning power of the human mind.
2. The empirical method is based on 'facts' obtained through the five senses.
3. Scientific research is a process that combines the principles of rationalism with the process of empiricism.
4. A quantitative research process develops from the description of the object under study, to the explanation of the relationship between the described facts, to the inferred prediction and finally to the identification of intelligent intervention.
5. Science is based on the following assumptions: natural and social laws exist and can be discovered by human beings; natural phenomena have natural causes; knowledge is founded on evidence; the advance of knowledge increases gradually and sequentially; and scientific observation is systematic and does not depend on the observer.
6. Distinctions have to be made between situations where a prediction can be made with certainty and situations where only a probabilistic explanation is possible.
7. The essential properties of scientific research are that it be empirical, systematic, replicable and transmittable.

Checklist

Keywords:

Check whether the meaning of these concepts introduced in this chapter is clear to you.

method of authority; rationalistic method; empirical method; probabilistic explanation; replicable, transmittable, objective, reductive, falsifiable observations.

Your research:
1. Can the topic of your research be investigated empirically?
2. Will the research process be replicable?
3. Does your research satisfy the five properties of scientific research?

CHAPTER 1 The different methods of acquiring knowledge

Exercises

1. Identify the various ways of knowing and discuss the advantages and disadvantages of each one.
2. What is meant by 'replication of scientific research'? What is required for replication and why is it important?
3. Explain the difference between probabilistic and deductive explanations. Give examples of each.
4. Analyse, using your own example, the positive and negative aspects of research being reductive.
5. Identify a social science research project that illustrates the four steps of research: description, explanation, prediction and intervention.
6. Is it possible to observe an event objectively? Discuss the role of the subjectivity of the observer.

Additional resources

1. Babbie, E R. 2004. *The practice of Social Research*, 10th ed. Belmont, CA: Wadsworth.
2. Strobel, N. 2010. *Astronomy Notes*, Columbus, OH: McGraw-Hill. Available at www.astronomynotes.com/scimethd/56.htm.Accessed 22 November 2012.

The scientific method applied to social reality

CHAPTER 2

This chapter explores science as an active, purposive reflection on the world and its laws. The source of knowledge is the outside world which people must interact with in order to understand it. There is a relationship between the action of people on nature and society, and the set of explanations. The starting point and basis of scientific knowledge is the direct contact of a person with an environment. This superficial knowledge is deepened, generalised and expressed in the form of theory. Facts and theory interrelate at each step of the learning process. This is reflected in the research process that expresses the systematic scientific method.

> **CHAPTER OBJECTIVES**
>
> Learners who have completed this chapter will be able to:
> - Compare and contrast social and natural sciences.
> - Compare and contrast quantitative, qualitative and mixed-methods research.
> - Analyse the relationship between fact, theory and observation.
> - Describe the process of scientific research, in quantitative, qualitative and mixed-methods research.

The distinction between natural and social sciences

Research usually arises from some need, so that it has a particular purpose to fulfil. Natural sciences investigate the properties and laws of natural phenomena. The development of natural sciences is at times determined by the needs of production, commerce and industry. This explains the development of astronomy, which was indispensable to pastoral and agricultural societies. Geometry was necessary for navigators. Mechanics was developed because of the need for large building operations. In the modern period, the development of chemistry, physics and the biological sciences is directly related to the demands of expanding industries.

On the other hand, social sciences investigate the properties and laws of *social* phenomena. The development of social sciences has its roots in the need for understanding, management and manipulation of social affairs.

The development of both types of science depends on the needs, values, aspirations and other characteristics of the particular society in which it takes place. Thus, many countries in Africa show a greater concern for developing techniques to reduce the spread of malaria than they do for research into heart transplants. Social sciences, however, are much more affected by some aspects of the society than are the natural sciences. Moreover, the actual objects of investigation and research problems of the social sciences introduce new methodological challenges. For ethical reasons, for instance, some experiments cannot be done on human beings and some variables cannot be controlled. Generally, there are so many uncontrolled factors due to the complexity of social reality that exact laws can rarely be found. Thus, most results are expressed as probability statements, a fact which is a reflection of some level of doubt. A physicist can express the laws of electricity with a formula and predict with certainty when a light bulb will glow. A sociologist, on the other hand, can only predict that, under certain circumstances, unemployment leads to an increase in crime. This textbook concentrates only on the social sciences. At this point, one needs to be aware of a controversy that developed in the 1960s and is still unresolved, about the adequacy of the positivist approach to scientific methods in studying social phenomena. The defenders of 'social sciences' argue that social science disciplines can be correctly understood as 'natural sciences of individuals in society', and that they are not qualitatively different from the well-established natural sciences. However, the differences between natural and social sciences demand an adjustment of the natural sciences' research methods to social reality. The methods and techniques must be modified and adapted according to the characteristics of social processes, but they are the correct ones for a successful understanding of social issues and the building of theories.

On the other hand, many people argue that the rigid scientific method is often incapable of grasping the fluidity of many social phenomena. These arguments are determined largely by the school of thought to which the critics belong. Their reluctance to consider social disciplines as sciences extends from the analysis of some failures of the empirical, scientific approach to the extreme of denying the existence of laws in social reality.

Relationship between facts and theory

A fact is an indisputable set of statements about reality. For example, it is a fact that the sun rises in the East and sets in the West. One does not need to embark on a research process to validate this fact; it has been established and can be demonstrated daily.

A theory may be defined as a set of ideas or statements that explain a particular social phenomenon. For example, learning theory may be used to explain anti-social and maladaptive behaviour at school. Social learning theory maintains that behaviour is learned and therefore a child may have learned anti-social and maladaptive behaviour from his family.

As mentioned earlier, science is based primarily on observations about the world. The scientific enterprise assumes that our fundamental knowledge is **perceptual**, that is, information about the environment perceived through our senses. Only external, superficial relations between information acquired by our senses can be known. Perception by itself is only one means of acquiring knowledge. On its own, however, perception falls short of true knowledge. One may know that green fruits are not ripe and should not be eaten, but what about watermelons? **Rational knowledge**, based on judgement and logical thought, provides explanations or reasons for the relationships between observations. The combination of observation and the process of logical thought provide a deeper understanding of the world. Thus, a description of facts can only be complete when both the direct information given by our senses and the deeper understanding based on reasoning and judgement are taken into account. There exists, therefore, a fundamental relationship between facts about the world, defined as empirically verifiable observations, and theory, as an explanatory framework.

- *Facts give rise to theory* since they raise a need for explanations of the observed phenomena. Observation of reality can lead to systematic research and the formulation of a general explanation or theory. Facts, the cornerstone of knowledge, are not the product of random observation, but should be both *selective* and *meaningful*.

- *Theory serves as a basis for the gathering of facts* since it specifies the facts to be systematically observed. If a theory stipulates that the failure of cooperative unions is related to the absence of particular managerial skills among the members, the observations will focus on the existence or absence of these skills, rather than on the size of the union, the age and sex of its members, or the climatic conditions under which the members live. Thus observations are not arbitrary or haphazard. They are guided by the underlying theory or concerns held by the researcher.

- *Facts allow a researcher to find support for, improve, disprove or formulate a theory.* Facts lead to a redefinition or clarification of a theory. A scientific explanation or theory must be subjected to empirical testing to determine whether it corresponds to observed reality. This means in practice that a theory allows a researcher to predict some facts. If the predicted facts are not observed during experiment or investigation, the theory is disproved and will need to be improved or reformulated. Equally, if some observed phenomena do not coincide exactly with the theoretical predictions, the theory must be reformulated. For example, if a theory states that violent behaviour in young people is a consequence of poverty, the existence of many violent middle-income children would disprove that theory. Any theory should provide an explanation of how relevant facts relate to one another.

- *The process of theory reformulation is extremely important to the advancement of science, and therefore of new knowledge.* If theories were not advanced, deeper understandings of social phenomena would not be achieved and knowledge would become stagnant. For the frontiers of knowledge to be pushed, theories need to be continually refined and improved.

- *Theories are typically not proved.* When data corroborate a theory, this is taken as evidence that the theory is tenable, that is, it remains a credible and viable explanation of the observed data. However, there is always the possibility that, at some point in the future, some observations or data might contradict the theory. Thus, social scientists usually accept that an existing theory is tentatively

the best explanation of the phenomena under study for the moment, but that it may yet be falsified by further data. For this reason, it is uncommon to speak of theories being proved. The notion of proof conveys a sense that a theory is incontrovertible, which is never the case.
- *Theory allows for a classification and conceptualisation of facts*. It summarises and provides explanations of how relevant facts relate to one another.
- *Theory predicts facts*. For example, under certain conditions, the law of supply and demand predicts the existence of an illegal market much in the same way as the laws of astronomy predicts the occurrence of an eclipse of the sun. A useful theory then allows social scientists to make predictions about future phenomena in the form of probability statements. Such statements then afford social scientists the opportunity to intervene to influence the course of events. Thus, if an economist understands the conditions that make an illegal market flourish, he or she would have some knowledge of what mechanisms to put in place to minimise the likelihood of this happening or to limit its extent.

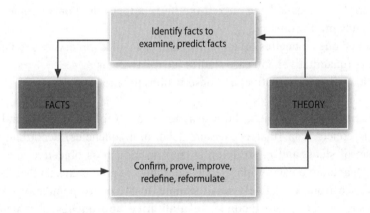

Figure 2.1 *Relationship between facts and theory*

Quantitative, qualitative and the mixed-method approaches

Quantitative methods emerged from the philosophical belief that the world runs according to natural laws and that the role of the scientist is to uncover or discover these pre-existing laws. Thus truth is assumed to be absolute and independent of the human beings that search for it. In comparison, qualitative methods emerged out of more recent philosophical beliefs that truth is relative and that knowledge is constructed by human beings. In other words, our understanding of the world is a product of our personal assumptions, biases and prejudices. As you can see, these are quite extreme philosophical positions.

In fact, most social scientists today adopt the position that while it is impossible for human beings to be completely objective in their study of themselves and their world, it is nevertheless possible to develop shared knowledge that is useful in understanding our world and solving the problems that our communities face. This pragmatic approach is the foundation of much of modern social science and many researchers combine quantitative and qualitative methodologies to develop knowledge about the world that can be used to improve the quality of life.

Social science research can either use quantitative or qualitative research or a combination of both approaches. The **quantitative approach** relies extensively on numbers and statistics in the analysis and interpretation of findings that are generalised from the sample to the population. On the other hand, the **qualitative approach** is often used when the problem has not been investigated before. Generally this method uses smaller samples, from which findings a better understanding of the phenomenon being investigated is produced. Sometimes, circumstances or the problem under investigation demand that both approaches be used in the same study in order to confirm or elaborate each other. This is called the **mixed-methods approach**. For example, a mixed-methods study might combine:

- structured questionnaires (quantitative) and open ended interviews (qualitative)
- surveys (quantitative) and case studies (qualitative), or
- questionnaires (quantitative) and observations (qualitative).

In the **quantitative approach**, the researcher tends to follow what natural scientists do: that is collect data (that is measurements or frequencies) according to a very specific set of steps, and in so doing attempt to remain as objective and neutral as possible. Quantitative data is analysed using statistical procedures so that findings can be generalised from a relatively small sample, to the entire population. Alternately, other researchers are more inclined to **qualitative approaches** in which the plan of the research is more flexible and circular. The researcher investigates a problem from the respondents' point of view. The focus of such a study is to determine what respondents think and feel about a particular phenomenon or issue. In other words, reality is interpreted from the respondent's frame of reference. These studies attempt to understand phenomena in their natural context, rather than the more controlled environment favoured in quantitative approach.

The distinction between the quantitative and qualitative approach notwithstanding, both are authentic scientific approaches to developing knowledge in the social sciences. Such knowledge as we have benefited from, and which posterity stands to learn from, was generated through the use of either one or a combination of these approaches.

CHAPTER 2 The scientific method applied to social reality

> **Example**
>
> A researcher may be appointed by the African Union to investigate whether it is possible and desirable to have a political structure such as an United States of Africa. The researcher could, in pursuit of this goal, conduct a survey in each country. The survey would demonstrate through numbers how many people are in favour of this proposed structure and how many are not. However, the results of the survey may not tell us why people voted in a particular way. If we want to establish the reasons for people's choices in voting, we may need to include on the questionnaire open-ended questions to establish why they are in favour of or against the establishment of a structure such as an United States of Africa.
>
> Alternatively, some focus group discussions may be conducted to establish how people feel about a structure like this. The findings generated from those focus groups could be used to confirm or refute findings generated in the quantitative survey.

A comparison between quantitative and qualitative approaches can be made based on the following criteria:

Table 2.1 *Comparison of quantitative and qualitative research*

Criterion	Quantitative	Qualitative
Structure/design	Rigid	Flexible
Size of the study	Often big	Likely to be small in size
Personal involvement of the researcher	Objective/neutral	Subjective
Reasoning	Seeks to generate findings and generalise from sample to population (deductive)	Seeks to understand the phenomenon under study from the sample (inductive)
Sample/s	Representative of the population	Not representative of the population
Type of collected data	Measurements; scores; counts	Oral and written expressions of opinions, feeling, etc
Theory	Tests a theory	Theory emerges as the study continues or as a product of the study
Hypothesis	Tests whether a statement of relationship between variables can be confirmed	May generate more theories and hypotheses
Data analysis	Statistics	Coding, text analysis
Analysis	Uses numbers and statistics	Uses recurrence of themes

continued ...

17

Table 2.1 *Comparison of quantitative and qualitative research* continued ...		
Criterion	Quantitative	Qualitative
Variables	Seeks to find relationship between variables (independent and dependent variables)	Seeks to understand the variables
Literature study	Extensive literature study is done at the beginning of the study	Literature study is sometimes delayed until data has been collected

Developing theory from facts

As mentioned before, there exists a fundamental relationship between facts and theory. This relationship is expressed through a succession of steps. Facts raise questions. These questions can in turn be condensed into a problem that is then given a temporary solution, yet to be tested, which is called the **hypothesis**. This step is not fortuitous but is related to a large framework, a more general building of knowledge, the underlying theory. Thus a hypothesis, a tentative explanation of certain facts, will become part of a theory as soon as it is verified, that is, supported by sufficient evidence.

Other forms of thinking that make the transition from empirical to theoretical knowledge possible are analogy and model-building. **Analogy** is a correspondence between a phenomenon or event that has been studied already and another phenomenon or event that resembles the first but has not yet been studied. Analogy permits one to draw conclusions based on the similarities between objects and certain of their properties. Comparing these objects or facts that have been identified as analogous allows one to infer some properties of the less well-known objects. For example, the first aeroplanes were built to resemble flying birds. In fact, many explanations of social phenomena are based on an analogy to biological processes like the growth of organisms. In understanding human behaviour, an analogy to animal behaviour is often used. Since it is much easier and more morally acceptable to experiment on animals, comparative psychology will study animals subjected to great stress (fear, hunger, lack of sleep) and infer, by analogy, some knowledge about human behaviour under the same conditions.

In **model-building**, one object or phenomenon, the well-known one, serves as the model. Here certain properties of the object have been singled out, represented in their pure, simplified form and then studied in the absence of the actual object. Ideal models are formed with the help of particular symbols. For instance, a commonly used model is the representation of certain properties of the earth's surface by geographical maps. Fine lines represent rivers, different colours represent vegetation or altitude, and circles of different size represent towns of various size. Of course, each map is a simplification of the object it describes and only represents some of its properties with symbols. In the social sciences one finds models of underdevelopment, such as Gunder

Frank's model of the centre and the periphery (Frank, 1983), or models describing the nature of a certain society, like the stratification model used by Evans-Pritchard in his anthropological studies of some African societies (Evans-Pritchard, 1962).

The relationship between facts, problems, hypotheses, models and theory

Analogy and model-building are therefore quite similar ways of discovering some properties of an object or phenomenon by utilising the existing knowledge of another object or phenomenon. The advantage of model-building is its reductive property, that is, only the main characteristics are considered. The characteristics that do not affect the process under study are ignored and the properties of the model can then be studied in the absence of the original object of study. A geographer can study the properties of a particular region through the use of adequate maps without actually travelling to that region.

Of course, the utility or danger of analogy and model-building depends on the adequacy of the analogy or model. The similarity of two chosen objects or events might be too superficial. The model might be an over-simplification of reality. Both flaws will lead to fallacious results.

The relationship between facts, problems, hypotheses, models and theory is summarised in Figure 2.2.

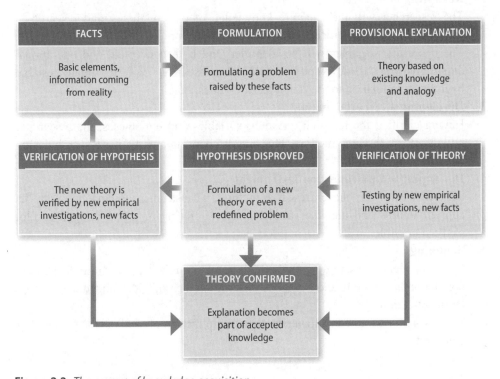

Figure 2.2 *The process of knowledge acquisition*

Steps in scientific research

The research process in the social sciences, although subjected to variation according to the particularities of the research problem, has a constant frame expressed in the form of a loose timetable. Some steps must be performed before others can take place. However, the research process is more cyclic than linear. This book analyses each of the components of the scientific research process in turn.

The best research results are based on careful planning of the whole process. What follows is a useful plan of action for research, but it is by no means the only one. Depending on the problem under investigation, varying degrees of flexibility may be required. Literature review, for instance, is an ongoing process that can be useful at different times during the research process. Also, some steps may be ignored when some specific methods of research are used. For instance, case studies seldom require statistical analysis and exploratory studies do not have hypotheses. The last step, dissemination of the results, is in fact a summary of the whole research process in words.

The **quantitative research** process generally involves the following steps:

1. **Selection and formulation of the research problem**
   During this step the researcher identifies an area of study and specifies one or more clear research questions.

2. **Reviewing literature**
   The researcher will then acquire knowledge of current theory and research in the field through the process of reviewing the existing literature on the subject. The necessary variables will be identified and both conceptual and operational definitions will be developed. Finally, the researcher will formulate testable hypotheses in relation to the stated research questions.

3. **Developing a research method**
   Having clarified the research question, variables and hypotheses, the researcher will develop a research method. This entails choosing a particular research design and sampling method.

4. **Developing a data collection instrument**
   On the basis of the chosen research method, an instrument is developed and its appropriateness and quality (validity and reliability) are tested through a pilot study, if possible.

5. **Sampling**
   Using the identified sampling method, the actual sample is drawn from the general population under study and a detailed description thereof is developed.

6. **Data collection**
   The research instrument is then administered to the sample and data is gathered or collected.

CHAPTER 2 The scientific method applied to social reality

7. **Data Analysis**

   Once data is collected it must be organised, and checked for accuracy and completeness. When this process has been completed the researcher will use a range of arithmetic and statistical tests to describe the sample data and generalise from this data set to the population from which the sample was drawn.

8. **Interpretation of results**

   At this point the researcher considers what the results of the statistical analysis can teach us about the research questions specified in step one. To what extent has the research answered the questions? To what extent can we trust those answers?

9. **Conclusions and recommendations**

   Based on the interpretation of the results, the researcher draws certain conclusions and makes considered recommendations. This may have to do with social policy or action, or the recommendations may point to further research.

10. **Dissemination of results**

    Finally the results are presented in different forms such as research reports, seminars and conference papers, books and, of course, peer-reviewed journal articles.

The **qualitative** research process is more difficult to describe since the steps are generally less linear. In fact, qualitative research often progresses in a circular fashion. Some stages may precede and follow others on the basis of pragmatism.

1. **Selection and formulation of the research problem**

   Qualitative research begins with a research question in the same way as quantitative research does. However, the question is typically more descriptive in nature, and while the different components of the question must be defined at a conceptual level, operational definitions and hypotheses are seldom specified.

2. **Reviewing literature**

   The purpose of reviewing literature is to learn first-hand what has been studied on the specific question and thereby increase the researcher's understanding of the concept under investigation so that he or she will ask more relevant questions. Sometimes, literature study takes place at the same time as data collection. In fact, unlike in the quantitative research, a comprehensive review of available literature may be deliberately postponed until the data collection stage.

3. **Developing a research method**

   At this point, the researcher determines the most appropriate way of gathering data that will shed light on the research questions.

4. **Developing a data collection instrument**

   In qualitative research, the most commonly used data collection tools are interviews and focus group discussions. These are used in the collection of spoken and written words. If the researcher wishes to collect data by means of an interview, then he or she first needs to design an interview guide.

21

5. **Sampling**

Since it may not be possible to study the whole population, the investigator may need to sample the population. In qualitative research, the main aim is to understand the phenomenon under investigation very deeply and therefore representative samples are not a requirement as they are in quantitative studies. The researcher needs to find a sample of participants that carries most of the characteristics associated with the phenomenon under investigation.

6. **Data collection and analysis**

In qualitative research, data collection and analysis often take place at the same time or as alternating processes in a cycle. Qualitative data includes words (written and spoken), artifacts, pictures and video. In the case of interviews, data collection may include the use of audio tape recorders and video cameras. Data collection and analysis may in turn lead to more literature study, making the process ever more flexible and cyclic.

7. **Interpretation of results**

During this phase, the researcher studies the results of the data analysis in order to gain some overview. To what extent have the research questions been addressed and answered? To what extent can these answers be trusted?

8. **Conclusions and recommendations**

As is the case in quantitative research, based on the interpretation of the results, the researcher draws certain conclusions and makes considered recommendations. These may have to do with social policy or action, or the recommendations may relate to further research.

9. **Dissemination of results**

Ultimately, as for quantitative research, the findings of the research must be shared with others. This may take the form of a report, a seminar or conference presentation, a book or a peer-reviewed journal article.

Finally, **mixed-methods research** is likely to follow either the quantitative or qualitative research process outlined above, depending upon which kind of data collection is dominant in the research design. Some mixed-methods research has quantitative data at its core and this data is then elaborated or explained with qualitative data. In this case a quantitative research process is likely to be followed. Other mixed-methods designs have qualitative methods at the core and thus follow a more qualitative research process. Of importance to mixed-methods designs is the point at which quantitative and qualitative data are mixed. This could happen during data collection, during the analysis of data, or only at the end of the research during the interpretation of the results. Mixed-methods researchers must describe in their reports why, how and when they combined the different kinds of data collected.

Whatever the approach employed, it is essential that the researcher is able to describe in detail the steps that led from the formulation of the research problem through to the final results and conclusions. This is the essence of the scientific method.

CHAPTER 2 The scientific method applied to social reality

Key points

1. Social sciences investigate social phenomena, whereas the natural sciences study laws and properties of natural phenomena.
2. A fact is an indisputable statement about reality and a theory is set of ideas that explain a social phenomenon.
3. Quantitative research emanates from the philosophy that the world operates on natural laws, whereas qualitative studies are informed by the philosophy that the world and the truth is not objective as meaning is socially constructed. Quantitative research is planned well ahead, and is rigid and objective whereas qualitative research requires a flexible plan, which allows for movement back and forth.
4. The quantitative approach uses scales and instruments in the collection of data whereas qualitative approach uses observation, interviews and focus group discussions.
5. Data analysis in quantitative studies happens at the end of the data collection stage whereas in qualitative research this occurs at the same time with data collection.

Checklist

Keywords:

Check whether the meaning of these concepts introduced in this chapter is clear to you.

quantitative and qualitative research; mixed-methods research; facts, theory and model; the research process.

Your research:
1. Is your research qualitative or quantitative? Provide reasons for your answer.
2. What kind of data will you obtain?
3. Which data collection tools are you going to use?
4. How are you going to analyse your data?
5. How are you going to disseminate your findings?

Exercises

1. Describe the differences between natural and social sciences. In what ways are they similar? Outline three examples that illustrate the relationship between facts and theory.
2. Find two examples of models or analogies used in the social sciences, which are not mentioned in this book.
3. What are the differences between theories, hypotheses and facts?

continued ...

4. Can you distinguish between quantitative and qualitative research in terms of:
   a. design
   b. process
   c. literature study
   d. data collection tools?
5. Read any article from a social science journal and identify the following:
   a. the topic
   b. the title of the study
   c. the research problem/question
   d. the research approach, whether quantitative, qualitative or mixed-method
   e. the hypothesis (if applicable)
   f. the theory or theoretical framework
   g. the research design
   h. the sampling procedures
   i. the data collection tools/instruments used
   j. the major findings.

Additional resources

1. Denzin, N K & Lincoln, Y S. (eds) 2011. *The Sage handbook of qualitative research*, 4th ed. Thousand Oaks, CA: Sage.
2. Tashakkori, A & Teddlie, C. (eds) 2010. *Handbook of mixed methods in social and behavioral research.* 2nd ed. Thousand Oaks, CA: Sage.

CHAPTER 3

Research ethics

Researchers typically have greater power than those who participate in their research. While most researchers are well-intentioned and honest people, there is always the potential for the rights of research participants to be violated, either knowingly or unknowingly. Often, issues arise that may affect participants adversely but are not considered by the investigator. This issue is so important to researchers internationally that a code of ethics has been developed over many years which is now recognised throughout the world. This chapter calls attention to the various ethical principles that must be considered when undertaking research of any kind.

> **CHAPTER OBJECTIVES**
>
> Learners who have completed this chapter will be able to:
> - Understand why ethics in research is important.
> - Understand the underlying principles of ethical research.
> - Understand particular ethical guidelines.
> - Apply the appropriate ethical guidelines to the process of research.

The need for ethics in research

As social researchers, our education, our position in society and our organisational affiliations give us knowledge and power that can be used for good or bad. Imagine a young social researcher who is completing her Master's degree in Sociology who visits a farm in order to interview farm labourers about their work conditions. These are poor people with very little education. She is wearing nice clothes, speaks like an educated person, arrives at the farm in her car, and introduces herself as a researcher from a particular university in the city. When she arrives she has a quick meeting with the farm manager and then walks out into the fields and approaches the workers. To each person she explains that her research will improve working conditions of farm workers, that participation is voluntary and that anything that they say to her will be kept confidential. As you imagine this scenario, ask yourself honestly whether you think these farm workers are really informed about the research, and whether their participation is truly voluntary?

One of the reasons why social scientists are so concerned about research ethics is that there have been many cases of abuse of people's rights in the name of social research. Some of the worst examples from the history of social science illustrate this.

In 1932, the United States public health service began a study to investigate the long-term effects of untreated syphilis in a sample of 399 African American men in the state of Alabama (Reverby, 2009). Members of the sample were diagnosed with syphilis, a very serious sexually transmitted disease, but treatment was deliberately withheld. The researchers wanted to see how the disease developed in the absence of treatment. The participants in the study were not informed of the aim of the research, the nature of their condition, or the fact that effective treatment was available for the disease. To make sure that participants returned for follow-up observations, the researchers offered so-called 'free treatments' that were really ineffective for syphilis. By the mid-1940s, the results of the study were clear. The mortality rate for participants with untreated syphilis was twice as high as that of the comparison group in the study, participants without syphilis. Nonetheless, the study continued until 1972 when a newspaper report called public attention to it.

During the Nazi era in Germany, experiments that involved extreme cruelty were conducted on prisoners in concentration camps. Under the direction of Nazi doctor Josef Mengele, studies were conducted to determine the effects of injecting certain poisons or germs into people, removing body organs, and conducting amputations without the use of anesthesia. Victims obviously suffered enormously, and many died during these experiments. These studies were conducted in the name of scientific inquiry, although it is now quite obvious that science was only an excuse to satisfy the cruel curiosity of the Nazi scientists.

In psychological research, several studies have been conducted that today would be regarded as unethical. Stanley Milgram (1974) studied the phenomenon of obedience, in which participants were made to administer shocks of incremental gradation to confederates, in order to determine how much authoritarian pressure from the researcher they could withstand before refusing to continue. In 1973, Philip Zimbardo (Haney, Banks & Zimbardo, 1973) conducted a study that involved a mock prison, using a sample of college students. Some participants in the study played the role of prison guards, while others played the role of prisoners. Zimbardo observed that the guards became extremely sadistic and displayed considerable cruelty towards participants, even though the conditions of the study were simulated and not real, while the prisoners became depressed and showed signs of extreme stress. The study had to be stopped after only six days.

In South Africa, it has been alleged that as many as 900 forced sexual reassignment operations were performed on gay and lesbian soldiers between 1971 and 1989. These operations were part of a broader programme of treatment and research that was designed to show that homosexuality could be cured through the use of aversion therapy, electro-shock therapy, hormone treatment, chemical castration and sexual reassignment surgeries. This continued long after the American Psychiatric Association removed homosexuality from the list of mental disorders, a fact that could not have been overlooked by the doctors and researchers responsible for the project (Kaplan 2001; Van Zyl et al., 1999).

CHAPTER 3 Research ethics

And yet research ethics are about much more than not abusing the human rights of the people who participate in our research. Ethics are also about making sure that we use our knowledge and skills to contribute to our societies and to the lives of all people.

Researchers' social responsibility in developing countries

Scientific research has the ability to generate accurate information which is an important resource. Think how much politicians spend on social research to determine how the population is feeling about key social issues. Thus social research is a source of power which can be used for social benefit, or abused for personal gain. For almost every new research finding, there are people who stand to gain from it, and there are people who might lose because of it.

Every country in Africa (as in many other parts of the world) is struggling with complex, chronic, social problems, which impact negatively on the lives of millions of people every day. Because these countries are not wealthy, it is imperative that the few available resources are used to generate the maximum benefit for the population. On the one hand, this is an argument for greater research spending, since so much is wasted on projects which fail because not enough time was spent on needs assessments, feasibility studies and so forth. On the other hand, the situation of developing countries demands that researchers think hard about the work that they do in order to ensure the greatest benefit to society. Four issues are relevant here.

1. *Highest quality practice.* Internationally, the quality of social research is extremely variable. Unfortunately, poorly performed social research devalues all social research. It is therefore important that social researchers are properly trained, supported and supervised while they are still inexperienced. It is very important that researchers critically review their own values and biases (see Chapter 13). The requirement that methodologies, results and conclusions are recorded in detail and made available to peer review is most important. Only if one knows exactly how a piece of research was conducted can the results be evaluated.

2. *Building capacity of all sectors of the community.* In some cases social research methodology is seen as being beyond the reach of the majority of people. Although it is true that some sophisticated techniques require a degree of specialised knowledge, virtually all problems can be usefully tackled using the methods explained in this book. It is important that a wider range of people learn how to conduct useful research so that they can benefit directly from these techniques and judge more accurately the value of research in which they have an interest.

3. *Relevance.* The question of the relevance of research is a controversial and political one in many circles. However, since the resources needed to support social research are somewhat scarce, it is safe to say that researchers should aim to make a useful contribution to society. While it is true that people disagree on what is useful and what is not, all social researchers should ask themselves what

27

contribution their work is making to society. This topic is covered in more detail in later chapters.

4. *Promulgation of results.* Too often important research findings are lost because of the manner in which findings are presented. It is part of the researcher's responsibility to make the results available in a form that is usable by the people who can benefit from them. In some cases publication in a journal is sufficient to achieve this. In other cases, the people who are most likely to benefit from the study are unlikely ever to read a scientific journal. In these cases it is required that researchers find other ways of making their findings known. If promulgation of results is not handled properly, then the research is unlikely to make a difference to society and the previous point about relevance becomes meaningless. Many Africans are greatly angered by researchers from the developed world who study our problems and our people (often in pursuit of degrees and academic recognition), but then never make their results and conclusions available to the people whom they have studied in a way that can make a difference to their lives.

What are research ethics?

The word 'ethics' is derived from the Greek word *ethos*, meaning one's character or disposition. It is related to the term 'morality', derived from the Latin term *moralis*, meaning one's manners or character. A moral issue is concerned with whether a behaviour is right or wrong, whereas an ethical issue is concerned with whether the behaviour conforms to a code or a set of principles. The idea of codes of good practice for different professions has been very well established since the Middle Ages and even before. The ethical code governing medicine originates with the Hippocratic Oath that dates back to the 5th century BC. Today, the ethical code of medical professionals who deal with life and death is understood by ordinary people all over the world.

But where do these ethical rules come from, and who decides what is ethical and what is not? The ethical codes of science are not based upon the values or rules of any particular society or religion. Instead they are based on the principle of reciprocity. Stated very simply, the principle of reciprocity is that we should treat others as we would like to be treated by others. At its heart this principle recognises that all individual human beings should enjoy the same rights and protections. As a result the ethics of science are closely connected to the philosophy of human rights, as laid down in the Universal Declaration of Human Rights.

The study of research ethics helps to prevent research abuses and assists investigators in understanding their responsibilities as ethical scholars. Research ethics places an emphasis on the humane and sensitive treatment of research participants, who may be placed at varying degrees of risk by research procedures. It is always the researcher's responsibility to ensure that his or her research is ethically conducted. In fact, before a single participant is contacted, the researcher must ensure that the research plan can pass an ethical evaluation. To this extent, ethical standards attempt

CHAPTER 3 Research ethics

to strike a balance between supporting freedom of scientific inquiry on the one hand, and protecting the welfare of participants on the other. In other words, researchers have the right to search for truth and knowledge, but not at the expense of the rights of other individuals in society. Similarly, participants have basic rights when they elect to participate in a research study, chiefly rights to privacy and to protection from physical and psychological harm. The goal of research ethics is to minimise the risk to participants. Many academic disciplines, including disciplines in the social sciences, have professional bodies that have published guidelines to help researchers think through ethical issues as they pertain to their research. Most published ethics guidelines have identified common principles of research ethics.

Principles of ethical research

Non-maleficence

The most basic principle of research is that participants must not be harmed by participating in the research project. It is important to note that harm may occur intentionally or unintentionally during the course of a research study, and thus the researcher must be aware of the various possible adverse events that are likely to occur throughout the duration of a project and beyond. Thus, research should never injure or harm participants. One consequence of this principle is that the use of placebos might be unethical since, by withholding effective treatment, a researcher might worsen the health of a research participant. If a particular research procedure produces unpleasant effects for participants, the researcher should have the firmest scientific grounds for conducting it.

Beneficence

It is important that research not only does no harm, but also potentially contributes to the well-being of others. At times this might place a researcher in a difficult position. What is beneficial to one group may not be so to another. Consider the case where, despite government efforts to promote new crops, commercial farmers have been slow to plant the new crops. A researcher is called in to find ways of ensuring that the farmers plant the crops required by the government. Whose interests are being served in this case? How might the research be adapted to serve the farmers' interests?

Part of the principle of beneficence is the question of competence. People who are professionally trained by accredited and acknowledged institutions are much more likely to be competent at what they do. Thus the qualifications of researchers are of considerable importance. The principle of beneficence requires social and behavioural researchers to conduct research that is effective and significant in promoting the welfare of people.

29

Example

Decades of social research on South Africa's mining industry has produced many controversial results. This industry has been linked to accelerated urbanisation, undermining family structures, disrupted rural economies, exacerbated social prejudice and racism, the spread of illness, and unethical labour practices. Even today, after a great deal of positive reform, there is ongoing concern about the conditions under which miners work and the safety of mining operations. However, a careful researcher who studies published social research of the 1960s and 70s in South Africa will find various scientific papers describing the great social benefits that miners enjoyed during this time. Mines were described as safe havens from the negative influences of the more politicised townships. Research that arrived at conclusions of this nature was clearly ideologically biased, racist and unashamedly supportive of the apartheid regime. The unethical nature of this kind of research is clear, as the findings unambiguously place the needs of an illegitimate government and a system of racial and class oppression above those of miners, their families and their communities.

Autonomy

The principle of autonomy incorporates the freedom of individuals' actions and choices to decide whether or not to participate in research. No person should be forced, either overtly or covertly, to participate in research. At the core of the principle of autonomy is the right to participate voluntarily in social research or decline to participate. In the past, prisoner populations have been used for medical and psychological research. Very commonly, these prisoners were unable to refuse participation. To this end, the principle of informed consent is of paramount importance. Participants need to be informed about the nature of the research project in which they are being asked to participate, so that they can make an informed decision about their participation. Thus, participants must be given clear and sufficient information on which to base their decision. Informed consent requires that all participants be fully informed of the nature of the research, as well as the risks, benefits, expected outcomes and alternatives before they agree to participate. The principle of autonomy can, however, affect the generalisability of results. People who agree to participate in research may differ from the many others who do not volunteer. This is known as the volunteer effect and is discussed in greater detail in Chapter 11 that deals with issues of sampling.

Justice

The principle of justice is based on the belief that all people should be treated equally. Thus, people should not be discriminated against in research on the basis of race, gender, disability, income level or any other characteristic.

Fidelity

The principle of fidelity implies faithfulness and keeping promises or agreements, specifically between the researcher and the participant. Thus, engaging in deception or breaching confidentiality is an ethical violation that infringes on a participant's rights.

Respect for participants' rights and dignity

As human beings, all participants have legal and human rights. No research project should in any way violate these rights when participants are recruited. It is necessary therefore to ensure that the dignity and self-respect of participants is always preserved. An important part of protecting people's dignity is understanding and respecting their culture. For example, in many cultures it is considered highly inappropriate to discuss certain topics with anyone other than one's closest confidants. A researcher concerned with women's health and contraception must therefore find ways to gather information about this important topic without offending the research participants.

Sometimes well-meaning researchers fail to respect clients' rights. Consider for example the case of a non-governmental organisation that offers counselling and legal assistance to rape survivors. To measure the impact of their work, they contract a researcher who telephones a random sample of past clients in order to find out how beneficial those clients consider the service to have been. Have the clients' rights to privacy and confidentiality been compromised? How might the study have been designed to better protect the clients' rights?

Important ethical guidelines

Often, the ethics of conducting a research project are not very clear-cut, but these overarching principles can serve to guide ethical decision-making by researchers. In general, when the ethical issues are not clear, it is important to consult. In addition to the overarching ethical principles described above, the following are important ethical requirements to which researchers must adhere.

Ethical review

Before a researcher proceeds with a particular study, he or she should submit a detailed proposal of the intended research to a process of peer review. This proposal should anticipate what ethical concerns might be raised during the implementation of the project and should explain how these concerns will be handled. Ethical review is handled differently in different countries, and unfortunately in some African countries the mechanisms of ethical review are poorly developed. It is essential that researchers abide by the laws of their countries, the ethical codes of their professions and the policies of their institutions. Where formal mechanisms of ethical review are not adequately developed, it is the responsibility of the researcher to find suitably knowledgeable and experienced peers to conduct a formal ethical review of the proposed research.

Ethical review is the most important tool by which professional researchers ensure that the ethical standards of our work are maintained. It is essential that all ethical concerns are resolved *before* the research project begins.

Informed consent and voluntary participation

As mentioned previously, participants have a right to know what the research is about, how it will affect them, the risks and benefits of participation, and the fact that they have the right to decline to participate or to discontinue their participation at any time during the process if they choose to do so. Usually a researcher or an assistant will take some time to explain to participants what the study entails and what is required of them in terms of participation. Each participant may then be asked to sign an informed consent form, which is an indication that they indeed understand what has been explained to them. Typically, participants receive a copy of the form for their own records. An example of an informed consent form is presented in the Appendix at the end of this chapter.

However, it is important to remember that informed consent may have different implications in different cultural contexts. Think about the situation described in the following example.

Example

An international aid agency is concerned about breast-feeding practices among women in rural Ghana. Researchers attend a clinic offering ante- and post-natal services in order to interview mothers of small babies. At first the women talk openly to the female interviewers. However, a few days into the study, women at the clinic begin to avoid the researchers and refuse to be interviewed. The researchers are made aware that various heads of household in the community have become angry that the new mothers are talking about private matters with a stranger. A community meeting has been held and the local authority has refused permission for the research to continue. Who has the right to consent in this situation? How might the researcher have avoided these problems?

Confidentiality

Confidentiality is an ethical requirement in most research. Information provided by participants, particularly sensitive and personal information, should be protected and not made available to anyone other than the researchers. Thus, data collected from participants should at all times be kept under secure conditions.

CHAPTER 3 Research ethics

Anonymity

The principle of anonymity is linked with confidentiality. A participant's data must never be associated immediately and obviously with his or her name or any other identifier. Usually, researchers assign a number to a participant's data to ensure that the data remain anonymous. Anonymity applies to all aspects of the research process, from the first time that the researcher makes contact with a potential research participant, to the publication of reports and findings.

Appropriate referral

Sometimes it may be the case that research participants' well-being (psychological, emotional, physical and/or social) may be compromised as a result of participation in research, for example, after a traumatic experience such as war, social turbulence or displacement. The possibility of this happening must always be anticipated by the researcher and processes need to be put in place to manage any negative consequences should they occur. This is most commonly done by arranging appropriate referral to a counselling centre, social work agency or medical facility.

Discontinuance

Participants must be given every assurance that that they are free to discontinue their participation at any time without being required to offer an explanation. Thus, at any time in the conduct of a research project, if a participant decides for any reason that he or she would like to stop participation, this wish should be respected. Participants should also be informed that stopping participation will not prejudice their receiving services, if the project is conducted at a clinic, government department, school or counselling centre.

This can be important, as some participants may feel that their social benefits may be affected if they do not agree to participate or if they discontinue their participation. In rare cases, there may be unavoidable negative consequences for the participant who withdraws from a study, such as developing drug resistance following withdrawal from tuberculosis treatment. In these cases, it is the responsibility of the researcher to ensure that the participant fully understands the consequences of his or her decision. The researcher should also take the necessary steps to get further assistance for the participant leaving the study (see Appropriate referral above).

Research with vulnerable populations

Vulnerable persons are those who may not have the necessary degree of understanding to give informed consent to participate in research. Examples of vulnerable persons include children, mentally ill persons, disabled persons, unemployed persons, refugees, asylum seekers and homeless persons. Whenever research involves vulnerable persons, the researcher must be sensitive to their needs and the fact that they may not fully appreciate the implications of requests to participate in research. At the same time, it is also inappropriate to be patronising or condescending to people and make assumptions about their competence that may be unfounded. In some cases, when it is not possible or appropriate to obtain informed consent from a participant (for example, a child), it may be necessary to obtain permission from a third party (for example, a parent). The following case example illustrates some of the challenges of working with vulnerable populations.

Example

In many African countries researchers are concerned about children who, as a result of the Aids pandemic, have become the household heads in their families. Such children may be taking care of younger siblings, providing financially and making important decisions for the family. Researchers identify such families through local civic associations and visit their homes in order to determine how they are surviving. What are the ethical issues that the researcher must consider in this case? What steps should the researcher take to protect the interests of this vulnerable group?

Deception

In deception, the researcher hides the true nature of the study from the participant. This is done to prevent the participants from altering their natural behaviour as a result of knowing that it is being observed. The following example serves as an illustration of deception.

Example

Imagine a researcher who wishes to study helping behaviour in public places. He or she may enlist the help of an assistant who pretends to be in distress in a place where many people are present. The objective of the research is to determine which passersby volunteer to help a person in visible distress, and which do not. As the assistant is not in genuine distress, there is an element of deception in the study.

Deception causes many ethical problems. If used, safeguards must be employed. The most common safeguards are:

- The researcher needs to ensure that the deception poses no serious or long-term risks.
- The researcher needs to explain the true nature of the deception to the participant in a debriefing, which occurs once all the data has been gathered.
- The debriefing should counter any lingering misconceptions, possible discomfort or risk that may have been generated by the deception.

CHAPTER 3 Research ethics

■ Debriefing should be done with care to ensure that participants are not left with bad feelings or doubts about themselves based on their performance in the study.

Ethics in analysis and reporting

Researchers are not allowed to change their data or observations. The fabrication or falsification of data is a very serious ethical transgression. There have been some examples in the history of social research where data have been fabricated or falsified. When reporting the results of a study, the researcher should report on technical shortcomings, failures, limits of the study, negative findings and methodological constraints. The final ethical responsibility always rests with the researcher.

In general, the researcher must always judge the research in terms of:
■ its value to science
■ the amount of risk it poses to the participants
■ whether the potential benefits outweigh the risks, and
■ whether adequate safeguards have been included to minimise the risks.

Reporting back to research participants

It is the duty of the researcher to ensure that the rights of participants to be informed of the results of the study are protected. This means that the researcher must present the results of every study to the research participants in a form that is easily understandable. Factors such as participants' home language, culture and education level must be considered. Foreign researchers have a duty to submit a report of their research to the appropriate authority of the host country.

Obtaining access to research participants by means of gatekeepers

Sometimes it may be necessary for a researcher first to approach a gatekeeper before approaching participants directly to participate in a study. For example, if you wish to research children attending school, it will be necessary to contact the school and even the relevant national or provincial educational authorities. The same applies to other institutions such as hospitals, prisons, private companies or commuters using the transport system, if participants are to be approached on the premises of these institutions.

Relationships with organisations

Research is often made easier by organisations or institutions that assist researchers in gaining access to particular groups of people. Many organisations will be interested in learning the results of the research that they have supported. They may want to use the findings to inform their own practice and policies. For this reason it is important that researchers make sure that they return to the organisations that have assisted them in data collection in order to pass on their results and conclusions. This is one way in which research can directly make a difference in the lives of people. Research is not only about knowing more about our world. It is about making informed decisions about what needs to be changed so that peoples' lives can be improved. Feedback should be provided in a form that can be easily understood by the audience. Not all organisations will be able to digest a scientific report. In such cases a meeting and discussion might be more appropriate.

Publication

Publication of research results is important, as it is a way of communicating the results to the scientific community. When research results are published, it is important that participants not be identified by name or in any other way that would make it possible for them to be identified. Publication credit must be given to all persons who have contributed to the research, either in the form of authorship or in the form of an acknowledgement. Plagiarism has become a serious problem at many institutions. Plagiarism is when a writer presents material or research findings as his or her own work when it is in fact the work of someone else. Plagiarism is essentially academic theft, and for this reason it is a serious offence.

Occasionally, publication presents some difficult problems to researchers. Consider the following case: An international agency concerned about education conducts research to see how a particular country's high school syllabi are changing over time. The results demonstrate that, in one country, the mathematics syllabus has been gradually simplified over many years. The education department demands that the agency not publish the research report because it will undermine confidence in the department. What should the agency do in this case?

A final word about ethics

Ethical considerations in research are always evolving and changing. It is very important that researchers keep up to date with the latest thinking about research ethics. When in doubt, it is always helpful to consult with others about ethical matters. It is recommended that research proposals always be subjected to scrutiny by ethics committees. Ultimately it is the researchers' responsibility to ensure that every study meets the highest ethical standards. Failure to do so may result in researchers being censured by their professional bodies, being dismissed by their employers, or even being prosecuted by research participants.

CHAPTER 3 Research ethics

Key points

1. Research ethics are designed to ensure that research takes place according to the highest moral standards, and that science does no harm to people or communities, either intentionally or inadvertently.
2. Research ethics are closely linked to human rights.
3. Research ethics are built on the principles of non-maleficence, beneficence, autonomy, justice and fidelity.
4. Ethical research is ensured through a process of ethical review.
5. Important ethical guidelines include informed consent, voluntary participation, the right to discontinue participation, the right to anonymity or confidentiality, as well as honesty in analysis and publication.

Checklist

Keywords:

Check whether the meaning of these concepts introduced in this chapter is clear to you.

non-maleficence; beneficence; autonomy; justice; fidelity; ethical review; informed consent; voluntary participation; confidentiality; anonymity; discontinuance; vulnerable populations; deception; and, plagiarism.

Your research:
1. Make sure that you consider all ethical principles while you are planning your research. There is no value in planning something that is ethically unacceptable.
2. Consult with others to check that your research plans are in fact ethical.
3. Make sure that your research proposal is reviewed and approved by the appropriate independent body before you begin the work.
4. If you have ethical concerns about your own or someone else's research, seek advice immediately.

Exercises

1. What are research ethics and why are they important?
   Why are research ethics important?
2. Discuss the basic principles of research ethics.
3. Is deception ever appropriate in research?
4. Why is it an ethical issue for research to be of high quality?
5. What is the difference between confidentiality and anonymity?
6. Design an informed consent form for a study that you will undertake.

Additional resources

1. Artz, L & Themba Lesizwe 2005. *Ethics relating to social science research with victims of violence and other vulnerable groups.* South Africa: Themba Lesizwe.
2. Institute of Education. n.d. *The Research Ethics Guidebook: A resource for social scientists.* University of London, www.ethicsguidebook.ac.uk
3. Social Research Association. 2003. *Ethical Guidelines.*

Appendix: Example of an informed consent form

(Name of institution)

(Name of principal investigator)

(Name of department) (Day telephone number) (Email address)

CONSENT FORM
(TITLE OF RESEARCH PROJECT)

INVITATION TO PARTICIPATE
You are being asked to participate in this research study because ....

PURPOSE..

PROCEDURES
As a participant, you will be enrolled in the study and ... *(State what the procedures are and what is expected of the participant).*

RISKS
Some of the questions on the questionnaires you will be completing may touch on sensitive areas. However, every effort will be made by the researchers to minimise your discomfort. You are encouraged to discuss with the research staff and/or coordinator any negative or difficult feelings or experiences you have as a result of participating in this research project. If at any time you feel you would like to stop your participation in the study, you will be free to do so.

COSTS AND FINANCIAL RISKS
There are no financial costs directly associated with participation in this project. Services from support staff are provided at no cost to you.

BENEFITS
There is no guarantee that you will benefit directly from the study. However, the investigators believe that it is likely that participants may benefit from attending the group interventions.

COMPENSATION
You will not receive any compensation for participating in this study.

ALTERNATIVES
Participation in this research project is entirely voluntary and you may choose not to participate.

continued ...

CONFIDENTIALITY

Every attempt will be made by the investigators to keep all information collected in this study strictly confidential, except as may be required by court order or by law. If any publication results from this research, you will not be identified by name.

ADDITIONAL INFORMATION

Your participation in this study is entirely voluntary, and you are free to refuse participation. You may discontinue your participation at any time without prejudice or without jeopardising the future care either of yourself or of your family members. If you discontinue participation in the project, you may request that we not use the information already given us. You are encouraged to ask questions concerning the study at any time as they occur to you during the programme. Any significant new findings developed during the course of the study that may relate to your willingness to continue participation will be provided to you.

DISCLAIMER / WITHDRAWAL

You agree that your participation in this study is completely voluntary and that you may withdraw at any time without prejudicing your standing within *(name of institution)*.

PARTICIPANT RIGHTS

If you have any questions pertaining to your participation in this study, you may contact the Principal Investigator *(name of principal investigator)* by telephoning (XXXX).

CONCLUSION

By signing below, you are indicating that you have read and understood the consent form and that you agree to participate in this research study.

_____   _____

Participant's signature   Date

_____   _____

Researcher's signature   Date

CHAPTER 4

Problem conception and background information

This chapter describes how to start a research project, how to identify and formulate a problem, how to pose a research question, and which factors to take into account before embarking on a project. The aim of gathering background information on theories and facts, in particular by literature review, is explored. Some guidelines are given on how to find information, as well as on how to review and abstract articles.

> **CHAPTER OBJECTIVES**
>
> Learners who have completed this chapter will be able to:
> - Source and identify research problems, questions and topics.
> - Initiate their own research projects.
> - Identify and formulate their own research problems and pose research questions.
> - Search for appropriate literature.
> - Compile a literature review.
> - Better Understand systematic reviews and meta-analysis.

Sources and identification of research problems

Although social reality provides innumerable questions, selecting a research problem or question is a delicate task. Out of the great variety of queries arising from the environment, one has to sort out those that are appropriate for scientific investigation. Only general guidelines on how to choose and formulate a research problem can be stated, as well as some criteria that should be satisfied for a successful research project. The difficulty of providing precise directives for the selection of research questions and problems arises from the diversity of possible topics and their sources.

Sources of research topics

1. *Observation of reality*. The most obvious source of research topics is contact with, and observation of, the external world. Many of the world's great scientific advances have been the result of nothing more than observation.

> ### Example
>
> It is often said that Sir Isaac Newton was sitting under an apple tree when an apple fell onto his head. He was fascinated by the acceleration of the apple to the ground and wanted to find out which force was responsible for this motion. He was prompted to research this phenomenon and his investigations led to the discovery of the gravitational force and the laws of motion as we know them today. This knowledge about gravity, the force pulling everything to the ground, was essential for the design of the first aircraft by the Wright brothers. In order to remain airborne, they needed to design a machine that could counteract the effects of gravity.

2. *Theory*. Theory is another source of research topics. If a theory is correct, one expects that events will unfold in pretty much the same way as predicted by that theory. Research is necessary to verify the correctness of the assertion that the particular situation will occur as spelled out in a theory. In psychology, Piaget's theory of cognitive development links the passage through different stages of reasoning to maturation rather than to education. If this is the case, there should be no essential differences in the cognitive development of school children and children who have never received any formal education. Neither should there be major differences between people of different cultures in this respect. Thus, this theory suggests many research topics.

3. *Previous research*. Previous investigations often inspire new studies because of contradictions between results or concerns about the procedures used. Alternately, ambiguous results may require further exploration. Finally, it might be useful to repeat earlier studies with different groups of participants. For instance, it may be suggested that some findings and interpretations are biased by the way in which data have been collected. Children may have been disadvantaged when asked to perform some tasks, not because of their lack of skill, but because of their difficulty in grasping instructions given in an unfamiliar language. Thus, new research should be undertaken where either a non-verbal task is used, or where the instructions are given to the children in their mother tongue.

4. *Practical concerns*. Very often, research stems from concrete problems encountered in the everyday life of a certain community. For instance, if students with tertiary education qualifications experience difficulty finding employment, the relationship between the content of courses being offered by the tertiary education institution and the demands of the job market should be investigated. Research carried out in response to practical concerns turns out to be applied in the sense that the findings emerging from that investigation are used to remedy a

CHAPTER 4 Problem conception and background information

particular unpleasant situation. Applied research is discussed further in the next chapters.

5. *Personal interest.* Sometimes, research projects are undertaken as a result of the personal interest of the researchers. In this case, the relevance of the research to the broader community is sometimes of less importance. Research out of personal interest may simply be to satisfy one's curiosity, or generate more knowledge. Such endeavours may fall within the realm of basic research, a topic which is covered in Chapter 5. One needs to be careful not to pigeonhole every research project as either applied or basic. Human nature and thinking is so complex that such a simplification is not always helpful. One never knows how an interesting advance in knowledge, which finds no application today, might be used in the future.

6. *Researching topics of interest to another party.* In many cases social researchers earn their money by taking on contract research which is paid for by another party. This other party might, for instance, be a business which requires some market research about a new project, a government department that wishes to test the feasibility of a new social policy, or a civil society organisation that needs evidence about a particular problem being experienced by the community. In each of these examples, the research topic is specified by the party that will pay for the research. Of course, this introduces many moral and ethical challenges relating to who may, and who may not, use research to generate knowledge. This topic will be discussed further in Chapter 7.

Identifying a research problem

In the identification of a research problem, one can distinguish three steps in narrowing the range of interest. These are: the selection of a topic area, the selection of a general problem, and the reduction of the general problem to one or more specific, precise and well-delimited questions. In general, the sources of a research problem are to be found in a combination of direct observations and experiences, theory, previous investigations and practical concerns.

The choice of the topic area may be dictated by various factors: intellectual or academic (the social organisation of cockroaches – topic: comparative social psychology), practical interest (the queuing at bus-stops – topic: urban public transport), or personal interest (why do I forget so quickly what is taught in lectures? – topic: learning, motivation, and memory). Nowadays, topics of research are strongly influenced by social conditions. It may be 'fashionable' to conduct research into a particular area during a particular period (such as issues concerning women and the disabled emphasised by the United Nations Decade for Women or the Year of the Disabled). The final two decades of the twentieth century have produced an enormous wealth of research on HIV and Aids. Today, a great deal of emphasis is given to war and violence, peace and security, governance, leadership and economic sustainability.

Social and financial incentives play an unavoidably important role in the choice of the subject matter for investigation.

Within a topic area, a general problem must be chosen which may be mainly of scientific and intellectual interest, or revolve around a practical concern. In either case, the objective might be for more information about a particular issue or it might be to explain the relationship between existing facts.

Example

A study of the use of oral contraceptives in an African population might aim at determining how many women use this form of contraception, taking into account women from different geographic areas (urban or rural), income levels, levels of education, age, number of children, and so on. A different study in the same area might aim to explore the relationship between the use of oral contraceptives and the health of women in the country. The first study aims at describing a phenomenon in greater detail, the second to understand the relationship between different variables. Both could be aimed at developing interventions in the health sector.

Both of these studies would involve very extensive research due to the enormous variety of variables involved. While the contraceptives themselves may influence the health of women directly, it is also likely that women's health will be indirectly affected by the fact of having fewer pregnancies. Also, how the contraceptives affect women's health is likely to be influenced by age, nutritional status, and many other factors.

Often social research involves a large number of different variables and can be extremely complex. Thus, after a general problem has been identified, one still has to find ways of reducing it to a specific and manageable **research question**.

A research question must be such that it can be handled in a single study or divided into a number of sub-questions to be dealt with in separate studies. One way of doing this is to list different possible answers to the general problem and to express them in the form of questions.

Example

Topic area
Instability of marriages

Research problem
What is the relationship between the level of social change in an African country and the rate of divorce?

continued ...

CHAPTER 4 Problem conception and background information

> *Question*
> What factors might be influencing divorce?
>
> *Possibilities include:*
> 1. age of partners at the time of marriage
> 2. differences in religious affiliation between partners
> 3. differences in the cultural backgrounds of the partners
> 4. employment status of partners
> 5. type of employment (industrial sector, informal sector, commercial sector, self-employed, etc)
> 6. type of marriage (customary or statutory)
> 7. method of selection of partner (arranged marriage, individual choice)
> 8. difference in the education levels of partners
> 9. difference in the socio-economic status of partners
> 10. financial situation of the family.
>
> Point 1 can, for instance, be expressed in the form of a specific, well-delimited and unambiguous research question: Are marriages between very young people (for example, under 23 years old) less stable than those between older people?
>
> Point 9 could be formulated as either: Does the rate of divorce vary between different socio-economic levels? or Is divorce more frequent in the higher socio-economic level than in the lower socio-economic level?
>
> Note that in the second formulation only two groups of the population are considered and expectations are expressed regarding what the difference will be. This formulation is more precise than the first and the study is therefore more narrowly delimited.

It is a common mistake among research novices to underestimate the extent of a research problem and to undertake investigations far beyond the time and money available to them, as well as beyond their abilities. As a general rule, inexperienced researchers are advised to reduce the research topic to as simple a question as possible. Chapter 6 provides further guidelines on how to achieve this.

An important issue in the search for, and identification of a research problem is that not every topic can be transformed into a research project. The first and most fundamental constraint is that only problems that are empirically based, that is, which deal with observable reality, can be investigated by means of the scientific method. This excludes all problems concerned with subjective issues such as value or moral judgements.

45

Another important constraint to be borne in mind when choosing a research problem is that, although the problem relates directly to **empirical reality**, the **feasibility** of data collection may be doubtful or impossible. For this reason, the proof of the existence or non-existence of God cannot be studied by scientific means. In other cases, data collection could harm the participants or interfere too much with their private lives. One cannot, for instance, separate a child from its parents when trying to examine the effects of lack of parental care. In addition, any project based on longitudinal study over several generations may never be completed since so much might change over that length of time.

Also, when there is almost no literature or theory about a problem, it may be very difficult to conduct certain types of studies. It is likely that more descriptive and exploratory research would be needed first. This research would help to identify and define the key concepts, and to develop methodologies for measuring and describing those concepts. Only when this research has been done, might other kinds of study be possible. Novice researchers in particular should think very carefully before launching research into relatively uncharted territories.

Based on the above, a well-chosen problem or question should satisfy as many as possible of the following criteria:
1. Be timely.
2. Relate to a practical problem or question.
3. Relate to a wider population.
4. Relate to an influential or critical population.
5. Fill a research gap.
6. Permit generalisation to broader principles of social interaction or general theory, or enhance our understanding of a particular situation.
7. Sharpen the definition of an important concept or relationship, or shed more light on a concept or relationship.
8. Create or improve an instrument for observing and analysing data.
9. Provide possibilities for a fruitful exploration with known techniques.
10. Have implications for a wider range of practical problems.

As mentioned in Chapter 2, the relevance of research must be judged in terms of the extent to which it facilitates intervention that leads to an improvement in society. This point has a particular connotation in developing countries where, in the past, the aim of research often did not correspond to the interests of the people or the country. Too often, academic researchers preferred to choose their topics of investigation for academic ambition, rather than for their social relevance.

CHAPTER 4 Problem conception and background information

Finally, before going ahead with the actual study, a researcher should check whether the following more general criteria are satisfied.

1. *Empirical testability*. The question must refer to empirical facts and be answerable through the observation of reality. The question should not be based on moral and ethical judgements, or cultural beliefs. Scientific research cannot answer such questions.

2. *Feasibility*. This refers to whether or not the proposed study is manageable, taking into account the available time and literature, financial means, the size of the sample, and the available methods or instruments for collecting data.

> ### Example
>
> It may not be possible to investigate the attitude of nurses towards patients in all the clinics of a large town within one month. Neither would it be possible to move conveniently from one clinic to another without sufficient funds for transport. On the other hand, if one wants to restrict the research to psychiatric nurses with at least 10 years' experience, the sample available in a single town may be too small.

Another hindrance to research feasibility is that the questions the researcher needs to ask may be too personal, too emotionally loaded or too dangerous to be answered honestly.

> ### Example
>
> Asking people in a country under dictatorship about how they are treated by the security forces if they do not support the regime, might get them into great trouble, or at least not produce reliable information. A more general example might be of asking prisoners how the warders handle them. To answer truthfully might result in fact in worse treatment.

3. *Critical mass*. This refers to the breadth, or scope of the research. Is the problem so narrow, specific or trivial that it is not worthwhile pursuing?

> ### Example
>
> When investigating the use of various methods of contraception, it may not be of much use to ask only female university professors whether or not they use contraceptives. Such a focus would be too narrow and almost trivial, as female university professors constitute a negligible part of the population of an African country, albeit with quite specific properties.

4. *Interest*. This refers to the motivation of the researcher to carry out the proposed research. Since conducting a research project is a long and demanding task, strong motivation is essential. Motivation that is only external (like the need to carry

47

out a research project as part of a course on research methodology) will often lead to a deficient, biased research outcome. If, on the other hand, the choice of topic is dictated by a deep-seated interest, the quality of the research is likely to be positively influenced by such interest. When the research process becomes challenging, it is interest more than anything that sustains the investigator to carry the project through.

5. *Theoretical value*. The importance of the theoretical relevance of research has already been reflected in many of the criteria given for a well-chosen problem. The general idea can be summarised by the question of whether or not the research will contribute to the advancement of knowledge in a particular field of research and how useful this knowledge will be for the further development of that field.

6. *Social relevance and practical value*. This refers to the relevance of the research results to society. What changes will the results effect in the actual life situation of those studied? How can the study results be adapted to the present situation so as to improve it? Are practitioners likely to be interested in the result? There has been a great deal of discussion and debate about the obligation of research projects conducted in Africa to be plainly pertinent to the needs of African societies. Much has been written about the fact that research projects in Africa are very often informed by the values and concerns of the developed world, which puts more resources into knowledge generation. This is a practical demonstration of the expression, 'He who pays the piper calls the tune'. As Africa develops, new powerful groups have begun to emerge within the continent too. Many people are more educated than others, have access to greater financial and technical resources, and they too use (and sometimes abuse) social research in support of their own interests and viewpoints. Thus, social relevance is not merely about undoing the legacy of colonialism and of redressing historical injustices, but also a question of defining and redefining our vision of a society in which citizens have the freedom to realise their potential, not only as individuals, but also as communities that make up the nation, and the continent as a whole. Thus, ideally there should be a clearly demonstrated relationship between research and social development.

In closing this section, note that, although ideas on how to proceed in choosing a research problem should have been clarified by the guidelines given above, the function of a research problem, to be discussed in the next chapter, constitutes a new step in the research process. However, this step cannot be meaningfully realised before the literature related to the problem has been carefully studied. A literature review often helps to clarify the question under investigation by showing how it is embedded within already existing facts and theories.

CHAPTER 4 Problem conception and background information

Literature review

Literature review involves a search and study of current writings on the problem under investigation. In order to conceive the research topic in a way that permits a clear formulation of the problem and the hypothesis, some background information is necessary. This is obtained mainly by reading whatever has been published that appears relevant to the research topic. This process is called the literature review. Although acquaintance with different theories and models, as well as research results, takes place, by necessity, before a clear statement of the problem can be formulated, a literature review is an ongoing process. This is the case not only because the relevant research results can be published by others at any time but also because, in the course of research, new aspects and problems arise requiring new information.

In conducting a literature review, the following three broad issues should be kept in mind: the purpose of the review, the literature sources and the reviewing techniques. Each of these issues is now examined in detail.

The purpose of the review

Why is a literature review necessary? What is to be gained? What should one look for? A literature review aims to achieve, among others, the following objectives:

1. To sharpen and deepen the theoretical framework of the research. That is, to study the different theories related to the topic, taking an interdisciplinary perspective where possible.
2. To familiarise the researcher with the latest developments in the area of research, as well as in related areas. In particular, the researcher should become acquainted with the problems, questions, hypotheses and results obtained by other researchers in order not to duplicate existing efforts but to widen and deepen them. Previous results are a starting point for new research.
3. To identify gaps in knowledge, as well as weaknesses in previous studies. That is, to determine what has already been done and what is yet to be studied or improved. In many fields of study, theories developed in one context are assumed to hold in other contexts too. For instance, we cannot assume that a finding derived from research with middle-class social science students in Los Angeles will automatically hold for middle-class students in Accra, but we can conduct a study to test the extent to which that finding is transferable to an African context.
4. To discover connections, contradictions or other relations between different research results by comparing various investigations.
5. To identify variables that must be considered in the research, as well as those that might prove to be irrelevant. This finding is often a result of the comparison of different investigations, done in different contexts.
6. To study the definitions used in previous works as well as the characteristics of the populations investigated, with the aim of adopting them for the new research. Often some definitions are found to be correct and unbiased so that they can be

49

adopted for the new investigation along with other basic characteristics of the population. By using the same definitions we facilitate comparisons between our research and the work of others.

7. To study the advantages and disadvantages of the research methods used by others, in order to adopt or improve on them in one's own research. It is unwise to impose research methods on a particular community without due regard to the culture of that community. Some research topics are easier in some cultures and much more difficult in others. Anthropologists speak about cultural relativism, the recognition that different theoretical frameworks and methodological approaches have different utility within different cultures.

It should be noted that, although a literature review is essential, it also carries some potential dangers. One may be influenced by the results of previous research, or one may accept without criticism their chosen characteristics and explanations so that one fails to discover new possibilities, and fails to observe without preconceptions or expectations. One may develop the tendency to emphasise mainly what has been brought to one's attention or to work within an already established framework, instead of exploring new approaches. For this reason some qualitative researchers prefer to delay the process of literature reviewing until after they have collected and analysed some or all of their data. Most researchers, however, prefer to conduct the literature review at the beginning of the process to ensure that their work extends and develops the work of others, and does not duplicate work that has already been done.

Sources of literature

Where is the information to be found? How does one locate the relevant articles, books and reports? The most common problem when starting a literature review seems to be the identification of relevant sources. Often the impression is created that nothing has as yet been written on the chosen topic, and the multiplicity of non-relevant literature can be overwhelming. To overcome this problem, the following procedure can be adopted.

1. To start with, information centres, subject abstracts, indexes or reviews should be consulted. The easiest starting point is the indexing system of a library in which different aspects of a topic would be noted. A listing of relevant books and articles could thereby be established. A discussion with the desk librarian could be useful for particularly difficult topics. Another very useful source of information is the abstract or index of the area under investigation. For instance, the *Sociological Abstracts* will provide researchers with a brief summary of all published articles in different areas of sociology. Bibliographies (such as *the International Bibliography of the Social Sciences*) and indexes (such as the *Book Review Index*) list citations necessary to find literature on specific topics. Abstracts are available electronically at all academic libraries and are easily searchable.

CHAPTER 4 Problem conception and background information

2. Over the past decades there has been an explosion of subject specific databases to support work in various fields. Thus, for example, the Education Resources Information Centre (ERIC) can be found at www.eric.ed.gov and contains the abstracts of a very wide range of journals dealing with education. Similarly, the PILOTS database is housed by the National Centre for Post-Traumatic Stress Disorder (PTSD) and can be found at www.ptsd.va.gov. It contains references for every academic paper, book and book chapter published worldwide that deals with PTSD. Although few of these databases are housed in the developing world, they remain excellent resources for identifying important literature in the field.

3. Professional, peer-reviewed journals (such as the *African Journal of Health Professions Education*, the *Africa Research Bulletin*, and the *African Journal of Aids Research)* are important sources for the most recent technical work. Such journals also often present reviews of books summarising the latest thinking in the field. Most journals also have a presence online where the researcher can look through the different issues and download relevant abstracts and often some full articles for free. Thus, for example, the *Africa Research Bulletin* can be located online at http://onlinelibrary.wiley.com/journal/10.1111/(ISSN)1467-825X. Also, many journals allow researchers to request updates by email whenever new material is published. This means that the researcher does not need to go looking for material but can have relevant material emailed to his or her computer.

4. General search engines on the internet are also a useful tool for starting a literature review. For example, Google Scholar (http://scholar.google.co.za/) contains academic material from many peer reviewed journals published around the world. Other important resources are Science Direct (http://www.sciencedirect.com/) and Highwire Press (http://highwire.stanford.edu). The internet has become an indispensible tool for any researcher.

5. The researcher should discuss the research problem with other social scientists that have experience in the area of the research problem. Again, email and the internet are invaluable in this regard. Several social network sites have groups that are dedicated to particular areas of interest and research.

6. Once an initial list of books and articles has been established, the next step is to expand the search in a more direct way. Whereas the initial list may cover a wide range of information, the new selection should focus more precisely on the present research problem. In the process of reading the material on the initial list, the most relevant items should be selected and their bibliography and references used to detect new sources of more precise information. In particular, it is useful to consult journals cited in articles since this starts a 'snowball' process, providing the researcher with a great number and variety of sources of information.

51

The reviewing techniques

How does one review and abstract relevant literature? Of the publications identified for reading, a certain number will be selected as being particularly relevant for the proposed research and they should be reviewed for use in the study. The question revolves around the type of information, which should be abstracted from these publications and how to present it. Reviews and abstracts should contain the information listed below.

1. The full reference, including topic or title, name(s) of author(s), name of journal or book in which the publication appears, the date and place of publication, and internet address for material download electronically. Very powerful software now exists which helps researchers store their reference material. Such programs can import the citation information, store it in searchable forms, and export in using the different scientific formats required by academic institutions and journals.
2. The purpose of the study as well as any hypotheses, research questions and variables.
3. The methodology used in the research, including a brief summary of sampling method, research design, the sample and population of interest, instruments used to collect data, and approaches to data analysis.
4. A summary of findings and conclusions, including the implications of the study and any weaknesses in the methodology.

The importance of a wide, comprehensive literature review cannot be emphasised enough. Because of the complexity of social issues, an interdisciplinary approach is encouraged. An economic issue always has some sociological, political and psychological aspects which are more or less evident and relevant. For example, to what extent is the productivity of a factory related to such economic variables as input, level of technology and style of management? How much is due to motivational factors, learning procedures and the political leaning of the trade union? Furthermore, some theoretical reasoning in one science can be applied by analogy in another science.

In writing a literature review it is important that the researcher tries to integrate the material from various journal articles and books. A literature review should not read like a list of short summaries. Rather it should consist of a discussion of the key issues relating to the research question. The views of different researchers who have already done work in the field should be presented in an integrated manner.

As the amount of literature available to the social researcher has multiplied in recent decades, new approaches to reviewing literature have emerged. Systematic reviews and meta-analyses are sometimes used to summarise large bodies of research and to reflect on the overall state of an area of enquiry.

A **systematic review** aims to comprehensively locate and synthesise research on a particular question or problem, using organised, transparent and replicable procedures at each step in the process. A systematic review follows a detailed design that specifies its objectives, concepts and methods.

CHAPTER 4 Problem conception and background information

> **Example**
>
> A researcher does a computer-based search for all papers published on the impact of education campaigns on mother-to-child transmission of HIV. The search produces more than 60 papers. The researcher reads them all carefully and records the following data from each paper:
> 1. From what country was the primary author?
> 2. In what country was the study conducted?
> 3. What research design was used in the study?
> 4. How was the sample created?
> 5. How large was the sample?
> 6. Was the sample rural, urban, peri-urban or mixed?
> 7. What measurement instruments were used?
> 8. What results were recorded?
>   The researcher then summarises the data she has collected from this set of papers, each one representing a unique research study. In this way a systematic review is produced.

Meta-analysis refers to a set of statistical methods for combining quantitative results from multiple studies to produce an overall summary of empirical knowledge on a given topic. In other words, meta-analysis is a more statistical form of systematic review. In meta-analysis the researcher calculates the same numerical expression, called an effect size, to describe every study included in the review. By doing this, the researcher is able to compare the effect sizes across various studies.

> **Example**
>
> Returning to the review of literature on the impact of education campaigns in preventing mother to child transmission of HIV, the researcher might notice that 24 of the studies follow a similar methodology that is amenable to meta-analysis. All of these studies measure mothers' knowledge of good nutrition both before and after the education campaign. Unfortunately mothers' knowledge of good nutrition is measured in different ways in different studies. However, by calculating an effect size for each study the researcher is able to compare the impacts that are recorded in all 24 studies. If the calculated effect sizes turn out to be close to zero, this would indicate that education campaigns have a very weak impact upon mothers' knowledge of nutrition.

Other background information

Although consulting scientific literature is an essential means of acquiring necessary background knowledge for starting a research project, it is not the only one. Much vital information and many personal experiences have never been published, making it necessary to talk to people as well. Useful background information can be obtained in direct discussion with people involved in a similar issue. Hopefully, these are people who have accumulated experience from which the researcher can learn. Nurses, relating their experiences, methods and difficulties in introducing family planning to the rural population, telling anecdotes or describing the reactions of women, will offer a variety of useful information to the health researcher. A conversation with a foreman or trade union official may give a labour-economics researcher insights into working conditions, worker morale and salary structures.

Information on a research problem can also be obtained by direct observation of, or even participation in, a relevant situation. Sharing the life of villagers can deepen the understanding of their problems and aspirations and open new perspectives on the type of research question to raise, or how to formulate the problem, taking into account the realities of village life.

In conclusion, after a thorough literature review, the researcher should have acquired an overview of the various theories and models which could be adopted for the planned research. The researcher/scientist should then be in a position to identify the theoretical framework (and model, if any) on which the research will be based. Moreover, an overview of other research done on the topic should have been gained, leading to a deeper understanding of all relevant studies.

Key points

1. Research topics can be sourced from observation, curiosity, personal interest, previous research and the desire to solve a particular practical problem.
2. In conducting research, the researcher needs to narrow down the research topic to a research problem or research question.
3. Not all research problems and questions satisfy the empirical testability criteria.
4. Before embarking on research, one needs to be sure that all the ethical imperatives are adhered to.
5. Research is often a time-consuming activity and so one needs to establish whether the following aspects are in place to sustain the process: interest, social and practical value, theoretical value and feasibility.
6. Quantitative research is preceded by a thorough literature study, whereas in qualitative research, literature study and data collection happen at the same time.
7. For one to do an adequate literature study, one needs to be familiar with the various techniques for doing so.

CHAPTER 4 Problem conception and background information

Checklist

Keywords:

Check whether the meaning of these concepts introduced in this chapter is clear to you.

research topic, research problem, empirical testability, feasibility, critical mass, systematic review, meta-analysis.

Your research:
1. What is your research topic?
2. What is your research problem?
3. Is your problem researchable? Justify your response.
4. Does your research project have practical value or relevance?
5. Does it comply with ethical norms and standards?
6. Is there adequate literature to support this?
7. Where are you going to obtain literature? Which sources?

Exercises

1. Discuss the empirical testability of each of the following research questions:
   a. Are religious people happier than non-religious people?
   b. Should ancestor worship be practiced more frequently?
   c. Are African people neglecting the rituals of traditional belief systems?
   d. Are bad things happening in the world because African people are neglecting the rituals of traditional belief systems?
2. The research topic is 'Changing attitudes to traditional beliefs in Sub-Saharan Africa'. Identify three different research questions that relate to this topic and satisfy the criteria for good research questions identified in this chapter.
3. What search words would you enter into a computerised library catalogue to find articles on the research topic mentioned in the previous question?
4. Why is it important that the researcher conduct a literature review?
5. Use one of the internet resources mentioned in this chapter to identify five research papers relevant to a topic that you are currently studying.
6. Write a brief literature review integrating the information from these five papers.

Additional resources

1. Little J H & Pillai, V. 2008. *Systematic reviews and meta-analysis. Pocket guides to social work research methods*. Oxford: Oxford University Press.
2. Sheafor, B W & Horejsi, C R. 2011. *Techniques and guidelines for social work practice*, 9th ed. London: Allyn & Bacon.
3. De Vos, A S, Strydom, H, Fouche, C B & Delport, L S L. 2007. Research.

CHAPTER 5

The types of research

In this chapter the different types of research are presented. Distinctions are drawn between quantitative, qualitative and mixed-methods research, between applied and basic research, and between exploratory, descriptive, correlational and explanatory research. Emphasis is placed on the relationship between the research problem and the type of research selected to investigate it. The characteristics of the problem, the initial level of knowledge, the properties of the variables, as well as the purpose of the investigation, all play a role in determining the type of research to be used. The opportunities and challenges relating to research over the internet are also discussed.

> **CHAPTER OBJECTIVES**
>
> Learners who have completed this chapter will be able to:
> - Compare and contrast quantitative, qualitative and mixed-methods research.
> - Compare and contrast exploratory, descriptive, correlational and explanatory research.
> - Identify the type of research used in a study.
> - Select the most appropriate research type for particular research problems.
> - Differentiate between primary and secondary data analysis.
> - Recognise the challenges and opportunities for conducting research using the internet.

Ways of classifying research

There are several ways of classifying research studies. One of the most important focuses on the methodology used. **Quantitative research** relies on measurement to compare and analyse different variables. By contrast, **qualitative research** uses words or descriptions to record aspects of the world. **Mixed-methods research** uses both measurements and descriptions in a complementary fashion to deepen the researcher's understanding of the research topic. The differences between these types of research are discussed in greater detail and illustrated below.

A second way of classifying research arises from the reasons for which the research is being conducted, that is to say, the research aim. Studies that primarily seek to increase human understanding of a particular aspect of society are often referred to as **basic social research**. By contrast, studies that primarily aim to solve a particular problem confronting a group of people are often referred to as **applied social research**. **Participatory research, action research, community needs assessments**, as well as

CHAPTER 5 The types of research

monitoring and evaluation studies tend to be more applied in nature and are discussed further in later chapters.

A third classification of research is between primary and secondary research. **Primary research** occurs when the researcher collects data with the specific intent of answering a particular research question. **Secondary research** occurs when a researcher uses data that has been collected for some other reason to answer a new research question. For example, a researcher who uses census data to track the migration of subsistence farmers to urban areas would be conducting secondary research, since census data is not collected specifically for the purpose of this research. Primary and secondary research are discussed further in Chapter 12.

A final, and more traditional way of classifying research is based on the demands of the research question. In cases where very little is known about the research topic, we speak of **exploratory research**. The purpose of exploratory research is to determine the breadth and scope of a particular topic, and to generate initial questions or hypotheses to guide more searching research.

Where the researcher is interested in describing a phenomenon, the research is called **descriptive research**. Descriptive research may be conducted from a quantitative or qualitative perspective. Patterns and trends in social phenomena such as the population characteristics, or the human development index of a country, can be described in figures and statistics. Descriptions can also take the form of verbal narratives and descriptions derived from interviews, essays, novels, and even poems and songs.

When the research question requires an understanding of the relationship between variables, the research is called **correlational research**. Both quantitative and qualitative methodologies can be used to determine the existence of a relationship between variables. Quantitative methods do this through statistical approaches (see Chapter 14) while qualitative methods do this through documenting the co-occurrence of particular themes in the data (see Chapter 15).

Finally, when the research question demands that the researcher explain the relationship between variables and demonstrate that change in one variable causes change in another variable, the research is called **explanatory research**. Explanatory research is used to test theories of how social scientists believe the world works. This is the most challenging form of knowledge production in the social sciences for several reasons. Firstly, it is philosophically challenging to prove that change in one variable *causes* change in another. Secondly, very few phenomena in the social sciences have a single cause, and causal pathways are seldom one-directional. Social scientists find that they are frequently studying complex systems with multiple causes and effects, often relating to one another in a cyclic or circular fashion. Thirdly, it is very difficult to filter out all the other factors that might confuse or obscure the particular causal relationships in which the researcher is interested.

Quantitative, qualitative and mixed-methods research

As mentioned above, **quantitative research** methodology relies upon measurement, counting, and the use of various scales. These are discussed further in Chapter 12. Numbers form a coding system by which different cases and different variables may be compared. Systematic changes in 'scores' are interpreted or given meaning in terms of the actual world that they represent. Numbers have the advantage of being exact. 'Three' means exactly the same thing to every person who knows the concept, and will mean exactly the same thing in different social, cultural and linguistic contexts. Another important advantage of numbers is that they can be analysed using descriptive and inferential statistics (see Chapter 14).

However, there are some kinds of information that cannot be recorded adequately using quantitative data. In many cases, language provides a far more sensitive and meaningful way of recording human experience. In these cases, words and sentences are used to qualify and record information about the world. These words might come from recorded interviews or focus groups, written responses to open-ended questions, diaries, letters, stories and other forms of literature, or from the field notes of a diligent observer of social phenomena. Research using this kind of data is called **qualitative research**.

There are advantages and disadvantages to both quantitative and qualitative research methods. The skilled social researcher carefully chooses the most appropriate approach to a particular problem. In many cases, the line between quantitative and qualitative methods is blurred. Often a researcher will provide opportunities for respondents to describe their experiences by including a couple of open-ended questions in a questionnaire composed largely of quantitative style items. At the same time, there are also ways in which text can be coded to produce numbers, and **mixed-methods research** attempts to combine the advantages of quantitative and qualitative methods and to avoid their disadvantages. Researchers using mixed-methods will collect both quantitative and qualitative data and then find ways of combining, or mixing, the two types. Mixing is not a simple process and can happen at different points in the research. Sometimes mixing occurs during data collection with both sorts of data being collected at the same time. At other times, the types of data are combined during the data analysis phase or only during the interpretation of data.

Example

When a researcher studies the nature of education in a community, she might do so in terms of the number of years of schooling that the majority of people living in that community have completed. In other words, 'education' is defined as the 'number of years of schooling' and the study is quantitative.

continued ...

CHAPTER 5 The types of research

> However, the researcher might prefer to ask people what they know, and how they learned what they know. In this case, members of the community might describe different educational techniques including experiential learning, learning by observing and copying other people in the community, learning by rote and so forth. They might speak about their practical knowledge and their understanding of their world. Here, language is the tool by which social reality is recorded and the research is qualitative.
>
> Finally, a research project might wish to think of education in both these forms, a more complex view of education in the community. This would be an example of mixed-methods research.

Basic and applied research

Sometimes the researcher's primary motivation is to contribute to human knowledge and understanding about a particular phenomenon. This is usually achieved by gathering more facts and information that may challenge existing theories and allow new ones to be developed. The actual utility or application of this newly acquired knowledge is of little concern to the researcher. This kind of research is called **basic research**.

At other times the researcher's primary motivation is to assist in solving a particular problem facing a particular community. This is referred to as **applied research** and is often achieved by applying basic research findings to a particular community's challenges. In this way applied research may assist that community to overcome their problem or at least design interventions to address it.

Example

> A researcher who studies the critical factors leading to the pollution of ground water in highly industrialised regions would be doing basic research, since her study aims to increase human understanding of water pollution. A different researcher who is concerned with protecting the drinking water of a particular community that is located near a water polluting factory would be doing applied research, since the purpose of his study is to solve a particular problem facing that community, probably using knowledge gained from basic research.

In many cases the distinction between basic and applied research is not very helpful. Almost no social research is completely without application, and even very specific local projects may teach important lessons about work in similar communities, if well conducted. The researcher who finds a good way of protecting the water supply of a particular community will be able to share that same plan with other people working in similarly threatened communities. In this way, that solution becomes part of the more general understanding of water pollution. Similarly, the general study of water pollution should yield some new ideas on how local water supplies might be protected. As such, the basic study finds application in the life of a particular community.

59

The social problems facing African countries in Africa and other parts of the developing world sometimes seem overwhelming. Ongoing wars, extreme poverty, global economic trends and diseases such as Aids present regular emergencies and chronic threats to many people on the continent. A great deal of Africa's scarce resources is spent on the struggle for basic health and safety for all of the continent's citizens. It is becoming clear that the most effective strategies for surmounting these challenges are based on a concerted effort by whole communities of empowered people. Individual, curative type interventions are enormously expensive and do not address the underlying social causes of many of these problems. Community-based projects with a preventative or resilience-building strategy appear to offer far more viable solutions. The various ways in which research methodologies are applied to community projects are discussed in later chapters.

Exploratory, descriptive, correlational and explanatory research

Whether research is exploratory, descriptive, correlational or explanatory depends largely upon the researcher's objective, or aim in conducting the research.

Exploratory research

Exploratory research is called for where limited knowledge or information exists about a particular subject and the purpose of the research is to gain a broad understanding of a situation, phenomenon or community. One must become more familiar with a phenomenon if one is to formulate more searching research questions or hypotheses.

Social anthropologists, for instance, are occasionally confronted with a situation where a certain group of people living in a remote area has virtually no contact with the outside world. Thus, before being in a position to search for an explanation related to the modes of living of these people, or some other characteristic, a certain amount of background information must be gathered. In this case, the most appropriate type of research is exploratory research, and because so little is known about the topic, qualitative methods are often used.

Example

A researcher is interested in understanding the way in which the social systems of rural people in Sudan are helping communities survive famine. Because some rural communities in Sudan are somewhat reclusive and isolated, relatively little has been published on how these societies are organised. The researcher must therefore begin with a broad ethnographic study in one particular community with the objective of identifying a more focused research question down the line.

CHAPTER 5 The types of research

Descriptive research

In other cases, enough background knowledge is available to permit quite a precise topic of investigation. For instance, a researcher may be interested in finding out the opinion of a group of people towards a particular issue at a particular time. Descriptive research might involve a survey (for example, a population census), a one-shot case study, or in depth qualitative descriptions of the phenomenon. Various types of information can be collected in many different ways. For social issues, interviews where the interviewees can confide freely, as well as diaries, personal documents and participant observation are all useful. The greater part of the data collected in these ways will be qualitative and more or less reliable, depending on the source of the data and the skill of the researcher. A case study of a particular village suffering from famine should also include quantitative data such as the number, age and occupations of inhabitants. The more diverse and relevant the questions asked, the better the case study is likely to be.

The choice of one or the other technique is rarely arbitrary and depends on the aim of the research and on the type of data available. Bear in mind that if an event occurs only rarely, conducting a survey would have to be excluded due to a lack of sufficient data. In other situations, a case study may be inadvisable because it is very time-consuming and the data may not be compared easily to other results. Descriptive research can be conducted using quantitative, qualitative or mixed-methods approaches.

Finally, the descriptive method is also used to test factual hypotheses, or statements that do not relate two or more variables but express facts about the world. 'The sun is shining now' and 'Lake Kariba is an artificial lake' are examples of factual hypotheses. In these cases, the researcher has only to observe directly whether the sun is shining, or consult some historical or geographical documents about the formation of Lake Kariba in order to confirm the hypotheses.

Example

A researcher conducting descriptive research on social systems might wish to describe the ways in which food is stored and distributed during times of famine. This is a much more focused research question and it should be possible to describe the food storage and distribution systems for communities of different sizes, and at different times of the year. Quantitative data might include the quantity of grain in storage at any time, or the amount distributed to each person per week. Qualitative data might include a description of how community leaders make decisions as to how much food is to be distributed.

Correlational research

When a researcher is able to make a statement or hypothesis predicting the relationship between at least two variables, the results obtained will provide more than a mere description of reality. In this case the researcher is beginning to formulate some theory about how different variables relate to each other. In some cases the relationship between variables can be stated precisely, while in others it cannot. In correlational research, the researcher states that two variables co-vary, that is, that they change simultaneously. They may change in the same or opposite directions, but they must change together. Note that correlational research does not give an explanation of how variables are related. It merely indicates that they are related, and provides an indication of the strength and direction of the relationship. Quantitative and qualitative methodologies use different approaches to identify and demonstrate relationships between variables.

Example

In the study of systems of food storage and distribution in times of famine, the researcher might propose that the amount of food distributed to a family is closely related to the age of the oldest man in the family. The researcher believes that families, in which the oldest man is relatively young, get more food than those where the oldest man is relatively old. In this case the researcher is stating that the variables co-vary in opposite directions, that is, families with younger men get more food, families with older men get less food. Note that the researcher is not arguing that families get more food *because* the oldest man is younger, merely that the two variables are related.

Explanatory research

When a causal relationship between variables can be stated, and an explanation can be found for the variation of at least one variable, the research is explanatory.

When using an explanatory research method, one acquires a deeper understanding of the relationships between variables than one does when using either correlational or descriptive methods.

Example

In the study of food storage and distribution in times of famine, the researcher might have a hypothesis that in these communities older men are expected to be able to take care of their families, regardless of climactic conditions. In other words, the researcher is saying that cultural norms around age and masculinity result in (or cause) families with younger men receiving more food than families with older men.

Causality of this kind is difficult to demonstrate, a topic that is discussed in more depth in the next section. Again, quantitative and qualitative methodologies have different ways of investigating causal relationships.

Criteria for selection of research type

It should be clear that the choice of the type of research, whether exploratory, descriptive, correlational or explanatory, cannot be arbitrary. It depends on the following factors:

1. *The object of research*. Does the researcher have enough information to establish a relationship between variables? Can the different variables be manipulated or controlled in order to permit a study of the effect of one variable on another? For example, a researcher working with people whose culture has not been studied in detail before, cannot begin to start making specific hypotheses until a comprehensive exploratory study has been undertaken.
2. *The aim of the research*. Does it benefit the researcher to establish a causal relationship, or is correlational or descriptive research more appropriate? For example, in pre-election times one might merely be interested in the proportions of the population that will vote for the different candidates (descriptive), or one might want to know the factors which influence voting behaviour in order to improve the chances of a particular candidate (explanatory).
3. *The nature of the data to be collected*. How sophisticated are the available techniques that will be used for data collection? Do they require further development before they can be used in more elaborate research? How many participants does the researcher have access to? For example, the impact of cerebral lesions on emotional states, or the effect of strikes on some aspects of the economy can only be observed in a few cases since a researcher cannot damage a person's brain nor provoke a strike for the purposes of research.

Demonstrating causality

The question of causality has in some instances been very controversial. Many philosophers of science insist that, just because two variables co-vary, that is, vary together, this does not mean that one causes the other. For example, if we find that people who are highly educated are also less racist, can we say that education causes a reduction in prejudice? Another explanation may be that highly prejudiced people may avoid education or lack the motivation, self-discipline and intelligence needed to succeed in school. This alternative explanation for the relationship is called a plausible rival explanation.

There are generally accepted criteria that need to be met in order to demonstrate that one variable is causally related to another, and these criteria are temporal order, association and the elimination of plausible rival explanations.

1. *Temporal order*. A cause must always precede an effect. There are never circumstances when a cause happens after an effect.

2. *Association*. When one variable causes another to vary, there must be a strong relationship or association between them. Stated statistically, there must be a correlation between them. Two phenomena are associated if they occur together in a systematic way. If a researcher cannot find an association, then a causal relationship is impossible. Yet, as illustrated above, one can find an association without causality. Correlation or association is a necessary but not sufficient condition for causality.
3. *Eliminating plausible rival explanations*. A researcher must show that the supposed effect is due to the causal variable and not to something else. When an apparent causal relationship is actually due to an alternative but unrecognised cause, this is called a spurious relationship.

An example is the strong relationship between shoe size and reading ability among children. Clearly, neither one of these variables causes the other. They are both caused by a third variable, which is age.

Potential errors in causal explanation

Developing a good causal explanation for any kind of theory requires avoiding common logical errors. It is easiest to think of them as fallacies or false explanations that may appear to be legitimate on the surface.

1. *Tautology*. This is a form of circular reasoning in which someone appears to say something new but is really talking in circles and making a statement that is true by definition. The statement 'Poverty is caused by having very little money' is an example of tautology. This statement looks like a causal statement but is not actually one. The absence of money is a description of being poor, but cannot be the reason why the person is poor. The relationship is true by definition and involves circular reasoning.
2. *Spuriousness*. To call a relationship between variables spurious is to say that it is false, an illusion. Researchers get excited if they think they have found a spurious relationship because they can show the world to be more complex than it appears on the surface. Because any association between two variables might be spurious, researchers are cautious when they discover that two variables are associated – upon further investigation, it may not be the basis for a causal relationship.

Testing a causal hypothesis

The five characteristics of a causal hypothesis are:
1. It has at least two variables.
2. It expresses a causal or cause/effect relationship between the variables.
3. It can be expressed as a prediction or future outcome.
4. It is logically linked to a research question and a theory.

CHAPTER 5 The types of research

5. It is falsifiable, that is, it is capable of being tested against empirical evidence and shown to be true or false.

How can a researcher test a causal hypothesis? Suppose that two variables, A and B, have been identified, and that a relationship is observed between them. In other words, the researcher has noted some form of regularity in the way in which the two variables vary in relation to each other. To use a concrete example, let A be malnutrition and B illiteracy. Their simultaneous existence can be interpreted in three possible ways.

1. Variable A is the cause of variable B or, in this case, malnutrition is the cause of illiteracy, as for instance, malnutrition affects the intellectual development of children, who are then unable to benefit from education and so do not learn to read and write.

2. Variable B is the cause of variable A or, in this case, illiteracy is the cause of malnutrition, since illiterate parents are unable to find employment and so have no means to adequately feed their children.

3. Both variables A and B depend upon a third variable, or in this case, both illiteracy and malnutrition depend on socio-economic factors in the system, such as distribution of wealth and services within the country. In developed areas of the country, children are well fed and go to school. In less developed areas, there is not enough food and there are very few schools.

The problem here is to find some criteria to determine which one of the three alternatives is correct. Firstly, what does a causal relationship between two variables imply? If A is the cause of B, then the occurrence of A, the cause, is a necessary and sufficient condition for B, the effect, to occur. By necessary condition we mean that B can never occur unless A occurs first. By sufficient condition we mean that wherever A occurs, B will occur. The *occurrence* of A can be either necessary or sufficient for B to occur but A is the *cause* of B if, and only if, the occurrence of A is a necessary and sufficient condition for B to occur. Then B is the effect of A and there is a causal relationship between B and A.

Under experimental conditions the researcher builds controls into the study design itself so as to eliminate plausible rival explanations for the effect. Thus, the experimental situation is isolated from the influence of all variables except the main causal variable. For this reason, the most effective and convincing method of demonstrating a causal relationship between two variables is to conduct an experiment, or controlled trial.

Fundamentals of Social Research Methods: An African Perspective

> ## Example
>
> Malnutrition is a necessary condition for illiteracy if, whenever illiteracy is encountered, malnutrition is also present (although malnutrition can be found without illiteracy). Malnutrition is a sufficient condition for illiteracy if, whenever malnutrition occurs, illiteracy is present (although illiteracy can be found without malnutrition). Finally, malnutrition is the cause of illiteracy if the latter occurs only when the former exists and does so as a prior or concommital condition. At the same time, illiteracy cannot be found among normally fed people, and nor can malnourished people be literate.

To decide which one of the three previous interpretations of the relationship between variables is correct, three checks must be performed. Only if all three conditions are satisfied is a causal relationship between A and B assured. These conditions are the following:

1. *Proof of the co-variance of A and B.* In other words, the researcher must demonstrate that a relationship exists between the variation of A and B. Using the above example, the researcher must show some regularity in the presence (or absence) of both malnutrition and illiteracy.
2. *Proof of the non-spuriousness of the co-variance.* In other words, the researcher must exclude a third variable which alone can determine the variations of both A and B. Using the above example, the researcher must exclude all other factors which might influence the presence (or absence) of both malnutrition and illiteracy.
3. *Proof of a stable time-order.* In other words, the researcher must demonstrate that the cause always precedes the effect or, in terms of the example, that malnutrition always comes before illiteracy.

If points 1 and 2 are proved, interpretations (i) and (ii) on the previous page may be correct. If A always precedes B (that is, there is a stable time-order) and point 3 is correct, interpretations (i) and (iii) could be correct. Taken together, it is clear that only interpretation (i) is possible, in other words, A is the cause of B.

From this short analysis it becomes obvious that the task of determining the existence of a causal relationship is a complex and difficult one. It is based on systematic comparison, manipulation and control of variables. The plan of how to proceed in determining the nature of the relationship between variables is called a **research design**. This constitutes the backbone of explanatory research and the quality of the research depends largely on the correct choice of design. Some research designs are presented in Chapter 10, together with a discussion of their relative weaknesses and strengths.

The purpose of correlational research is often only to detect the existence of a relationship between variables (co-variance) that suggests a possible base for causality. In this case, correlational research is useful as a first step to explanatory research. Correlation does not necessarily imply causation, but causation always implies

CHAPTER 5 The types of research

correlation, since if A causes B, A and B must vary together. Note that correlational research is at times the only possible research method. Often explanatory research is not feasible. This is the case when it is not possible to manipulate the variables or to assess the time-order.

Furthermore, in the case of a non-causal relationship, a correlational study can assess the type and strength of the relationship between two variables. For example, one can correlate the productivity of a shoe factory with the type of technology used, the state of repair of the machinery, the number of workers, their skills, wages and conditions of service, the availability of raw materials, spare parts, etc. Each of these factors should, to a different extent, contribute to the variation in the productivity of the shoe factory. A correlational study will allow for an evaluation of the importance (or strength) of each relationship, or the contribution of each factor to productivity. This is of great practical relevance. It will also indicate whether each of these factors promotes productivity (positive correlation) or inhibits productivity (negative correlation). Therefore, a correlational study is not only useful when no clear causal relationship exists, but it also allows for an estimation of the strength of the relationship between two variables even when one variable is influenced by many others. Moreover, this type of research does not involve elaborate research designs.

In conclusion, the four types of research (exploratory, descriptive, correlational and explanatory) are applied to different aspects of the same research topic. For instance, concentrating on the results of an election, one could explore the range of voter attitudes, describe the political trends expressed by the number of seats won in parliament by each political party, correlate the level of education of the voters with their level of involvement in the election process, or analyse the cause/effect relationship between voting preferences of parents and that of their children, and thereby attempt to explain voting behaviour.

To conclude this section, some examples of bad and good research questions for these four different kinds of research are offered.

Example

Bad research questions

Not empirically testable, non-scientific questions
Should prostitution be legalised?
Should capital punishment be implemented in South Africa?

General topics, not research questions
Treatment of alcohol and drug abuse.
Sexuality and ageing.
Capital punishment and racial discrimination.
Urban decay and gangs.

continued ...

> **Questions that are too vague and ambiguous**
> - Do police affect delinquency?
> - What can be done to prevent child abuse?

Example

Good research questions

Exploratory
- How do young Zambian mothers experience health services in their country?

Descriptive
- How has the infant mortality rate in Zambia changed over the past 10 years?
- What factors do doctors feel explain changes in the infant mortality rate over the past ten years?

Correlational
- Is the infant mortality rate in particular hospitals related to the average income of people living in the surrounding area?
- Do mothers with better education have greater access to healthcare?

Explanatory
- Have changes in the training of medical personnel caused a drop in the infant mortality rate?

Research and the internet

The growth of the internet over the past 20 years has produced many new opportunities (as well as some dangers) for social researchers. Africa has the lowest internet penetration of all the continents. Only about 6% of Africans have access to the internet, compared to about 35% of people globally. This is sometimes referred to as the 'digital divide'. However, advances in cellular phone technology are giving more and more African people access to the internet.

In the short term, though, a central concern about any research conducted over the internet in Africa is that it can only ever reach people with access, a serious distortion of the general population. And yet there are populations, such as business executives or information technology professionals who will all have access to the internet. For research on these groups, the internet provides many advantages and opportunities.

CHAPTER 5 The types of research

1. Data collection can be quicker and more affordable. For example, questionnaires can be emailed and interviews can be conducted using voice over internet protocols.
2. The researcher can reach respondents over a very broad geographic area, such as the whole of Africa, or even the whole world.
3. Respondents can participate in data collection from the privacy and comfort of their own homes.

Of course, the internet is itself a source of enormous amounts of data. For example, market researchers pay close attention to what kind of people visit which sites on the internet, how long they spend on those sites, and how often they return to them. This kind of data can provide important insight into the attitudes, beliefs, values and aspirations of internet users.

Other uses of the internet are discussed in more detail elsewhere. The use of online databases for literature searches and access to published material was discussed in Chapter 4, and the advantages and disadvantages of emailed questionnaires are discussed in Chapter 12.

Without doubt, the growth of the internet and changing patterns of internet access are some of the most important factors changing the way in which social research is conducted today.

Key points

1. There are several different ways to divide the field of social research.
2. Quantitative, qualitative and mixed-methods research approaches are distinguished primarily by the form of data collected.
3. Basic and applied research are distinguished by the desired outcome: pure knowledge or social intervention.
4. Primary and secondary research are differentiated by whether the data was collected specifically to answer the current research question, or for some other reason.
5. Exploratory, descriptive, correlational and explanatory research are distinguished by the aims of the researcher and thus the methodologies employed.
6. A demonstration of causality demands (a) demonstration of co-variance; (b) refutation of alternative explanations; and (c) demonstration of a stable time order.
7. The growth of the internet and increasing access to online resources offer both opportunities and dangers to the social researcher.

Checklist

Keywords:

Check whether the meaning of these concepts introduced in this chapter is clear to you.

quantitative research; qualitative research; mixed-methods research; basic research; applied research; primary research; secondary research; exploratory research; descriptive research; correlational research; explanatory research; causality; tautology; circular reasoning; necessary and sufficient conditions; and, spuriousness.

Your research:

1. Ensure that you understand precisely what kind of research you are conducting. Is it quantitative, qualitative or mixed-methods? Is it basic or applied? It is primary or secondary? Is it exploratory, descriptive, correlational or explanatory?
2. If you are conducing explanatory research, make sure you are familiar with the demands of demonstrating causality. How will you demonstrate co-variance? How will you refute alternative explanations? How will you demonstrate a stable time-order?
3. If you are using the internet, make sure that you are not working with an extremely biased sample. (Refer to Chapter 11 for more details.)

Exercises

1. A researcher is interested in the impact of crime on tourism. Suggest two quantitative and two qualitative research questions relating to this topic.
2. Describe the difference between applied and basic social research. What are the relative advantages and disadvantages of each?
3. Choose a research topic and formulate an exploratory, descriptive, correlational and explanatory research problem related to aspects of your topic. Possible examples are:
   a. the employment conditions of industrial workers in your country
   b. the economic development of a particular region
   c. recent educational reforms in the primary school curriculum
   d. the effectiveness of an Aids education campaign.
4. What extra demands are made on research design by explanatory research as compared to correlational research?
5. Suggest a research question which you think would be ideal for internet-based research. Explain why you chose this question.

Additional resources

1. Babbie, E R. 2004. *The practice of social research*, 10th ed. Belmont, CA: Wadsworth.
2. Babbie, E R &, Rubin, A. 2010. *Research methods in social work*, 7th ed. Belmont, CA: Brooks/Cole.

CHAPTER 6

Research questions and variables

The purpose of this chapter is to learn how to develop a good research question. The research question is the focal point of the entire study and determines the type of research, the design of the research, the way the sample is created, the way data is collected and analysed, and ultimately the way in which the results are reported. Every research question also highlights the most important concepts or variables that are to be studied in the research. In some kinds of research, research questions are stated somewhat broadly. In others, research questions are stated very precisely and might be accompanied by very specific research hypotheses.

> **CHAPTER OBJECTIVES**
>
> Learners who have completed this chapter will be able to:
> - Formulate a research question.
> - Identify the various concepts or variables associated with a research question.
> - Appropriately define and operationalise variables.
> - Where appropriate, formulate testable hypotheses.

Formulation of the research question

In Chapter 4 we discussed various sources of research topics and described how important it is that researchers have a deep interest or passion for their research work. In fact, inexperienced researchers are often so enthusiastic about their research that they begin to work too quickly, without giving enough time to carefully designing the research question on which they will be working. Very often, research questions are defined too vaguely. An important rule when formulating a research question is that it should be specific rather than general. When a question is specific and focused, it becomes a more answerable research question than if it remains general and unfocused. For example, the question, 'What are Ugandans' attitudes towards contraception?' is extremely vague. The question, 'What are the attitudes of Ugandan women attending antenatal clinics in Kampala towards the female condom?' is much more focused and specific.

Background information obtained from the literature review and other sources helps to position the research question within the theoretical framework and existing results. As is often stated, a well-formulated problem is already a half-solved problem. A research question is usually expressed as a general question about the *relationship between two or more concepts or variables*.

> ### Example
>
> Let us consider the development of a women's cooperative in Zambia as a research topic. This is a very broad topic, and there are many different research questions that we might ask, for instance:
>
> 1. *Are the credit facilities available to women's cooperatives adequate?* In this case, important aspects of the research would be (a) the financial needs of the cooperatives (perhaps measured as an average amount per year in Kwacha); and (b) the credit facilities currently available from banks and other institutions. Of course, the financial needs will themselves be determined by other factors, such as the size of particular cooperatives, and any profit available for reinvestment from the previous year. The credit available will also be determined by other things, such as the economic climate in the country and the cooperative's past credit record.
> 2. *How do family obligations relate to the time that women make available for work at the cooperative?* This is a very different question relating to the same research topic. In this case the researcher would need to investigate many aspects relating to the family obligations of cooperative members. These would include marital status, number of children, the age of children, whether other people in the family are working, whether other people in the family can take responsibility for household chores, and whether there are any old people or sick people in the family who need to be taken care of. All of these will need to be compared with the number of hours per week that women actually work at the cooperative.
> 3. *What factors motivate Zambian women to join cooperatives?* For this question the researcher would be interested in a potentially wide range of factors. These might include the desire to contribute money to the family, the desire to have some money of their own, the desire to learn new skills and competencies, and the desire to socialise with more people outside of the family.

This example shows us that a single research topic can produce many research questions, and that it is important to decide exactly which question it is that you are working on before you begin. The research question itself always includes various concepts or variables. It is very helpful to identify and define these carefully. How to achieve this is discussed in the next sections.

Concepts, variables and constants

As we described in the previous chapter, different kinds of research use different languages. The word '**concept**' refers to a particular idea that can be described in words. As such it is more closely associated with qualitative research. The word '**variable**' has a similar function in quantitative research. 'Variable' means that something varies and that its variation can be measured. For the sake of simplicity, we will generally use the word 'variable' in these chapters. One can measure variation with numbers

CHAPTER 6 Research questions and variables

as in quantitative research, or one can describe variation with words as in qualitative research. In a mixed methods study you will, of course, be doing both.

Since a variable is something that varies from one observation to the next, it needs to be contrasted with a **constant**, which does not vary. If you recruit a sample of people into a study, it is likely that the members of the sample will vary in age and therefore age is a variable. They may also vary in terms of intelligence, socio-economic status, linguistic group or gender. All of these are variables. If you only recruit men into a sample, then gender is a constant, that is, it does not vary in terms of your sample. Similarly, if you only study children in Grade 1, then school grade is a constant, but age and gender might be variables.

> ### Example
>
> Consider a crowd gathered at a sports stadium. The people are of different sexes, different age groups, different social backgrounds, from different residential areas, and so on. All these differences of sex, age, social background, place of residence, etc are variables that have to be given particular values. They are thus converted into variables with different levels. The variable 'sex' has two levels or two different values that it can take, namely 'male' and 'female'. The variable 'age' can take many more values, such as 'below 20 years', '21–30 years', or any number between 0 and 100. But all the people gathered could have some common property, something that is constant. They may all be citizens of the same country or they may all have come to the stadium to watch the same event, that is, they may all share the same interest. Such concepts are constants.

Identification of the variables

Much of social science research involves understanding the relationship between variables. Suppose that a problem has been formulated in a way that relates two or more variables. It may be relevant to ask such questions as: 'Which are these variables and how are they related? Do they all have the same importance? Do they all vary at the same time? Do changes in one variable cause changes in another variable?' Different variables may play particular roles in a certain problem. Some variables may be the ones influencing other variables, determining the values of these affected variables. These are the **independent variables** (indicated by **IV**). Other variables may be subject to other causes so that their values are influenced by the values of other variables. These are the **dependent variables** (indicated by **DV**). Independent and dependent variables are the two most important types of variable. As the names indicate, both are tied to each other by a certain relationship: the variations in one (the dependent variable) are a function, or a consequence, of the variations in the other (the independent variable). Put another way, changes in the IV cause changes in the DV.

73

Example

It is well known that the height of a child (DV) depends on its age (IV). To prove this assertion, a researcher will have to take many children of different ages, say 1, 3, 5, 9, 12 and 15 years old, and measure their respective heights. In so doing, the independent variable 'age' will be given different values or levels by the researcher. In some cases, the researcher manipulates the independent variable. Then the corresponding measured values of the other variable, the height of each child, will be compared to the age. A certain regularity should become evident: the height of the child (DV) should vary according to the age (IV), or younger children should be shorter than older ones. Obviously, it is not because a child measures 98 cm that she is five years old, but rather she is 98 cm (small) because of being only five years old.

Independent and dependent variables are defined more precisely as follows:

- The **independent variable** is that factor which is measured, manipulated or selected by the researcher to determine its relationship to an observed phenomenon that constitutes the dependent variable.
- The **dependent variable** is that factor which is observed and measured to determine the effect on it of the independent variable, that is, it is that factor that appears, disappears, diminishes or amplifies, in short, varies as the experimenter introduces, removes or varies the independent variable.

In order to clarify and illustrate these very important points, three examples will be considered.

Example

Sociological example: Regarding the question about the possible causes of divorce, the independent variable, which is the age of the partners at the time of marriage, is given two sets of values: married when under 23 years of age and married when 23 years or older. The researcher, when selecting the participants, will categorise them, using this criterion. Then, by measuring the values taken by the dependent variable, that is, the stability of the marriage measured in terms of the number of years without divorce, the researcher will be able to draw a conclusion about the effects of marrying young on divorce rates.

Health example: The kindness that a nurse displays in treating a very anxious patient will depend to some extent upon the working conditions in the hospital. A researcher might describe the tone of voice and facial expressions of nurses working in different hospitals to show how the quality of working conditions (IV) affects nurses' bedside manner, that is, their behaviour towards patients (DV).

continued...

CHAPTER 6 Research questions and variables

> **Economic example:** The output in the number of bags of maize per hectare (dependent variable) may be a function of the quantity of fertiliser used (independent variable). The researcher will manipulate the last variable by choosing different levels or quantities of fertiliser to be used per hectare and will then measure the output in maize per hectare for each level of the independent variable. The output of maize is clearly expected to vary according to the amount of fertiliser used.

Another kind of variable is the **moderator variable**. In the simple example of the relationship between the age and height of children, a researcher could argue that other factors also influence the height of a child. These include the child's sex, the height of his or her parents and the quality of the child's diet. These additional variables affecting the dependent variable are called moderators. In other words, the **moderator variable** is that factor which is measured, manipulated or selected by the researcher to discover whether or not it modifies the relationship between the independent and dependent variables. Since moderator variables share some of the characteristics of independent variables (in that they are measured or manipulated by the researcher to observe the effect on the dependent variable), they can be thought of as 'secondary independent variables'.

Example

> **Sociological example:** To return to the example about the causes of divorce, the economic circumstances of a couple or the birth of a child shortly after marriage could be moderator variables. If the couple is economically self-reliant the negative or adverse effects of the youth of the couple on the stability of the marriage could be reduced. The necessity to care for a new born might strengthen the ties between a very young couple who may otherwise have felt the need for an early divorce.
>
> **Health example:** In the example of research on nurses' bedside manner in different working conditions there might also be important moderator variables. For example, differences in socio-economic status between the nurse and the patient might moderate the effect of the working environment. It is conceivable that patients who are viewed by nurses as coming from a lower class are treated worse than other patients when the working conditions in the hospital are stressful. In this case the social class of the patient moderates the impact of stressful work conditions on the bedside manner of the nurse.
>
> **Economic example:** When studying the maize output per hectare, the moderator variable could be the amount of water available. Using a system of irrigation which allows the experimenter to manipulate the amount of water supplied per hectare, one could study the effect of different quantities of water on the output where the amount of fertiliser used is the same. In other words, knowing that the output (dependent variable) will increase as a function of the use of fertiliser (independent variable), it must be checked how this increase is accelerated or decelerated by the amount of water used (moderator variable).

Most of the phenomena studied in social sciences cannot be explained by the effect of only one independent variable. The variation in the independent variable can usually only *partly* account for the variation in the dependent variable. More of the variation will be explained or accounted for by introducing secondary independent and moderator variables. But, the simultaneous variation of many variables will make an assessment of the role of any one particular variable impossible. This is illustrated in the next example.

Example

A researcher is interested in the health of young children in a particular community and how it is affected by the fact that a new clinic has been opened in the area. A comparison of children's health before and after the opening of the new clinic reveals a general improvement. However, the researcher also notes that the average income of families in the communities has risen during the past year. In this case it is extremely difficult to tell whether the improvement in children's health is due to the improved healthcare facilities or the improved economic situation of their parents.

One way to overcome this kind of problem is through the control of certain variables.

Control variables are those factors that are controlled by the researcher to cancel out or neutralise any effect they may otherwise have on the observed phenomenon. For instance, when measuring the height of children as a function of their age, one should control for their health condition, since malnutrition has a negative effect on growth. Practically, it means that children of the same nutritional background (control variable) but different ages (independent variable) should be compared on the basis of their height (dependent variable). Note that, depending on the aim of the research, the quality of the diet given to children or the health condition of the children could be considered as a moderator variable.

Example

Sociological example: When looking at the causes of divorce, the role of culture could be controlled by choosing only couples belonging to the same ethnic group, or the role of education could be neutralised by selecting couples with similar levels of education.

Health example: When looking at nurses' bedside manner, it would be possible for the researcher to design the study so that nurses' manner is only measured when they are interacting with a person from a similar social class to that from which they themselves come. In this way the effects of the patient's social class are eliminated from the research and it becomes possible to examine the effect of working conditions more clearly.

Economic example: When looking at the maize production, the quality of the soil or meteorological conditions could be controlled for by choosing only sample hectares under cultivation in the same area.

CHAPTER 6 Research questions and variables

Two other variables, both related to the independent variable, often play an important role. The **antecedent variable**, as indicated by its name, appears before the independent variable and determines it.

> ### Example
>
> **Health example:** The hospital working conditions (the independent variable) may be strongly influenced by the economic situation of the area in which the hospital is located. It is conceivable that nurses who feel trapped in a situation with poor working conditions, because there are no better employment opportunities in the area, will feel particularly frustrated by their anxious clients.
>
> **Economic example:** For the maize output per hectare, the independent variable, which is the quantity of fertiliser used, may be strongly influenced by the financial situation of the farmer who can or cannot afford to buy as much fertiliser as he or she would like to. Thus the research could have been to analyse the output of maize as a function of the wealth of the farmer.

Note that if the antecedent variable is held constant, the relationship between independent and dependent variable still exists.

> ### Example
>
> **Health example:** Even if one takes nurses working in a more affluent part of the country where there are opportunities for improvement, the different working conditions in different hospitals will still influence the bedside manner of the nurses.
>
> **Economic example:** One selects only farmers of the same economic position: those who utilise different quantities, but the same quality of fertiliser. The output of maize will still vary.

Conversely, if the antecedent variable is allowed to take different levels, but the independent variable has a fixed level, the dependent variable will not vary.

> ### Example
>
> **Health example:** The researcher chooses hospitals from many different parts of the country that all have stressful work environments. In this case, no matter in which part of the country the data is collected, nurses will be less considerate towards their patients.

The **intervening variable** is in some ways the opposite. It is a consequence of the independent variable and it determines the variation of the dependent variable. It falls between the independent and dependent variables, so that, if it is held constant, the latter will not vary.

> **Example**
>
> **Health example:** Continuing with the example of the nurses working under stressful hospital conditions, we can imagine that the working conditions will also affect the way hospital managers treat the nurses whom they manage. In other words, because of the stressful work conditions, managers are often very rude to nursing staff. The managers' behaviour (intervening variable) is a consequence of the hospital conditions (independent variable) and influences the nurses' behaviour (dependent variable). If the researcher selected only nurses working under managers who were always respectful mangers (regardless of their own working conditions), we might see that the nurses' bedside manner was also more compassionate and patient. Thus by holding the intervening variable constant, we have reduced the variation in the dependent variable.
>
> **Economic example:** If the use of fertiliser has, as a consequence, the need for more weeding (which is a time-consuming activity proportional to the quantity of fertiliser used), the intervening variable could be the time needed for weeding. If this time is held constant, there will not be a significant variation of the output of maize, since the crop would have been harmed by the lack of weeding. One would also consider the quantity of fertiliser used as an intervening variable when the independent variable is the financial situation of the farmer.

It is useful to think of antecedent, independent, moderator, intervening and dependent variables as being connected in a causal chain or network. It is part of the social researcher's function to explore these various causal links. However, the researcher should also be watchful for accidental connections and extraneous variables.

An **extraneous variable** is a variable that influences both the independent and dependent variables, giving the false impression of a relationship between them.

> **Example**
>
> Often people who are afraid of hospital treatment will comment that, for the same age group, the death rate in hospitals is much higher than outside hospitals. Although nobody will contest this statement, can one infer from this covariation (being admitted to hospital and dying) that one is the cause of the other? Or, are they both due to a third variable, the ill health of people admitted to hospital?

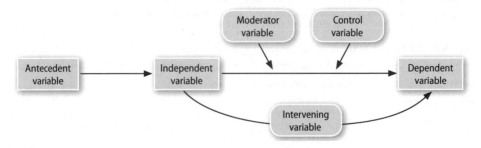

Figure 6.1 *Relationship between different types of variables*

CHAPTER 6 Research questions and variables

A final example illustrates this relationship again.

Example

The research of a sociologist focuses on the effect of background sound on employees' performance of clerical tasks in a large enterprise.

1. The independent variable is the sound environment and has four levels:
   a. total silence
   b. incoherent street noise
   c. classical music
   d. modern popular music.
2. The dependent variable is the work performance of a group of employees in a specific set of clerical tasks.
3. Moderator variables might include the type of task (simple or complex), the age of the employee (below 25 years, 25–40 years, more than 40 years), and the cultural background of the employee (African or Western).
4. The control variable is sex, since it is presumed that male and female employees perform differently in clerical tasks. Thus, the sample is constituted only of women.
5. The antecedent variable is the acoustic nature of the office and includes the type and height of the ceiling, size of the hall, the presence of windows, the arrangement of the furniture, and the existence or otherwise of a carpet. The level of background noise will be influenced by all these factors.
6. The intervening variable is the stress or the soothing effect of the sounds and has two levels: stressful and soothing.

In quantitative research it is essential that these six types of variable are correctly identified and defined. Only when this task has been completed can the researcher begin to specify hypotheses and explore ways of testing them. The same kinds of variables can be identified in qualitative research too. However, because qualitative research emphasises the complex interactions of many variables within their real world context and employs a more fluid process, it is less important in this case to clearly identify and define every variable at the beginning of the study.

Note that variables take on various roles in relation to different research questions. In other circumstances, the independent variable could actually depend on a different variable, or the dependent variable could serve as an independent variable predicting the variation in yet another variable.

Example

The instability of marriage, measured through the rate of divorce, which was the dependent variable in the sociological example, could become an independent (or moderator) variable in a study investigating the impact of marriage instability on performance at work. Moreover, the independent variable, age at time of marriage, could become a dependent variable when investigating the impact of education or of residential area on age at marriage. It could be asked: 'Do people with secondary school education marry later than people with primary school education?' or 'Is the age at time of marriage of the urban population higher than that of the rural population?'

Lastly, having identified all the variables, criteria must be established whereby their different values may be measured. In other words, the variables must be defined in a way that allows a systematic and accurate description or measurement of their variation.

Conceptual and operational definitions

Verbal communication among human beings would be impossible without the existence of words expressing concepts. When one speaks of a table or a tree, of patience or of efficiency, one uses words to describe the empirical world, something which exists, in an abstract way. People share a general idea or a concept of what a table is, allowing all objects considered as tables to be classified under this category, even if they differ in shape, colour or material. The same is true of more abstract concepts, such as who is a patient person or what is an efficient organisation.

The main functions of concepts are, firstly, to facilitate communication among human beings. Secondly, concepts aid in the classification of the elements of reality and their generalisation. By observation of some plants, one may distinguish between particular characteristics and thus classify one plant as a 'tree', another as a 'flower'. The concept 'tree' can be applied, by generalisation, to all other plants sharing the same characteristics. Thirdly, in research, concepts are the building blocks of theories. The concepts of assimilation and accommodation are cornerstones of Piaget's theory of cognitive development – the concepts of supply and demand constitute fundamentals of classic economic theory.

But for concepts to be useful, they must be defined in a clear, precise, non-ambiguous and agreed-upon way. For an exchange of views to take place, the participants must 'speak the same language'. They must attribute the same meaning to the concepts they use. This is particularly important in research.

The two types of definition useful for our purpose are conceptual and operational definitions. A **conceptual definition** is the definition of a concept in terms of a set of other concepts. Thus, a courageous person is a brave person, or a person able to control fear in the face of danger, or a person who remains calm in the face of threatening events. A hungry person is someone who needs food. Since concepts are still to be defined by other concepts, they form a chain until one encounters primitive terms.

CHAPTER 6 Research questions and variables

These primitive terms, like colours, sounds and odours, cannot be defined in terms of other concepts. Instead, their meaning is conveyed by direct experience, such as 'blue as the sky', 'hot as fire' and 'hard as rock'. Concepts like sky, fire and rock used in this analogy are things that one can see or experience.

A conceptual definition cannot be true or false, but it may or may not be useful for communication. Below are some properties that conceptual definitions should have in order to be useful.

1. *A conceptual definition must denote the distinctive characteristics of that which is defined.* It must include all things belonging to this class, but only these things. For example, defining a fish as an animal living in water would include whales and shrimps, neither of which are fish.
2. *A conceptual definition should not be circular.* In other words, it should not describe something by using the same concept. For example, an impatient person should not be defined as a person lacking patience.
3. *A conceptual definition should be stated positively*, expressing the properties shared by the objects and not the properties they lack. For example, a book cannot adequately be described as not being a mode of transportation.
4. *A conceptual definition should be stated in clear and unequivocal terms* to avoid different interpretations. For example, defining a substance as being a drug could lead to two interpretations: medicinal or narcotic.

Even a very well-formulated conceptual definition does not fulfil the need of a researcher who wants to assess the existence of some empirical phenomenon. This is the function of an **operational definition**. Thus an operational definition not only gives precise indications as to what the fundamental characteristics of a concept are, but it also gives precise indications about how to observe, describe or measure the characteristics under study. Stated in another way: an **operational definition** is based on the observable characteristics of an object or phenomenon and indicates what to do or what to observe in order to identify these characteristics.

Instead of defining a hungry person as a person needing food, a researcher who finds it difficult to assess the existence of this need will prefer one of the following definitions: a person who has been deprived of food for 24 hours, a person who can eat a loaf of bread in less than 10 minutes, or a person whose blood sugar level is lower than a specified level. Although these three definitions are quite different, they share a common property: they indicate a way of observing, describing and measuring the phenomenon under investigation. If a researcher wants to be convinced that a certain person is hungry, any one of these three methods can be chosen and other researchers will agree that the person is hungry on the basis of the given definition.

Clearly, a concept may be described by more than one operational definition. Depending on the aim of the research, an adult can be defined as 'physically grown to full size and strength' (biological approach), as 'economically self-reliant' (economic approach, excluding students and the unemployed) or as 'enjoying the right to vote' (legal approach, relative to the country's constitution). Some constraints, like the unavailability of direct information or the need to obtain information through secondary sources, will influence the way concepts are operationalised. For instance, if one cannot assess the wealth of research participants by direct evaluation of their income, one can define their wealth by what is observable in their way of living: residential areas, ownership of houses, ownership of luxury items like cars, television sets, stereo sets and furniture. A particular operational definition may even be unique for the particular situation, or research for which it has been conceived.

Within the multiplicity of possible operational definitions, three types can be constructed, as seen in the above example of a hungry person. The first type is an operational definition that indicates the operations that must be performed in order for the phenomenon under study to occur. For example, to make sure that the participant will be a hungry person, the researcher should deprive the participant of food for 24 hours. The second variant is an operational definition that indicates how a particular person or object possessing the characteristics under study will operate or act. Thus a person who, when presented with a loaf of bread, will eat it in less than 10 minutes, could be defined as being hungry. If a person takes more than 10 minutes to eat the loaf one can assume that this is not the case. The third variety is an operational definition that indicates some intrinsic properties of a person or phenomenon that possesses the characteristics under study. For instance, by measuring some property of a person, in this case the level of sugar in the blood, one can assess whether or not the person is hungry (low blood sugar levels).

The more unique an operational definition is, the more useful it is, since it discriminates accurately between elements that possess the characteristics under investigation and those that do not. In short, the most important feature of operational definitions is their ability to indicate measuring devices or assessment techniques to determine the level of the variables so defined. In our operational definitions of a hungry person, the first definition requires the measurement of the period a person has not eaten, the second definition relies on the time needed for a person to eat a loaf of bread, and the third definition suggests the measurement of blood sugar levels. By comparison, the initial conceptual definition of a hungry person − one who needs food − did not indicate how the person's need for food should be measured.

Hypothesis formulation

Essentially, research problems are questions about relationships among variables, and hypotheses are tentative, concrete and testable answers to such questions. In other words, a **hypothesis**, which is a suggested answer to a question, has to be tested empirically before it can be accepted and incorporated into a theory. If a hypothesis is not supported by empirical evidence, it must be rejected and the researcher is obliged to suggest another one. In this sense, the role of hypotheses is not only to suggest

CHAPTER 6 Research questions and variables

explanations for certain facts or problems but also to guide the investigation. While it is possible to develop hypotheses in qualitative research, the formal statement and testing of hypotheses is more commonly associated with quantitative research. This is because qualitative research is often more exploratory and descriptive in nature.

The following are the main characteristics of usable hypotheses.
1. *A hypothesis must be conceptually clear*. All variables identified must be clearly described, using operational definitions.
2. *A hypothesis should have empirical referents*. This property is an essential feature of a scientific approach to problems. It is fulfilled as soon as operational definitions have been found for all the concepts appearing in the statement of the hypothesis. Particular care should be taken to avoid moral judgements, attitudes and values. Expressions like 'good', 'bad', 'ought to', 'should', and the like are not scientific.
3. *A hypothesis must be specific*. This property reflects the fact that the range of the problem must be narrow enough to allow a precise, well-delimited investigation. If the problem is too wide, the hypothesis will be too general and thus not testable. Again, good operational definitions will safeguard against this pitfall. A hypothesis such as 'peasants are more prejudiced than workers' may sound interesting, but, unless 'peasants', 'workers' and, above all, 'prejudiced' have been given operational definitions, the hypothesis is not testable. 'Prejudiced' as such, without specifying that the prejudice is directed toward other racial groups, nationalities or foreign foods, may be beyond measurement. Moreover, a specific hypothesis makes mention not only of the independent and dependent variables, but also of the moderator and all control variables. As mentioned above, the effect of working conditions on nurses' bedside manner can only be reliably analysed if all other factors which could also influence bedside manner, such as nurses' training and the patient's social class, have been taken into account. Thus, the conditions under which relationships between variables are examined must be stated explicitly. In the example of the maize production, the effect of a certain fertiliser can only be reliably proven if all other factors that could also influence the production, such as quality of soil, period of fertiliser application and meteorological conditions have been controlled.
4. *A hypothesis must be testable with available techniques*. Although some investigations may be relevant and specific, it may not be possible to carry them out because of a lack of instruments or methods to measure or describe one or other of the variables. One can easily measure the temperature of a sick child, but how does one measure a lack of affection that affects the child's health? Thus, when formulating a hypothesis, it is very important to ensure that adequate techniques of observation and measurement are available. One way to go about this is to study carefully the operational definitions and be sure that they clearly indicate the methods of measurement or description.

83

The criteria for formulating a usable hypothesis emphasise the importance of adequate operational definitions of all variables. These, added to the correct identification of all variables, constitute the fundamentals of a good research project.

A final word is included about the way in which a hypothesis can be formulated. When a causal relationship between two variables is suspected, it is possible in some cases to determine precisely the direction (positive or negative) of this relationship.

Hypotheses concerning the cause of marriage instability could be variably formulated as follows:

1. The young age of the partners at the time of marriage (under 23 years) has an effect on the stability of their marriage.
2. The young age of the partners at the time of marriage (under 23 years) has adverse influences on the stability of the marriage.
3. The young age of the partners at the time of marriage (under 23 years) has positive influences on the stability of the marriage.

The first formulation is **non-directional**, since it does not indicate the direction in which the dependent variable will be influenced by the independent one. The second and third formulations indicate a negative and positive influence respectively and they are thus called **directional** hypotheses. Whether a hypothesis is presented in a non-directional or a directional form depends on the extent to which the researcher is able to predict the type of relationship between variables. Of course, because a directional hypothesis is more precise and gives more information, it is preferred. More information about testing hypotheses using quantitative methods is provided in Chapter 14.

Replication

Knowledge rarely advances on the basis of one test of a single hypothesis. In fact, it is easy to get a distorted picture of the research process by focusing on a single research project that tests one hypothesis. Instead, knowledge develops over time as researchers throughout the scientific community test many hypotheses.

Researchers are a sceptical group and thus support for a hypothesis in one research project is not sufficient for them to accept it. The principle of replication says that a hypothesis needs several tests with consistent and repeated support to gain broad acceptance.

Disconfirmation

The strongest contender, or the hypothesis with the greatest empirical support, is accepted as the best explanation at the time. This logic suggests that the more alternatives we test a hypothesis against, the greater our confidence in it becomes. A

CHAPTER 6 Research questions and variables

curious aspect of hypothesis testing is that researchers treat evidence that supports a hypothesis differently from evidence that opposes it. They give negative evidence more importance. The idea that negative evidence is critical when evaluating a hypothesis comes from the logic of disconfirming hypotheses. Disconfirmation is associated with the idea of falsification and with the use of null hypotheses. The **null hypothesis** is a hypothesis that states that the variables in question are not in fact related. Thus, if our hypothesis is 'The young age of the partners at the time of marriage (under 23 years) has adverse influences on the stability of the marriage', the associated null hypothesis would be 'The young age of the partners at the time of marriage (under 23 years) does not influence the stability of the marriage'. Thus a hypothesis is never proved, but it can be disproved. A researcher with supporting evidence can say only that the hypothesis remains a possibility or that it is still in the running.

Negative evidence is more significant because the hypothesis becomes 'tarnished' if the evidence contradicts it. Thus negative and disconfirming evidence shows that the predictions are wrong. Positive or confirming evidence for a hypothesis is less critical because plausible rival hypotheses may make the same prediction. A researcher who finds confirming evidence for a prediction may not elevate one explanation over its alternatives.

Example

A man stands on a street corner with an umbrella and claims that his umbrella protects him from falling elephants. His hypothesis that the umbrella provides protection has supporting evidence. He has not had a single elephant fall on him in all the time he has had his umbrella open. Yet, such supportive evidence is weak. It is also consistent with an alternative hypothesis — that elephants do not fall from the sky. Both predict that the man will be safe from falling elephants. Negative evidence for the hypothesis, that one elephant that falls on him and his umbrella crushes both, would destroy the hypothesis for good.

Many researchers, especially those conducting experiments, frame hypotheses in terms of a null hypothesis based on the logic of the disconfirming hypotheses. They test hypotheses by looking for evidence that will allow them to accept or reject the null hypothesis. Most people talk about a hypothesis as a way to predict a relationship. The null hypothesis does the opposite. It predicts no relationship.

Example

A researcher believes that students who live on campus in dormitories get higher grades than students who live off campus and commute to college. His null hypothesis is that there is no relationship between residence and grades. Researchers use the null hypothesis with a corresponding alternative hypothesis or experimental hypothesis. The alternative hypothesis says that a relationship exists. This researcher's alternative hypothesis is that students' on-campus residence has a positive effect on grades.

85

For most people, the null hypothesis approach seems like a backward way of hypothesis testing. Null hypothesis thinking rests on the assumption that researchers try to discover a relationship, so hypothesis testing should be designed to make finding a relationship more demanding. A researcher who uses the null hypothesis approach only directly tests the null hypothesis. If evidence supports or leads the researcher not to reject the null hypothesis, he or she concludes that the tested relationship might not exist. This implies that the alternative hypothesis is false. On the other hand, if the researcher can find evidence to reject the null hypothesis, then the alternative hypothesis remains a possibility. The researcher cannot prove the alternative. Rather, by testing the null hypotheses, he or she keeps the alternative hypothesis in contention.

The reason for this roundabout way of doing things is that the scientific community is extremely cautious. It prefers to consider a relationship to be false until mountains of evidence show it to be true. This is similar to the legal idea of being innocent until proven guilty beyond reasonable doubt. A researcher assumes, or acts as if the null hypothesis is correct, until reasonable doubt suggests otherwise.

Formulating a research question and a hypothesis do not have to proceed in fixed stages. A researcher can formulate tentative research questions, then develop possible hypotheses. The hypotheses then help the researcher state the research question more precisely. The process is interactive and involves creativity. Researchers use general theoretical issues as a source of topics. Theories provide concepts that researchers turn into variables, as well as the reasoning or mechanisms that help researchers connect the variables into a research question. A hypothesis can both answer a research question and be an untested proposition from a theory. Researchers can express a hypothesis at an abstract, conceptual level or restate it in a more concrete, measurable form.

Key points

1. Broad research topics must always be narrowed down to clearly defined research questions.
2. Research questions typically refer to a relationship between two or more concepts or variables.
3. Variables change from one observation to another whereas constants remain the same.
4. The research question concerns the influence of the independent variable(s) upon the dependent variable(s).
5. The relationship between the independent and dependent variable(s) is also influenced by moderator, control, antecedent and intervening variables.
6. Researchers should be careful to ensure that the relationship being studied is not the result of some other extraneous variable that has not been included in the study.
7. All concepts and variables must be carefully defined with both conceptual and operational definitions.

continued ...

CHAPTER 6 Research questions and variables

8. Hypotheses state a potential solution to the research question and may be directional or non-directional.
9. Science demands that results are replicated, or that the same hypotheses are tested in several studies, before the findings are accepted as being generally true.
10. Science proceeds by searching for evidence that a hypothesis is not true. This is called disconfirmation.

Checklist

Keywords:

Check whether the meaning of these concepts introduced in this chapter is clear to you.

research topic; research question; variable; constant; independent variable; dependent variable; control variable; moderator variable; antecedent variable; intervening variable; extraneous variable; conceptual definition; operational definition; hypothesis; directional hypothesis; non-directional hypothesis; null hypothesis; replication; disconfirmation.

Your research:
1. Have you formulated a clear and concise research question?
2. Have you identified all the variables of importance to your research question?
3. Have you decided which variables are to be the independent and dependent variables?
4. Have you identified any antecedent, intervening, moderator and control variables?
5. Have you developed clear conceptual definitions of all variables?
6. If appropriate, have you developed clear operational definitions for all variables?
7. If appropriate, have you developed testable hypotheses?

Exercises

1. In the following statements, identify the independent (IV), dependent (DV), control (CV) and moderator variables (MV).
   a. The less first-year male students are supervised in their tutorial work, the more they develop initiative and self-reliance as far as their reading is concerned. Female students, given the same conditions, develop less initiative.
   b. When food suppliers sell food made from local produce, the price of the end product is determined mainly by the level of technology and the cost of labour used in production. When imported produce is used, the cost of the end product is determined mainly by currency exchange rates.
   c. The frequency of attendance at nightclubs for young people between 16 and 20 years of age varies with the days of the week. The fluctuations are particularly strong for young men.

continued ...

87

2. Referring to the statements presented in the previous exercise, formulate an operational definition for each variable.
3. Why do researchers use operational definitions?
4. Formulate at least one directional and one non-directional hypothesis for each of the following questions:
   a. Is there a relationship between the involvement of women in cash-crop agriculture and the health conditions of their children?
   b. Does the introduction of more modern farming equipment in a village have a positive impact on the diet of inhabitants?
   c. Is there a relationship between the marital status of women (married or single) and their participation in decision making at work?
   d. Is there a difference between the professional identities of teachers working in private and government educational institutions?
5. Criticise and improve upon the following hypotheses:
   a. Urban life conditions are better than rural ones.
   b. The way people describe themselves is strongly influenced by the way their partners describe them.
   c. A religious person is more understanding than other persons.

Additional resources

Babbie, E R. 2010. *The practice of social research*, 12th ed. Belmont, CA: Thomson Wadsworth.

CHAPTER 7

Participatory and action research

The history of science in Africa is characterised by scientists from outside the continent studying and writing about Africans. African people were virtually never included in the design and analysis of the research and so had no control over what questions were asked, and what conclusions were reached. Participatory and action research is one way of giving ordinary people a central role in what research is done, how that research is conducted, and what results and conclusions are reached. In this way, research becomes more relevant to the day-to-day lives of ordinary people, and the power imbalances between those who create knowledge and those who use that knowledge are addressed.

> **CHAPTER OBJECTIVES**
>
> Learners who have completed this chapter will be able to:
> - Understand the importance of both action and participation in research in Africa.
> - Negotiate and plan a simple participatory action-research project.
> - Design simple participatory research methodologies.
> - Recognise the strengths and weaknesses of participatory action-research projects.

Participation in knowledge generation

Paulo Freire, the famous Brazilian teacher, philosopher and critical thinker, argued that:

> ... apart from inquiry, apart from the praxis, individuals cannot be truly human. Knowledge emerges only through invention and re-invention, through the restless, impatient, continuing, hopeful inquiry human beings pursue in the world, with the world, and with each other.
>
> (*Pedagogy of the Oppressed*, 1970)

Freire believed that what makes us truly human is the way we constantly create and recreate meaning about our world. He believed that knowledge is created through people struggling, debating, observing, analysing and arguing with each other about how to make the world a better place in which to live. When one group creates meaning about another group, the former wields power over the latter. For example, early anthropologists and theologians spent a great deal of time in Africa studying African people. The focus of their research was in large part determined by their own interests and values as researchers, rather than the interests and concerns of the people they studied. They were more interested in topics of African sexuality and intertribal wars than in African philosophical systems or technological innovations. These researchers painted a picture of Africans as primitive and unable to govern themselves, a position that was used to justify several hundred years of colonial oppression and exploitation.

In other words, Africans were excluded from a research process through which they and other people around the world came to understand them and their world better. They were excluded from the process of generating knowledge. Only when people are involved in the work of producing knowledge about themselves and their own world can they be free to define themselves. Participation in knowledge generation is the principle of self-determination applied to research. Participatory action research (PAR) is one way in which people can be more involved in the production of knowledge about their own lives.

In contrast to the other kinds of research previously discussed, participatory research is distinguished by two characteristics: the relationship between the people involved in the research, and the use of research as a tool for social change, as well as for increasing human knowledge. Thus, the conventional roles of researcher (the expert) and participants (naive objects unaware of the research hypotheses) are changed. **Participatory research** encourages the active participation of the people whom the research is intended to assist. In this way, it empowers people to be involved in all aspects of a project, including the planning and implementation of the research, and any solutions that emerge from the research. Everybody involved in the research project works together as a team.

Participatory research techniques focus on particular problems facing communities and attempt to use research (and the resulting action) as a tool to bring about social change. As such, the nature of participatory research is predominantly applied. Such social change is achieved through the democratic collaboration of social researchers, community members and various other parties. Together, and as equal players, the participants investigate the problem and its underlying causes (including socio-economic, political and cultural factors) and then take collective action in order to bring about long-term solutions to that problem.

Participatory research uses all the conventional tools of social research. However, tools that acknowledge the value of the opinions and thoughts of all people, such as focus groups, indepth interviews and participant observation, tend to be more popular than structured interviews, questionnaires and simple observation. As a result, there is no one way of doing participatory research.

A form of participatory research that is growing in popularity is action research, an approach that suggests a particular complementary relationship between action and research.

Steps in action research

Participatory research is not necessarily action research, although action research is always participatory. Beyond the characteristics of participatory research introduced above, **action research** demands that the social scientist and the community work as

CHAPTER 7 Participatory and action research

equal partners in the planning and implementation of a project. Each brings valuable resources to the project. Furthermore, action and research take place alternatively in an ongoing learning process for everyone involved. Because of this dynamic process between researcher and community, and between research and action, there is no general formula for doing action research. One can, however, sketch a very broad framework that describes how action-research projects often proceed.

1. *Request for assistance*. Ideally the initiative for an action-research project comes from members of a community who find themselves in difficulty. The idea should never come from social researchers who believe (rightly or wrongly) that they know what is best for a particular community and set out to demonstrate to the community the best way to proceed. Very often requests for assistance come to social scientists via social workers and others in the front line of service delivery. This is because community members themselves are often not aware that the services of social scientists are available to them. They are, however, familiar with people who work within the community and it is to these people that problems are first referred. In this way, frontline workers play a very important role in bringing the challenges facing communities to the attention of social scientists. They can also help social scientists achieve a better understanding of what is happening on the ground.

> ### Example
>
> Parents and teachers of a secondary school are concerned about the high dropout rate at the school. As a result they call a meeting to discuss this problem. At the meeting various possible reasons for the dropout rate are discussed, but it soon becomes clear that the problem is complex and that no easy solution is likely to emerge. As a result, the group decides to ask the school counsellor for assistance. The counsellor, being unequipped to solve this problem, puts the community representatives in touch with a social scientist who then facilitates an action-research process in order to help find a solution.

There are, however, times when the social scientist (who usually enjoys a high level of education) has information that is not available to some communities. A community may be in difficulty without knowing it.

> ### Example
>
> A good example can be found in the Aids pandemic. Social scientists became aware of the spread of HIV and the effects of Aids long before people in rural areas who had little access to media and other sources of information. Such communities could be unaware of the danger. In these cases, the social researcher is obliged, where possible, to make information available and to formulate the problem so that communities may respond effectively to it.

At all times, however, the social scientist must be wary of disempowering a community by dictating what problems that community is facing and how such problems ought to be solved.

2. *Negotiation.* Negotiation most often occurs between the social scientist and representatives of the community. This raises an important ethical issue for the social scientist. In some cases, community representatives may not be truly representative of the community. It may be necessary for the social scientist to check whether the situation, as presented by the community representatives, accurately reflects the will of the majority of people within that community. This is called an '**accountability gap**'. Also, the social scientist and the community representatives should make sure that every person or organisation that may have something important to contribute to the project is present to discuss the problem. This list may include religious, labour, political, youth and other kinds of groups, as well as government, non-government and funding organisations.

At this point all the participants should establish a broad ethical framework based on mutual trust, within which they can work together. In other words, if the representatives from any group feel that they will not be able to work usefully with people from another group (for whatever reason), this should be discussed during this phase. In a community where rival gangs exist in violent conflict, one gang may refuse to participate in the project if the other gang is present. In this case a process of mediation is needed before the project can begin. Opposing religious groups and political parties may experience similar problems.

Once a comfortable working relationship has been established, it is time to consider the goals of all the groups that will be involved in the project. In most cases these goals will be different. Consider an action-research project involving only two parties or co-researchers: the community and a team of social scientists. The community desires a solution to its particular problem. The social scientists hope to identify a more general solution adaptable to a range of similar problems that may be experienced by other communities. For the social scientists' goal to be met, the community may have to participate in a far more complex project than its original one. Similarly, if the community's goal is to be achieved, the social scientists cannot stray too far from the specific details of the problem at hand. Thus both the social scientists and the community must reach a compromise on the goals of the project. The complexity and importance of negotiation increase when more than two parties are involved in the project.

CHAPTER 7 Participatory and action research

Example

Returning to the example of the high school dropout rate mentioned previously, the concern about school dropout was raised by the local parents and teachers. It is likely that these adults will have many things to say about how the children in the community think and feel. But this is a kind of accountability gap. An action researcher might suggest that some school children are invited to the meeting to hear what they have to say about the reasons that some children are leaving school prematurely.

We can imagine that this group of concerned people from the community (teachers, parents, children, religious and civic leaders, and so on) plus the social researcher would have many different ideas about the causes and solutions to the problem. The parents might be angry with the teachers who they feel are not doing enough to keep the children in school. They think the solution is for the teachers to do their job better. The teachers might think the problem lies with the parents who do not do enough to motivate or discipline their children. The children may feel that neither the parents nor the teachers really care about their well-being. Perhaps the researcher strongly believes that a particular kind of teaching is the problem and believes that changing the teaching style will solve the problem. Everyone has their own priorities and beliefs. Part of the action researcher's job is to create space for everybody to contribute to the discussion and help members of the community to arrive at some shared goals that everybody can be happy with. This can be very challenging.

Some writers suggest that the best way to resolve these difficulties is to construct a formal action-research contract. Such a contract would outline exactly what each party is expected to contribute to the project and what each party can expect to gain from the project. Table 7.1 contains an illustration of such a contract.

Table 7.1 *A simple action-research contract*	
Community	Social researcher
To provide: ■ active participation ■ first-hand practical knowledge of the problem on the ground ■ material resources ■ skills	To provide: ■ active participation ■ academic knowledge and theory ■ academic and research skills ■ access to material resources ■ skills training
To receive: ■ a solution to their particular problem ■ a solution for future similar problems ■ skills to solve future problems ■ skills training and access to resources	To receive: ■ a general solution to similar problems applicable to a range of similar communities ■ increased understanding of the problems faced by some communities ■ development of theory ■ publication

In deciding upon the various roles of the co-researchers it is important to constantly think critically about power. Who will the decision makers be? Who will be paid for their time on the project, and who will be expected to donate their time for free? Many action-research projects are managed by a committee of people including both the social researcher and representatives of the community. Sometimes the social researcher, as well as community members who are part of the data collection and analysis processes, are paid for their time and expertise. Whatever the arrangements, as soon as such a contract has been agreed upon, the participants are ready to enter the next phase.

3. *Planning*. In the third phase of an action-research project, all the groups involved must work together to find a way of solving the community's problem and of meeting all the goals set out in the action-research contract. Essentially, this phase involves three distinct tasks. First, the co-researchers must find a way of defining the problem that is clear and acceptable to everyone. Very often this is not as straightforward as it sounds. The co-researchers may have different ways of explaining the world. Reaching a point of shared understanding might require long and patient discussion. Secondly, the co-researchers must determine exactly what information is needed in order to find a solution to the problem, and how that information is to be collected. This is the essence of the action-research project because at this point the co-researchers decide what their specific aims are and how these aims are to be achieved. Also at this point it is necessary for the participants to decide how the data will be collected. Finally, the co-researchers must break the action-research project down into manageable tasks and distribute responsibility for each of these tasks amongst the participants.

> ### Example
>
> Back to school dropouts. Through careful discussion the community decides that perhaps the best way to proceed is to have senior students who are still in school conduct in-depth interviews with their friends who have left school prematurely. The researcher will help the group develop an interview schedule (see Chapter 12). The interviews will be recorded and transcribed. The analysis will be conducted by a specially selected group that includes the researcher, two experienced teachers, two parents and the children who conducted the interviews. The results will be summarised and presented at a community meeting called to discuss exactly this problem. The research group will come up with some recommendations that will be discussed at that meeting. A detailed budget is drawn up which includes some small amounts to pay the children for their work. A committee is set up to oversee the project and to ensure that the money is spent properly. This committee comprises the school headmaster, the researcher and the elected chair of the parents' committee. People are excited to be actively involved in solving a serious problem in their community.

CHAPTER 7 Participatory and action research

It is during the negotiation and planning phases that the participants build up a rapport, or sense of cooperation. A good relationship between everyone involved is essential for the success of the action and research involved in the final stages.

4. *Implementation.* Once the co-researchers have made a plan about how to proceed with the project, implementation can begin. It is during this phase that action and research take place. Very often implementation begins with a period of research where the resources and needs of the community are systematically assessed and the necessary information to guide appropriate action is gathered. This process then informs some kind of action which the action-research partners undertake together. Thereafter, the results of the action are assessed and a further period of research (although this time of an evaluative nature) is initiated. Depending on the results of this research it may be necessary to develop or completely redesign the original action undertaken. In this way, action and research continue as alternate processes in the search for solutions to the community's problems. The relationship between action and research is illustrated in Figure 7.1.

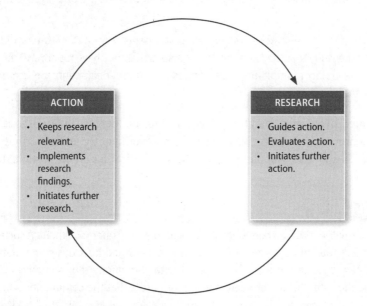

Figure 7.1 *Relating action and research*

Example

Continuing our previous example, when the interviewers talk to their friends to find out why they left school, they discover that in fact there are many different reasons. However, there is one common thread. All the children who dropped out come from among the poorer families in the community. These children felt pressure from their parents to either earn some money, or to take care of smaller children while their parents were out looking for work. It quickly becomes clear that the question of school dropout is closely connected with poverty. The research committee thus recommends that an affordable crèche for smaller children be started next to the school so that older children will not have to leave school to take care of their younger siblings. It is also suggested that the school should ensure that all maintenance of the school grounds and property should be done by parents of children at the school, thereby trying to create a few jobs for local people.

After these ideas are implemented, the research team suggests that a new cycle of research be started. This cycle will compare the dropout rate in previous years with the dropout rate following the implementation of these ideas. The research will check to see how well the ideas were being implemented (how many children attended the crèche? how many parents got some small jobs at the school?), as well as whether they make a difference to the dropout numbers.

In addition the social researcher will write a policy paper for the Department of Education explaining the study that they have done, the results that they have found, and the solutions that they are trying to implement. She hopes that these ideas might be useful to other schools in the area too.

This repeated cycle of research and action, with neither possible without the other, produces a process of ongoing learning and empowerment for all the participants in the study. Here is another example to highlight the cyclical nature of participatory action research.

Example

Consider a small, peri-urban community facing problems of unemployment. A social scientist agrees to facilitate an action-research project in order to address this community's needs. The first step would be to identify and meet with community representatives in order to determine the extent of the problem and the resources that the community is prepared to commit to the project. At this point, other role players will also be called in. These might include investors, funding agencies, small business support agencies, training institutions and the like.

continued ...

CHAPTER 7 Participatory and action research

After discussion, the co-researchers may decide that before any action can be undertaken, it is necessary to collect some background information. What skills are currently available in the community? What sorts of self-employment schemes are available and which are the previous sources of employment for community members? Moreover, a wide range of social and cultural variables may influence the income-generating possibilities within the community. On the basis of this information, the committee may choose to develop a farming cooperative in order to provide work for some community members, as well as to provide sustenance for the rest of the community. Simultaneously, the community may wish to embark on an extensive programme of skills training in management and accounting to run the cooperative better. This could involve development agencies and outside funders.

After a few months it will be necessary to evaluate the progress being made. This will entail investigating the functioning of the newly formed cooperative. Here it may be discovered that the cooperative is experiencing problems due to the diffusion of responsibility for tasks, lack of commitment to (or belief in) the project, or the lack of specific skills, such as marketing of the agricultural products. Further action will have to be taken in order to address these new concerns. Also, it may be discovered that even with new skills, community members are still unable to find employment. At this stage the co-researchers may wish to discuss and implement self-employment initiatives based within the community. Again, these will have to be developed and evaluated in the future, thereby initiating further action and research.

Throughout this process, both the social scientist and the community are gaining valuable knowledge, experience and skills. The social scientist is gaining first-hand experience of the problems encountered by particular communities and the effectiveness of different solutions. This experience will be extremely valuable in dealings with other communities. Apart from the obvious advantages to the community of removing a particular obstacle to its well-being, its members are also learning more about their own problems and resources, as well as problem-solving strategies that will serve the community well for a variety of other difficulties which may arise in future.

Using action research in developing countries

Action researchers are often criticised by social scientists who are accustomed to conventional research methods.

In an action-research project extraneous variables are difficult, often impossible, to control. It is therefore very difficult to be sure positive results are due to the action taken by the co-researchers.

> **Example**
>
> A community sets up a transport system for taking pregnant women and mothers with young children to hospital in an attempt to lower the infant mortality rate. At the same time, the government installs a freshwater supply to the community. If a decrease in infant mortality is measured, it is not possible to determine the respective contributions of either of these two life improvements.

The close relationship between 'researcher' and 'participants' makes it quite difficult for the 'researcher' to be objective, and the research is, therefore, vulnerable to all kinds of bias.

> **Example**
>
> In the failing cooperative of a previous example, a social scientist that has developed a strong rapport with the people responsible for the cooperative may be reluctant to admit that the source of the cooperative's problems is the lack of commitment to the project by the members.

The necessary narrow focus of research (to a particular community with a particular difficulty) prevents the social scientist from generalising research findings to other communities.

> **Example**
>
> Imagine two communities afflicted by civil violence. Whereas in one instance the people have a good relationship with the police, in the other the police are not trusted at all. In this case, solutions generated in one community are unlikely to be applicable in the other, and vice versa.

Action researchers usually respond to these criticisms by acknowledging that action research is not the only form of research available and that for some kinds of problems action research is not appropriate. However, in developing countries, where communities are in great need of immediate solutions to vital survival problems, where social researchers are few and far between and often quite ignorant of the reality to be addressed, and where financial resources are scarce, action research is a particularly valuable tool. Action research,

1. is concerned with solving particular problems facing communities.
2. helps individuals, organisations and communities to learn skills and access resources so that they can function more effectively in future.
3. provides a way of spreading the understanding gained through research to people and communities who can benefit from those findings.
4. attempts to understand the individual and the community within a broader social context.

CHAPTER 7 Participatory and action research

5. facilitates communication between social researchers and communities in need of assistance.
6. shakes the 'ivory tower' of many social scientists and makes their work directly beneficial to society.

Key points

1. The capacity to create knowledge is an important form of social power that can be used for good or ill.
2. Participatory action research is concerned with making the tools of knowledge creation available to ordinary people in society.
3. Participatory action research depends on careful negotiation and planning, as well as critical reflection on the balance of power within relationships and communities.
4. Participatory action research tends to be cyclical. Research leads to action, which leads to more research, and so on.
5. Participatory action research is particularly important in developing countries with urgent social and community needs and where power of knowledge generation has been abused in the past.

Checklist

Keywords:

Check whether the meaning of these concepts introduced in this chapter is clear to you.

participatory/action research; representation; accountability gap.

Your research:
1. Have community representatives played a meaningful role in all aspects of the research process?
2. Have you facilitated a process to clearly define the roles and responsibilities of all parties?
3. Have you explored opportunities for ongoing cycles of action and research?

Exercises

1. Look through a local newspaper and identify a problem in your neighbourhood or community.
   a. Describe this problem concisely.
   b. How would you go about initiating a participatory action-research project to solve this problem?
   c. What people do you think should be involved in the project and how will you ensure accountability to the community?
   d. What research would you like to do?
   e. What might an action-research contract look like for this project?
   f. What action do you think might flow from this research?
   g. What research might follow this action?
   h. How would you ensure that this project had some benefit beyond your own community?
2. What strategies might one employ to prevent an accountability gap from developing within a particular community?

Additional resources

1. *Action research*, a peer reviewed journal available at http://arj.sagepub.com/
2. Freire, Paulo. 1970. *Pedagogy of the oppressed*. Boulder: CO, Paradigm.
3. Reason, P & Bradbury H. (eds) 2008. *The Sage handbook of action research: Participative inquiry and practice*, 2nd ed. London: Sage.

CHAPTER 8

Research and community development

There are many ways in which research methodologies can be employed by communities to access accurate information and to facilitate effective community development projects. One of these ways is by conducting needs assessments to determine both the most pressing and the underlying needs of particular communities. Based on a needs assessment, it is possible to develop a theory of change that is the foundation upon which community projects are built. These theories can be tested using pilot projects. Finally, feasibility studies test whether a project is likely to be successful before a great deal of scarce resources is spent on an untested idea. This information can be used to develop projects and interventions that will make a real difference to the quality of life of people in the community.

CHAPTER OBJECTIVES

Learners who have completed this chapter will be able to:
- Plan and conduct a community needs assessment.
- Develop a theory of change.
- Test a theory of change with a pilot project.
- Plan and conduct a simple feasibility study.

Research and community projects

Applied social research has an important role to play in the planning, management and implementation of community projects. In many parts of Africa the needs of communities are great and the resources available to address those needs are few. For this reason it is imperative that the available resources are used to the greatest possible effect. We cannot afford to waste precious resources on community development projects that do not achieve the desired goals. Social researchers have an important role to play in this regard. We can help to identify which community needs should be given priority so that when addressed, they produce the greatest positive results for the greatest number of people. We can also design research to identify the critical steps upon which a project depends, as well as the pitfalls that must be avoided at all cost. In this way researchers are able to predict the likelihood of success under different conditions, thereby supporting developers in achieving their goals. Finally, researchers are able to analyse the actual implementation of small, pilot projects, thereby identifying further problems or opportunities which could not be recognised before the project actually started, information that is extremely important when it comes to multiplying the size of the project or bringing it up to scale so that it achieves its planned results.

Unfortunately, good research is expensive and takes time. All too often development agencies and governments are not prepared to spend the time and money necessary. Rather than doing the research, they focus on those goals they believe ought to be prioritised, they use the methods that they think will work, and they go directly to the full-sized project without taking the time to test their ideas. Nobody living in Africa has to look very hard to find well-intentioned community development projects which failed to deliver the promised results. Whether one investigates the areas of housing development, job creation, safety and security, healthcare, or any number of others, you will always find good ideas that were not properly researched and so were ultimately unsuccessful. It is important to know that the money and time spent in doing rigorous research is usually well worth the money and time saved on failed or partially successful projects. This is one area in which development agencies and government could learn a lesson from the private sector. Large retail corporations never launch new products or open new stores without extensive, time-consuming and expensive research. They want to be sure that their idea will work before they invest large amounts of money.

In this chapter we will explore three areas in which social research supports the implementation of large-scale community development projects: needs assessment, pilot projects for testing intervention strategies, and feasibility studies.

Needs assessment

The first step of any community intervention is a detailed analysis of the particular challenges facing that community, and the available resources with which those challenges may be met.

Usually community-based organisations, local leaders and other representative structures believe that they have a fairly good idea of the challenges facing their community. It is important to assess the extent to which these role players actually do understand the concerns and needs of all people within the community. (Refer back to the discussion of accountability gaps in Chapter 7.) It is important to examine the extent to which community representatives have analysed the causes of the underlying community's problems. It is essential that scarce resources are put to the best possible use so that the community derives maximum long-term benefit.

Of course, different community members have different needs. When resources are scarce, these needs might exist in competition with one another. Often young people would like money to be spent on sport and recreation facilities, while their mothers are more concerned with better public transport to get their children to school. Shopkeepers, on the other hand, might want to spend public funds on better lighting outside their shops so that they can safely stay open after dark. Difficult decisions must often be made about the best way to use limited resources. Good choices can only be made when decision-makers are in possession of all the relevant facts. With the correct information it is possible to prioritise the various needs and to tackle those that affect the community the most profoundly first. It might be that better public transport

CHAPTER 8 Research and community development

will benefit the greatest number of people, allowing those with jobs to get to work, children to get to school more safely and customers to get to the shopkeepers' stores more conveniently. Perhaps sport facilities and street lighting must wait until more funds become available. Very often these decisions have far-reaching consequences for the community and many different factors must be weighed. In many cases a natural sequence starts to emerge.

> ### Example
>
> Money that is spent on building a new crèche to assist working mothers with small children cannot also be used to start a brick-making project for unemployed adults. It might be best to first start the brick-making project which would reduce the cost of building a crèche. However, if the participants on the brick-making project include many mothers of young children, building the crèche first would increase participation in the project.

Many of the research techniques discussed in this book (refer to Chapters 5 and 12) can be used to conduct a needs assessment. These techniques include qualitative, quantitative and mixed-methods approaches, and may use observation, interviews, questionnaires, focus groups, or perhaps the analysis of public records and documents. One approach that is often used is the needs assessment survey.

The **needs assessment survey** is a survey of various facets of the community in order to define the different concerns of all the community's members. The first step in a needs assessment survey is to negotiate entry into the community itself. Most communities have people who control access to the members of that community. These people are sometimes referred to as **gatekeepers**. In rural communities the gatekeepers might be traditional leaders or a council of elders, in urban communities they might be a group of elected councillors or party officials. Access to a school will be controlled by the principal or parent-teacher association, and access to a state hospital might require permission from a senior official in the country's Department of Health. While negotiating entry, the researcher will gain valuable insight into how the community runs, who has the most power and who has very little power, what tensions exist between community groups, and what political alliances are in operation. This understanding is important for the researcher to ensure that all groups are represented in the needs assessment. It is especially important that those groups whose voices are unlikely to be heard at community meetings or through structures that claim to represent all the people of the community, are heard. Groups that are not sufficiently represented often include women, children, the elderly and the disabled. In some communities people from particular ethnic backgrounds or who follow particular religious beliefs find themselves without a voice in the usual structures. These people should also have a chance to discuss the problems facing their community.

One of the features of good needs assessment research is that it is participatory in nature. True participation requires that everyone in the community understands the purpose of the research and how the results will be used. It also requires the use of research tools that are sufficiently simple to be clear and transparent to everyone in the community. That is to say that everybody should be able to understand in a step-by-step manner how the results are to be arrived at. Researchers have developed a range of creative tools to conduct this kind of research. One such method is described in the following example.

Example

In a small rural community, a researcher asks the traditional leader to call a community meeting at which all interest groups in the community are represented. At the meeting, the researcher facilitates an informal brainstorming session to produce a list of problems and needs in the community. People put up their hands and make suggestions. Each suggestion gets written on a sheet of paper together with a simple picture so that illiterate members of the group can remember all the items that have been suggested. When someone suggests that the police in the community treat people badly, a picture of a man in uniform beating someone is drawn. When another says that vendors are leaving a mess on the main street, a picture of a very messy market place is drawn. The researcher regularly reminds everybody about all the needs and problems that have been mentioned. Once the list is complete and about ten different concerns have been raised, the researcher hands everyone at the meeting three pebbles and instructs them to place one pebble on the picture of each of the three problems that they feel is most important to be solved. Each person wanders around, debating with friends and neighbours, and placing the pebbles where he or she feels they should go. In the end the researcher counts the number of pebbles on each picture and reports back on the results to the people present.

While this very simple technique can be criticised in many ways, it does have the advantage of real participation and transparency. Even people with very little education can understand the purpose, method and results of a process like this. A similar process could be used in a factory or a vendors' market. An alternate approach could be to divide the community into different interest groups and have each group brainstorm and rank the community problems independently. The researcher's job then involves comparing the priority concerns of the different groups. Whatever method is used, it is imperative that all results are compiled and made available to the community in either written or verbal format, depending upon what is most appropriate.

The following real-life example illustrates some deeper points about needs assessment.

CHAPTER 8 Research and community development

> ### Example
>
> In the years 1984 and 1985, west Sudan suffered a two-year drought which resulted in widespread famine, since rural communities in that area depend wholly upon rain-fed subsistence farming. The immediate concern of providing sufficient food to prevent widespread starvation was partly met by international relief agencies. However, when the rains did start again in 1986, rural communities did not return to their original way of life and many people continued to starve.
>
> The results of a needs assessment revealed that two factors prevented the region from regaining its self-sufficiency. There were no seeds to plant crops, and there was no workforce to farm the land. A closer investigation of the community and its history revealed the underlying causes of these problems.
>
> When the famine struck, many men had moved to urban areas to find other sources of income (and thus food for themselves and their families). Those farmers who stayed had survived by eating their seed supplies. Younger women who were no longer employed in farming had taken over the upbringing of their children, a role usually performed by grandparents. With the food shortages and the loss of their role in the community, the old people had become a burden and many had moved away to the cities and were begging on the streets. When the rains returned, the seeds had been eaten, many men had moved away and the women were caring for children where before they had been free to farm the land.
>
> Thus a problem of not having enough food has its roots in problems of urbanisation and migration, as well as family and community structure. Supplying food will never solve this community's problems. However, the establishment of a 'seed bank', the development of more effective irrigation systems and a range of other projects, including the introduction of new farming techniques and literacy classes, enabled the community to adapt to its changed circumstances.

What this example demonstrates is that identifying a problem does not mean that its causes are immediately understood or that solutions are easily apparent. Most community problems have multiple underlying causes and it is the task of the researcher conducting a needs assessment to uncover those causes. Unless the deep causes of a problem are addressed, the problem will only be solved in a superficial manner. It is likely that a similar problem will emerge in the same community in time. In the same way that it is necessary to treat the cause of an illness rather than the symptom, it is important to address the source of a problem, rather than its effects.

105

Example

In the previous chapter we discussed a problem where many children were leaving school prematurely, something that was of great concern to many adults in the community. Thus the first question facing the research team was:

Question one: Why are many children leaving school prematurely?
Answer: Following the in-depth interviews with children who had left school, the researchers discovered that some children were dropping out of school to take care of younger siblings while their parents were at work. This finding then suggested a different question for the researchers to consider.

Question two: Why do these parents not find other solutions for the care of small children?
Answer: The researchers followed up the interviews with children who had left school, with interviews with parents of small children. Through this second process they discovered that the neighbourhood is new and that people came from different areas to settle here. As a result, families don't really know their neighbours. So while many people share the same problem, they have not been able to find a collaborative local solution. Also, because the community is new, there is no crèche in the neighbourhood and it is time-consuming and expensive to transport children to the next suburb where there are several affordable crèches. (Perhaps some other questions could be asked at this point.)

Question three: Why has nobody opened a crèche in this neighbourhood?
Answer: Perhaps the answer to this question is that a couple of women have tried to open a crèche, but the local authority which is responsible for ensuring the quality of childcare facilities is extremely inefficient. As a result the administrative work necessary to get the proper licences and permissions has proved too expensive and time-consuming, and the women had given up.

After this needs assessment, the problem looks very different. There is no crèche in the neighbourhood because local women are unable to get the necessary permission to open such a facility. As a result working parents must choose to spend more money than they can afford to take small children to a crèche in a neighbouring area, or they must pull older children out of school so that they can work in order for the family to survive. Immediately this new understanding of the problem suggests some affordable solutions. For example, the local government could consider a project to assist local women to register one or more local crèches and, in so doing, also address some of the problems in the local authority. Not only would this create jobs in the area, but it would also allow older children to stay in school. Alternatively, the parents could organise some kind of communal transport arrangement to take small children to crèche in the neighbouring area.

CHAPTER 8 Research and community development

As we have seen from this example, needs assessments often involve digging more and more deeply into a community problem. At each level the researcher is asking a new 'Why?' question. 'Why is this the case in this community?' For each answer to the 'Why?' question there is often another 'Why?' question, until the researcher starts to understand the root causes of the problem. In most cases, it is very difficult to address any need unless the root causes are considered. For example, an education campaign to keep young people in school by educating them about the consequences of dropping out is unlikely to be successful if the real reasons why children are dropping out remain unchanged.

A range of research techniques might be used to gather the information needed to understand the root causes of community problems. This allows one to prioritise the problems with the aim that any community-based project creates the maximum good for the most people. As in the previous examples, the information emerging from the needs assessment should place community leaders and decision-makers in a better position to make the right choices for the future well-being of their community. Very often those choices involve some kind of community-based project which must be carefully planned and implemented.

Pilot projects

A sound needs assessment provides the foundation for a community project. The results of the needs assessment identify the priority needs or problems within the community and the root causes thereof. Having done this work, it is possible to plan a pilot project to solve the problems.

A **pilot project** is a project that is run on a limited scale, for example, with a single small community over a short period of time, in order to test the effectiveness and community support for the proposed solution. Since pilot projects are trials of a possible solution to the community's problems, it is essential that they involve a large research component.

The development of a pilot project depends upon the community developers being able to explain a theory of change. A **theory of change** describes in a step-by-step fashion how the particular community project activities are intended to produce the positive outcomes or changes hoped for by the community. Often a theory of change is presented as a flow chart. We illustrate this by returning to the example of the drought in west Sudan.

107

> **Example**
>
> In addressing the starvation resulting from the two-year drought in west Sudan, a theory of change must explain how the proposed actions (the creation of a 'seed-bank', the introduction of more effective irrigation systems and the provision of literacy classes) will produce the desired outcome (people in the region will have enough to eat). A possible, simple theory of change is presented in the following flow chart.
>
>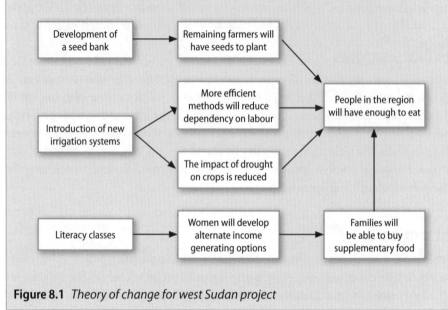
>
> **Figure 8.1** *Theory of change for west Sudan project*

Immediately the logic of the proposed project becomes clear. At this point the critical researcher will start to identify and question the assumptions being made. Let's consider a few of these assumptions for this example. This project seems to assume that there are enough farmers to cultivate sufficient crops to feed the people in the region. Is this in fact true? Can we assume that farmers will be able to adapt their farming methods to the new irrigation systems? Is it possible that they will resist the change and continue to use old methods, even though these are not as efficient? We seem to be assuming that the women who used to work in the fields want to learn to read and write. Is this true? Even if it is true and they do become literate, are they really going to get jobs? Even assuming they do get jobs, will they use the money they earn to buy food, or will they move their families to the city where more and better jobs are available?

Each of these questions could be answered by independent research studies. An economist and agricultural specialist could investigate the number of farmers remaining in the area and the predicted output of each farm to determine the overall expected yield. A sociologist could study farmers' attitudes to new technologies, and a labour specialist could investigate the availability of jobs for the newly literate women in the community. This would certainly take a great deal of time and effort. Another possibility would be to run the project on a very limited scale and see how successful it

CHAPTER 8 Research and community development

actually is. By investigating each step in the theory of change as it happens in the real world, as experienced in a pilot study, one is able to develop the intended action and thereby produce greater impact. Most importantly, if the project has not been thought through carefully and thus does not succeed, limited resources have been wasted in the failed attempt to solve the problem.

Theories of change will be discussed again in Chapter 9 with regard to project monitoring and evaluation.

Feasibility studies

Even after completing a thorough needs assessment and a successful pilot study, it is difficult to predict what will happen when the project is scaled up. **Scaling up** refers to the process of expanding a small pilot project until its effects are felt across a whole district, province or country. For example, a new teaching format has been successfully tested in three schools (pilot project) and is then included in the curriculum of all schools in the country, or a new store layout is tested in one outlet and when sales improve, the company decides to renovate all its outlets across the country in the same way. It is relatively easy to manage a small pilot project, whereas it is much more challenging to run an enormous community development project which involves many people, large budgets and potentially a wide geographical area.

Feasibility studies try to identify further problems and obstacles that might arise when a large and expensive project is implemented. Again, a process of checking assumptions must be followed. Can we assume that the conditions that held for a pilot project will continue to hold in the same way on a large-scale project? What new problems will arise as a result of the expanded scale of this project, and how do we solve them? What opportunities might arise as a result of the scale and how can we make the most of these? We illustrate this process by continuing our discussion of the example from west Sudan.

Example

Assuming that in a pilot project in one community we discovered that there were sufficient farmers remaining to provide food for their community, can we assume that this will be true for all communities? Or, might there be some communities without any remaining famers? If that is the case, is it possible for farmers from one community to supply people beyond their own community? Would they be willing to, and would they be accepted by the other community?

continued ...

109

> Also, given that we are now talking about implementing this project across the entire area of west Sudan, how will the seed travel from the seed bank to the farmers? Will the famers be expected to travel to the seed bank to collect their seed? And if so, will they be able and willing to do this? If the seed will be delivered to the farmers, how much will this cost? How long will it take to do? Will it be possible to deliver the seed in time for planting? Perhaps we can employ some of the women who used to work in the fields to drive the trucks which deliver the seed, thereby creating some local employment?

These questions are all concerned with the problems and opportunities associated with increasing the scale of a project.

A feasibility study must do two things:
1. It must help project planners to identify each of the assumptions underlying the scaled up project plan. In other words, what have the planners assumed will happen as a result of the project?
2. It must estimate the likelihood of each of these assumptions being met. Where the assumptions have a good chance of being met, the project can go ahead as planned. But, where the planners have made risky assumptions, it may be better to rethink the project or at least develop contingency plans.

In conclusion, the value of scientific information (see Chapter 2) should not be underestimated. A clear-minded analysis of the plan for a community-based project might lead to substantial savings in the long run. Many projects are weakened by inadequate planning and the failure to systematically consider other possible outcomes of the intervention. However, when needs assessments are thoroughly conducted, pilot projects are carefully tested and the feasibility of scaling up is carefully worked through, successful community development projects have the capacity to make significant positive changes to our societies and the overall quality of people's lives.

Key points

1. Community development in Africa uses scarce resources to solve complex problems. It is essential that existing resources are used to maximum effect.
2. Social research methods offer a variety of tools to support efficient and effective community development work.
3. Needs assessments help communities and developers to identify the most pressing needs or problems experienced in the community, as well as the root causes of those problems.
4. Needs assessments should be conducted in a way that is participatory so that all groups within the community are represented.

continued ...

CHAPTER 8 Research and community development

5. Techniques of needs assessment should endeavour to be participatory; everyone in the community should be able to understand the purpose, methods, analysis and results of the research.
6. Needs assessments allow us to generate community projects to address the identified needs. The logic of proposed community projects should be described in a theory of change.
7. A theory of change enables the project team to check the assumptions upon which the success of the community project rests.
8. One way to test those assumptions is to run a pilot project of limited scope, duration and expense.
9. A feasibility study examines the probability of the pilot project being equally successfully implemented when it is brought up to scale, rolled out among more communities or across a wider geographical area.
10. Feasibility studies also involve testing the assumptions underlying the process of implementing a large-scale project.

Checklist

Keywords:

Check whether the meaning of these concepts introduced in this chapter is clear to you.

community development; needs assessment; participation; gatekeepers; theory of change; pilot project; checking project assumptions; feasibility study.

Your research:
1. In conducting a community needs assessment, have you found a way to ensure that the views of all relevant groups within the community have been considered?
2. Are you using tools and methodologies that are clear and transparent to everyone in the community?
3. Have you dug deeper using 'why' questions to identify the root causes of the problem or need?
4. Have you given detailed feedback of the results to the community?
5. When designing a pilot project, have you clearly articulated your theory of change?
6. When conducting a feasibility study, have you considered all the difficulties and opportunities involved in larger scaled projects?

Exercises

1. Identify and critique a community project from your own community or neighbourhood.
   a. Describe the project briefly.
   b. What kind of needs assessment was conducted before this project was undertaken?
   c. Do you feel the root causes of the problem are being addressed? Explain.
   d. How could the researchers have explored the root causes more deeply?
   e. What other 'Why?' questions would you ask?
   f. Construct a 'theory of change' flowchart to explain the logic of the proposed project.
   g. List the assumptions underlying this theory of change.
   h. Do you feel these assumptions are likely to be met? Explain.
   i. What opportunities do you see for expanding this project to other communities?
   j. What new problems might arise in implementing this project on a larger scale?
2. Explain what is meant by a needs assessment being 'participatory'.
3. What tensions do you foresee in the relationships between social researchers, community representatives and project developers? How would you as a social researcher handle these tensions?
4. African countries struggle to create sufficient employment opportunities for young people. Imagine that you were employed to conduct a needs assessment and pilot intervention in a small rural town in your country. How would you proceed?

Additional resources

Phillips, R & Pittman, R H. (eds) 2009. *An introduction to community development.* New York: Routledge.

Project monitoring and evaluation

CHAPTER 9

In this chapter we discuss the important work of monitoring and evaluating the progress and impact of community projects. These functions depend on knowledge and skill in social research. **Monitoring** is a process whereby key indicators relating to the activities and outputs of a project are constantly measured. By keeping a watchful eye on such indicators, project managers can quickly tell when a project is, or is not, reaching its goals, where the project might be failing, and possibly how to fix the problems. **Evaluation** studies are used to assess the impact that a particular project has had, analyse why it did or did not achieve its goals, or suggest ways in which impacts might be increased or even multiplied in future. Monitoring is typically conducted by someone working within a project and thus has an internal perspective. Evaluation may happen from an internal or external perspective, and reflects on the overall success of the project. Both these research activities are intended to increase the effectiveness and efficiency of interventions. Moreover, monitoring and evaluation work may also generate knowledge that is transferable to other projects and contexts.

CHAPTER OBJECTIVES

Learners who have completed this chapter will be able to:
- Develop SMART indicators for utilisation in monitoring and evaluation studies.
- Develop a simple monitoring frame for a community development project.
- Differentiate between diagnostic, formative and summative evaluation aims.
- Design simple evaluation studies to achieve one or more of these aims.

Project indicators

As discussed in previous chapters, social research has various important roles to play in the broader world of community development. In Chapter 7, the importance of participatory and action-research was discussed. In Chapter 8, we considered the role of social research in helping communities to identify and prioritise their needs, as well as to plan and test community interventions. In this chapter we explore ways in which social research can be used to enhance community projects and reflect on their effectiveness and efficiency.

> **Example**
>
> The department of education is concerned that insufficient students from rural communities are graduating from secondary school with the mathematical skills needed to enter scientific fields of study at tertiary level. The department develops a pilot project to be run in 50 rural schools. They plan to develop teaching materials containing fun mathematical games and challenges at Grade 10 level. Mathematics teachers from the selected schools will be trained to use these materials. These teachers will then enrol interested Grade 10 students in mathematics clubs within the schools. These clubs will meet in the afternoons and students will have a chance to develop additional mathematical skills in an enjoyable way.
>
> Using the information from Chapter 8, we can construct a very simple theory of change.
>
>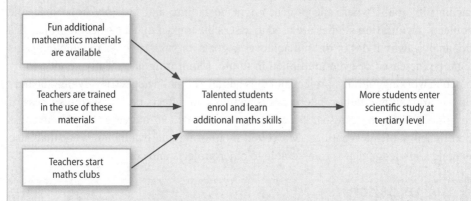
>
> **Figure 9.1** *A simple theory of change*
>
> The department also sets some targets for this project. In the first year, project managers plan to run the project in 50 schools, and hope to enrol twenty Grade 10 students per school. They must, therefore, produce enough materials for 50 clubs and 1 000 students. The department is hopeful that of these 1 000 students, at least 50 will enter a field of scientific study at tertiary level after completing their final school exams.

This example will be developed further as the different aspects of monitoring and evaluation research are discussed.

Selection of indicators

The terms 'monitoring' and 'evaluation' are often confused. They are actually different enterprises, which rely on different methods and have different objectives. However, both monitoring and evaluation require the identification of indicators. **Indicators** are dependent variables that provide information about the progress or impact of a particular project or intervention. Thus, for example, the quantity of produce, measured in tons, reaped from fields would be an indicator of the effectiveness of different irrigation systems used in those fields. If the tonnage is high, the irrigation must have been good. If the tonnage is low, the irrigation system was probably somewhat ineffective.

CHAPTER 9 Project monitoring and evaluation

By measuring indicators during the course of a project, project managers are able to monitor day-to-day progress, and quickly tell when something has gone wrong. By comparing measurements of indicators taken before a project with measurements of the same indicators taken after the project, a researcher is able to evaluate the overall impact of the project. (This is a pre-test/post-test design that will be discussed further in Chapter 10.)

Indicators should be identified for every step in the theory of change. Monitoring research is concerned with indicators that reflect on day-to-day activities and intermediate milestones or outputs of the project. Evaluation research is concerned with the indicators of overall impact. So, to fulfil both the monitoring and evaluation functions properly, it is essential that indicators are found to help keep track of each action and each anticipated outcome in the theory of change.

Usually monitors and evaluators have a choice of many different indicators for each step of the process. The selection of the best indicators for a particular project can be a very sensitive matter. One needs to consider the accuracy of the indicator as well as the cost and time needed to collect the data. Very inaccurate indicators will be of little help in drawing precise conclusions about the effectiveness of a project, but it is equally unhelpful to create a situation in which it takes more time and money to monitor a project than it does to actually implement it. Remember that monitoring and evaluation are tools to facilitate good community development work, but they should not drain resources away from that work.

Researchers commonly use the acronym SMART to assist them in selecting appropriate indicators. SMART stands for:
Specific
Measurable
Accurate
Realistic
Time-bound.

Specific means that an indicator should measure only that aspect of the theory of change that it is intended to measure. Indicators are used to identify points at which the project is failing (in the case of monitoring) or has failed (in the case of evaluation). An indicator that is not specific, that is, which measures more than one aspect of the theory of change, will not help the researcher identify exactly where the problem lies.

Measurable means that an indicator can be expressed quantitatively, in other words, that is it possible to collect the necessary data. Unfortunately, and as has been discussed in Chapter 1, there are some aspects of life which are virtually impossible to measure.

115

Accurate means that the indicator is sufficiently sensitive to consistently pick up changes in the project. Some indicators might produce different results when being measured by different people, or may miss subtle changes in the aspect of the project being monitored.

Realistic means that the data can be collected given the time, finance, number of monitoring personnel and technologies available to the researcher. There is no value in selecting an indicator that takes so much time to apply or costs so much that the project timetable and budget is overwhelmed by the monitoring process. This means that researchers must be very practical when planning a monitoring or evaluation framework.

Time-bound means that an indicator should be collected according to a certain timetable. In some projects the indicator might be measured on a daily basis, although for bigger community projects, indicators are usually measured on a monthly, quarterly or even annual basis.

The researcher setting up a monitoring and evaluation project should work through the letters of this acronym for every indicator that is considered. We illustrate this by returning to the example of the maths clubs.

Example

Looking at the theory of change outlined above, the researcher focuses on the point where teachers are trained in the use of the new mathematics materials. What indicators might tell the researcher whether or not this step in the process is being achieved? Some different options are considered.

1. The researcher could count the number of teachers who attend the special training courses. This is specific, as it relates only to this aspect of the theory of change, it can be measured, it is not a lot of work to count attendees at a course, so it is realistic, and it could be measured on a weekly basis so that the researcher would know how many teachers are being trained per week and how soon the project managers can hope to have completed this step. The problem is that this indicator is not accurate because it measures whether teachers attend, but not whether they actually learn anything. Saying that teachers have been trained implies that they have acquired the skills on which the future steps of the project depend.

continued ...

CHAPTER 9 Project monitoring and evaluation

2. The researcher could go to the maths clubs and observe the teachers using the skills taught in the training in interaction with students. This is specific, since it relates directly to the skills taught in the training, it is measurable and it would be accurate. The problem is that this would mean sending observers to 50 different schools in different places. This would either require a large number of observers or a great deal of time. Either way this indicator does not seem to be very realistic.
3. A third option, which can be part of the training, would be to ask each teacher to role play a class presentation using one of the games, thereby demonstrating his or her mastery of the new material. The trainer would then rate the teacher's performance at that task. This indicator is specific, measurable, accurate, realistic and time-bound. Therefore, this is an indicator that could well be used for this project.

Note that a monitor who noticed that the majority of teachers were consistently being given low scores by the trainers would be able to identify a problem in the presented theory of change in time to save the project. Perhaps the training course is not long enough, perhaps the materials are inadequate, or perhaps the teacher selection process is flawed. Whatever the problem, it becomes clear that something is not going well if the teachers are not able to master the new materials.

This is the value of monitoring. When a problem is identified, the project team can stop and think about how to fix the problem before spending more time, money and energy on a project that is unlikely to be successful.

In larger projects where more resources are at stake, researchers are usually encouraged to have at least two indicators for each component of the theory of change. This is because different indicators measure different aspects of the project and different kinds of complementary information can be very helpful. Often researchers will choose one quantitative and qualitative indicator for each step. As a result the vast majority of monitoring and evaluation studies are in fact mixed-methods studies.

Measuring indicators

Once indicators have been selected, the researcher must develop some way of collecting data on each of them. Some indicators are extremely simple and collecting data on them may be quick and easy. For example, to monitor attendance at meetings one merely needs a record of the meeting noting who was present, and to monitor the delivery of textbooks to schools, one merely needs to collect delivery notes signed by the school principal. These are pieces of data that already exist in the normal administration of day-to-day work.

Other indicators are, of course, much more difficult to measure. For these indicators the researcher must develop some kind of data collection instrument. How this is done is discussed in detail in Chapter 12.

117

Project monitoring

Project monitoring is a tool for managing the ongoing implementation of a project. It is important that a monitoring framework be established during the planning phase of a project. To be effective, it must be in place before the implementation phase begins. The following steps outline a method for establishing a monitoring framework.

1. *Identify at least one indicator for each activity or outcome in the theory of change*. If resources allow, two or more indicators should be identified, including a mix of quantitative and qualitative options.
2. *Design an instrument to measure each indicator on a regular basis*. Such instruments should not be overly complex or unwieldy.
3. *Set clear targets for each indicator* to show when an activity has been completed, or an outcome reached.
4. During implementation, *measure each outcome regularly* and compare the results with the targets so as to be constantly aware of which aspects of the project have been successfully completed, which aspects are progressing smoothly and where any problems might lie.
5. *Produce regular brief reports* to keep all participants and stakeholders up to date on the progress of the project.

Monitoring becomes an important management tool since it allows for the setting of suitable goals and deadlines, provides targets for everyone involved in the project and gives early warning when things are not going as planned. In this way, problems can be quickly solved and the chances of the project achieving its stated objectives are greatly enhanced.

Example

Let us return to the example of maths clubs. One of the activities planned is the enrolment of students in maths clubs. The target is to have 1 000 students enrolled, and managers think that they could expect the first clubs to start enrolling students after approximately three months. They hope that all 1 000 will be enrolled within a six-month deadline. Teachers starting clubs are expected to submit lists of names of students enrolled to the project managers on a monthly basis. This allows the project managers to track a key indicator, namely the number of students enrolled. Every month the managers add up the number of students enrolled and they compare this figure with the targets. Based on this information they produce the chart depicted in Figure 9.2.

continued ...

CHAPTER 9 Project monitoring and evaluation

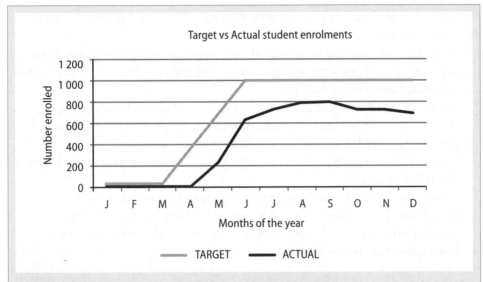

Figure 9.2 *Comparison between student enrolments and targets*

Stakeholders can learn a lot from this chart. Firstly, although students were expected to start enrolling in April, in fact, they only started enrolling in May. The figure for April is still zero. They enrolled quite steadily for the first few months as expected (the target and actual lines are roughly parallel) but enrolment drops off before the project reaches the target of 1 000 students. Most worrying is the fact that the data suggests that students are actually dropping out of the project already. The highest enrolment total was in September but it dropped noticeably by December.

Had the project managers been watching this monitoring data more closely, they might already have been able to develop a strategy in July to find extra students to enrol, and the project might still have been able to reach its target. This is the purpose of well-conducted monitoring.

Project evaluation

The methods of social science can be used to assess the design, implementation and usefulness of social interventions. This type of research is called **evaluation research**. Social interventions are most often thought of as sophisticated programmes (such as drug rehabilitation programmes, campaigns against malnutrition, skills training courses or the introduction of appropriate technologies to promote small-scale industry). Actually, any attempt to change the conditions under which people live (no matter how simple, or who is responsible for it) can be thought of as a social intervention. As has already been shown, one of the central concerns of social research is action. Evaluation research aims to test interventions to see how effective they are and therefore represents an important means of linking action and research in a constructive manner. Social interventions may benefit from evaluation research in a number of ways. Three of the most important ways are listed below.

1. Evaluation research may be used to identify neglected areas of need, neglected target groups and problems within organisations and programmes. This is referred to as **diagnostic evaluation**.

2. A comparison of a programme's progress with its original aims is another of the functions of evaluation research. This may serve to adjust the programme to the particular needs and resources of the community within which it is situated. Evaluation designed to promote the future effectiveness of a programme is called **formative evaluation**.

3. Finally, evaluation research can furnish evidence of the usefulness of a programme. In this way a programme may gain credibility with funding organisations, as well as the community within which it is operating. This is known as **summative evaluation**.

Although different, each of these three types of evaluation is complementary and most evaluators are expected to think about all of them simultaneously.

Diagnostic evaluation

Diagnostic evaluations are designed to inform researchers and project managers about the present situations within communities, highlighting current problems, trends, forces and resources, as well as the possible consequences of various types of intervention. Thus, diagnostic evaluation is a technique for gathering data which is crucial to the planning of a new project. As such, it is important that this research is carried out before a project is designed. The different ways in which diagnostic evaluations assist organisations and communities are explained further below.

Firstly, it often happens that an organisation or community is aware that something is going wrong, but is unable to identify exactly what the problem is. In other words, organisations and communities often find it difficult to define their problems in a precise manner.

Example

A community suffers from a high incidence of youth crime. Community members may well be aware of the problem, but have not managed to determine whether the majority of youths are committing crimes or whether there is only a small group of delinquents. They do not know whether the crimes are all of a particular type or very general in nature.

CHAPTER 9 Project monitoring and evaluation

Secondly, diagnostic evaluation can help communities and organisations in societies that are undergoing rapid social change. Such organisations or communities might desire change, but may not fully understand how such change will affect them. Diagnostic evaluations can serve to map out the full range of probable outcomes of any project.

> ### Example
>
> An organisation wishes to change its management structures through affirmative action procedures. Although the goal of this action is clear, the project managers are convinced that affirmative action may lead to fears and hostility among current managers. This might result in little support for new managerial staff. It is clearly important that the full implication of this type of programme are thought through well in advance.

Thirdly, during the initial planning stages of a project, it is useful for the project manager to specify the project's broad aims in a couple of points. These broad aims may be usefully broken down into several more manageable objectives that should be stated explicitly and in detail. This would allow them to be evaluated (using other evaluative research techniques) at a later date. The specification of both the broad aims and the various objectives must be guided by carefully conducted diagnostic research.

Finally, the researcher and the project manager should investigate problems that may arise during the course of the project. Where such problems cannot be avoided, contingency plans should be established to overcome them, so that the project may achieve its objectives.

> ### Example
>
> The question of appropriate methods to generate community policing in developing countries provides a clear illustration of the role of diagnostic research in social intervention.
>
> It is important, firstly, to understand that the pressure to adopt community policing principles and strategies comes primarily from government. Such methods entail quite drastic changes in the values, attitudes and perceptions of all parties if authoritarianism is to be replaced with democratic participation.
>
> In order to plan an effective community-policing programme, it is important to understand the current attitudes and values of people in both the target community and the existing police service. Members of the community may be distrustful of members of the police service, due to their experiences of policing in the past. Members of the police face a loss of status and power and, as a result, may be resistant to change. On the other hand, the community can expect to be better protected and enjoy more security, whereas the police will experience fewer threats and more acceptance from the community.
>
> *continued ...*

121

> So, it is vital to consider the ways in which people from both groups may react when the new policing strategy is put into effect. Community members may refuse to support the police in their work, and members of the police may resist or even undermine the action, hoping thereby to restore the old methods of policing.
>
> Plans for changes to the current approach to policing which are based upon an understanding of people's attitudes, values and expected responses are far more likely to be successful than those which are not.

Diagnostic evaluation might also be useful in the maths club example.

Example

> A diagnostic evaluation of the maths club project might investigate whether students are not pursuing careers in science, not because they lack confidence or ability in mathematics, but because scientific careers are viewed as not generating enough money, as lacking social value or as merely being boring. A diagnostic evaluation might also explore whether teachers and students are actually likely to invest additional time and energy in extra-curricular activities, such as maths clubs.

Clearly, the diagnostic evaluation is trying to understand the successes or failures of a project by looking at the root causes of problems and how they are addressed by the intervention.

Formative evaluation

Formative evaluation relates to the development and implementation of a programme. Its aim is to shape the programme so that it will have the greatest beneficial impact upon the target community. Formative evaluation is an evaluation of the programme in order to improve it. Longer term interventions use formative evaluations at regular intervals during the life of the programme to ensure that it adapts to changes in social reality and thus continues to produce the greatest possible benefit. The questions that the social scientist must consider are of both a theoretical and a practical nature. On a theoretical level, the social scientist must consider whether the content of the programme has been adequately adapted to the social reality and whether conceptual definitions have been adequately operationalised. This is especially important when the particular body of social theory has its roots in the United States of America, Europe or parts of the world where the social reality is very different to that of Africa. All too often social scientists wrongly assume that conditions and people are the same all over the world, and that theories developed in far-off places are just as valid locally. On a more practical level, the social scientist must think about problems such as the availability of resources for the project, the most effective ways of using those resources, potential areas of difficulty in the programme, and so on.

CHAPTER 9 Project monitoring and evaluation

There are many different ways of carrying out formative evaluations and the method depends largely upon the project being assessed. Very often, however, the evaluation relies heavily upon the social scientist's experience of similar programmes, understanding of social reality and theoretical knowledge. In some cases, social scientists may not have all the available information needed for a satisfactory formative evaluation.

One very useful method that does not depend on the social scientist's expertise in the area of the programme is the **reputability study**. This technique involves the researcher identifying experts from within the community, from academic institutions, from government and non-governmental organisations, and elsewhere. Note that 'experts' are not only people with academic qualifications or important positions. People from the community in which the programme is to be run (who may have no qualifications or titles) are experts on conditions prevailing in the community, the nature and extent of community problems, the community's likely reaction and many other aspects which might affect the programme. The choice of experts is a sensitive issue and one should be careful to ensure that a wide range of people are represented so as not to have bias in the final results. The researcher interviews the experts (either individually or as a group) and presents an overview of the programme. The experts are asked for their opinions on the way the programme has been planned and the method of implementation. Their comments and criticisms form the base of the formative evaluation. Formative evaluations and reputability studies are almost always qualitative in nature.

Example

In the example of the maths clubs, a reputability study might be conducted after one year of implementation. Many clubs have been started, many students have been enrolled and teachers are doing the work of making mathematics more enjoyable and challenging to young people. And yet, the attendance is not as high as expected and many students are dropping out. The project seems to be working, but not really well, and the Department of Education wants to know how the project might be improved.

A formative evaluator decides to conduct a reputability study. To do this, she constructs a panel of 'experts'. These experts include students who are active participants in the maths clubs, students who enrolled and then dropped out, teachers who are running maths clubs, principals in schools in which maths clubs are running, parents of children participating in the maths clubs, managers from the education department, and independent advisors who have run other projects promoting mathematics education in African countries. The evaluator interviews each person separately and compares and contrasts the different responses. Through a qualitative analysis (see Chapter 15) some clear patterns emerge, which in turn are translated into recommendations to the Department of Education.

Summative evaluation

Another broad aim of evaluation research is summative evaluation. Summative evaluations set out to determine the extent to which programmes meet their specified aims and objectives. This information is used to gain credibility with various groups of people, particularly potential funders and future target communities. Moreover, successful programmes may be replicated in other communities. If the designers of a programme can demonstrate scientifically that their programme has had certain positive effects, then people are likely to be much more enthusiastic about the programme being implemented in their community. They are also more likely to receive funding for similar programmes. Although summative evaluations ought to happen at the end of a programme, they are often carried out at regular intervals during the life of long-term programmes as well. The process of summative evaluation research generally occurs according to the following five steps.

1. *The identification of the aims and objectives of the programme.* The programme is thought of as the 'treatment', that is, it is one level of the independent variable (the other being 'no treatment'). Summative evaluation compares the 'treatment' group with a 'no treatment' group to see whether the 'treatment' has caused any positive change in the former. To assess the change, the researcher must know what the 'treatment' is designed to achieve. The identification of the programme's aims and objectives requires close cooperation between the programme developers and the social scientist carrying out the evaluation. Unless the social scientist knows exactly what the programme hopes to achieve, the evaluation cannot proceed to the next step. The question of whether or not the aims and objectives were adequately chosen falls in the domain of formative evaluation and is not considered here.

2. *The formulation of the aims and objectives in measurable terms.* At this point it is important for the researcher to translate the aims and objectives into observable changes that can be measured in the target community. The variable that is expected to change will become the dependent variable of the evaluation research. In other words, the conceptual definitions of the programme designers must be translated into operational definitions so that they can be studied through the methods of social science. (Refer to Chapter 6 for a discussion of conceptual and operational definitions.) Typical questions that the evaluator may need to consider are: How might people from the target community behave if the programme is successful? What should they be able to do? What type of action is expected from them? What statements on the behaviour of these people can be used to assess whether or not the aims and objectives of the project have been fulfilled? Note that all these questions relate to observable behaviours, rather than self-reports. Almost all programmes aim to induce observable changes of behaviour that can be accurately measured and studied. However, some programmes also produce effects that are less easily observed in people's actions, such as emotional and

CHAPTER 9 Project monitoring and evaluation

psychological changes. These may be measured by asking people for subjective reports of their own experiences, or by creating situations where these are likely to be translated into observable behaviour. No matter what kind of measure is chosen, it must be directly relevant to the aims and objectives of the particular programme.

3. *The construction of the instrument of measurement.* An instrument must be found or designed which is capable of accurately measuring the dependent variable chosen in the previous step. A wide variety of such instruments is available to social scientists, including carefully designed psychometric and sociometric tests, interviews, questionnaires and observation techniques. The most common of these instruments are discussed in detail in Chapter 12.

4. *Designing the evaluation study and data collection.* Designs used for summative evaluation are discussed in detail in the next chapter. Note that in order to carry out a summative evaluation, it is necessary for the researcher to compare the group that received the 'treatment' with a similar group that did not receive the 'treatment'. These two groups represent the two levels of the independent variable discussed in step one. The groups must be similar to start off with. Thus, if the group receiving the 'treatment' changes positively, the researcher can conclude that the 'treatment' has been successful. Summative evaluations are almost always quantitative in nature because inferential statistics (see Chapter 14) allow the researcher to estimate whether differences are real or merely due to chance factors.

5. *Reporting back.* Once the evaluation has been completed, the researcher should present the findings to those responsible for the intervention, the participants and any other interested parties. This must be done in such a way that the methods, results and conclusions of the evaluation can be easily understood, even by people with little experience of social research.

Example

A simple summative evaluation of the maths club project might count the number of students who register in scientific fields of tertiary study from the 50 schools included in the project, and compare that with the number of students registering for similar studies of 50 similar schools that were not involved in the project. If more students from the schools with the maths clubs went on to register for studies in the sciences, the evaluator would be able to conclude that the project had successfully achieved its aims.

A further example is included to illustrate the differences between summative and formative evaluation.

Example

A development organisation in KwaZulu-Natal, South Africa, aims to help unskilled people to find employment and to become productive members of the community. It is hoped that these people will be able to bring resources into the community and thus improve their own, their families' and their community's living conditions. The organisation is situated in a large urban community and sets out to provide training in practical skills such as carpentry, metal work and bricklaying. At the end of the first year of operation, the organisation asks an outside researcher to carry out both formative and summative evaluations on the programme.

The *summative evaluation* will be considered first. Step 1 of the research is to determine the exact aims and objectives of the project. The overall aim of the project is community development, but, in order to achieve this aim, several objectives have been specified. These are to help unemployed people to find work by providing them with skills required by the market place. In a more complex real world situation, the researcher should also look at exactly what group of people the project aims to benefit, how these people are selected, and so on. In this simplified example, the aims and objectives as specified above are sufficient.

In Step 2 of the summative evaluation, conceptual goals are translated into observable measures. Such measures may be operationalised as whether or not a person finds a job within six months after completing a training course, or whether they have mastered a particular skill or set of skills. Moderator variables such as the amount of effort put into the job search might also need to be considered.

Step 3 requires the researcher to find or construct an instrument to measure the concepts operationalised in Step 2. Whether or not a person finds a job within six months can be easily and accurately determined through observation and ongoing communication with the trainees. Whether or not a person has mastered a skill would most appropriately be measured with some kind of practical test of ability. Such a test would have to be carefully designed in order to distinguish clearly between trainees who have and have not mastered their chosen skills.

Next the researcher must choose a research design. (Refer to Chapter 10 for more details.) Unless prior notice of the need for evaluation was given to the evaluator by the project managers, it will be impossible to carry out a pre-test/post-test design at this stage. In fact, this more complex design requires that the trainees be assessed prior to the training. If the training has already begun when the evaluation is commissioned, the possibility of using the pre-test/post-test design is lost. This is just one of the reasons why it is important that managers give evaluators ample warning of their evaluation requirements. For this example it is assumed that the researcher is using a post-test-only design. An important part of the design is to find an appropriate comparison group. In this case, a comparison group would be a similar group of people from a neighbouring community perhaps, who are similarly unemployed and unskilled.

continued ...

CHAPTER 9 Project monitoring and evaluation

A comparison of the different skills of people from the two groups will allow the researcher to evaluate the effect of the skills training programme and these results must be presented to the project managers in a way that is easily accessible to them.

The *formative evaluation* requires a different approach to the problem. In this case the researcher is trying to find out how the training programme may be improved to better achieve its aims in future. With this in mind, the researcher may choose to interview the participants in the programme. This would include trainees, trainers, potential employers, as well as the programme managers. Questions should cover a broad range of topics relating to the functioning of the programme. Some areas of interest may be the content of the training courses, the methods of training employed, the teaching skills of the trainers, the structure of the organisation, the setting of the training, etc. These interviews are likely to uncover a variety of problem areas within the programme, and these can then be presented to those responsible for the project so that adjustment and 'fine-tuning' can be performed and the whole project improved.

Some concluding comments on evaluation

Firstly, although presented separately in this chapter, diagnostic, formative and summative evaluations are all interrelated and occur side by side in the course of ongoing interventions. During diagnostic evaluation, background circumstances highlighting the need for an intervention, as well as the forces which are expected to influence the intervention, are identified. The aims and methods are assessed using formative evaluation and recommendations for improving the project are discussed. Finally, the summative evaluation determines whether the aims have been met. If not, those responsible for the programme must consider further diagnostic and formative research in order to isolate and resolve problem areas. Comprehensive and integrated programme evaluation, which uses all three forms, maintains ongoing effectiveness, facilitates flexibility in response to changing circumstances and ensures credibility and the ongoing survival of programmes.

Secondly, very few interventions have only one aim. In most cases, programmes have several related goals and it must be decided whether the evaluator is to investigate all or only one of the intervention's goals.

Thirdly, the evaluation process demands a very close working relationship between those responsible for the planning and implementation of an intervention and the evaluators. In some cases this relationship may be difficult to maintain, particularly where the results demonstrate that the intervention is not meeting its stated aims. In these circumstances it is the responsibility of both parties to work together to resolve the problems in the intervention in order to ensure maximum benefit to the target community.

Fourthly, the question of who should evaluate interventions is often a difficult one. Researchers should remember that it is impossible for one person to be both 'a player' and 'the referee'. Insiders (people who have helped to plan and implement a project) are the most knowledgeable about the area, but also the most subjective. Outsiders may not understand the aims and objectives of the project as well as an insider, but are likely to be far more objective. The question of who should evaluate an intervention must be decided by those responsible for the intervention and depends upon a number of questions: Are there insiders available who have the skills to conduct an evaluation? Are the funds available to employ outside evaluators who are often more expensive? And how important is an external reviewer to the evaluation?

Finally, some evaluators consider it their task to carry out a cost-benefit analysis comparing the input and output of an intervention. In virtually all cases, the cost of an intervention must be taken into account when measuring its effectiveness. Although for sophisticated programmes cost-benefit analyses require the additional skills of an accountant, the costs of most interventions can be investigated by a social researcher using the methods discussed above.

Key points

1. Monitoring is a tool for project management that makes use of social research knowledge and skills.
2. Monitoring depends on the identification and monitoring of SMART indicators at regular intervals.
3. Evaluation can be diagnostic (identify problems and underlying causes of success or failure), formative (develop recommendations for future improvement), or summative (determine the extent to which a project has achieved its stated aims).
4. Evaluation is a delicate process requiring the researcher to manage the relationship with project stakeholders carefully.

CHAPTER 9 Project monitoring and evaluation

Checklist

Keywords:

Check whether the meaning of these concepts introduced in this chapter is clear to you.

theory of change; monitoring; evaluation; indicator; SMART indicator; diagnostic evaluation; formative evaluation; summative evaluation; reputability study.

Your research:
1. Make sure that there is a clear theory of change before you begin any kind of monitoring or evaluation work.
2. Identify SMART indicators for each activity and outcome in the theory of change.
3. Develop instruments to measure your indicators at regular time intervals.
4. In evaluation research think carefully about your relationship with project managers.
5. Be clear as to the needs of project managers. Do they want formative, diagnostic or summative information, or do they want a combination of the three types?
6. Design your evaluation research around the needs of project stakeholders.

Exercises

1. Identify SMART indicators for each of the following project components:
   a. a meeting of factory workers to discuss new working hours
   b. nurses in casualty washing their hands between consultations with patients
   c. the ambulance drivers to arrive at motor vehicle accident scenes
   d. motorbike riders' respect for the rules of the road.
2. Discuss the differences between monitoring and evaluation.
3. Find a report or description of a community project being run in your area. Work out some questions that an evaluation of this project should answer. Plan a diagnostic, formative and summative evaluation of the project.

Additional resources

1. Gudda, P. 2011. *A guide to project monitoring and evaluation*. Bloomington, IL: AuthorHouse.
2. International Development Evaluation Association (IDEAS) – www.ideas-int.org
3. South African Monitoring and Evaluation Association (SAMEA) – www.samea. org.za

CHAPTER 10

Research planning and design

In the previous chapters, different types of research were introduced, amongst them research types that are based on testing hypotheses as well as those of a qualitative nature, such as exploratory studies that do not. Whether it is correlational, explanatory or exploratory research, the planning and designing of a research project is a delicate task. Although in quantitative research, this process is usually based on probabilistic reasoning, it must leave as little doubt as possible as to the validity of the results. In order to achieve this, the researcher must logically exclude all reasonable explanations, other than the one that he or she wishes to demonstrate. The testing procedure must therefore satisfy some criteria of logic and rigour. These are expressed for different situations and problems in procedures to be followed, namely the research designs. In qualitative research, however, although the planning of the main steps of the process is important, the researcher is essentially guided by the data collection and its consequences, rather than by a predetermined plan.

The present chapter aims to introduce some planning issues, as well as the most common research designs used in social science, as well as an indication of which type or research they are best suited for.

> **CHAPTER OBJECTIVES**
>
> Learners who have completed this chapter will be able to:
> - Explain the fundamental principles of research design.
> - Distinguish research designs in qualitative research from those in quantitative research.
> - Develop appropriate research designs for particular research questions.
> - Identify and avoid a broad range of biases that affect research design.
> - Evaluate the internal and external validity of any research project.

What is a research design?

A **research design** relates directly to the answering of a research question. Because research is a project that takes place over an extended period of time, it is unthinkable to embark on such an exercise without a clear plan or design, a sort of blue print. A design in quantitative research is a detailed outline for the testing of a hypothesis, spelled out in clear and definite terms. It is a specification of the most appropriate operations which need to be performed in order to test a specific hypothesis under given conditions. This design is not, however, to be confused with **research management** which is a plan to guide the researcher through the research process. In quantitative research, the vital

CHAPTER 10 Research planning and design

question facing the scientist is: What steps should be taken in order to demonstrate that a particular hypothesis is true and that all other possible explanations have been rejected? On the other hand, the concept of research design in qualitative research is more flexible, sometimes cyclical and much less detailed than it would be in the case in quantitative research. In the qualitative case, as the many steps of literature review, theory building, sampling and data collection do not constitute separate activities but are continuously interrelated (see Chapter 2), the planning and design of the entire process must remain dynamic.

The purpose of research design is to ensure high **internal validity**. In quantitative research, internal validity is concerned with the question, 'Do the observed changes in the dependent variable actually relate to changes in the independent variable?' In other words, internal validity examines the extent to which a particular research design has excluded all other possible hypotheses that could explain the variation of the dependent variable. We call this eliminating plausible rival explanations or isolating the dependent variable. In order to achieve high internal validity in quantitative research, a research design must control as many extraneous variables as possible. In qualitative research, internal validity is sometimes referred to as credibility (see Chapter 13) and is concerned with whether the researcher's method of data collection and analysis (see Chapters 12 and 15) addresses the research question adequately. Will the researcher be able to develop a convincing argument in anser to the research question from this study design?

Example

A researcher observes a high incidence of depression in a poor community. She suspects that the cases of depression are caused by long-term unemployment. In order to lobby for a job-creation programme in the area, she has to demonstrate the correctness of her hypothesis. She has, therefore, to plan a study which shows that in this particular community, depression is largely due to unemployment and not, for instance, to the past history of the people, their age or gender, or the poor living conditions within the community. Alternatively, if her aim is to study the effect of depression on the community in terms of the mental health of the affected families, she could base her research on interviews done not only with family members but also teachers. However, in the course of the research, she might find out that nurses at the local clinic or some village elders have different views on the issue that should be investigated. She might also discover that some characteristics of the village itself, such as its reliance on agricultural activities rather than on industrial ones, have a particular effect on the mental health of subjects. Thus her exploratory research design is continuously reshaped by the new information she gathers.

In order to achieve the objectives of social research, the scientist requires a carefully thought out strategy. The first steps in constructing solid research planning and design require the researcher to answer several fundamental questions about the research. These questions relate to the focus, the unit of analysis and the time dimension of the problem at hand. These concepts are explored below.

131

The focus of research

Social research can be used to explore almost any topic in the social world, although with differing degrees of accuracy, certainty, confidence and success. However, it is useful to try to classify the most common of these topics, since they sometimes require different types of research design. The focus of research may be understood in terms of three different categories: conditions, orientations and actions.

1. *Conditions* are studied when the researcher wishes to explore the current state of the respondents of the research. For example, a researcher who measures the unemployment rate in 20 West African cities is interested in the current condition of the labour markets in those cities. Similarly, a researcher interested in the health of elderly people in rural areas might measure their heart rate after light exercise. This kind of study would be located within the quantitative paradigm, since variables such as unemployment rate and heart rate presuppose numeric measurement. The same holds true if the present conditions related to unemployment (or health of a community) are investigated qualitatively through the use of focus groups composed of members of the community under investigation.

2. *Orientations* are concerned with participants' attitudes, beliefs and lifestyles. Researchers interested in religious and political views would, for example, be interested in orientations. Attitudes, beliefs and lifestyles can only be quantified and therefore measured numerically with difficulty. Thus, they remain qualitative in nature. However, an association may be found between respondents' attitudes, beliefs and lifestyles that might be correlational and therefore quantitative. In studying orientations the researcher is provided fertile ground in which to conduct a mixed-method study using both qualitative and quantitative dimensions.

3. *Actions* are also very often the focus of research. These actions may be observed directly or may be reported by the actor or others who observed the actor. For example, a study of how people travel to work in urban areas might involve extensive observations of road, taxi and bus routes as well as trains (direct observation), or alternatively it might rely on interviews with workers or employers (an indirect method).

In most cases, conditions, orientations and actions are not mutually exclusive and the social researcher must be sensitive to all of them simultaneously. For example, the relationship between unemployment and depression involves all three. Experiences of being without work are likely to depend upon the length of time participants have been unemployed and their current level of savings (conditions), their beliefs about themselves, their futures, and their families (orientations), as well as the amount of energy they spend each day looking for, or trying to create, work (actions).

CHAPTER 10 Research planning and design

The unit of analysis

The second important factor that the researcher must consider when planning an appropriate research design is that of the **unit of analysis**. This becomes particularly important when the researcher begins to draw a sample (see Chapter 11) with which to work. The unit of analysis is the person or object from whom the social researcher collects data. The unit of analysis may be at a micro (individual, family, group), mezzo (organisation, community) or macro (national) level. One of the aspects that clearly distinguishes quantitative from qualitative studies is the procedure involved in selecting the units of analysis (for more details, see Chapter 11). In quantitative studies, where the underlying purpose is generalisation of the findings to the entire population, selection of participants is done largely through probability samples. In the case of explanatory studies the principle of random assignment must also be observed. In situations where participants have not been randomly selected, the researcher should exercise caution before generalising findings to the entire population: the data from such a unit can only describe that unit. However, when combined with similar data collected from a group of similar units, the data provides an accurate picture of the group to which that unit belongs.

In qualitative research, the selection of the unit might change in the course of the research. For instance, in the previous example, the researcher might have planned to interview only the members of the families affected by unemployment. Other types of units, such as teachers and nurses, might have to be added in the course of the research.

> ### Example
>
> A researcher is interested in the physical health of people in a rural community. Using a medical screening procedure, she collects data from 100 carefully sampled people (the units of analysis of this study) living in that community. By analysing the data from these 100 different people, a general estimate of the health conditions in this particular community can be constructed.
>
> In a different approach, the status of physical health of that community might be studied through the perceptions, attitudes and feelings that the community has about their own health situation. From discussions with villagers, a researcher might establish the health conditions of the community as perceived by its members.

Although many people believe that social scientists always focus exclusively upon the phenomenological experiences of individual people, this is not always the case. There are several possible units of analysis which fall into broad categories.

- *Individuals* are the most common unit of analysis. In this case, the researcher investigates the conditions, orientations, actions, attitudes and beliefs of a group of individual people. When the individual is used as the unit of analysis, the people that actually take part in the study are often selected because they belong to a particular group, such as police officers, women, people with cancer, and so forth.

133

- *Groups of people* are also sometimes studied. Some examples of research where the unit of analysis is more than one person are studies of siblings and identical twins, marital relationships, family functioning and small-group functioning. In this case an entire group (and not each of its members) constitutes one unit and can be compared to another group (another unit).
- *Organisations* with formal structures constitute a particular kind of group that is often used as the unit of analysis for social research. In this case, questions of interest might relate to proportions of employees from different social groups, organisational structure, profit and communication channels.
- Occasionally, the unit of analysis is a *period of time*. For example, a researcher may wish to determine whether there is a systematic change in infant mortality in a given community over a 20-year period (each unit is one year), or how much rain falls each month over a year (each unit is one month), or how some cultural beliefs or values evolve through time.
- Finally, a common unit of analysis is a particular *social artifact*. Social artifacts are the products of social beings and can be anything from poems and letters to automobiles and farming implements. A systematic analysis of such artifacts may provide valuable information about the individuals and groups that created or used them.

It is very important that the researcher keeps the units of analysis clearly in mind throughout the research process. It is often very tempting to draw conclusions about one unit of analysis when, in actual fact, the research is focused on a different one. This is called the **ecological fallacy**.

Example

A comparison between rural communities, which have relatively few young men, and peri-urban communities, with their large numbers of young men, reveals that the peri-urban communities tend to have a higher incidence of alcoholism than the rural ones. The researcher uses this to argue that young men are more likely than other groups within the community to abuse alcohol.

The data does not, however, show this. The possibility exists that men and women of all ages consume more alcohol when living in a peri-urban area due to the greater stresses of living near a city and the easy availability of drink. The researcher has made the error of drawing conclusions about individuals when the research examined groups of people (different communities).

CHAPTER 10 Research planning and design

The tendency of researchers to focus on particular units of analysis is another potential flaw in social science research. This is a form of *reductionism* and was mentioned in Chapter 1. Psychologists tend to focus on the individual, but sociologists investigate groups of people, as do economists. Anthropologists focus on group behavior and social artifacts, whilst historians often consider only social artifacts. This represents a flaw, because most social phenomena can only be explained if one understands the dynamics operating at a number of different levels.

Example

In recent years large numbers of people have immigrated to South Africa from various other African countries. Some rapidly become integrated into South African society, while others remain isolated and may experience physical, emotional and social problems. To understand why some people adjust quickly and others do not, the social scientist must consider the political and economic realities of the country from which these people have come, as well as their personal ability to form friendships in a new place and adapt to different social norms. In other words, it is necessary to investigate some aspects of the individuals, as well as the social context from which they came.

It cannot be denied that social scientists with backgrounds in different disciplines are often trained to operate with particular units of analysis only. It should be remembered that virtually nothing in the world is dependent only upon one of those levels and that, in order to be effective in one's work, one needs to consider social reality at many levels simultaneously. This is one reason why multidisciplinary collaboration is so important.

The time dimension

A third fundamental aspect of any research is the manner in which it deals with time. Observations may all take place at a particular time or may be deliberately stretched over a long period.

When all data is collected at the same time, the research design is **cross-sectional**. The discussion of correlational research in Chapter 5 is relevant here. The researcher using this design attempts to understand a topic by collecting a *cross-section* of information relevant to that topic. For example, a survey of nutrition patterns and infant mortality across a variety of living conditions may reveal differences between peoples' nutrition and the conditions under which they are living, as well as a relationship between these factors and infant mortality. The inherent difficulty with cross-sectional designs is that, because they do not allow the researcher to measure change over time (since all the data is collected at once), it is very difficult to demonstrate causality. In the above example, the researcher may be able to demonstrate that infant mortality and nutrition are related, but will not be able to show that poor nutrition is a cause of infant mortality. (Refer to the requirements of causality discussed in Chapter 5.)

135

Nevertheless, the immediate nature of cross-sectional designs, as well as the relative ease of data collection, makes these designs the most common choice for social scientists.

Longitudinal designs spread data collection out over time. For example, a researcher interested in unemployment in Nairobi between 2000 and 2009 conducts a broad yearly survey in the city in order to find out what proportion of the population is employed at any one time. Data collection occurs several times, in 2000, 2001, etc. (Note that the survey must take place during the same period of each year in order for the results to be comparable.) Once all the data has been collected, the researcher may be able to demonstrate that there is a predictable trend in the level of unemployment in Nairobi, information that may be useful to job-creation programmes, town planners and many other people.

Evaluation research (discussed in Chapter 9) may be cross-sectional or longitudinal in nature. Some longitudinal designs are introduced below.

- *Cohort studies* use a type of longitudinal design that tracks particular age group/s over time. For example, the 'Birth to Twenty' project running in South Africa (Richter et al., 2007) is recording the development of hundreds of South African children over the first 20 years of their lives. These researchers record a wide range of physical, emotional, social and educational variables relating to children's development.
- *Tracer studies* are used to 'trace' people, or to follow their lives over a period of time. In most cases, the data is collected at only one point, which is cross-sectional (perhaps 10 years after graduation or release from prison). As such, the tracer study is not strictly longitudinal, but produces data that simulates a longitudinal design.

Types of research design

Every project requires a research design that is carefully tailored to the exact needs of the problem. Of the many different designs that have been developed by social scientists over the years, only the few that are most frequently used are presented here. More complex designs can be studied in specialised books.

Research designs have two essential components. The first is observation. At some point in every research project, the researcher must observe and record differences in the different variables involved in the research. Some research designs require that the researcher observe more than one group, at more than one time. The second essential component of research design is the analysis of the relationships between the variables. This may be done in quantitative research by manipulating certain variables in order to observe the effect on other variables, or by observing corresponding changes in more than one variable. In qualitative research, this analysis is done by comparing information and then selecting further participants to help to clarify the relationship.

CHAPTER 10 Research planning and design

Three categories of research design can be distinguished for quantitative research according to the level of scientific rigour involved in proving the causal relationship, or the aims of the qualitative research.

- **Pre-experimental (exploratory and descriptive)** designs (see also Chapter 5) are essentially the methods of qualitative research. They satisfy the aim of the researcher to describe and understand a phenomenon. As instruments for quantitative research, pre-experimental designs are the least adequate in terms of scientific rigour and thus are least likely to establish a clear causal relationship between the independent and dependent variables. In cases where quasi-experimental or experimental designs are not possible, the quantitative researcher is forced to use a pre-experimental design, as these have far fewer requirements than the other designs. Three pre-experimental designs are presented below:
  - one-shot case study
  - pre-test/post-test design
  - intact group comparison design.
- **Quasi-experimental designs** are designs which do not meet the exacting criteria of experimental designs, but which manage to approximate experimental conditions. Although these designs have fewer requirements than experimental designs, they can achieve a similar level of scientific rigour. They often provide correlational relationships between variables. Four quasi-experimental designs are presented:
  - contrasted groups design
  - post-test-only cohort design
  - pre-test/post-test cohort design
  - time-series design.
- **Experimental designs** are the most rigorous of all the designs and have strict requirements. They provide explanatory relationships between variables. Three experimental designs are presented:
  - pre-test/post-test control group design
  - post-test-only control group design
  - factorial design.

Although the designs are presented here in order of increasing scientific rigour, it should be noted that experimental designs were developed before quasi-experimental designs. The latter were developed to accommodate the constraints of social reality that could not be accounted for using the former. Thus quasi-experimental designs appear as alternatives to stricter experimental designs.

Pre-experimental designs

Pre-experimental designs are largely qualitative and often use small, non-probability samples (see Chapter 1). Descriptive and exploratory research respond to the need of qualitative researchers to gain a deeper understanding of a particular social phenomenon. Quantitative researchers sometimes use exploratory designs to find out whether a full, detailed and rigorous investigation is possible. This is a way of generating hypotheses which can be tested later with more sophisticated research designs.

One-shot case study

In quantitative research, a one-shot case study is most often used to determine whether an event (or intervention) has any effect upon a group of participants. The dependent variable is measured after the event (post-test) and conclusions are drawn.

Qualitative research uses this method extensively: the most common use being case studies and focus groups.

A one shot case study is represented in Figure 10.1 below.

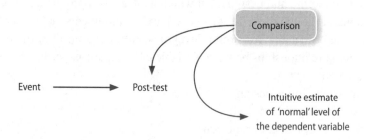

Figure 10.1. *One-shot case study*

> **Example**
>
> *Quantitative research:* A factory manager is concerned about the daily number of absentees. A system of monitoring attendance is introduced (the event) and thereafter the number of absentees (the dependent variable) is recorded every day. Finding that the number of absentees is low, the manager concludes that the new monitoring system is a success.
>
> Unfortunately, this conclusion is not really justified. The central objection is that, without some measure of what the absentee rate was like before the monitoring device was installed, it is very difficult for the manager to argue convincingly that absentee rates after the installation are any lower than they were to begin with.
>
> *Qualitative research*: The same factory manager considers that, in order to overcome absenteeism, he has to understand its causes and be informed about the best motivators for his staff. He requests a social researcher to conduct focus groups to investigate this issue.

In quantitative research, the lack of an initial measure of functioning, often referred to as the **baseline**, makes it very difficult to convincingly demonstrate change resulting from the event and therefore does not exclude plausible alternative explanations as mentioned in Chapter 5. Thus the one-shot case study is generally regarded as uninterpretable and, when used, is vulnerable to many criticisms. The following design is used to overcome this problem.

Pre-test/post-test design

In the pre-test/post-test design, the quantitative researcher measures the dependent variable before (pre-test or baseline) and after (post-test) the treatment or event that is expected to bring about a change. As a result, the scores for the dependent variable can be compared at two points in time, and the difference between the before and after scores may be due to the event that occurred between them. The same can be achieved in qualitative research, when the perceptions of a situation before and after some event are compared, for instance, by comparing the attitude of young people towards alcoholism before and after a public campaign against drunk driving.

In quantitative research, the pre-test/post-test design is the most common one for impact studies or summative evaluations (discussed in Chapter 9). In this case the event is the intervention that is being evaluated.

The design is presented diagrammatically in Figure 10.2.

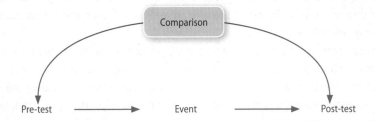

Figure 10.2 *Pre-test/post-test design*

> **Example**
>
> Using this design, the manager of the factory is required to measure the daily absentee rate before installing a new monitoring system. The new system is then put into operation and, shortly thereafter, the absenteeism rate is measured again. A finding that the absenteeism rate has dropped from ten workers per day (pre-test) to four workers per day (post-test) represents a difference of six. Since this change occurred after the new system came into operation, the manager has far more convincingly demonstrated that the monitoring system is effective in reducing absenteeism. A qualitative approach might investigate through focus groups the change of work motivation, or of feelings towards leadership before and after the installation of the monitoring system.

However, from a quantitative viewpoint, even this approach raises some concerns. It is not impossible that other changes occurred at the same time as the event (the installation of the monitoring system) and those changes, not the monitoring system, might have been responsible for the change in the dependent variable. This is particularly true when a long period of time has elapsed between the pre- and post-tests. These changes threaten the validity of the study's conclusions that the changes observed between the pre- and post-tests occur as a result of the intervention, with a plausible alternative explanation that the changes might be due to a spurious variable (see Chapter 5).

One of the problems with a single group design lies in the impossibility of determining what might have happened if the intervention had not been made. This is called a **counterfactual condition**. These other changes that might be confounding the study are of two different types: those that occur within the environment and those that occur within the participants.

Events that arise within the environment are referred to as **history**. In the absenteeism example it is possible that the workers' attendance was influenced by a fear of losing their jobs due to increasing unemployment, changes in weather conditions which made it easier to get to work, or the end to a flu outbreak in the area. Any of these reasons could be used to explain the change in the absentee rate and the manager therefore has still not demonstrated conclusively that the device works.

Events that arise within the participants are referred to as **maturation**. It is also possible that the workers' attitude to their job has changed and, as a result, they are staying away from work less often. Again, this confounds any change that might have occurred due to the installation of the new monitoring device and the manager cannot show that it actually works.

In cases where participants must be tested (such as tests of memory or driving skill) a bias called the **test effect** may arise. Participants may become bored with the test procedure, or they may become practised and thus improve, or they may become fatigued. In other words, this bias results from a change in participants' responses to the test instrument with repeated usage.

Instrumentation refers to changes in the measuring device or procedure over the course of the study. So, for example, having used one person to conduct the assessment interview at pre-test, and another person to do it at post-test, might account for changes in post-test scores. If tests are subjectively scored, this may account for variations in scores that are therefore not due to the intervention.

When participants drop out of a study, the scores that remain at post-test may not be representative of the original sample that was recruited for the study. This is referred to as **attrition** or **mortality**.

A final source of error in the pre-test/post-test design is that of **regression towards the mean**. All variables fluctuate somewhat due to chance. It is possible that the initial measurement (pre-test) was not an accurate reflection of the dependent variable. As a result, the second measurement (post-test) is likely to be different but closer to the actual level of the dependent variable, regardless of the effect of the event. Using the previous example, it may have happened that on the day that the initial measurement was taken, an unusually high number of people were absent from work. As a result, it is likely that the second measurement will be lower, even if the new monitoring device has no effect.

Intact group comparison design

Instead of using only a single group, the intact group comparison design uses two groups, one of which is affected by the event or treatment, while the other is not. Instead of comparing the performance of one group before and after the event or treatment, this design compares the scores of two groups, only one of which was affected by the event or treatment. Since both performances are measured at the same time, the intact group comparison design overcomes the difficulties of history, maturation and regression towards the mean. This design is presented diagrammatically in Figure 10.3.

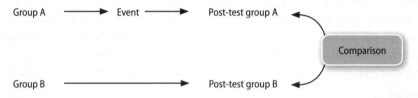

Figure 10.3 *Intact group comparison design*

Example

Quantitative research: This design requires that the factory manager or researcher has access to two factories. The workers of factory A are to be the experimental group. The workers of factory B are to be the comparison group. The new monitoring device is installed in factory A in order to deal with the problems of absenteeism. Shortly thereafter, the daily absentee rate is measured for both factories (post-test). If the absentee rate is lower for factory A than for factory B, the manager can argue that the monitoring device works.

Qualitative research: Here, using focus groups or individual interviews in both factories, it is possible to assess the difference in attitudes between the two groups of workers in respect of punctuality, work conditions and leadership.

Looking at the quantitative approach, one can see that, while this design does overcome problems of history, maturation, test effect and regression towards the mean, it unfortunately introduces new problems of its own. The difficulty with this design is in demonstrating that the two groups are similar to begin with. In the previous example, it may be that working conditions in factory B are a lot poorer than those in factory A and that the absenteeism rate is higher for factory B anyway. The possibility that the groups were originally different, or may react differently to the same event or treatment, is the crucial weakness of this type of design.

Any group that exists prior to a research study is called an intact group. The issue of not being sure that two such groups are equivalent is a problem for many studies that try to examine the differences between pre-existing groups.

Quasi-experimental designs

Quasi-experimental designs allow the researcher to maintain a higher level of control and rigour than is possible in pre-experimental designs, even when the demands of experimental designs cannot be met.

One of the hallmarks of a true experimental design is random assignment of participants to treatments. Random assignment allows the researcher to control many of the threats to internal validity. A true experimental design always includes random assignment of participants to conditions, manipulation of the independent variable and comparisons between groups. However, this may be too expensive, too difficult to conduct or even unethical, and is therefore seldom possible to achieve! It may be simpler to evaluate naturally occurring differences in treatment settings. Thus, quasi-experimental designs may be used to provide preliminary support for verifying potentially important treatments. The major identifying characteristic of a quasi-experimental design is the lack of random assignment of respondents to conditions.

> ### Example
>
> A researcher wants to evaluate the effectiveness of a programme to delay the onset of sexual activity among secondary-school students in Dar-es-Salaam. School-age adolescents are most at risk for HIV and early sexual activity is a risk factor. A quasi-experimental design may involve providing the programme to one class of Grade 10 students and withholding it from another and then assessing at a later time if the programme was successful. The study is quasi-experimental, as participants have not been randomly assigned to conditions, yet there is manipulation of the independent variable (treatment versus no treatment) and a between-conditions comparison (one class versus another class).

Contrasted group design

One solution (but not the best) to the problems of the intact groups design is to use groups that clearly contrast. In other words, the researcher's goal has changed from finding similar groups to finding groups that are essentially dissimilar, or contrasting in their main characteristic. If the researcher knows that groups are only different in terms of one aspect (the independent variable) and records a difference between the groups in terms of another aspect (the dependent variable), then she can conclude that the differences in the dependent variable are related to the differences between the two groups. Note that the important difference between this design and the others discussed so far is that this design does not allow for an independent event or treatment, but is based on differences that already exist between the two groups. This design is illustrated in Figure 10.4.

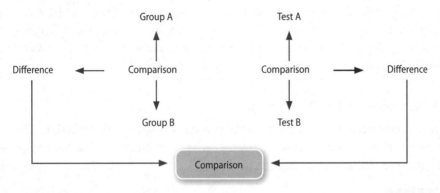

Figure 10.4 *Contrasted group design*

> **Example**
>
> One may wish to assess the influence of the education of parents on the performance of their children in mathematics. To carry out this research design the researcher forms two groups of children, those whose parents have a university degree and those whose parents did not complete high school. The researcher matches the children in terms of sex and age. These are contrasting groups of children since the education of their parents is clearly different. By comparing the differences in mathematics scores for these two groups of children, one can infer that parental education has an effect upon performance. Clearly, if the maths performance of the two groups of children is not different, then one would infer that the educational background of parents has little influence on children's maths performance.

Cohort designs

Cohorts are likely to be similar to each other since their environment is the same except for the treatment variable. For example, the Grade 6 class at a school in 2005 is likely to have similar demographic characteristics to the Grade 6 class at the same school in 2006. Cohort designs are strengthened when the researcher can argue that the two cohorts share similar environments, except for the interventions that they receive.

This design is similar to the one-shot case study design except that the post-test cohort tests age groups after the passing of time. These testings occur at different points in time because the cohorts follow each other through the system such as a school system, a university system or workers undergoing a training programme.

> **Example**
>
> A lecturer wants to test the effectiveness of new teaching materials, in teaching research methods to undergraduate psychology students.
>
> In 2002 the lecturer uses the old materials and tests the students at the end of the semester. In 2003 she uses the new materials and tests the students. Thereafter she compares the students' marks for both years and makes an inference about whether the new materials are more or less effective than the old.

Pre-test/post-test cohort design

A more sophisticated cohort design is the **pre-test/post-test cohort design**. The main advantage of this design is that the researcher is more confident that the groups were similar at pre-test, that is, prior to treatment.

> **Example**
>
> A researcher wants to test the effectiveness of a psychological treatment with students at a university counselling centre. Every student attending the centre undergoes a pre- and post-counselling assessment. At the beginning of the semester when students come, she might give them cognitive therapy, and the students who come for services later in the semester receive solution-focused therapy. The researcher can then compare the change in scores on the first cohort (the cognitive therapy group) with the change in scores on the second cohort (solution-focused group). This is a pre-test/post-test cohort design.

Time-series design

Time-series designs represent an improvement over the one group pre-test/post-test design of the pre-experimental group. Rather than relying on a single measurement before and after the event or treatment, several measurements all before (pre 1, pre 2 and pre 3) and after (post 1, post 2 and post 3) the event or treatment are made. This allows one to observe the effects of history and of maturation, test effects and regression towards the mean. This is achieved by comparing each measurement with the measurements that were taken before and after it. Differences between those measurements taken before the event (for example, pre 3–pre 2) and between those taken after the event (for example, post 2–post 1), but not between the before and after measurements, must be due to such variables as regression towards the mean, history, maturation and test effect. The biases can be taken into account when differences due to the treatment are examined and interpreted. The most important difference is thus the one between the before and after measurements (that is, post 1–pre 3) since this must be due to the event or treatment. Putting all this information together allows the researcher to draw conclusions about the effect of the event or treatment, taking into account the effect of the various confounding variables.

The limitation of this design lies in the difficulty of obtaining a series of repeated measures. It is often difficult to test the same group of people six to eight times. Further, over time some group members may no longer be available (attrition), which changes the composition of the group. This bias is called experimental mortality and is discussed in greater detail later in this chapter. Time-series design is illustrated in Figure 10.5.

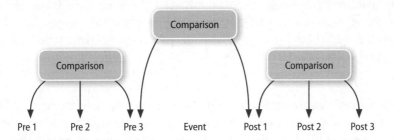

Figure 10.5 *Time-series design*

Example

Returning to the example of the factory manager and the problems of absenteeism, using a time-series design, the level of absenteeism can be measured several times before the new monitoring device was installed. Differences between these initial scores are due to secondary factors such as regression towards the mean, history, maturation and test effect. A similar set of records from after the monitoring device had been installed would provide complementary information. By comparing the level of the scores before and after the installation, the manager would be able to tell whether or not the new device made a significant difference. Typically, the data of such a study could be graphed as shown in Figure 10.6.

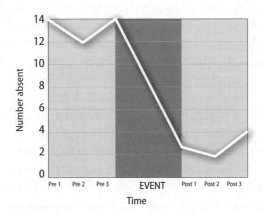

Figure 10.6 *Charting time-series data*

Example

A further example illustrates the usefulness of time-series design. Moganu and Rumish (1994/2000) present the following analysis of the incidence of tuberculosis in Botswana.

During the period 1975–1985 the number of new cases of tuberculosis reported each year dropped by between 2% and 8%. From 1985–1990 the incidence of tuberculosis did not change significantly. However, in the period 1990–1994 the number of reported tuberculosis cases increased by 200% per year. Clearly something important has changed, but what? The answer is found in the fact that nearly all of the new cases reported in the last four-year period also tested positive for HIV.

Many other quasi-experimental designs intended for coping with different problems of social reality exist and are discussed in more advanced texts. A researcher confronted with a particular problem should consult specialised literature on the subject.

Experimental designs

Most experimental designs that meet the objectives of explanatory research are characterised by their use of randomisation to create two or more equivalent groups. The use of randomisation negates the difficulties of ensuring that the groups are identical. (The symbol 'R' is used in the following diagrams to identify groups that have been generated using random procedures.)

Randomisation

Randomisation requires that every participant involved in the study has an equal chance of being assigned to any of the groups of the study. This can be achieved by first identifying the entire group of participants, then randomly dividing this group into two or more subgroups (depending on the chosen design) through the use of random number tables, coin flipping or various other randomisation techniques.

It is important that some systematic random technique of determining which subject falls into which group is utilised. Arbitrary assignment to groups is not necessarily random. (Techniques for generating random numbers are introduced in Chapter 11.) It is important here to distinguish between random selection and random assignment. **Random selection** means that each member of the population has an equal chance of being selected into the sample. **Random assignment** means that each member of the sample has an equal chance of being assigned to any of the conditions or groups in the study. The terms 'random assignment' and 'randomisation' mean the same thing.

When two groups are created using randomisation they are most likely to be equivalent. This is particularly true when the researcher is working with large groups. The smaller the groups, the less sure the researcher can be that they are actually equivalent. The advantage of randomly generated groups is that the researcher starts

CHAPTER 10 Research planning and design

the experiment with two (or more) equivalent groups. If only one group is subjected to the treatment, the researcher can be reasonably sure that any difference between the groups thereafter is due to the effects of the treatment and nothing else. The group that does not receive the treatment is called the **control group**, while the group that receives the treatment is called the **experimental group**. The purpose of a control group is to compare treated participants with non-treated participants. In this way the effect of treatment versus no treatment can be examined.

Placebo control group

The placebo control group is another type of control group. Respondents or participants in a placebo control group are led to believe that they are receiving a viable treatment, although in reality what is given to them is supposed to be ineffective.

So, in a study of the effectiveness of counselling to reduce anxiety among cancer patients receiving surgery, the placebo control group might participate in a discussion group with no active group counselling. The reason for doing this is that it enables the separation of the specific effects of a treatment from the effects due to client expectations, receiving attention from an experimenter or a group leader or therapist, and other non-specific factors.

The **Hawthorne effect** is relevant here in accounting for the differences between pre- and post-test scores. This effect was discovered during a study of worker productivity in the United States. Workers in a factory were assigned to either a treatment group or a no treatment group. The treatment group received an intervention designed to increase productivity, such as better lighting and various other things. The control group received nothing, but was simply studied by the researchers. They received only the attention of the researchers, and without receiving any active intervention, the participants in the control group also increased their productivity. This change in post-test score for the control group was explained as the effect of receiving attention from the researcher. It should be noted that the data obtained in the original Hawthorne study has been criticised as being flawed. Nonetheless, it is generally accepted in research that just by receiving attention from a researcher, participants' post-test scores might change.

Matching

Of course, it is impossible to randomly assign participants to groups when the independent variable cannot be manipulated. An obvious example of a variable that cannot be manipulated is sex. Almost all people are either male or female and the researcher can do nothing about it. The same is true of religious affiliation, cultural background, income, age, place of residence and many other characteristics. When one of these factors is the independent variable, the researcher must use other techniques to establish equivalent groups. One procedure is **matching** the elements of the group. In this case, the control for the equivalence of the two groups is based on having knowledge of the

147

main characteristics of the elements, persons, events or objects to be investigated. The researcher forms pairs of members having identical characteristics considered relevant to the research. The members of each pair must differ in terms of the independent variable only. For the example of absenteeism, the workers could be matched on such properties as age, sex, skill, health, family situation and work experience. Each member of each pair is then randomly assigned to a different group. In this way, the two groups so constituted will have equivalent properties and they are called **dependant groups** (see Chapter 11 for dependent samples and Chapter 14 for statistical tests).

Another method of **matching**, which has the advantage of being more efficient especially in the case of large groups, is aimed at forming groups that have the same global characteristics. For instance, the two groups must have the same number of males and females, the same average height, and the same number of skilled workers. Of course, the matching is not as precise as in the first case, but it is essential that the matching is done for all relevant factors. Where important factors are neglected in the matching process, the groups are no longer equivalent for the purposes of the research, and the results are compromised.

The choice between randomisation and matching often does not exist. Matching procedures can only be used if enough variables relevant to the research are known. If, for instance, age is an important factor, but the experimenter is not provided with the ages of participants, no matching can be done on the basis of age. Moreover, if the number of variables to control is large, it will become increasingly difficult to find enough individuals with the same combination of characteristics. Furthermore, in very large groups, the matching procedure becomes very time-consuming, tedious and costly.

It is only through the creation of equivalent groups by randomisation or matching that the following experimental designs are possible.

Pre-test/post-test control group design

The pre-test/post-test control group design requires participants to be randomly assigned to two groups, one of which becomes the experimental group while the other is the control group. Note that a control group is similar to the comparison group of the intact group's design, except that it is arrived at through random assignment. Both groups are measured at the beginning of the study. Thereafter, the experimental group is subjected to the event or treatment.

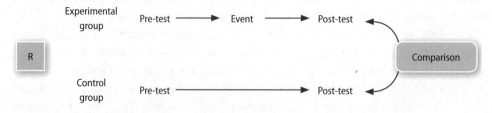

Figure 10.7 *Pre-test/post-test control group design*

CHAPTER 10 Research planning and design

Following the treatment, both groups are measured again. Now the researcher can compare the pre-test and post-test scores of the experimental group, as well as the post-test scores of the experimental and control groups, in order to assess whether the event or treatment made any difference to the scores of the experimental group. This is illustrated in Figure 10.7.

> **Example**
>
> The factory manager of the earlier examples would first have to assign the factory workers randomly to two different groups. Random assignment means that one can assume that these groups are equivalent. In other words, it is expected that the proportion of absentees in both groups is about the same. The next step is to collect absentee data from both groups (pre-test). Thereafter, the new device is put into operation on the one group only. This becomes the experimental group. The other group continues as before and is the control group. Shortly thereafter, the manager must again record the absentee rates of each group. By comparing the pre-and post-test scores for the experimental group, as well as the post-test scores for the experimental and control groups, the manager can tell how much difference the new device has made and how much change was due to the other variables which confound the pre-test/post-test design of the pre-experimental group.

Because of randomisation, the two groups can be expected to be equivalent at pre-test. However, it is possible that they will differ, in which case the difference in the pre-tests is taken into account when comparing the post-test results. Note that this design also allows the researcher to measure the effects of history, maturation and regression towards the mean at the same time as providing a powerful method for impact studies or summative evaluations. It is the design of choice where the possibility of random assignment exists.

Weaknesses of the design

It is possible that giving a test twice – a pre-test and post-test – might sensitise participants to the material, and this may make post-test scores different to what they might have been without a pre-test. However, if the two groups are truly randomly assigned, then this effect will be the same for the control group and so therefore no real threat to internal validity.

On the other hand, it may be a threat to external validity (see more detail at the end of this chapter and in Chapter 13). The treatment may or may not have had an effect on post-test scores but the fact that participants had a pre-test might have affected the way in which they responded to the post-test.

149

> **Example**
>
> A pre-test questionnaire about attitudes towards HIV might cue respondents to reflect on the topic of HIV and also to process information differently while receiving a programme about awareness of HIV.

It is also possible that treatment in itself might not have an impact on post-test scores, but there may be an interactive effect of the pre-test and the treatment that results in substantially higher scores on the post-test. The effect of this might be that the researcher believes that a programme is excellent and therefore promotes it. However, when the practitioners implement the workshop without the pre-test, they find a much weaker treatment effect than they were expecting. This is a serious problem, and it is what is meant by a threat to external validity.

Post-test-only control group design

An experimental design that has virtually all the experimental rigour of the pre-test/post-test control group design is the post-test-only control group design. Randomisation aims at ensuring that the experimental and control groups are identical except for the fact that only the experimental group receives the treatment or event. Therefore the pre-test/post-test comparison incorporated into the previous design may be superfluous. The simpler design represented by Figure 10.8 does away with the pre-testing.

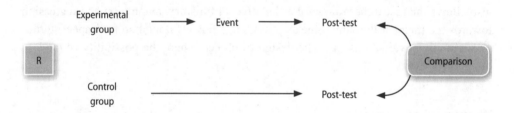

Figure 10.8 *Post-test-only control group design*

> **Example**
>
> Using this design on the absenteeism problem, the researcher would again divide the workforce randomly into two equal groups but install the new monitoring device in the work area of one group only. Note that this is done without pre-testing. Shortly thereafter, the post-test measurement is taken of both groups and the results can then be compared.

Example

A second example is taken from education. This design is very useful for assessing the efficiency of a new teaching method. A class of pupils is randomly divided into two groups. One group, the experimental one, is subjected to the new method, while the control group continues to be taught using the old method. After a certain period, both groups are given a competency test to assess their progress in the subject. Note that if the pre-test/post-test control group design had been used, it would have meant constructing two equivalent competency tests, one to be given before the treatment and the other after the treatment. Not only is it technically difficult to construct two tests to assess the same knowledge content and skills but, also, the pupils' results in the second test would be influenced to various degrees by their experience of the first test. This would make an assessment of the effects of the new teaching method difficult to gauge.

Since all the data is collected at one time, the problems of maturation, history, test effects and regression towards the mean do not arise. Bear in mind that it is impossible for the researcher to be certain that the two groups are indeed equivalent to start with, but when a random assignment technique is used and there are enough participants in the study (at least 30 in each group), the researcher can safely use the post-test-only control group study.

Factorial designs

Factorial designs can be thought of as generalisations of either the pre-test/post-test control group design or the post-test-only control group design. The important difference, however, is that factorial designs can incorporate two or more independent variables, whereas the previous designs only allow for a single independent variable. A factorial design with two independent variables, each having two levels, will be studied here. Call the variables x and y, and their levels x_1, x_2, y_1, and y_2. The following figure illustrates how an analysis of the relationship between these two independent variables demands four experimental groups in the design.

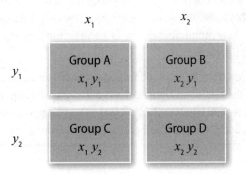

Figure 10.9 *Factorial design with two variables*

Thus this design requires four groups *(Group A* to *Group D)* and in an experimental design it is required that these groups are constructed using randomisation. Depending upon the size of the sample and the particular needs of the researcher, the groups may be pre-tested. As for designs with only one independent variable, the pre-test is not essential, but can provide extra information. Once the groups have been exposed to different combinations of the two (or more) independent variables, they are then post-tested. The researcher then searches for differences between the levels of the independent variables, that is between x_1 and x_2, and between y_1 and y_2. Such differences are called main effects. Further, the analysis may reveal that there is an interaction between the two variables. This means that both variables in conjunction are producing a particular pattern of results that cannot be explained in terms of only one of the variables. Figure 10.10 illustrates a post-test-only factorial design with two variables, each with two levels.

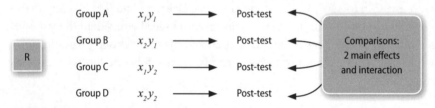

Figure 10.10 *Factorial design*

Example

Imagine that the factory manager of the previous examples wished to examine the effects of different work hours or shifts, as well as the use of the monitoring device on absenteeism. There would therefore be two independent variables, each with two levels: work hours with day (x_1) and night (x_2) shifts, and the monitoring system without (y_1) or with the device installed (y_2). To put the design into effect, the manager randomly assigns each person in the workforce to one of four groups. Random assignment implies that these groups are equivalent for all other variables. Each group then gets a different combination of the independent variables as follows: Group A works the day shift (x_1) without the new monitoring device (y_1). Group C works the day shift (x_1) but with the new monitoring device (y_2). Group B works the night shift (x_2) but without the new monitoring device (y_1) and Group D works the night shift (x_2) with the new monitoring device (y_2).

Once the four groups have been working under these conditions for a short period, the manager measures the rate of absenteeism for each group. A comparison of groups A and C with groups B and D reveals whether the shift makes any difference. A comparison of groups A and B with groups C and D reveals whether the new monitoring device makes any difference.

continued ...

By examining the scores of all four groups, the manager is able to discover whether the new monitoring device and the shifts interact. A possible interaction is presented in the chart shown in Figure 10.11.

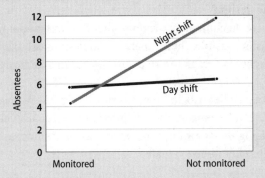

Figure 10.11 *Charting an interaction effect*

Note that the lowest level of absenteeism was recorded for the group that was monitored and worked the night shift. The group that was monitored and worked the day shift produced the next lowest score of absenteeism. The third lowest absenteeism score came from the group that was not monitored, but which worked the day shift. The highest level of absenteeism was recorded for the group that was not monitored and which worked the night shift. From these results, the manager can conclude that when workers are monitored, the levels of absenteeism for the day and night shift are quite similar, whereas, when not monitored, workers resort to absenteeism much more often during the night shift than the day shift.

Developing a research design

Very often research is hampered by constraints of resources, participants and time. Rarely can any of the designs discussed in this chapter be imposed directly onto actual research projects. Rather, these designs explain the logic of social research and should serve as a foundation for good research design. The researcher's work is complicated by many sources of bias and error which must each be dealt with as effectively as possible in order to ensure the highest quality of research.

In developing a design for a particular research problem, there are several questions to be considered.
1. Is a cross-sectional or longitudinal design more appropriate? Studies involving change over time virtually always use longitudinal designs. Cross-sectional designs are most useful for describing populations, and differences between populations, at a particular moment in time.

2. If a longitudinal design is used, how many repeated observations will be made? How will the problems of history, maturation, test effect and regression to the mean be addressed? Is there any danger of experimental mortality affecting the usefulness of the design?
3. Is it possible to create equivalent groups either through randomisation or matching? If this is possible, then experimental designs are the most appropriate. If not, the researcher is forced to use a quasi-experimental design.

It is important for social scientists to be very critical of their own and their colleagues' research designs. The following section explores the critical evaluation of research designs by summarising the common sources of bias in designs, as well as the criteria against which designs should be evaluated.

Summary of sources of bias in research design

Because every research project has its own particular set of problems, a complete list of the possible sources of bias in research does not exist. The quality of both quantitative and qualitative research can be affected to different extents and in different ways by these factors. There are, of course, many other sources of bias that relate more specifically to methods of data collection, subject selection, data presentation and analysis. These are discussed in other chapters and only those relating to research planning and design are dealt with here.

History and maturation

History refers to changes which occur in the world, other than those intended by the researcher, and which might affect the results. Maturation refers to changes that occur within participants and thus confound the researcher's design. These effects are particularly problematic to designs that require that data be collected at more than one time. One common solution is to collect data at a single point in time only. Post-test-only designs are advantageous in this respect. A second solution is pre-test/post-test control group and time-series designs, where repeated measurements allow the researcher to estimate the effects of history and maturation. These effects are then taken into account in the interpretation of the results. Clearly, when qualitative data are collected, the same issues and solutions are valid.

Regression towards the mean

Regression towards the mean arises when researchers base their conclusions upon single measurements. If a pre-test score is unusually high due to chance factors, the post-test score is likely to be lower, regardless of any changes due to the experimental variables. The most effective solution to this problem is the repeated testing adopted

CHAPTER 10 Research planning and design

by time-series designs. In the case of qualitative research, the freedom of selecting the participants as the research develops, gives the opportunity to compensate for this tendency.

Test effect

In quantitative research, prior exposure to a test or measurement technique can bias a person's responses. This is particularly problematic when participants are tested and retested, as in all pre-test/post-test and time-series designs. Particular test effects are boredom (when exactly the same test is repeated), practice (as participants learn how to respond to the test) and fatigue (particularly evident when the test procedure is lengthy). To counter these effects, the researcher should reduce the number of times that participants are tested, vary the test slightly so as to reduce boredom and practice effects, and use shorter tests to reduce fatigue. Alternative instruments are technically very difficult to construct and are also draining on resources. The same is true for qualitative research.

Instrumentation

Some of the many difficulties of developing appropriate instruments are discussed in a later chapter. However, instruments present a problem for design as well, particularly when different instruments are used to test the same concept. The researcher must be sure that the instruments are equally sensitive and accurate, otherwise changes between the two measurements might be due to differences in the instruments and not due to any differences within the participants. Also, instruments constructed for use in developing countries should be sensitive to people's lack of experience with advanced technology, as well as to differences in culture. Where possible, instruments should be pre-tested with a pilot study in order to check their appropriateness, accuracy and, where more than one instrument is used, their equivalence.

Sometimes, when measurement instruments are used in inappropriate ways, very powerful reactive effects can be produced. For example, it is not uncommon for potential employees undergoing a selection procedure to be subjected to instruments that were designed for the measurement of mental illness. In this case, potential employees will be extremely sensitive to being turned down for reasons of mental health, and are unlikely to respond truthfully to the instrument. This defeats the purpose of the selection assessment. Although data collection in qualitative studies rely more on natural methods, such as interviews and focus groups, the way in which they are conducted should be in accordance with cultural and other social and environmental factors.

Experimental mortality

Often participants drop out of a research project during the data-collection procedures. This is particularly true of research that takes place over an extended period of time. Time-series designs in particular are vulnerable to this source of error. Although experimental mortality produces difficulties for data analysis, the most important problem relates to the design of the research. It is possible, if not likely, that the people who drop out of a study are systematically different from those who remain with the study until the end. This may result in biased findings. The researcher should design the research so that it is convenient for people to participate until the end, and should impress upon the participants the importance of their continuing cooperation.

Reactive effects

When participants are aware of being observed, they behave in unnatural ways, that is, they 'react' to being observed. One example of a reactive effect is test anxiety. The measuring instrument may increase the arousal levels of some participants and thus influence their scores. Similarly, some participants try to please the experimenter and provide those results that they believe are desired. Others will do just the opposite and try to confound the study in order to find out how the researcher will react.

A well-known reactive effect is the Hawthorne effect. The Hawthorne effect occurs when participants of a study feel that their selection makes them a privileged group and, as a result, they perform differently to how they would otherwise.

The most effective way of countering this source of bias is to use unobtrusive techniques of data collection. In other words, if the participants are not aware that they are being observed, there is no reason to expect them to act unusually. Of course, this is not always possible and then the researcher should attempt to collect data in a way that causes the least disturbance to participants' lives. Practically, this may mean collecting data in participants' usual environments, using techniques that do not require special skills or unusual apparatus.

Selection bias

Since many studies incorporate more than one group of participants, it is important that the quantitative researcher be sure that these groups are equivalent to each other in all respects except for the independent variable of the study. When the independent variable is beyond the researcher's control and a quasi-experimental design has to be used, there is little that can be done. When the researcher is in control of which participants fall into which group, there are two techniques that can be used to ensure that the groups are similar. The best technique for a large group of participants is random assignment, which was discussed earlier in this chapter. This entails assigning the participants to different groups on the basis of a randomisation procedure. When the researcher has only a few participants and has reason to believe that randomisation might not result in

CHAPTER 10 Research planning and design

equivalent groups, the option of matching is available. This issue affects the qualitative researcher far less, as she can select participants in the course of her research and therefore has much more flexibility in order to avoid this bias.

Note that questions of history, maturation, test effects, reactive effects, instrumentation and attrition apply for both quantitative and qualitative research. Regression towards the mean is not a problem that qualitative researchers need to think about.

Relationship between internal and external validity

As explained at the beginning of this chapter, good research design leads to high **internal validity**, where the researcher is able to answer the research question convincingly. The potential of a design to achieve this aim is referred to as the validity of the design, and it is measured in terms of two separate but related dimensions: internal and external validity.

External validity is concerned with the question, 'To what extent do the results obtained in this study apply to the population being studied and to contexts different to those of this specific study?' In qualitative research, external validity is often referred to as transferability. External validity examines the extent to which the results of the study can be generalised. The researcher must consider two factors in order to achieve high external validity. Firstly, the sample must reflect the experiences of the population as fully as possible: in quantitative research the demand is for a representative sample, while qualitative researchers use a range of other methods to ensure that their study includes the full range and depth of respondents' experiences. These topics are discussed in greater detail in Chapter 11.

Secondly, the researcher must ensure that the study simulates reality as closely as possible. The conditions and situation must be seen as normal, depicting the usual reality of the participants. This means that the tests and tasks that are required of the participants must be planned so as to minimise the whole range of reactive effects. When people behave differently due to their participation in a research project, the findings are immediately less valid than they would have been had the participants behaved as they would every other day of their lives. Techniques for ensuring less reactivity include making data collection as unobtrusive as possible and testing people within their usual surroundings.

Unfortunately, internal and external validity tend to be inversely related. That is, studies with high internal validity often have low external validity and vice versa. Studies that take place in a particular social context have high external validity but cannot control the wide variety of real-world variables that could interfere with the effect of the independent variable on the dependent variable. Thus these studies have low internal validity. Similarly, studies that take place within more controlled environments have high internal validity, but they may be so far removed from everyday reality that their external validity is low. Very seldom does a design achieve high levels of both internal and external validity. In most cases social scientists tend to design studies that

157

Fundamentals of Social Research Methods: An African Perspective

have either high internal or external validity and then compare their study with other studies in the same field that have high validity on the other dimension.

Sometimes, in intervention research, the distinction is made between efficacy and effectiveness research. **Efficacy studies** test the success of one treatment over another under tightly controlled lab-like conditions. Thus, in an efficacy study, the researcher tries to control and isolate the variable of interest. One is only interested in whether the treatment works under ideal conditions. The researcher might provide transport and childcare for participants, and even compensate them to participate in the study. This will ensure compliance with the treatment and reduce attrition rates. Studies of this nature have very good internal validity, but less external validity. In the real world it is often not possible to give people transport, childcare and pay them to come for treatment. In fact, it is supposed to be the other way round. In the real world we conduct **effectiveness studies**, to see if there is actually uptake of the service and what its effect is if people have competing demands on their time. Do they still come for treatment, do they come regularly, on time, for the full duration of the treatment course, or not? Under these circumstances, is the treatment effective? This is the main difference between efficacy studies and effectiveness studies.

Key points

1. A design in quantitative research is a detailed outline spelled out in clear and uncertain terms for testing of hypotheses. It is a specification of the operations to be performed in order to test a specific hypothesis under given conditions

2. In the qualitative case, as the many steps of literature review, theory building, sampling and data collection do not constitute separate activities but are continuously interrelated, the planning and design of the entire process remain more flexible.

3. The purpose of research design is to ensure high internal validity. In quantitative research, internal validity is concerned with whether the observed changes in the dependent variable actually relate to changes in the independent variable. In qualitative research, internal validity is concerned with whether the researcher's method of data collection and analysis adequately addresses the research question.

4. When dealing with research design, three aspects must be considered: the focus of research, the unit of analysis and the time dimension.

5. There are three types of research designs: pre-experimental (exploratory, descriptive), the quasi-experimental, and the experimental designs.

6. Experimental designs, in particular, use some specific methods such as randomnisation, placebo control group and matching.

continued . . .

158

CHAPTER 10 Research planning and design

7. Many sources of bias can be identified in research: history and maturation, test effect, instrumentation, experimental mortality, reactive effects, selection bias and regression towards the mean.
8. The validity of the research design is assessed in terms of its internal and external validity. The relationship between these designs leads to delicate decisions as they are inversely related.

Checklist

Keywords:

Check whether the meaning of these concepts introduced in this chapter is clear to you.

cross-sectional designs; longitudinal designs; counter factual condition; pre-experimental, quasi-experimental and experimental designs; test effect; maturity; history; attrition/mortality; regression towards the mean; matching and randomisation; internal and external validity; one-shot case study; pre-test/post-test design; intact group; comparison design; contrasted group design; post-test-only cohort design; pre-test/post-test cohort design; time-series design; pre-test/post-test control group design; post-test-only control group design; factorial designs.

Your research:
1. Make sure that you understand the advantages and disadvantages of all the design.
2. Make sure that you have selected the most appropriate design to address your research question.
3. Have you considered all the possible sources of bias and have you found solutions to avoid or neutralise their effect on your research?
4. Have you checked the internal validity of your design?

Exercises

1. Take any of the research problems or hypotheses mentioned in earlier chapters and develop a couple of different research designs that could be used. Compare and contrast the advantages and disadvantages of the different designs you have chosen.
2. Explain the role of history, maturation and test effect in a pre-test/post-test design, and why these biases do not affect a time-series design.
3. Develop an example similar to the ones presented in this chapter. Apply the pre-test/post-test and time-series designs. What are the relative advantages and disadvantages of the two designs?

continued ...

159

4. What is the weakness of using a comparison group instead of a control group, and what is the role of random assignment? What is the difference between random selection and random assignment?
5. Why are experimental and even quasi-experimental designs challenging for qualitative research?
6. Compare the importance and role of research designs in qualitative research to those in quantitative research.
7. Complete the following table:

Design	Advantages	Disadvantages
One-shot case study		
Pre-test/post-test design		
Intact group comparison design		
Post-test-only cohort design		
Pre-test/post-test cohort design		
Time-series design		
Pre-test/post-test control group design		
Post-test-only control group design		
Factorial designs		

Additional resources

1. Campbell, D & Stanley, J C. 1963. *Experimental and quasi-experimental designs for research*. Chicago, IL: Rand-McNally.
2. Leedy, P D & Ormrod, J E. 2012. *Practical research planning and design*, 10th ed. Boston, Mass: Addison Wesley.

CHAPTER

11

Sampling

The purpose of this chapter is to introduce the concept of sampling. Why in research is it advantageous to restrict the investigation to a small but well-chosen group of participants (the sample) and how can we know that that accurately represents a much wider group (the population)? How is it possible, as required by quantitative research, to generalise the results obtained from a sample to the whole population? In the case of qualitative research, how can one obtain a detailed and specific description of a complex phenomenon? What are the different methods of sampling, and what are their strengths and weaknesses? What biases or other errors could be introduced at the sampling stage of the research process? These are some of the questions discussed in this chapter.

> **CHAPTER OBJECTIVES**
>
> Learners who have completed this chapter will be able to:
> - Discuss the rationale for and difficulties associated with sampling.
> - Compare probability and non-probability sampling.
> - Identify and evaluate the sampling method used in any study.
> - Select the most appropriate sampling method for a particular research question.
> - Carry out the sampling procedures required by a particular method.
> - Determine the most appropriate size for a sample.

The purpose and types of sampling

How does one judge if the customer service of Bank A is better than that of Bank B, that Shop C is better equipped than its competitor D, or that a shirt of Make X is of a higher quality than a shirt of Make Y? Judgement is usually based on experience, either personal or reported by others. One might observe how many times and for how long customers have to wait in a bank before being attended to, or ask the bank customers to express their opinion about the personnel working in the bank. Equally one could investigate how often an item is found in Shop D when it was not available in Shop C, and so on. On the basis of few observations one can generalise, or infer, properties of the whole and draw conclusions.

Sampling theory is the scientific foundation of this everyday practice. It is a technical accounting device to rationalise the collection of information, to choose an appropriate way in which to restrict the set of objects, persons or events from which the actual information will be drawn.

Without doubt, if one wants to collect accurate information about a group of persons or objects, the best strategy is to examine every single member or element of the group.

But it is also possible to reach accurate conclusions by examining only a portion of the total group. This assessment of only a portion of the group is commonly used in both the social and natural sciences. Medical assessments of blood characteristics of a patient are done after analysis of just a few drops of blood. Similarly, the interviewing of just a few students can allow an inference about the attitudes of the whole class towards a particular lecturer. Admittedly, many factors might reduce the accuracy of the results based on a small section of the whole group, but these are not of immediate concern and will be dealt with later.

The entire set of objects or people that is the focus of a research project and about which the researcher wants to determine some characteristics is called the **population**. It could be a population of all the cars assembled at a particular factory during 2005, all the houses in a town, or all the primary school teachers in the country. The subset of the whole population, which is actually investigated by a researcher and in the case of quantitative research whose characteristics will be generalised to the entire population, is called the **sample**. A sample might consist of every tenth car produced in that factory, every fiftieth house in that town or 100 primary school teachers selected from a list of trade union members. In each sample, a car, a house or one primary school teacher constitutes an element or **unit of analysis**. Specific values or quantities that relate to the population as a whole, such as the average age of all primary school teachers, are called **population parameters**. When the corresponding values or quantities are drawn from the sample, such as the average age of the 100 teachers constituting the sample, they are called **sample statistics** or simply **statistics** (see Chapter 14). Statistics are therefore estimates of population parameters.

Sampling theory

As explained in Chapter 5, quantitative and qualitative studies do not have the same aim, nor do they use the same methods. Most often, quantitative research aims at testing a hypothesis on a **representative sample**, so that the results can be generalised to the whole population. It is thus deductive and tends to simplify the complexity of reality. On the other hand, qualitative research aims at acquiring a deeper insight into a complex phenomenon that might be quite specific and unique, and which appears in different ways in the various units of the population. Qualitative research is concerned with studying people in their natural context. It is thus inductive and holistic. It does not aim at generalising the results to the population, but aspires towards some aspects of the new knowledge and understanding being transferrable to other units of the population.

For example, a quantitative research project might aim at testing the hypothesis that matriculants' results are higher in urban schools than in rural ones by collecting data in selected rural and urban schools. A qualitative research project might investigate the emotions experienced by matriculants during exams: some matriculants might describe feelings of general stress, fear, anxiety, excitement, feeling paralysed or exhilarated, and experiencing health disorders, such as sleeplessness, lack of appetite, stomach

CHAPTER 11 Sampling

pains, etc. Clearly the selection of the appropriate sampling method is determined by the type of research, as discussed in Chapter 5.

Quantitative sampling theory is the study of the relationship between a population and the samples drawn from it. Since the aim of research is to determine some characteristics of a certain population, one of the objectives of sampling is to draw inferences about the unknown population parameters from the known sample statistics. These are obtained by collecting data from the sample. The process of generalising from findings based on the sample to the population is called **statistical inference**. Sampling means abandoning *certainty* in favour of *probability*. Because a large part of the population has not been investigated, statements made about the population on the basis of what has been found to be true for the sample are of necessity probability statements. One is aware of introducing possible error by asserting that the units that had not actually been studied would produce the same results as those studied. Here probability is understood as the likelihood of an event happening, an element being found or a statement being true. An example of a probability statement is: If the average age of a sample of primary school teachers is 34 years, the average age of the whole population of teachers probably lies between 32 and 36 years. In many instances, if the sampling or selection of a sample is correctly and carefully carried out, the margin of error can be accurately calculated.

The *main advantages of sampling*, as compared to the collection of data on the whole population, are the following:

1. Gathering data on a sample is less time consuming. If a student population numbers 4 000 it would take a researcher at least 4 000 hours to conduct a one-hour interview with each student. It would take only 200 hours, or 5% of the time, to interview a sample of 200 students.

2. Gathering data on a sample is less costly since the costs of research are proportional to the number of hours spent on data collection. Moreover, a large population may be spread over a large geographical area, involving large travel expenses. Such expenses are likely to be decreased by reducing the number of respondents to be studied. Other expenses, such as the cost of reproducing data collection instruments like questionnaires, will also be reduced.

3. Sometimes, sampling may be the only practical method of data collection. This is the case in studies where the property under investigation necessitates the destruction of the object. When testing the resistance of an object to wear and tear, such as testing the lifespan of an electric light bulb, one must wait till the bulb is 'dead'. It would be inadvisable to test an entire population, for example, the annual output of a light bulb plant, as the plant would have no bulbs left to sell. This is called destructive sampling and in this case testing can only be realistically conducted on a sample.

4. Sampling is a practical way of collecting data when the population is infinite or extremely large, thus making a study of all its elements impossible.

163

The limitations and weaknesses of sampling will be discussed separately for each type of sampling, and again in the discussion of sampling errors at the end of this chapter.

Main sampling concepts

Good sampling must satisfy different criteria for quantitative and qualitative research.

1. *Quantitative research.* A sample is considered to be adequate if it enables the obtained results to be generalised to the whole population. It is also based on an estimate of how representative the sample is of the whole population, that is, how well, in terms of probability, the sample statistics conform to the unknown population parameters. This last topic will be introduced here but elaborated upon in Chapter 14. The sample is selected before starting data collection and analysis.

2. *Qualitative research.* A sample is considered to be adequate if it allows all possibilities or aspects of the researched phenomenon to be identified. In other words, when the researcher reaches the conclusion that collecting more data and increasing the sample does not bring any new information, **data saturation** has been achieved. It is based on an estimate that further expansion of the sample will not bring any further element to the research. Because of this approach, the sample is partly selected in an ongoing way during the process of data collection and analysis.

In both cases, one has to have a well-defined population and an adequate sample.

A well-defined population

As mentioned above, a population, sometimes referred to as a 'target population', is the set of elements that the research focuses upon. In the case of quantitative research, the results obtained by testing the sample should be generalised to the entire population. In the case of qualitative research, the results obtained are exhaustive to all researched aspects found in the population. It is essential to describe the target population accurately. This can be done most effectively by clearly defining the properties to be analysed. In quantitative research it is done by providing an operational definition, thus allowing measurement (see Chapter 6). Once this is done it should be possible to compile a list of all elements of the population under investigation or at least to determine whether or not an element belongs to that population. In this way the population will be well defined.

CHAPTER 11 Sampling

> **Example**
>
> In defining the student population of a university, it would not be adequate to draw up a list of students living on campus. Such a list would exclude students residing off campus and part-time students. An attendance list of students at lectures will not constitute a population either, as it excludes correspondence students and absentees. The population will only be clearly determined when the term 'student' is given an operational definition, for example, 'a person who is registered at a university for the purposes of studying', or more narrowly, 'a person who studies full-time on the premises of a university'. It is important to note that the results obtained on a sample drawn on the basis of the narrow definition of a student can neither (in quantitative research) be generalised to the broader population, nor (in qualitative research) describe all aspects of that broader population, which also includes part-time and correspondence students. This is an error often made and overlooked.

Once an operational definition is given, boundary conditions can be established which make it easy to ascertain whether or not an element belongs to that population. A sample can then be easily selected from the population.

Although social scientists are often involved in constructing samples from populations of human beings, there are many other possibilities as well. Consider the economist who is interested in economic indicators over an extended period of time. She will sample from a population of dates. A historian interested in a particular person's life story might use a sample drawn from the population of all of that person's written correspondence. A geographer might work with a sample of water catchment areas while a sociologist might look at the attendance at a sample of different churches. Whatever the unit that comprises a particular population, the same basic sampling methods apply.

The sample

Because of the very different aims and methods of quantitative and qualitative research, the discussion of samples and sampling for each is presented separately.

Quantitative sampling: Although a sample is, by definition, a subset of the population, to be useful it must have all the properties of the population so as to be representative of the whole. To follow up the example of the students, selecting a sample of only very dull or very brilliant students would be wrong, because this group of students would not represent the whole of the student body. Thus one of the major issues in sampling is to determine samples that best represent a population so as to allow for an accurate generalisation of results. Such a group is called a **representative sample**.

The first means of ensuring a representative sample is the use of a complete and correct **sampling frame**. This is the list of all units from which the sample is to be drawn. To use a telephone directory for selecting a sample would be wrong as it would include only people owning a phone. Such a sample could never be representative of an urban population in a developing country. It might at best represent high-income

165

urbanites, but usually not even that. An inadequate sampling frame that discards parts of the target population has been the cause of many poor research results. Particular care must be taken to avoid this pitfall.

It must therefore be stressed that an adequate sampling frame should not exclude any element of the population under investigation. An even stricter requirement would be that all elements of the population should have the same chance of being drawn into the sample, or at least that the probability of this happening can be specified. In consequence, sampling theory distinguishes between probability or random sampling, and non-probability sampling.

Probability or **random sampling** is when the probability of including each element of the population can be determined. It is thus possible to estimate the extent to which the findings based on the sample are likely to differ from what would have been found by studying the whole population. In other words, the researcher can estimate the accuracy of the generalisation from sample to population. A sample is randomly selected when each member of the population has a known chance of being selected for the sample.

Non-probability sampling is when the probability of including each element of the population in a sample is unknown. In this case it is not possible to determine the likelihood of the inclusion of all representative elements of the population into the sample. Some elements might even have no chance of being included. It is thus difficult to estimate how well the sample represents the population and this makes generalisation highly questionable.

Probability samples are of a much higher quality because, when properly constructed, they are representative of the population. Although it is difficult to determine the extent to which non-probability samples are representative of the population, they have some practical advantages. When the necessary population lists are not available, non-probability sampling remains the only possibility for the researcher. Also, non-probability sampling is almost always cheaper, faster and often adequate for homogenous populations. Finally, it should be noted that to some extent, the disadvantages of non-probability sampling could be reduced by enlarging the sample. Non-probability sampling is thus frequently used in the social sciences.

In the following section, the most common sampling procedures will be examined. These are:
1. Probability sampling, which includes:
   a. simple random sampling
   b. interval or systematic sampling
   c. stratified random sampling
   d. multistage probability sampling.
2. Non-probability sampling, which includes:
   a. convenience or availability sampling
   b. purposive or judgemental sampling

c. quota sampling

d. cluster sampling.

Probability sampling for quantitative research

Simple random sampling

Firstly, it is important to clarify what is meant by 'random' since, in everyday language, it is often used to mean 'accidental'. It is not random to choose the first ten students who enter a lecture theatre, or students sitting in the front row. Neither is it random to choose ten students with average test results. In all these cases some underlying criteria were used to select the samples, which might have properties peculiar to them. For example, the first students arriving for the lecture may be the most dedicated ones. The ones sitting in the front row may have poor sight or may want to attract the attention of the lecturer. Even the sample of 'average' students does not represent the heterogeneity of the student population. Random, in the scientific sense, expresses the idea of chance being the only criterion for selection. Thus, the selection of an element from a population is called random when the chance, likelihood or probability of being included in the sample can be calculated for each element of the population.

Accordingly, simple random sampling is a sampling procedure that provides equal opportunity of selection for each element in a population. There are various techniques for selecting randomly. The most common are the lottery techniques where a symbol for each unit of the population is placed in a container, mixed well and then the 'lucky numbers' drawn that constitute the sample. The symbol for each unit of the population could be the names of participants written on identical pieces of paper, or a number assigned to each participant. Of course, sample size must be established beforehand, otherwise one would not know how many 'symbols' to draw.

A more sophisticated method, particularly useful for large populations, is the use of **random number tables** or **electronic random number generators**.

Interval or systematic sampling

This type of sampling is very similar to the previous one. This technique, instead of relying on random numbers, is based on the selection of elements at equal intervals, starting with a randomly selected element on the population list.

In the example of selecting 50 units out of a population of 500, the length k of the intervals is determined by the following ratio.

$$k = \frac{500}{50} = 10$$

i.e. $$k = \frac{N}{n}$$

$$= \frac{\text{Size of population}}{\text{Size of sample}}$$

(Note that the symbol N represents the number of units of analysis in the population, while the symbol n represents the number of units in the sample.)

In this example every tenth unit should be selected for the sample. The starting element should be any number between 1 and 10, or in the general case, between 1 and k. Thus, if the starting element selected is 4, the 50 sample elements will be 4, 14, 24, 34, 44, ..., 484, 494. This sampling procedure is simpler and quicker than the use of random numbers. It would be most convenient, for instance, when undertaking research that involves sampling houses in a town. Following a pre-chosen street, and having determined the size k of the interval, one can select every k-th house for the sample.

Unfortunately this method also has constraints. Like simple random sampling it relies on the availability of a complete, unbiased population list. Moreover, this list must not have any cyclical or periodic characteristics. This can be clarified using the previous example. If, at regular intervals along the predetermined street, there are houses with peculiarities, such as corner houses containing shops, one should compare the length of this interval with k. If the two intervals coincide, the consequence may be that too many corner houses with shops, or none at all, are selected for the sample. In both cases, the sample will not accurately represent the population, but give a distorted image of it. An even more trivial mistake would be to adopt a six-day observation cycle when comparing the volume of sales in different supermarkets: Mondays in shop A, Tuesdays in shop B, Saturdays in shop F. Surely, the large difference in sales between shops A and F can be attributed more to the Saturday shopping habits of people than to intrinsic properties of the shops?

Thus, when a peculiar regularity is detected in a list and the peculiarity coincides with the size of the interval k, the list should either be rewritten to avoid this regularity or another method of sampling should be adopted.

Stratified random sampling

As mentioned previously, simple random sampling, and even systematic sampling in its purest form, are seldom used in social sciences research because they are cumbersome for large populations. But they become useful tools when used as part of other random sampling techniques, such as stratified and multistage sampling. More about multistage sampling later.

The principle of stratified random sampling is to divide a population into different groups, called strata, so that each element of the population belongs to one, and only one, stratum. Then, within each stratum random sampling is performed using either the simple or the interval sampling method. Although many samplings are performed, each is done for a relatively small population only. This increases the availability of adequate lists and facilitates selection of a simple random sample without decreasing the quality of the sample in any way.

CHAPTER 11 Sampling

Example

Assume that research is being conducted on the attitudes of a rural population towards cooperative production. The size of the rural adult population is 8 000. It is expected that attitudes will vary with the sex and ages of the participants. The composition of the population regarding these two variables (sex and age) is:

Age	Females	Males
20–40	2 000	1 500
Over 40	2 500	2 000
Total	4 500	3 500

Figure 11.1 *Population composition*

A random sample of 500 people is to be drawn, taking into account the differences in age and sex. Since the proportions of the different strata within the sample must be the same as for the population, the size of each stratum must be calculated in proportion to the total population. The ratio of sample to population is given by:

$$f = \frac{n}{N} = \frac{\text{size of the sample}}{\text{size of the population}}$$

In the present example:

$$f = \frac{500}{8\,000} = \frac{1}{16}$$

Each category of the population must be multiplied by this fraction to obtain the corresponding category of the sample. The results are as follows:

	Population		Sample	
Age	Females	Males	Females	Males
20–40	25%	18,75%	125	93,75
Over 40	31,25%	25%	156,25	125

Figure 11.2 *Stratified sample*

Rounding off 156,25 to 156 and 93,75 to 94, one checks that the total size of the sample is 281 women + 219 men, which equals 500.

The next step of the procedure is to use a simple random or systematic sampling method to draw the different samples: a sample of 94 males out of the stratum of 1 500 males between 20 and 40 years, a sample of 125 males out of the 2 000 men of 40 years and older, and so on. The last step is to combine all individuals of the four subsamples to form the desired sample of 500 persons who are to represent the total population of adult rural dwellers in the attitudinal study.

Fundamentals of Social Research Methods: An African Perspective

To clarify the advantage of stratifying a population, an extreme case is given. Suppose that, using the previous example, it is suspected that men are strongly opposed to co-operatives while women vigorously support them. Suppose also that the population is very heterogeneous and that due to urbanisation, men constitute only 10% of the population. In other words, out of the population of 8 000 people, 800 are men and 7 200 are women. When selecting a sample of, for instance, 100 out of this population, using simple random sampling, chance factors may strongly distort the proportions of men and women. For such a small sample it is possible that only four men (4%) will be selected out of the 800 men, and 96 women out of the 7 200 women. This gross under-representation of men will heavily distort overall research results and the finding might be that the total adult population is strongly in favour of cooperatives, which does not reflect reality. The distortion is caused by the sampling method, in this instance, simple random sampling. (Note that only for very large samples can one be assured that the composition of the population will be reflected in the sample when simple random sampling is used.)

Stratified sampling, on the other hand, by preserving proportions even of very small samples, will allow for any small minority to be properly represented. Of course, if the population is very homogenous with no marked differences of opinion between sexes, or if both sexes are fairly equally represented (48% vs 52%, for instance), simple random and stratified sampling will lead to similar results.

Even stratified random sampling presupposes a definite population with a known composition, and the correct choice of the criteria for stratification is crucial. However, it offers great accuracy, even for small samples, and reduces costs of sampling considerably.

Multistage probability sampling

One of the major constraints of simple random, systematic and stratified sampling is the availability of complete lists of elements or units. Often such complete lists do not exist. For example, each school may have an up-to-date list of its pupils, but no national list may be available. Similarly, a village headman might be able to help in compiling a list of all widows or orphans in his village, but such information is very seldom found in a birth-and-death register at national level. At grass roots level many small income-generating groups that are more or less structured and more or less temporary may have been formed, but few may be formally registered as cooperatives or as members of a union. Such groups, in the main, remain informal and are known only within their direct environment. For these cases another type of sampling must be used. The principle underlying multistage sampling is to start by sampling a population which is much more general than the final one. In a second stage, on the basis of the first sample, a new population is considered, one that is less general than the first one, and a new sample is subsequently determined. The procedure is continued until the population to

CHAPTER 11 Sampling

be investigated is reached and a final sample is drawn. At each stage sampling is done in a random way, using one of the three previously mentioned sampling techniques.

Example

Suppose that a researcher would like to investigate the health conditions of orphans aged below 10 years in the whole country, using a sample of 500 orphans. It is unlikely that a list of all these orphans in the country exists, and so multistage sampling must be used.

The researcher should follow the following steps:
1. Obtain a list of all the districts in the country (level one). Use simple random sampling to select five districts.
2. For each of the five districts selected get a list of administrative wards (level two). Use simple random sampling to identify five administrative wards in each district. This will produce a total list of 25 wards.
3. For each of the 25 party wards get a list of administrative branches (level three). Use simple random sampling to identify 10 branches in each ward. This will produce a total list of 250 branches.
4. At branch level it should be possible, with the help of branch authorities or representatives of the community, such as church officials, to compile a list of all the orphans under 10 years of age (level four) living in each branch's area. Use simple random sampling to select two orphans from each branch, thereby producing a final list of 500 orphans as required.

In summary, the sampling units considered in this example were districts, administrative wards, administrative branches and then orphans. The elements of each population were qualitatively different (geographical areas, administrative units and human beings) and decreasing in their generality. Preceding units contained subsequent units. The specification of each unit and its corresponding sample constituted a stage and each stage was characterised by a random sample. In this case there were four stages.

While not as accurate as simple random sampling, the advantage of multistage sampling become apparent when other sampling methods fail due to a lack of complete lists of elements for a population under investigation. Even if a complete list of populations can be compiled directly, multistage sampling can cut down expenses by reducing the cost of compiling long lists and by reducing the travel expenditure necessary when respondents are spread over a large area. In fact, if a complete list of orphans was available and a simple random sample of 500 was selected, these 500 orphans would be spread all over the country. This would mean high travel costs and a great deal of travel time. Multistage sampling, by selecting only a few geographical areas (five districts), reduces travel costs and time, and permits careful planning of the data-collection process.

171

Non-probability sampling for quantitative research

Convenience or availability sampling

This sampling method, the most rudimentary one, consists of taking all cases on hand until the sample reaches the desired size. The interviewer will choose, for instance, a convenient place where he or she is assured of finding many people: a supermarket, a bus stop or a bar. Obviously, this can introduce serious biases, as men will be over-represented in bars, and old and wealthy people will be under-represented at bus stops. Taxi drivers, waiting at a stand for customers, would welcome a chat with the interviewer but might not be representative of a population. Students are the usual 'guinea-pigs' of social scientists though still not representative of the whole population. This makes generalisation based on such samples extremely risky, although the samples so chosen are convenient for researchers in terms of time and money.

Purposive or judgemental sampling

This sampling method is based on the judgement of a researcher regarding the characteristics of a representative sample. A sample is chosen on the basis of what the researcher considers to be typical units. The strategy is to select units that are judged to be the most common in the population under investigation. For instance, a typical school pupil may be thought of as being '12 years old, male, Catholic and having parents in a clerical profession'. Only students meeting these criteria will be chosen for the sample. The great danger in this type of sampling is that it relies more heavily on the subjective considerations of the researcher than on objective criteria. Although it has some value, especially if used by an expert who knows the population under study, this technique often leads to non-representative samples.

Quota sampling

This sampling method is the non-probability equivalent of stratified sampling. The purpose here is to draw a sample that has the same proportions of characteristics as the population. However, the sampling procedure, instead of relying on random selection, relies on convenience.

> ### Example
>
> Suppose that the population under study is estimated to consist of 40% men, 25% of whom are above 40 years and 15% of whom are between 20 and 40 years, and that of the 60% female population, 30% are in each of the above age groups. If one intends to draw a sample of 200, one would have to interview people in each category as they come (that is, by using accidental sampling) until one has gathered a group of 80 men (40% of 200) of whom 50 are above 40 years and 30 between 20 and 40 years. The female subsample would have to consist
>
> *continued ...*

> of 120 women, 60 in each age category. This sample would also be drawn by interviewing any available woman in each of the desired categories, stopping the interviewing process when the desired number of women in each age category has been reached.
>
> If, for some reason, one group is incomplete, for instance if one could find only 30 women above 40 years instead of 60, the researcher would have to weigh the result of this group by multiplying it by two. In other words, the inadequacy of the sample can be corrected in the analysis by weighing the results of different strata in terms of their proportions within the population.

Although much less accurate than stratified sampling this method is often more convenient and economical. No lists need be compiled and all data can be collected at an arbitrary location.

Cluster sampling

Finally, the very useful technique of multistage quantitative sampling has an equivalent in non-probability sampling, which is called cluster sampling. The process is the same as described above except that the use of simple random sampling is replaced by a non-probabilistic selection method, such as the availability of the elements or the convenience of reaching them.

Other sampling possibilities

Independent versus related/dependent samples

As already mentioned in Chapter 10 when dealing with randomisation of groups, two or more groups or samples might be selected in such a way as to make them independent. Each unit is drawn randomly from the population and is also randomly assigned to one or other group. Groups formed in this way constitute independent samples. Alternatively, groups or samples can be related, usually when their elements have been matched by specific properties. In such cases, they are called related or dependent samples.

Example

> A researcher wishes to draw two samples of men and women from a large corporation's workforce. However, in her study she wishes to control for age and seniority within the company. Therefore, she must find pairs of men and women who have similar ages and seniority within the company. In other words, they are the same for the variables she wishes to control (age and seniority) but differ in terms of the variable that she is studying (sex). Two senior managers both aged 43, one being male and the other female, would be such a pair. Similarly two 20-year-old entry-level staff would also be a pair if one was male and the other female.

173

When researchers draw up samples in this way, every member of the sample has a partner somewhere else in the study and so the samples can no longer be thought of as independent of each other. They are related or dependent.

Sample size: How large should a sample be?

Students and new researchers involved in quantitative research often ask, 'How large does my sample have to be?' The best answer is, 'It depends.' It depends on the kind of data analysis the researcher plans, on how accurate the sample has to be for the researcher's purposes, and on population characteristics.

Generally speaking, a large sample is more representative but very costly. A small sample, on the other hand, is much less accurate but more convenient. A census, which is a survey of the whole population, will be more accurate than a survey using a restricted sample, but it will be very expensive and its results may take so long to analyse that they become outdated.

However, a large sample size alone does not guarantee a representative sample. A large sample without random sampling or with a poor sampling frame is less representative than a smaller one with random sampling and an excellent sampling frame.

The size of the sample is an important determinant of the **statistical power** of the research. Statistical power refers to the likelihood that inferential statistical tests (see Chapter 14) will be able to test the research hypotheses adequately. Smaller samples have less statistical power than larger samples. The major criterion to use when deciding on sample size is the extent to which the sample is representative of the population. This can be expressed in terms of probability. One usually needs to have a 95% chance that the sample is distributed in the same way as the population. Formulae exist for determining a sample size that satisfies such a given level of probability, but they fall beyond the scope of this book. One should, however, note that the more heterogeneous a population is, the larger the sample must be to represent the characteristics of the population correctly. The rule of thumb for choosing a sample size is that is should be at least 5% of the population, but this remains quite an inaccurate guideline, though it is certainly usable when precise formulae are not available.

A researcher's decision about the best sample size depends on three things:
1. the degree of accuracy required
2. the degree of variability or diversity in the population
3. the number of different variables to be examined simultaneously in the data analysis.

All else being equal, larger samples are necessary if one wants a high degree of accuracy, if the population has a great deal of variability or heterogeneity, or if one wants to examine many variables in the data analysis simultaneously. Smaller samples are sufficient when less accuracy is acceptable, when the population is homogeneous, or when only a few variables are examined at a time. The analysis of data on subgroups

CHAPTER 11 Sampling

also affects a researcher's decision about sample size. If the researcher wants to analyse subgroups in the population, he or she needs a larger sample.

Sampling errors and related problems

As has been repeatedly mentioned, the purpose of sampling theory is to select samples, which reproduce as closely as possible the characteristics of a population. This aim is never completely achieved due to two types of error.

The first type of sampling error is due to **chance factors**. It may happen that, in a particular sample, one element and not another has been included. This type of error is the inevitable result of sampling and can never be completely eliminated, but the sampling error can be calculated statistically.

The second type of sampling error is due to **bias in selection**, arising primarily from faulty technique. These biases are frequently avoidable. They may or may not be deliberate. For example, an interviewer may fail to take into account one criterion, such as the age of respondents, or the respondents themselves may give incorrect information about their age. Some strata of a population may be over- or under-represented in a sample. For example, a sample that contains 50% rural and 50% urban respondents would under-represent the rural population and over-represent the urban population of virtually all less industrialised countries today.

Even when a representative sample has been drawn, a very important source of bias is **non-response error**. This type of error comes about when an element of the sample does not respond to a measurement instrument or is not available for some unknown reason. As a consequence such elements are excluded from the group, which changes the constitution, and thus the representativeness, of the sample. There are many reasons for non-response. Firstly, it may not be possible to interview or test a person because of illness, language differences or other factors. Secondly, it may be that the chosen respondents cannot be found because of changes in residence or name, or because of death. Thirdly, the selected person may be absent whenever the interviewer calls, purely by chance. Lastly, the person can refuse to collaborate and not answer questions or give information.

The issue of biases related to a sample will be discussed again in Chapter 16 where all possible sources of bias in research are summarised.

Sampling for qualitative research

Coming back to the aim of qualitative research, to investigate in depth a certain phenomenon, it becomes clear that probability sampling methods are too rigid and do not allow seldom occurring elements to be sufficiently represented and studied. Therefore, since qualitative research does not concentrate on the 'average' person (representative of the population at large) but rather on the diversity of cases, non-probability sampling is used.

175

The three types of non-probability sampling introduced under quantitative sampling, convenience or accidental, purposive or judgement, and quota sampling are the most frequently used. In qualitative research these techniques do not have the disadvantages mentioned for quantitative research since generalisation to the target population is not the criterion for sample quality. In addition, one should mention the very useful **snowball sampling**, a sub-category of accidental sampling. Some sub-categories of purposive sampling, such as maximum variations sampling, extreme/deviant case sampling and critical case sampling, as well as theoretical sampling, will be described below.

Convenience or availability sampling

As described under quantitative sampling, this is a very handy sampling procedure based on the availability of the units of the target population.

Snowball sampling (also called chain or referral sampling)

A more sophisticated sampling technique, particularly useful for identifying people not listed or difficult to find, is to identify a few participants and then to rely on each participant to guide you to the next one, etc. Through this method one can increase the size of the sample but also develop a network, for instance, of specialists: one astrologist or palm reading practitioner might introduce the researcher to a colleague, facilitating, access to that person.

Let us illustrate some of these possibilities.

Example

In research on homeless people, one might have met one or two people accidentally, and after interviewing each one, requested them to identify and give contact details for one or two other homeless people. For instance, the researcher might have observed two men who often sleep under a highway bridge at night. Contact is made with them and they are willing to speak about themselves, their life and present difficulties, be it to find food or to escape the attention of the police. They also mention that other homeless people use different tactics for survival. If they are willing to disclose where to find these other people and even to accompany the researcher to meet them, new respondents are found. The same process might repeat itself if these new participants can assist in locating a further group of homeless people.

This method could also be used to locate and interview pregnant women not attending pre-natal clinics, or rural women who are emergent leaders, or vegetarians not belonging to a religion that prohibits the consumption of meat. This technique is very helpful to gain access to participants when the framing of the target population is not possible. But it could also be used in social research related to a certain innovation

CHAPTER 11 Sampling

in, for example, computer technology: after identifying a few engineers in this field (through a literature review, for instance), one would gain access to many more such specialists if every participant would phone a fellow-computer engineer and motivate him or her to participate in the research.

Qualitative approach to purposive or judgemental sampling

As the name indicates, this type of sampling rests on the assumption that the researcher knows what type of participant is needed. In quantitative research, the most 'representative' element will be looked for. In qualitative research, on the contrary, the element that is the most complex and rich in information will be the most valuable. The researcher will thus purposefully choose participants on the basis of some specific criteria that are judged to be essential. There are many ways of reaching a deeper knowledge and understanding through the choice of more sophisticated purposive sampling, some of which are described below.

Extreme or deviant case sampling

This method concentrates on getting information from the most extreme cases, the 'exceptions to the rule'. Highly unusual manifestations of the researched phenomenon, obviously not representative of the target population, may sometimes be the most revealing cases. Here the assumption is that comparing these extreme cases might lead to a better in-depth understanding of the underlying factors of a problem. Studying learning processes in children, one might sample the strongest and the weakest children in each class. But one might also be interested in studying the few children who react negatively to the introduction of an otherwise very successful learning programme. Researching the importance of some managerial skills, one might choose to study very successful and very poorly performing businesses.

Critical case sampling

In some instances, one can assume that some cases have key position. They are particularly useful and can assist in deciding on the importance or the prevalence of some explanations. For instance, a teacher will assess the level of difficulty of an exam paper by stating: 'If student A can pass this test, then all others can!' Here studying the case of A allows generalising and applying the results to the entire class. This method has the advantage of reducing the sample to the few cases most likely to give a lot of essential, relevant information.

177

Maximum variations sampling

In this case the researcher aspires to having the most heterogeneous sample. For instance, studying causes or triggers for divorce, the search for a great diversity in the sample will include a wide range of professions without taking into account their frequency in the total population. Thus uncommon professions (animal breeders and astronomers) will be given the same importance as common professions (coal miners and receptionists). In general, maximum variation samples will thus contain extreme or deviant cases, critical cases and typical cases in which nothing is unusual. The importance here is to have the widest possible range of cases. This will yield a rich variety of variation for the phenomenon under study. However, for such samples to be all-inclusive, they will also be relatively large and costly.

> **Example**
>
> The government has introduced e-toll fees on a heavily utilised highway. The population, expecting a general increase in transport costs and therefore of all commodities, reacts strongly against the principle of paying for using this road, as well as the amount to be charged per kilometer. Being faced with this very strong reaction by the community at large, a research programme is developed. In order to investigate all possible aspects of this phenomenon, maximum-variations sampling will be adopted to include extreme socio-economic classes, from the very rich highway users to workers rarely using even public transport on that road, from private car and motorcycle owners to bus and taxi drivers, heavy vehicles drivers and owners, daily users, as well as occasional users. Also distinction will be made between short-distance travellers and those who have to use the entire length of the toll road.

Quota sampling

Proportional quota sampling has been described under quantitative sampling. To this method one can add a less restrictive one, non-proportional quota sampling. The principles are the same, but here the researcher does not make a concerted effort to reach the numbers or quota corresponding to the proportions in the population. What is important is to have all categories represented in the sample. One is satisfied if the information given by the participants of a certain quota has reached **saturation**.

Combination or mixed purposeful sampling

Often a combination of various sampling methods is chosen to arrive at the most appropriate sample. This flexibility is particularly helpful when dealing with triangulation (see Chapter 13). Most important, always, is that the sampling strategy focuses on and fits the aim of the research, the method and instruments used, as well as the available resources.

CHAPTER 11 Sampling

Sampling process and sample size: when is enough, enough?

As evidenced in the examples above, an important difference between quantitative and qualitative sampling is that, in the first case, the sample and the sample size are determined before data collection, whereas, in the second, once the type of sampling has been decided upon, the units constituting the sample are identified parallel and concomitant to the data collection. Moreover, in the ideal case, the data collection will continue as long as new elements or facts are found and will stop when no new details are available (also called **sampling to redundancy**). Thus the size of the sample is not determined in advance but becomes a consequence of the exhaustion of new discovery or data **saturation**, as defined earlier. Unfortunately, in reality, time and money sometimes demand some compromise.

The importance of good sampling

The quality of research, whether quantitative or qualitative, is directly related to the sampling procedures, the adequacy of the technique chosen, as well as the professionalism of implementation and the appropriacy of the sample size. Even though the aims and procedures for different types of research can be quite different, in the end the importance of the quality of sampling will reappear when evaluating the validity and trustworthiness of the findings in Chapter 13.

Key points

1. The purpose of sampling is to provide various types of information of a qualitative or quantitative nature about a population by examining a few selected units.
2. Quantitative sampling emphasises the representivity of the sample, allowing for generalisation of the results to the target population.
3. Qualitative sampling aims at the identification and understanding of a complex phenomenon experienced differently by the various units of the population.
4. The main distinction between probability (or random) sampling and non-probability sampling is related to the type and aim of the research, with probability sampling used nearly exclusively in quantitative research and non-probability sampling being particularly well suited to the aims of qualitative research, although it may also be used for quantitative research.
5. Sampling is based on a well-defined population and must be determined by the aim of the research.
6. Errors introduced into the sampling process (such as chance factors, bias in selection, non-response error, incorrectly identified criterion, etc) play an important role in the end product.
7. The optimal size of a sample is determined, in the case of quantitative research, by the need for the sample to be representative of the whole population, in the case of qualitative research, by the need for all the possible answers or information to have been collected.

179

Checklist

Keywords:

Check whether the meaning of these concepts introduced in this chapter is clear to you.

sampling; population; population parameter; sample; unit of analysis; sample statistics; statistical inference; representative sample; sampling frame; probability sampling; non-probability sampling; all types of sampling presented in this chapter: simple random sampling; interval or systematic sampling; stratified random sampling; cluster sampling and multistage probability sampling; accidental or convenience sampling; snowball or chain/referral sampling; purposive or judgemental sampling; extreme/deviant case sampling; critical case sampling; maximum variation sampling; chance factor; bias in selection; non-response error; sampling to redundancy; data saturation.

Your research:
1. Does your sampling fit the aim of your research?
2. Is it realisable? Does it take into consideration your constraints in terms of availability of resources, participants, time and finance?
3. What type of sampling error are you envisaging?

Exercises

1. What is the rationale for using samples? Should samples be used only when it is impossible to obtain a complete list of a population?
2. Explain the difference between probability and non-probability sampling, and in particular, between:
   a. simple random sampling and accidental sampling
   b. stratified sampling and quota sampling.
3. In conducting a survey, interviewers are instructed to single out 400 respondents, 160 of them urban and 240 rural, because the population of 12 000 is split 40/60% between urban and rural areas. It is indicated that the rural population is stratified by sex in the proportion of 3 200 men to 4 000 women, while in the urban population there are 2 000 women and 2 800 men.
   a. Which sampling procedure(s) would give the best results? Explain why.
   b. Calculate the strata required for a sample of 400 people, where stratified random sampling is to be used.
4. A public nurse would like to understand the reasons for some young mothers in a rural community not taking their babies to the under-five clinics for vaccination. What methods of sampling could she choose? Describe in detail how you would collect the data on her behalf.

continued ...

CHAPTER 11 Sampling

5. How would you conduct a multistage sampling in the capital city of your country in order to obtain a sample of 100 unemployed young men aged 14–18 years old? How would you proceed using accidental sampling? Analyse the biases introduced by using this last method.

6. In order to find out about commonly bought food and household items in a town, a researcher stands at the check-out counter of the town's largest supermarket for two days (Mondays and Tuesdays) for one month. All items bought by every fourth customer are recorded. Identify the type of sampling used and discuss the adequacy or biases inherent in this method.

7. A representative sample of 1 000 people in a town must be obtained for an investigation into reading habits. Which of the following methods of obtaining the sample is most appropriate, and why? Why are the others less appropriate?
   a. Choosing 1 000 names from the telephone directory.
   b. Stopping people at random outside a mainline bus station.
   c. Asking 10 libraries to supply 100 names.
   d. Asking 1 000 university students to participate in the study.
   e. Standing outside libraries and asking 1 000 people to be involved in the study.
   f. Since none of the above would give rise to a representative sample, what sampling procedure would you develop to take into account all the different groups within the total population?

8. Comparing probability and non-probability sampling: a primary school master wants to investigate how many parents help their children with their homework. The target population is well-defined as comprising all the pupils registered at that school. He could select a sample of 50 children by putting all the names of the pupils written on pieces of paper in a tin and randomly drawing 50 tickets. But he prefers a more convenient method for him: he stands at the school gate on a Monday morning and interviews the first 50 children arriving at that time. Analyse the two methods and indicate their strengths and weaknesses. How would he proceed if he wanted to draw a cluster sampling? What would the advantages of that method be?

9. The same primary school master would like to improve the good functioning of the school based on the opinion of the parents. In order to have not the most representative, but the widest range of opinion for this qualitative research, how should the sampling be done?

10. Wanting to introduce new services into the health department of her town, a mayor needs to know the wide range of opinions on health service delivery in her constituency. How would she proceed to get a maximum variation sampling? She observes that, on a specific issue related to hospitals, a few individuals strongly disagree with the majority of the community. How might a study of these people enrich her understanding of the situation?

Additional resources

1. Babbie, E R. 2012. *The practice of social research*, 13th ed. Belmont, CA: Wadsworth.
2. Babbie, E & Rubin, A. 2010. *Research methods in social work*, 7th ed. Belmont, CA: Brooks/Cole.

CHAPTER 12

Data collection: Basic concepts and techniques

A research project stands or falls on the quality of the data on which it is based. An excellent research design and a very representative sample are not sufficient to ensure good results if the analysis relies on incorrect data. The importance of constructing an appropriate and accurate instrument for measuring and collecting data cannot be stressed too much. Before dealing with different techniques of data collection, some basic concepts about data must be discussed: in particular, different scales of measurement. These depend on the type of research and the type of data being collected. A further purpose of this chapter is to demonstrate the construction of tools necessary to collect data and the way in which the information should be recorded. The reader will not only find guidance about choosing the most appropriate method of data collection, but also some practical guidelines on how to proceed with that collection, with particular regard to the preparation of useful questionnaires and interview schedules.

> **CHAPTER OBJECTIVES**
>
> Learners who have completed this chapter will be able to:
> - Understand the relationship between the type of research and the method of data collection.
> - Identify and use the various scales of measurement in an appropriate way.
> - Collect data through simple and participant observation.
> - Develop structured and unstructured interview and questionnaire schedules.
> - Develop internet-based surveys.
> - Conduct focus groups.
> - Contrast various research methods and select the most appropriate data collection techniques.
> - Check data sets for completeness, accuracy and uniformity.

Facts, data and measurement

Facts are empirically verifiable observations. Data consists of measurements collected as a result of scientific observations. Here the word measurement is used in its general sense and need not necessarily be expressed numerically. For example, one can measure the intensity of an attitude or feeling. A person's views on an educational reform might be positive, neutral or negative. The fact that a person takes a definite position towards an issue becomes data once it is expressed as a measurement. Experiences or emotions described by a participant become data, once recorded scientifically.

Data can be classified according to the way in which it is collected or in terms of its intrinsic properties. When researchers collect their own data for the purpose of a particular study, that data is called **primary** data.

Data collected in this way is most appropriate to the aims of research, since the data gathering is directed towards answering the specific questions raised by the researcher. Very often, however, researchers must use data collected by other investigators either in connection with other research problems, or as part of the usual gathering of social data for a population census. Such data is known as **secondary** data. The suitability of such data for a particular research problem may not be very good, since the purpose of its collection might have been slightly different to that of the new research. The data might have been based on different operational definitions and little may be known about other possible biases in the data collection, such as sampling biases. Thus, when research is based on the analysis of secondary data, great care must be taken in its interpretation. This will be detailed later in this chapter when analysing the record method.

Data consists of facts expressed in the language of measurement. The type of measurement used is closely related to the type of facts. The size of a table can be expressed in numbers (of centimetres), giving **quantitative** data. The colour of that table can be described by its quality of being red-brown, dark-brown or white, which yields **qualitative** data. Some properties of objects, persons or events cannot be quantified. This may be due to their nature, or the present non-availability of adequate measuring instruments. In some cases, quantitative measurements would be meaningless to the research, for example, describing the colour of a table by its wavelength. Whether data is quantitative or qualitative is very important since it determines how that data can be utilised.

There is a tendency to consider numerical (quantitative) data more reliable and easier to utilise, in particular for statistical techniques, than qualitative data. However, science is inconceivable without non-numerical data to assist in interpreting numerical data or to describe new aspects of a certain phenomenon. Disregarding qualitative information leads to an incomplete description of social reality. Moreover, in specific areas of social reality, purely qualitative research is often the most adequate method of investigation, and involves sophisticated techniques introduced later in this chapter.

Relationship between types of research and methods of data collection

In Chapter 5, different types of research were discussed. Some methods of data collection were mentioned, among them: observation, use of questionnaires or interviews, and the use of more sophisticated instruments. It was noted that the same method of collecting data could be used for different types of research. Observation is at the core of case studies, but also of field experiments. Questionnaires can be used to explore or describe a situation, but also to assess a correlation between two variables. In other words, the same method of data gathering can be adapted to different types of research, provided

CHAPTER 12 Data collection: Basic concepts and techniques

that the research design and the way the collected data are going to be analysed are directly related to the chosen type of research.

Scales of measurement

Quantitative measurements can be compared in terms of magnitude (for example, comparing the size of two buildings, measured in metres). The types of scales used to measure things express a broader aspect of measurement: the sets of rules utilised for the quantifying (assigning numerical scores), or the classifying (assigning a quality) of a particular variable. The presence or absence of three properties determines the type of scale.

1. The existence of *magnitude*, which allows the comparison of different amounts or intensities so as to assess whether two values or levels of a variable are the same, or if one is greater or less than the other.
2. The existence of *equal intervals*, which allows magnitude to be expressed by a certain number of units on a scale, all units on the scale being equal by definition.
3. The existence of an *absolute zero*, which is a value indicating that the measurement of a variable is meaningless in circumstances in which the variable is non-existent.

On the basis of these three properties, four different measurement scales exist: nominal, ordinal, interval and ratio.

Nominal scales are the most rudimentary. They name rather than measure by simply classifying information into categories or groups. These categories cannot be compared to one another, as they are qualitatively different. Thus, nominal scales do not satisfy any of the three properties outlined above. When classifying the variable 'sex' into the two categories of 'male' and 'female', one uses a nominal scale. The same is true when measuring the marital status (single, married, divorced, widowed) or the tribe, region or country of origin of the respondents. Even feelings can be classified using nominal scales: a person may be happy, sad, angry, etc. Nominal scales are the ones most commonly used in qualitative research, for example, when asking participants to describe an experience, or when recording their opinions.

Ordinal scales are more complex and informative than nominal scales. They allow comparison and establish rank-order between different values of a variable. It is thus possible to state that one value is greater or less than another. The feelings of the respondents are not just classified into happy or unhappy, but into very happy, happy, indifferent, unhappy and very unhappy, thus enabling the comparison of degrees of happiness between different people. Of course, this type of measurement still does not allow one to assess if person A is twice as happy as person B because, even though a relative magnitude can be given to the feelings of persons A and B, there exists no unit with which to measure them. Thus, only one property of scales is present, that of magnitude. Other examples of variables measured on the ordinal scale are the grade that a student gets on an essay, or the tax bracket into which an employee falls.

Many types of ordinal scales have been developed and are utilised frequently in all sorts of investigations and research projects. The **Likert scale**, for instance, offers three to five alternatives to assess the degree of agreement with a certain statement and assigns a certain point value to each possible answer. Thus, when asked for their response to the statement: 'In developing countries, staple food should be subsidised', respondents might choose between 'totally agree' (5 pts), 'no opinion' (3 pts), or 'totally disagree' (1 pt).

When many dimensions or criteria are combined and summarised in a single measurement, the result is called an **index**. Commonly used in everyday life, for instance, is the Consumer Price Index (CPI). Here, the cost of living is summarised on the basis of the price of a list of essential commodities (including food, housing, transport, education and medical costs, etc) in a certain place at a certain time. This, then, allows a comparison across countries or years, such as 'the CPI in South Africa is higher than the one of Zambia', or 'the CPI in Botswana has increased by 5% in the past six years'. The same can be done with attitudes, etc to create an Index of Tolerance or one of Xenophobia.

The same principle is applied often in psychology, and leads to the concept of **typology concept**. For instance, categorising a person as an introvert or an extravert is based on a personality type concept (based on a theory, such as the Jungian one). Here, a person is assessed on the basis of many personality criteria, which, combined, determine a certain profile or personality type. The same can be done in totally different domains, such as a linguistic typology.

Interval scales are an improvement over both nominal and ordinal scales in the sense that a comparison between different values of a variable is made more accurate by the introduction of equal intervals or units of measurement. For example, after the concept of 'employment' has been operationalised, a person is classified as employed or unemployed on a nominal scale, employed full-time, employed part-time or unemployed on an ordinal scale, or employed for a certain number of hours per week on a scale possessing equal intervals (one hour). In the latter case, a person employed for 40 hours a week is employed for twice as long as a person working only 20 hours a week. Here the unit underlying the scale is the hour. Typical examples of interval scales are all the scales based on the set of real numbers. For example, the money owned by somebody might be US $3000 (or rand, kwacha, shillings), while another person might be US$ 1500 in debt, which is expressed by a negative number (US$-1500). Note that this scale has magnitude as well as equal units of measurement; values of 0 as well as negative amounts are all meaningful. In other words, this scale has no absolute zero.

Ratio scales possess the three properties of magnitude, equal intervals and an absolute zero. A person can be 22 years old but nobody is minus five years old. Before birth, which, in this case, is the absolute zero, age does not exist and therefore cannot be measured. The unit, or equal interval, is the year and so a comparison can be made

CHAPTER 12 Data collection: Basic concepts and techniques

between a 40-year-old father and his 20-year-old daughter. The father is twice as old as the daughter. As a further illustration, consider the performance of students, as measured during their period of schooling. Their performance writing an essay is measured with an ordinal scale by letters like A = excellent to E = failure. But suppose that the same students are asked to write a multiple-choice test. In this case, a point is attributed to each correct answer and the performance of a student is expressed by the number of points achieved (with 1% as the unit). In this case a number below zero is meaningless as zero denotes total failure. The scale used is thus a ratio scale.

Note that when using a nominal or ordinal scale the researcher is classifying respondents by placing them into different categories. Interval or ratio scales, on the other hand, demand that a score is recorded for each subject. This difference is crucial when the researcher begins to analyse quantitative data using statistical methods. (See Chapter 14.)

Both interval and ratio scales have the danger of ceiling and floor effects. **Ceiling effects** occur when a scale does not permit sufficiently high scores, resulting in all responses clustering at the top of the scale. For example, an examination that is too easy will result in all students getting high scores and the examiner will not be able to differentiate the excellent students from the average ones. Similarly, **floor effects** occur when a scale does not permit sufficiently low scores, as illustrated by an examination that is much too difficult, and where all students fail.

It is important to note that many variables can be measured using more than one type of scale. For example, while it is possible to categorise each family in a village as living above or below a set 'poverty line' (thus comparing them on an ordinal scale), it is also possible to record the family's feelings about their economic situation (using a nominal scale), as well as to measure the exact income of each family (thereby using a ratio scale). In fact, in the latter case, if the researcher allows for the fact that families might be in debt, the scale would be an interval one. The choice of scale depends upon the nature of the research question as well as what is possible in a particular research situation.

Methods of data collection

Social scientists can choose whether they wish to use unobtrusive methods, where the participants in the research are not aware of being studied, or reactive methods, in which participants react to stimuli such as questions presented by the researcher. The most frequently used method of gathering information is by asking respondents to express their views directly. Although a variety of methods are presented, the emphasis in this chapter is placed on interviews, questionnaires and focus groups.

Observation

Although a seemingly straightforward technique, observation must be pursued in a systematic way, following scientific rules, if usable and quantifiable data are to be obtained.

Simple observation, also called **non-participant observation**, is the recording of events as observed by an outsider. For example, an observer placed at a road junction can observe traffic and record the number of cars passing, or the number of pedestrians crossing, the road, the speed of the cars, the number and causes of accidents, etc. A researcher can observe the social behaviour of people interacting in bars, shops, pleasure resorts or at political rallies, by recording the number of times people who do not know each other exchange words, the topic and length of their conversations, the way in which the interactions start and end, and so on. The weakness of this method is that people who feel that they are being observed may change their behaviour, become uneasy or stop their activities altogether. Thus, although simple (or non-participant) observation is based on the assumption that the observer merely records facts without interaction with the observed, in reality the observation itself introduces biases as people become aware of being observed.

To avoid this indirect interference with the observed person, a more complex form of observation, called **participant observation**, may be used. In this case, the observers join the community or group under investigation as one of its members, sharing in all activities. Becoming an insider allows a deeper insight into the research problem, since the researcher enjoys the confidence of participants and shares their experiences without disturbing their behaviour. This method has been found particularly useful for anthropological research and studies of minority groups, such as prisoners or homeless people. The down side of this method is that researchers may lose objectivity, and there are also ethical concerns if the participants are not informed of the researchers' role. Moreover, by being directly involved with a group and its daily concerns for an extended period of time, the researcher may become emotionally engaged and thereby lose his detachment from both the people and the events. Also, because notes may have to be taken down secretly or from memory, inaccurate information may be recorded.

Participant observation is a very demanding way of gathering data and may involve extended periods of residence among respondents. For this reason, a **modified participant observation** method, which restricts the researcher to participation only in major events, such as village meetings or ceremonies, is often preferred.

The third type of observation is done under **laboratory** conditions. It is a hidden observation of the behaviour of one or more persons in a room with one-way windows or false mirrors. In this case, although the negative aspects of laboratory experiments are present (see below), the distorting factors associated with simple or participant observation are removed.

CHAPTER 12 Data collection: Basic concepts and techniques

In all three cases one should keep in mind the following rules:

1. Observations serve clearly formulated research purposes. Thus, they must be planned systematically, with clear guidelines of what to observe and how that observation is to be done.
2. Observations should be recorded in a systematic, objective and standardised way.
3. Observations should be subject to control in order to maintain a high level of objectivity. Thus, many observers must be able to record the same phenomena or events, in the same way, with the same results.

Observation as a method of data collection has some major limitations that must be noted. Not only is it costly and time-consuming but, moreover, it cannot be applied to many aspects of social life. One cannot directly observe attitudes or beliefs, for example. Neither can one easily observe phenomena related to the private spheres of life (such as aspects of family life) or phenomena spread over a long period of time (such as the career of a politician). Biases due to the subjectivity of the observer can be partly alleviated by the introduction of mechanical devices, such as tape or video recorders, as long as the participants are not aware of their presence. But other limitations remain and these make it necessary to introduce alternative techniques.

The record method or unobtrusive measures

As will be shown later, collection of data by experiment, interviews and questionnaires is essentially based on an interaction between the researcher and the respondent, the latter reacting to a situation created by the former. Similar to observation, the record method, on the other hand, is an unobtrusive/non-reactive research method. The information about the respondent is gathered without direct interaction by use of public documents. The researcher uses archival records, published statistics like demographic records of births and deaths, judicial records like court decisions or election results, crime statistics and educational data. She will also refer to institutional publications, data published by the private sector, as well as personal documents, biographies, historical documents, medical and other scientific records.

In some cases, respondents are not aware that they are the subjects of a study and this eliminates some biases. However, in recent times the use of information has become much more controlled and people have to sign for their data to be included in research studies. Unobtrusive measures are endangered by many other sources of error. The records used may contain institutional biases. Reports are usually written in such a way as to safeguard the interests of the parent institution and to fulfill some short- or long-term goals. They will therefore present facts to support the efficiency of the institution, or the need for more funds, etc and the facts presented may therefore be distorted. One very common bias is introduced by mentioning only some facts and by hiding others. For instance, political considerations may result in inflating or deflating the sizes of different ethnic groups within a country.

Another source of error is related to erratic record collection and preservation. Collection of some data may be stopped for political or financial reasons, or records may be destroyed (by accident, such as fire, or willingly by an overthrown regime seeking to cover up facts), and in some areas no research may ever have been conducted. A third limitation of the record method arises from the secrecy of certain data. Many sources of information exist that are not available to social scientists and some research topics may be prohibited. These may include multinational transactions, police records, military issues and court cases, among others. More generally, when an important decision is taken, the end result is communicated to the public but often not the process leading to it, the type of discussions or arguments used, or the internal conflicts expressed at the time. These constitute important pieces of information that are inaccessible to researchers.

Lastly, bias may arise from a lack of information on the actual way in which the recorded data was collected, the sample characteristics, the operational definitions, the instruments used and any bias introduced by the person who collected the data. A population census is a good example in which these types of problems surface frequently.

The record method can be used as the only source of data in a given research, but it has been found more useful to combine it with other complementary methods. There is a major difference between data compiled by survey method, using questionnaires for instance, and data presented in records. The latter only give the properties of a group of individuals, an aggregate of much separate information, whereas the former permits the retrieval of data concerning a particular individual.

For example, data related to school performance as presented in ministry records would only indicate the average performance of each school in the country. Data compiled in a survey should allow for the compilation of schools' average-performance rates, while at the same time indicating the specific performance of individual learners.

It is important that researchers evaluate the instruments and procedures that were used to gather information. How such evaluation is to be done is the subject of the next chapter.

The experimental method

The experimental method was discussed in Chapters 5 and 10. Data collection through experimental techniques does not rely on what the participant says, but on how he or she behaves. This removes an important source of bias (see below the advantages and disadvantages of self-report) but the method still has intrinsic weaknesses when dealing with the complexity of social issues.

CHAPTER 12 Data collection: Basic concepts and techniques

In social research, the demands of social reality necessitate the introduction of quasi-experimental designs. Pure experimental research, done in a laboratory, can only be used in a few particular situations, mainly in psychology, and even more rarely in developing countries where the more flexible field experiment is widely applied. The presentation of the experimental method is therefore brief. A laboratory experiment is the most controlled method of data collection. It simulates certain characteristics of a natural environment, but only as far as these do not affect the control and the manipulation of the independent and other variables. The main distinction between this method and all the others is that only a laboratory experiment allows the manipulation of one variable at a time in order to study its effects on other variables.

This characteristic is realised through a high level of standardisation that guarantees that the experimental conditions are repeated exactly in all details and each time, which ensures a high degree of reliability (see Chapter 13). All conditions are standardised.

1. The presentation of the experiment and the testing situation, the environment within the laboratory, must be the same for all participants in a study (as opposed to interviews which can be conducted in different environments with conditions more or less conducive to concentration).
2. The instructions must be identical and given to the participants by an experimenter who remains neutral, avoiding any personal interference with the respondents.
3. The instruments must be identical, which is why they are most often produced under copyright to ensure standardisation and avoid even slight modifications.
4. The recording and evaluation of the results must be done systematically and usually quantitative measurements are recorded.

Even when great care is taken to achieve the highest scientific standards, laboratory experiments are often inadequate for social research. The laboratory environment remains very artificial, notwithstanding efforts to simulate real-life situations. People react to the artificial set-up, which modifies their behaviour considerably. Thus, the results obtained cannot be easily generalised to real-life situations. Moreover, participants often seek to discover how they should behave so as to do well in the experiment and to conform to what they believe the experimenter expects of them.

A remedy for these weaknesses is to conduct the experiment in a natural environment, maintaining as much control of the different variables as possible. Thus, a decrease in scientific rigour is compensated for by a more natural behaviour of participants who are not aware of being subjected to an experiment. In fact, many social phenomena cannot be analysed other than by **field experiment**. The following example contrasts laboratory and field experiments.

> ### Example
>
> Cooperation versus competition can be studied in a laboratory, as was done by Mintz (1957). This researcher provoked a certain behaviour in participants by confronting them with the following problem: A jar was connected to a source of water and as the level of the water in the jar rose, participants had to extract cones attached to a string before the rising water reached those cones. The difficulty lay in the narrowness of the neck of the jar, which did not allow more than one cone to be pulled out at a time. Thus, to avoid jamming the cones in the bottleneck and losing time, the participants had to cooperate and develop a common strategy.
>
> The feeling of emergency and threat which would promote cooperative behaviour or, on the contrary, a very competitive one to save one's own cone, is difficult to awaken in this quite artificial set-up, even when financial incentives or other motivators are introduced. In a field experiment, however, many 'natural' situations can be devised, using sports events, school life or incidents in the street. One experiment in which a fire was simulated in a cinema was conducted in order to observe how spectators would react at exits in their attempt to escape. It was perceived that disorganised behaviour, like pushing and queue jumping was detrimental since, in fact, it slowed down the escape process. In this particular case, the concern of participants was genuine so no artificial incentives were required. The people involved were completely unaware of being the subjects of an experiment and thus the results can lead to valid generalisations.

However, the duplication of this field experiment may cause problems since the sample was a non-probability one (refer to Chapter 11 on Sampling) and very little was known about the participants. In particular, some of them might have realised much later than others the danger of the situation, depending on where they were located, their concentration on what was going on, and other factors. In the laboratory set-up, on the other hand, all conditions are fixed and so all the participants tend to perceive the situation in the same way.

Self-report methods

By definition self-reports involve the research participant reporting on his or her own experience. The assumption is that the report is honest and accurate and reflects the true state of affairs.

The methods considered here are various types of interviews and questionnaires, as well as focus groups.

The advantages and disadvantages of self-reports are discussed below.

CHAPTER 12 Data collection: Basic concepts and techniques

Advantages of self-reports

- Easy to administer.
- Can be administered in group format.
- Do not always require special expertise on the part of the administrator.
- Simple to use and require little training of the subject.
- Can assess private thoughts, feelings and behaviour in private settings. For instance, in a study to assess the extent of sexual activity among adolescents, participants might lie in an interview, but be more open in filling in anonymous questionnaires.
- Participants can be asked to report on feelings or thoughts or behaviour in a hypothetical way, such as how they would respond in certain situations that might be unethical to arrange experimentally, eg, how they might respond to a sexual advance by a classmate.
- Self-reports give a sense of how things bother the person in terms of their experience. One can assess anxiety, for example, by measuring physical variables physiologically, but a self-report gives a better sense of how anxiety actually bothers a person and to what extent it is a source of distress.

Disadvantages of self-reports

- Participants can lie to make themselves look good.
- Participants can respond in a way that they think the researcher might want them to respond.
- Participants can respond in a way that makes them appear more distressed than they actually are so that they can receive services that might not otherwise be accessible to them.
- Participants may respond in a socially desirable way, that is, in a way that they feel is more acceptable to other people.

Interviews and questionnaires

There are many possible ways of gathering information directly from participants if such information cannot be obtained from observation. These methods all have advantages and disadvantages.

The first of these methods is the **interview**. An interview involves *direct* personal contact with the participant who is asked to answer questions relating to the research problem. One way of getting people to express their views is the **non-scheduled interview**, which consists of asking respondents to comment on broadly defined issues. Those interviewed are free to expand on the topic as they see fit, to focus on particular aspects, to relate their own experiences, and so on. The interviewer will intervene to ask for clarification or further explanation, but not to give directives or to confront the interviewee with probing questions. Usually no time limit is fixed for completing an interview of this kind.

193

The non-scheduled interview is very useful in exploratory research where the research questions cannot be narrowly defined. It is also an excellent technique when no comparison is sought between the responses of different participants, but when each participant is considered as a specific case, such as in a case study. The interviewer is present mainly to record the information. However, it is also essential to direct the flow of ideas and, by intervening and asking questions, one can influence an interview in many ways. The quality of personal contact can induce a respondent to speak with more or less confidence. The interviewer's presence may enhance comprehensiveness and objectivity in the recording of information, but it can also inhibit interviewed people from expressing their true opinions or feelings.

Frequently there is a need for more specific and detailed information that can facilitate comparison of the reactions of different participants. In this case, the interviewer has a much more precise goal and the types of questions to be answered by all interviewees are fixed. A **non-scheduled structured interview** is conducted. It is structured in the sense that a list of issues for investigation is drawn up prior to the interview. The list should contain some precise questions and their alternatives or sub-questions, depending on the answers to the main questions. But it is a non-scheduled interview in the sense that the interviewer is free to formulate other questions as judged appropriate for a given situation. Respondents are not confronted with already stated definitions or possible answers, but are free to choose their own definitions, to describe a situation, or to express their particular views and answers to problems. Here again, the influence of the interviewer can be considerable. It is therefore important that one refrains from influencing the respondent by the way one asks questions. At the same time one should be alert, and where information appears to be missing, ask for it to be supplied. Remember that improper recording of answers can result in incomplete and biased information. This type of interview presupposes some prior information, an understanding of the problem under investigation and a need for more specific information. A non-scheduled structured interview is very useful in qualitative research as well as for a **pilot study** (Chapter 8). These interviews assist in the formulation of accurate and precise questions followed by a representative or even exhaustive, set of possible answers as used in multiple-choice questions.

The most structured way of getting information directly from respondents is by means of a scheduled structured interview. This method is based on an established set of questions with fixed wording and sequence of presentation, as well as more or less precise indications of how to answer each question. This questionnaire must be presented to each respondent in exactly the same way to minimise the role and influence of the interviewer and to enable a more objective comparison of the results. In order to be useful and reliable, the questionnaire must satisfy a range of criteria. Bear in mind that questionnaires can be used without direct personal contact with respondents. These are **self-administered questionnaires**, and are completed by respondents themselves, without the assistance of an interviewer. This can be done either by distributing the questionnaire and collecting it once it has been filled out, or by mailing it and asking

CHAPTER 12 Data collection: Basic concepts and techniques

respondents to send it back. It is then called a **mail questionnaire**, which is definitely a *non-personal* method of gathering data. Nowadays, the internet is increasingly being used for surveys and information is often collected by emailing questionnaires.

Lastly, questionnaires can be completed not individually, but by a group. In such 'focus groups', the questions at stake are discussed and different responses are given.

In summary, the following techniques are available:
1. non-scheduled, unstructured interviews
2. non-scheduled, structured interviews
3. scheduled, structured interviews
4. self-administered and mailed questionnaires (posted or emailed)
5. focus groups.

Example

Suppose that a survey is to be conducted on the diet of an urban population. *A non-scheduled, non-structured interview* might consist of giving some general guidelines to the interviewer, such as: 'investigate the eating habits of the participants and their families, how such habits vary with season and age of the family members, and how stable these habits are'. A *non-scheduled, structured interview* will indicate more information to be gathered by the interviewer, for instance: 'investigate the diet of the participants and their families with reference to:
1. the consumption of meat, milk and other sources of protein
2. the consumption of vegetables and fruit
3. the consumption of starchy food.'

Determine the regularity of these three broad food categories, taking into consideration the seasons and the age of consumers. Investigate the adaptation of the diet to the needs of children.

A *scheduled, structured interview* could be conducted by using a questionnaire containing some of the following questions (where the appropriate answer must be ticked).

1. Do you eat meat?	2. Do you eat fish?	3. Do you drink milk?
℔ Never	℔ Never	℔ Never
℔ Less than once a week	℔ Less than once a week	℔ In tea or coffee only
℔ Once a week	℔ Once a week	℔ In porridge only
℔ Twice a week	℔ Twice a week	℔ Just plain milk
℔ Once every second day	℔ Once every second day	℔ Other (explain) ....
℔ Once a day	℔ Once a day	....

continued ...

195

> A *self-administered questionnaire* may not be suitable in this case, as many low-income, urban respondents do not have the necessary reading and writing skills. If their literacy level is high, respondents could be sent the kind of questionnaire illustrated above, accompanied by a covering letter with instructions.
>
> A *focus group* of 10 housewives could also be formed to investigate the eating habits of the villagers.

Comparison of the different methods

The aim of the five methods illustrated above is to convert information given directly by a person into data, as opposed to gathering information by the observation of that person. The type of information gathered directly is mainly:

- what people know: knowledge, factual information
- what people like or dislike: values, preferences, interests, tastes
- what people think: attitudes, beliefs
- what people have experienced or are experiencing.

Since this information is gathered by questioning people rather than by observing their behaviour, some basic conditions must be met to assure objectivity.

Firstly, the respondents must cooperate. They must be willing and motivated to share their knowledge.

Secondly, respondents must express what they perceive as their reality rather than what they wish reality to be, what they think it ought to be, or what they believe is the best answer to satisfy the researcher.

Example

A member of a small village cooperative is asked to comment on the cooperative's work atmosphere and team relationships. This villager is expected to assess whether the contacts among members are cordial, friendly, neutral, ambivalent, or even tense and hostile. To deny the existence of tension because 'we are all Christians', or to exaggerate poor relationships in order to make the story more interesting will negatively affect the level of objectivity of the study.

Thirdly, respondents must be aware of what they feel and think and be able to express it in order to communicate the information. This may be a problem with young children who are unable to analyse their feelings or accurately describe their experiences. In this case, observation of their behaviour will yield more objective information than direct questioning. Inability to analyse feelings or to describe problems can also occur in adults, especially when they are asked questions foreign to their way of thinking.

CHAPTER 12 Data collection: Basic concepts and techniques

In the light of the aforementioned difficulties, researchers should always keep the following in mind when using interviews:

1. To what extent are the respondents prepared to cooperate and what factors might influence cooperation? These factors might include lack of time, fatigue, other priorities, social norms and values, culturally diverse customs and personal beliefs. In many African cultures issues of sex and sexuality are not discussed publicly or with people of the opposite sex.

2. To what extent will a question influence the respondents to show themselves in a good light, to answer so as to please the researcher, or to distort reality in other ways? For example, a woman with an abusive husband may wish to present herself and her family in a positive light, and thus be unwilling to discuss domestic violence honestly.

3. To what extent do the questions ask for information that the respondents do not have, do not understand properly or are not sure of? In other words, to what extent do the questions force respondents to guess the answers? For example, asking a woman how much her husband earns will produce difficulties if she does not know how much he actually earns.

Advantages and disadvantages of unstructured or semi-structured interviews

As pointed out earlier, unstructured and semi-structured interviews are very helpful in exploratory research, as well as when considering a pilot survey prior to the formulation of a final questionnaire. These methods help to clarify concepts and problems, and they allow for the establishment of a list of possible answers or solutions which, in turn, facilitates the construction of more highly structured interviews. In particular, they facilitate the elimination of superfluous questions and the reformulation of ambiguous ones. They allow also for the discovery of new aspects of the problem by exploring in detail the explanations supplied by respondents.

Example

Why are women more conservative in their farming practices than men, when at least in principle, both groups have equal access to the advice of agricultural extension workers and to training courses? How do social and family constraints act on women to discourage them from attending courses? Unstructured interviews can encourage these women to describe their own experiences. The resulting detailed and extensive list of reasons could lead to a classification of all the factors at stake. Among these may be such reasons as non-availability of child care, husbands' apprehension about their wives sleeping outside the village, negative attitudes of male agricultural trainers towards women, and so on.

The wealth and quality of the gathered data are strongly dependent on the skill of the interviewer and the confidence she inspires in respondents. The types of question asked, and encouraging comments made at the correct moment, are also very important.

197

The weakness of unstructured interviews lies partly in the fact that if the interviewers are not competent, they may introduce many biases. In particular, recording the comments of participants is a delicate matter because of the great variety of answers and their complexity. Moreover, interviews are time-consuming and thus expensive. One way of reducing the costs associated with this technique is to conduct interviews over the telephone. However, such an approach excludes a considerable part of the general population, especially in African countries with poorly developed communications infrastructures.

Advantages and disadvantages of structured interviews

Structured interviews have a different aim to unstructured ones. Based on categories of answers already known, their aim is mainly to determine the frequency of various answers and to find relationships between answers to different questions. This is achieved by comparing the responses of large numbers of participants. The competence and influence of the interviewer are much less important and the recording of answers is usually quite straightforward. Moreover, compared to self-administered questionnaires, questionnaires filled out by an interviewer have definite advantages.

Firstly, they can be administered to respondents who cannot read or write. This is particularly useful for large sections of the population in less industrialised countries, as well as for poor sectors of the population and young children.

Secondly, they help overcome misunderstandings and misinterpretations of words or questions. As a result, the answers given are clearer. This is possible because in case of doubt the interviewer can ensure that respondents correctly understand the questions. Interviewers can also ask respondents for explanations concerning some of the answers.

Thirdly, interviewers can ensure that all items on the questionnaire have been considered and that respondents did not omit difficult questions. The interviewer can reassure respondents and encourage them to persevere.

However, structured interviews have quite important disadvantages. To begin with, personal interviews are costly in terms of time and money. Interviewers have to spend a certain number of hours interviewing each participant separately and they may also have to travel extensively to reach respondents. These constraints normally result in a small sample for study.

The employment of many interviewers in data collection enables researchers to deal with large samples more quickly than if only one interviewer collects all the data. But, unless interviewers have been carefully trained, there is a danger that they will subtly affect respondents' answers. This will lead to serious disparities in the results and reduce their comparability. Finally, the presence of an interviewer can be perceived as a handicap as far as anonymity and respect for the private life of the interviewees are concerned. The respondents may be embarrassed by questions which touch on confidential and private issues in front of an interviewer, whereas they would answer more freely and honestly if left alone to fill in a questionnaire. Moreover, such factors

CHAPTER 12 Data collection: Basic concepts and techniques

as the social status, sex and age of an interviewer can affect the respondents' answers. For instance, female interviewers may collect more and better results from female respondents than male interviewers on topics involving sexual practices, birth control or wife beating.

Advantages and disadvantages of mailed (posted or emailed) questionnaires

The most important advantage to using posted questionnaires is that a large coverage of the population can be realised with little time or cost. It is relatively easy to select 2 000 or even 5 000 people in different areas of a country and send them questionnaires by mail.

Also, since respondents are asked to mail back the filled-out questionnaires without indicating their name, anonymity is assured and this will make it easier for them to answer honestly. At the same time, bias due to the personal characteristics of interviewers is avoided, as no interviewers are used. Some types of questions, which might require reflection or consultation before answering, may also be more appropriately dealt with when the respondent has more time in which to answer and is not under pressure from an interviewer waiting for a response.

Although these advantages seem to be considerable, self-administered questionnaires in general, and mail questionnaires in particular, have many disadvantages, especially when used in developing countries. The main prerequisites for the use of mail questionnaires are a sufficient level of literacy and familiarity with the language used. These are not usually satisfied by a large proportion of the population of less industrialised countries. In countries where a number of different languages are spoken, respondents may be obliged to participate using a language other than their home language. A related issue is that, when sending out questionnaires, it is usually not possible to assess in advance whether or not the respondent has this minimum level of literacy. For this reason, and because of social and cultural constraints, people other than the chosen participant may fill out the questionnaires. In particular, many heads of household consider it their prerogative to answer for their wives, daughters or other dependants. Similarly, managers may ask their secretary or other subordinates to fill in the questionnaire for them.

Moreover, the response rate for mailed questionnaires tends to be very low. Very often out of the total number of questionnaires sent out, only 20 to 40% are returned. Many factors contribute to this poor return. The respondent may never have received the questionnaire due to poor mail service in rural areas, or, in the case of women, they may have married and changed their name and residence, or the questionnaire may have been confiscated by their husband. It could also be that the participant lacks interest and has misplaced the questionnaire or cannot be bothered to fill it in or is too busy to fill it in. To these unreturned questionnaires must be added the high number of incorrectly or incompletely filled-out ones that will have to be discarded. It is very common for respondents of self-administered questionnaires to skip over difficult or embarrassing questions, thereby spoiling the whole questionnaire.

This low response rate has important negative consequences for the quality of the research. The representativeness of the sample may be undermined since non-respondents are usually quite different from respondents. They may have particular features such as being poorly educated, old, female, with no stable residence, or be suspicious of research. Their absence from the sample will constitute an important bias. It is possible to increase the response rate by using a covering letter convincing respondents of the relevance of research, by adding a self-addressed, stamped envelope to the questionnaire, and by keeping the questionnaire short and well formulated. Nevertheless, low response rate remains a source of bias in the mail-questionnaire method.

Because of some of the problems mentioned above, questionnaires should have simple and straightforward questions. The type of answer expected and how the answer should be recorded must also be unambiguous. The need to avoid misunderstood questions in investigating complex research issues prevents researchers from using this technique for data collection in many cases.

In addition to all the reasons mentioned above, emailed questionnaires have the very restrictive condition of only reaching people who have access to the internet which, in rural areas of Africa, is a small minority. Moreover, anonymity is not ensured, and there is no certainty about the identity of the actual respondent. However, for certain types of research questions, in the business and academic world in particular, internet-based questionnaires have become a very efficient method of data collection.

Focus groups

A type of interview that is being used more and more commonly is the focus group. Ideally, a focus group consists of between six and ten respondents who are interviewed together. It is important that the focus group participants are carefully selected according to explicitly stated criteria. The focus group is conducted in an unstructured or semi-structured way. In other words, the researcher or facilitator of the focus group draws up a list of broad questions, topics or themes. These are used to develop a discussion among the focus group participants. It is important that the researcher has a good understanding of the topic before drawing up the list of questions or themes. Depending on the nature of the research question and also on the participants, it may be necessary for the facilitator to work in a more or less structured manner.

The advantages of using focus groups are that participants are able to discuss the issues in question with each other. One person's ideas may set off a whole string of related thoughts and ideas in another person. Similarly, one participant may disagree with and question the remarks of another. When this happens there is an opportunity for the whole group to explore the disagreement in detail, thereby producing a much deeper understanding of the problem. A careful record of the debate between participants can give the researcher much deeper insight into a topic than would have been gained from interviewing all the participants individually.

CHAPTER 12 Data collection: Basic concepts and techniques

Another important advantage of this technique is that it provides an opportunity for participants to learn from each other, and perhaps to resolve important dilemmas with which they are confronted. They can provide checks and balances for each other, which is very useful when dealing with incorrect information, extreme attitudes or factual errors.

Moreover, this is a quick and cheap way of collecting information from many participants, in particular with adults with a low level of literacy, and children. It is very useful in action research where part of the researcher's goal is to help address a particular problem facing a particular group of people.

However, its limitations include that participants might influence each other or even be dominated by one member who might skew the session. For this reason, the skills and experience of the facilitator in balancing the discussion is essential for the quality of the collected data.

Example

A researcher is interested in agricultural development in rural communities. She selects six women who are involved in setting up rural agricultural projects to participate in a focus group. It is likely that their discussion (facilitated by the researcher) will be very useful in identifying all the concerns that must be taken into account in this kind of project. At the same time, the sharing of ideas and experience might also assist all those women (and the projects in which they are involved) to become even more effective.

Many African cultures make constant use of small groups to address concerns within the community. For this reason, the focus group method of data collection might feel more comfortable for many people and may therefore be the method of choice.

There are, however, many potential dangers in using focus groups and the success of this approach depends in large part upon the skill of the group facilitator. Group facilitation is aimed at ensuring that a safe environment for uncensored communication is created. In particular, the facilitator should ensure that everyone in the group has real opportunities to contribute, and that the group does not prevent some members from freely expressing their ideas. Some members of the group might tend to dominate and they would need to be restrained by the facilitator. Others might find it extremely difficult to express their thoughts and they would need encouraging. People with more education, or more self-confidence, or better linguistic skills will tend to speak more than others. Thus the results of the focus group may be biased by those people who contributed most to the discussion.

201

> **Example**
>
> A researcher wishes to identify the chief sources of workplace stress within a large corporation. He randomly selects eight people from the company and puts them together in a focus group. As it happens, this group comprises a senior manager, three junior managers and five lower level employees. It will be very difficult for the junior employees to speak openly in front of the other members of the focus group. Even if they are courageous enough to express their opinions, they may not have the skills to do so as effectively as their seniors. In this case, the researcher would be better advised to use individual interviews or to set up separate focus groups for people with different levels of seniority within the company. It can also happen that the senior manager wants to use this focus group set-up to justify his actions or impose on the participants, or he could adopt a 'neutral' behaviour of non-participation, which could greatly disconcert the other members.

The problems of group dynamics are addressed through the skill of the facilitator and through the careful selection of group members. Wherever possible, all group members should be equally comfortable with the language of the group, have similar levels of education, social status, and so forth.

Another important factor relates to the composition of the group. Biases due to social desirability are extremely important in focus groups. It is difficult for people to speak honestly and openly about some issues to a single interviewer. It is very much harder to speak about those issues to a group of peers, especially when the group members know each other. Thus, focus groups are not the best method of data collection when the research topic touches on sensitive subject material.

In summary, although there are many important advantages of using focus groups, there are also potential pitfalls. The researcher must carefully consider the reasons for using the focus group technique and pay strict attention to the composition and facilitation of groups.

Data collection in practice

Constructing a questionnaire

Whether conceived to be filled in directly by a respondent or by an interviewer, a questionnaire remains a complex instrument of data collection. In a previous chapter, sampling theory was studied as being a science in which very precise procedures can be followed and sampling errors can be estimated. In the case of the construction of a questionnaire, however, although general guidelines can be given, as well as some suggestions on how to avoid particular pitfalls, there are few specific rules. There are many types of questions, question formats and interviewing techniques available to the researcher, and there is usually little chance of assessing whether a questionnaire, constructed differently, might have led to better results.

CHAPTER 12 Data collection: Basic concepts and techniques

Here are some general guidelines.
1. *Do not begin to develop a questionnaire by drafting questions. Instead, use the following procedure:*
    a. List the specific research issues to be investigated by the questionnaire.
    b. Decide what kind of data is needed to study those issues. Here the use of dummy tables (empty tables showing how the data will be presented) could help to anticipate how the data would actually be utilised in the analysis. Constructing such tables will lead to the identification of the variables to be considered.
    c. Formulate specific questions to measure those variables.

> ### Example
> Consider again the study concerning the relationship between the involvement of cooperative members in terms of time available and regularity at work, on the one hand, and their family commitments on the other. Let us assume that some of the issues to be investigated are:
> - the different family and social constraints and how they affect the work of the cooperative
> - the average time spent on cooperative activities
> - the timetable of cooperative members and how often it is not followed
> - the reasons for not respecting the adopted time schedule.
>
> A dummy table reflecting some of these points might look as follows:
>
>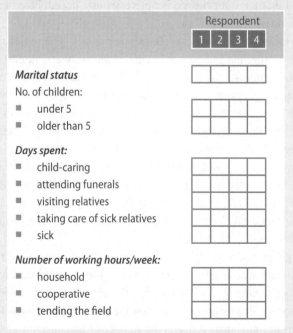
>
> *continued...*

> Some suitable questions might be:
> a. Are you single/married/divorced/widowed/separated?
> b. How many dependent children live with you?
> c. How many dependent children are below the age of five years?
> d. How many days during the last six months did you stay at home to attend to a sick child?

2. *Always take into account the needs, interests and problems of respondents.*
   These are, in fact, more important than academic factors. In other words, design a respondent-centred questionnaire or interview.

   An interview or self-administered questionnaire should never be of such a length that respondents become tired to the point of refusing to collaborate. If this happens, they will use any means to end the exercise, thus reducing the quality of their answers. Depending on the circumstances, the type of respondent, and the topic, a questionnaire should take between 15 and 90 minutes to answer. Multiple sessions should be avoided.

   There are a number of precautions one must take in the case of interviews.
   - The time and venue must be convenient to respondents.
   - Long interviews at places of work, during short lunch breaks or on the street can be regarded as disturbing to interviewees. Interviews may be more acceptable when done after working hours at the home of the participant, provided that the interviewee is not very busy, accepts the venue, and can thus concentrate on the interview.
   - The environment should allow for some privacy. The majority of respondents prefer that other people do not listen to their answers, in particular if some of the questions are quite personal. A further reason for preventing family members, neighbours or colleagues from listening to the interview is that if they are 'contaminated' by hearing another person's answers, the researcher will not be able to include them in the sample. Thus, with the exception of focus groups, interviews in public should be avoided.
   - Cooperation of respondents should be gained by using official permission and support, such as from village authorities, and by explaining the aim of the research and the relevance of the study. One should stress that the respondents have been specially selected and one should reduce suspicion by emphasising the confidentiality of the interview.
   - The language and vocabulary used should be adapted to the respondent (see questionnaire wording in 3 below). When translation into a local language is needed, great care should be taken in the choice of words. Double translation (for example, from English, into Tswana or Shona and back to English) done by different translators reduces the danger of inaccurate translation.

CHAPTER 12 Data collection: Basic concepts and techniques

- Difficulties arising from interviewers' personalities should be reduced. Interviewers must avoid being impatient, hurried and aggressive. They should also not be too friendly and accommodating. They must be aware of their own influence on respondents in order to control them. Thus, they should try to adapt to the environment in which the research is conducted, even in their way of dressing and behaving. Interviewers should guard against the respondents' developing negative or biased attitudes towards the interview as a whole.

3. *The researcher should give great attention to the wording of questions.*
   Questions should be simple and short.
   - Complex questions should be broken up into several simple ones.
   - Questions should be unambiguous. Words which are too general, too vague or which could give rise to different interpretations should be replaced with more specific terms. For instance, words like 'often', 'many', 'enough' should be replaced by 'three times a week', 'ten', and 'two meals a day'. Expressions like 'dependent children' should read 'children you are responsible for and who are living with you even if not your own'. Words like 'drugs' should be replaced by 'medicine', or 'aphrodisiac', according to the need.
   - Questions should be understandable. Use vocabulary adapted to the level of education of the participants. Avoid technical expressions and sophisticated language.
   - Questions should not be double-barrelled, that is, contain two questions in one. If one is asked to answer 'yes' or 'no' to the question, 'Do you like to go to the cinema and have a good laugh?' One excludes in a yes/no answer the possibility of going to the movies for reasons other than to laugh. Thus, a double-barrelled question should be divided into two.
   - Leading questions should be avoided. These are questions that favour one type of answer over another, or associate a particular response with an important personality. Questions starting with 'Don't you agree that …', or ending with '…is it not so?' are leading questions. For instance, 'Don't you agree that students are very irresponsible?', 'Students are very irresponsible people, is it not so?' or 'Do you support the statement of the Prime Minister that students lack a sense of responsibility?' induce biased answers and should therefore be avoided.

4. *The researcher should structure the questionnaire carefully.*
   - A logical sequence of questions which exhausts one topic before shifting to the next is the most meaningful approach. Often an even more structured method called a **funnel questionnaire** is used.

- One starts with very general questions and proceeds, by successively narrowing the scope, to the focus of the problem under study. Before asking the opinion of respondents on a particular event involving, for example, a politician, one might investigate the general interests and hobbies of the respondents, their political views and affiliations, and their sources of information.
- The inverted funnel sequence, also called a **filter questionnaire**, is based on the same principle, except that one reverses the process and starts with very specific issues that later lead to more general ones. Both methods can be used to instill confidence in respondents and to permit discovery of inconsistencies.
- The repetition of the content of a question, formulated in different ways and placed in different parts of the questionnaire, is another method of checking the veracity of answers and the honesty of a participant. This is particularly useful for topics on which the respondent may have reason to lie, to cover up something or to impress the interviewer. This is often the case with social status and financial questions.
- The tendency of participants to answer all questions in a specific direction regardless of the content of the questions, called a **response set**, must be counteracted. This is mainly done by breaking the monotonous sequence and format of questions and response categories. An example of this pitfall and its correction (from an attitude questionnaire containing statements on a five-point scale) is given below.

Example

	Strongly agree	Agree	No opinion	Disagree	Strongly disagree
TV weakens the sight					
TV develops passivity					
TV curbs creativity					
TV develops aggression					

continued ...

CHAPTER 12 Data collection: Basic concepts and techniques

All four statements express a negative view about television. Participants are thus likely to adopt a certain 'set' answer and to apply it to all the questions without analysing them. This could be avoided by reformulating the questions as follows:

	Strongly agree	Agree	No opinion	Disagree	Strongly disagree
TV weakens the sight					
TV develops creativity					
TV reduces aggression					
TV develops passivity					

In the example the first and last statements reflect a negative attitude. Much more than can be dealt with here could be said about such pitfalls and how to avoid them when designing a questionnaire. Interested readers should consult more specialised literature on the topic.

The following potential mistakes should be considered when implementing the above guidelines:

1. Is the question necessary? How will it be used to address the problem or test the hypothesis?
2. Does the respondent have the necessary information to answer this question? Is the participant willing to do so?
3. Is the question respondent-centred?
4. Will the question be interpreted similarly by all respondents?
5. Is the question neutral or does it favour a particular answer?
6. Is the wording of the question adequate?
7. Is the organisation of the questionnaire logical but not monotonous?

Types of questions

The first distinction to be made concerns the content of questions. A question can seek either factual information or opinion.

Factual questions request objective information about the respondents, such as their social background or related personal data. Questionnaires usually contain factual questions related to characteristics such as age, sex, marital status and level of education. It is debatable where factual background (personal) questions should be placed in the questionnaire. In some societies, the placing of enquiries about personal matters (such as level of education and income) at the beginning of a questionnaire is resented and can lead to a refusal to participate.

Factual questions seem easy to answer since they are straightforward and do not influence the respondent. But a common mistake is to allow ambiguity. For example, if a farmer is asked how many animals she has on her farm, she may count livestock only and not mention cats and dogs. This question is ambiguous. The truthfulness of a factual answer does not only depend on the willingness of respondents to tell the truth but also on their knowledge and memory. A wife asked to determine the income of her husband may not want to disclose it, may want to impress the interviewer by inflating it, or she may have reasons to depreciate it. She may also be ignorant of her spouse's income and just make a wild guess to please the interviewer. A person asked how much he spent on clothing in the past year may not remember all the details and therefore give an incorrect answer. Because of such difficulties, a researcher must make sure that participants are in a position to answer factual questions.

Sometimes it is possible to check the veracity of factual answers by referring to other sources. In the case of the woman who is ignorant of her spouse's income, it may be possible to check that income with the spouse directly. However, the researcher must be very careful not to violate the subject's privacy. Checking a person's income with their employer without their express permission would be an invasion of their privacy.

Opinion questions are more problematic, since the respondent is the only person who knows the true answer. There are also many factors that may introduce distortions in the answer. As already mentioned, the respondent may be influenced by what she considers socially desirable. Because racial prejudice is neither morally nor socially acceptable in most societies, a racially prejudiced person might feel uneasy and avoid openly disclosing such feelings. This should be taken into account when formulating research questions. Questions should be stated in such a way that the answers are socially acceptable. For instance, 'Some people feel that personal interracial contacts are a source of conflict and should be discouraged. Do you support this statement? Yes/No/No opinion'. This form of presentation allows respondents to express their attitudes without discomfort, since it is implied that they share those attitudes with other people. This would not be the case if the question were stated as 'Personal interracial contacts should be discouraged. Yes/No'. Note that opinions and attitudes expressed in questionnaires do not always reflect actual behaviour.

Example

These three possibilities are illustrated with an investigation into work relations conducted among employees of firm A. For all questions, the respondents have the choice of answering 'yes' or 'no'.

Statement:
The manager of firm A lacks democratic skills in his work relations with the staff.

continued ...

CHAPTER 12 Data collection: Basic concepts and techniques

> *Direct question:*
> Is your manager democratic in the way he deals with matters of the firm?
>
> *Indirect questions:*
> - Does the manager of firm A discuss affairs of the firm with staff?
> - Does he take into account the suggestions and wishes of staff?
> - Does he make decisions after consensus has been reached among members of staff?
> - Does he tend to impose his decision on staff?

Information can be gathered in different ways. The participant might be confronted with a statement that must be assessed, or with a question. In the latter case, it could be a direct or indirect question. **Statements** have the property of being more impersonal and therefore allow a shorter formulation. **Direct questions** are also brief and to the point. **Indirect questions**, used especially when dealing with delicate issues, allow the purpose of the question to be less obvious, and give respondents the impression that they are stating a general opinion rather than having to commit themselves, and so they are more likely to be more honest. The disadvantage is that a greater number of indirect questions is needed to gauge an opinion or a fact than would be necessary if direct questions were used.

Another concern is how to present a question in order to obtain a certain type of answer. Here the distinction is between the need for a long, detailed answer, reflecting the individuality of respondents, and a short answer, chosen among given categories. The types of questions considered below are unstructured or open-ended questions, as well as structured ones of great variety such as multiple-choice or checklist questions, scaled answers and ranked answers. To this list one should also add contingency questions and fill-in questions. Each of these has special functions, advantages and disadvantages, the main distinction being between open-ended (unstructured) questions and structured ones.

Open-ended questions leave the participants completely free to express their answers as they wish in as detailed or complex, as long or as short a form as they feel is appropriate. No restrictions, guidelines or suggestions for solutions are given. Consider the following questions:

> What are your future plans?
> ....
> ....
>
> How do you explain the present situation on campus?
> ....
> ....
>
> What major problems does your country face today?
> ....
> ....

209

Structured questions indicate a range of possible answers. They give a choice of answers (for example, multiple-choice questions) or guidelines on the procedures to follow (for example, ranking questions). Sometimes only two possibilities are given (such as 'Yes/ No', or 'Agree/Disagree'), which allow for very little differentiation. Adding a third, neutral possibility like 'No opinion', or 'Not applicable' increases the flexibility of the answer somewhat. When more possibilities exist, a checklist is appropriate, where the respondent is asked to tick either only the most adequate, or all the suitable answers. Consider the following structured alternative to the open-ended question, 'What led you to study at the university?'

Your decision to study at the university was mainly determined by:
- [ ] your parents
- [ ] your social environment
- [ ] your interest in a particular scientific field
- [ ] your ambition to have a lucrative profession

When a list is not exhaustive, an additional last choice might be:

- [ ] Any other reasons (state them)
....

In this last instance the structured question contains an open-ended answer option, which makes the whole question better adapted to all situations.

Some multiple-choice questions have a particular structure in the sense that the suggested answers are ranked, usually using an ordinal scale. This is the case for questions on opinions and attitudes where a statement is made and the respondents must decide how much they agree with it. The most frequently used scale for such questions is based on three points (such as 'I like/no opinion/I dislike').

To obtain more differentiated answers, one can use a five-point scale, as in the following example:

How suitable do you judge the applicant to be for the coordinator position?
- [ ] highly unsuitable
- [ ] unsuitable
- [ ] no opinion
- [ ] suitable
- [ ] highly suitable

Ranking questions are used when a set of possibilities is offered and the participant must assess the importance of each of them relative to the others. Here is an example.

CHAPTER 12 Data collection: Basic concepts and techniques

Rank, in order of decreasing importance, the relevance of the following factors in your choice of a profession.

Rank

- ☐ Money
- ☐ Social contact
- ☐ Type of occupation
- ☐ Social position
- ☐ Intellectual interest
- ☐ Humanitarian relevance

Contingency questions are a special type of structured question, which apply to subgroups of respondents only, namely the ones who have given a particular answer to a previous question. To give a very simple example, when collecting data the following alternative exists:

Do you have children?	If 'yes', how many?
☐ Yes	☐ Boys
☐ No	☐ Girls

Lastly, **fill-in questions** constitute a transitional type of question, between open-ended and structured, since no format is suggested but only a short format is expected. The following questions are examples of this type of question:

Name the feeling you experienced when smoking.

....

What emotion was painted on her face?

....

To the first statement, one may answer 'excitement and peace', to the second simply 'grief'. Thus responses can be kept quite brief.

Advantages and disadvantages of open-ended and structured questions

The main distinction between the two types of questions is that open-ended questions are not based on preconceived answers. They are thus well suited to exploratory studies, case studies or studies based on qualitative analysis of data. Answers may be quite complex and not easily comparable to those of other respondents. Their recording and scoring can therefore be more difficult. By contrast, structured questions, by restricting the number of possible answers, may produce bias if important categories are left out. Their quality is largely determined by a good pre-analysis and pilot study or survey using open-ended questions to discover the major possibilities and to classify them. They have the great advantage of being simple to record and to score, and they allow for easy comparison and quantification of results.

As mentioned earlier, some negative aspects of structured questions, like over-restrictive response possibilities or the exclusion of important ones, can be greatly reduced by adding an open-ended option. The two types can be used to gain the confidence and cooperation of participants in different ways. Open-ended questions may relieve the anxiety of participants to giving 'false' answers since they can speak more freely. But easy, structured questions will also reassure participants who recognise that they are able to answer precise, straightforward questions without difficulty.

As already mentioned in the guidelines, attention should be paid not only to the content of questions and the level of precision that one wishes the answers to have, but also to sustaining the interest of the participants by avoiding monotony in the questionnaire. Such considerations influence whether one selects open-ended or structured questions and how or if one mix both types of question within a study.

Ensuring the quality of questionnaires

Once a questionnaire has been constructed, one has to check its quality (see also Chapter 13): Is it well structured? Are the questions presented in a suitable order? Is the formulation of the questions appropriate to the type of respondents? Are the questions meaningful for the selected respondents: not threatening, boring or invasive? Are the choices offered as answers for multiple-choice questions relevant and exhaustive?

All these issues are particularly relevant if the questionnaire is to be completed without an interviewer to assist the participants.

In order to check on all these issues, a small pilot study (see Chapter 8) can be done. Presenting the questions to a few people who share the characteristics of the sample but do not belong to the group, will allow the researcher to identify all the potential flaws. In particular, is the language and vocabulary used appropriate and adapted to the respondent? Are some formulations ambivalent? Are some questions eliciting the same answer from all respondents, thus showing that the question is trivial and can be deleted?

A great advantage of checking the quality of a questionnaire through a pilot study is the opportunity to identify all the possible answers to multiple-choice questions. To do this, the question is presented as an open-ended question and the various answers collected in the study then serve to establish the multiple-choice options. A pilot study also allows one to check that the instructions explaining how to complete the questionnaire are clearly stated and understood by all.

Finally, one must assess the quality of a questionnaire against the following list:

- Are all the questions relevant to the purpose of the research?
- Are there superfluous or trivial questions?

CHAPTER 12 Data collection: Basic concepts and techniques

- Is the questionnaire well structured to facilitate the flow of questions?
- Are the questions well formulated, clearly stated, unambiguous and do they use appropriate language and vocabulary?
- Are the questions formulated in a non-suggestive way, no leading questions?
- Are the questions precise and to the point?
- Are the multiple-choice answers relevant and exhaustive?
- Are the questions neither too intrusive nor embarrassing?
- Are neutral answers such as 'I don't know' or 'No opinion' given as choices?
- Are the instructions clear and unambiguous?

Editing the questionnaire

Suppose that a survey or any type of research based on the collection of data through interviews or questionnaires has been conducted. Once the data have been collected, the researcher is confronted with piles of interview or questionnaire forms filled in by interviewers or by the respondents themselves. Before even starting to compile and code the information, one has to make sure that each question has been answered and that the answer is properly recorded. That is, one needs to check for the *completeness* of the questionnaires. An even more delicate task is to try to check the *accuracy* of the answers. Are there inconsistencies between the answers to different questions? Finally, one must check for *uniformity* in the interpretation of the questions and of the multiple-choice options. These three controls of completeness, accuracy and uniformity constitute the main tasks of the editing process.

The **completeness** of each questionnaire is often essential in research where even one missing answer may demand that the whole questionnaire be discarded. Sometimes, if a question has been omitted by a respondent or, in the case of an oral questionnaire or interview, if the interviewer has forgotten to record the answer, it may be possible to enter the type of answer that the respondent might have given, or for the interviewer to recall the general meaning of the answer. In delicate cases, one might even try to contact the respondent directly to ask him or her for the missing information. If the unanswered questions relate to objective information, such as residential area or marital status, the researcher may be able to find the appropriate data by cross-checking with other information sources. Problems may occur when some questions are not answered and it is difficult to decide whether it is due to the unwillingness of the respondent to provide the information or because the question was not applicable to the respondent.

To judge the **accuracy** of the answer is even more difficult. Inconsistencies in a questionnaire may have various causes, including misinterpretation of the question or answer, lack of concentration, carelessness or even purposefully misleading answers. Errors due to carelessness are often easily detected. There is an obvious contradiction between the answer 'No' to 'Do you have children?' and 'Three' to 'If yes, how many?' Sometimes the wrong answer is ticked by mistake or the tick is not clearly placed.

As mentioned, the variety and accuracy of some factual answers may give rise to concerns and be difficult to assess. If there is any doubt, one should find other sources to double-check the information. Although precautions will have been taken to avoid ambiguity in the questions when constructing the questionnaire, **uniformity** of the understanding of the questions and answers must also be checked. This could be as simple as a misunderstanding between the meaning of 'Not applicable' and 'No opinion'. Similarly, a variation in understanding between 'income' and 'assets' would result in great differences in the amounts indicated by respondents. These errors are difficult to correct at this late stage, but it is very important that the researcher is at least aware of them when interpreting the results.

Finally, editing can be done in two ways. The first method is based on the editing of one question at a time, that is, analysing one or a few answers given by the participants in all the questionnaires, then another small set of questions, etc. The second method focuses on the questionnaire, that is, analysing one questionnaire after another, going through all answers given by each respondent. The first method allows for the detection of inaccuracies in the answers and lack of uniformity in the interpretation of the questions, but not of inconsistencies within the same questionnaire. The second method will allow better judgement of each individual case as a whole. However, although it is preferable to edit all the collected data, it is sometimes too costly and too time-consuming and so only a sample of questionnaires (or of questions) is edited. This may have a negative impact on the quality of the research.

Conducting interviews

Before data can be analysed, it has to be produced (or selected from an existent field). The quality of the data collected is crucial to the quality of the analysis.

All research participants create meaning and there are differences in terms of the manner in which they do so. Participants may not hear the question in the same sense/ frame as that of the interviewer or other interviewees and they may genuinely understand the question in a different way. This may be because they have their own personal or hidden reasons for responding in a particular way, or are motivated to disguise the meaning of at least some of their feelings and actions.

Interviewing requires a great deal of skill and experience in order to counteract these problems. Here are some suggestions for good interviewing:
1. Use open-ended rather than closed questions – the more open the better.
2. Elicit stories. This has the virtue of anchoring people's accounts to events that have actually happened. This forces such accounts to engage with reality, even if compromising it in the service of self-protection. Eliciting stories from people is not always a simple matter, especially from those who feel their lives lack sufficient interest or worth to justify 'a story'.

CHAPTER 12 Data collection: Basic concepts and techniques

3. Follow up using respondents' ordering and phrasing. This involves attentive listening and possibly some note taking during the initial narration in order to be able to follow up themes in their narrated order. By doing this, the respondent's own words and phrases are used in order to show respect and retain the interviewee's meaning frames. As always, the follow-up questions should be as open as possible and framed so as to elicit further narratives.

The method entails a single, open, initial question that is also an invitation, 'Please, tell me about…'. In focused interviews the art and skill of the exercise is to assist narrators to say more about their lives without the interviewer offering interpretations, judgements or otherwise imposing her own relevancies, and thereby destroying the interviewee's flow.

Facilitating a focus group

Preparing a focus group starts with the selection of a small group of six to 10 people, taking into consideration the aim and the situation before deciding whether to choose a homogeneous or heterogeneous group. The advantage of a homogenous group is that participants may feel more supported in their views and so speak more easily. The advantage of a heterogenous group is that the contrasting viewpoints within the group may encourage a deeper discussion of the issue. However, in heterogenous groups, the facilitator must pay close attention to power dynamics and encourage silent people to express their views. The venue should be appropriate and the participants must be aware of the purpose of the meeting. The duration should be of about one hour. With the participants sitting comfortably in a circle, the facilitator should explain the aim and the process of the meeting and reinforce the motivation of the respondents to be both active and free in their contributions.

Starting with issues of great interest and familiarity to the participants will activate the discussion. The questions must always be formulated in a neutral and open way, so as not to suggest any tendency or bias. It is also important for the facilitator to reinforce the motivation and the enthusiasm of the group by emphasising how valuable their contributions are. Moreover, the facilitator also has the delicate task of dissipating negative feelings, avoiding personal confrontation and addressing disagreements among the participants, noting, however, that debates are useful to clarifying ideas. Managing the smooth interaction and participation of all the people present also means inviting the contribution of too silent and passive individuals, as well as kindly reducing the speaking time of more dominant participants. One must avoid the formation of cliques and separate close friends in order to increase diversity of opinion. At all times, the facilitator has to remain neutral, never taking sides and always remaining calm and polite.

Finally, with permission of the participants, a continuous record of what is discussed must be made, either by taking notes or by making a tape/digital recording.

215

Fundamentals of Social Research Methods: An African Perspective

Table 12.1 *Data collection – advantages and disadvantages of various techniques*		
Technique	Advantages	Disadvantages
Questionnaire	▪ Easily standardised ▪ Time and cost effective ▪ Very little training of researchers	▪ Difficult to interpret respondents' responses ▪ Difficult to check that respondents understand the questions ▪ Low response rate and high response bias
Mailed questionnaire	▪ Easily standardised ▪ Time and cost effective ▪ Very little training of researchers ▪ Reaches a geographically diverse sample	▪ Difficult to interpret respondents' responses ▪ Difficult to check that respondents understand the questions ▪ Very low response rate and high response bias ▪ Questionnaire may not be fully completed

Emailed questionnaire	▪ Easily standardised
	▪ Time and cost effective
	▪ Very little training of researchers
	▪ Reaches a geographically diverse sample
		▪ Difficult to interpret respondents' responses
		▪ Difficult to check that respondents understand the questions
		▪ Very low response rate andhigh response bias
		  — Questionnaire may not be fully completed
		  — Difficult to ensure anonymity

Standardised interview	▪ Relatively easily standardised ▪ Can be sure that respondents understand questions ▪ Can clarify and interpret respondents' responses ▪ Better response rate	▪ Very time-consuming and expensive ▪ Research assistants need training ▪ May introduce interviewer bias ▪ Bias due to social desirability
Exploratory interview	▪ Does not impose structure on interview ▪ Can access what respondents ▪ feel is important ▪ Useful for generating hypotheses	▪ Very time-consuming and expensive ▪ Research assistants need training ▪ Very difficult to standardise and analyse ▪ Bias due to social desirability

continued ...

CHAPTER 12 Data collection: Basic concepts and techniques

Table 12.1 *Data collection – advantages and disadvantages of various techniques*

Technique	Advantages	Disadvantages
Focus groups	■ Participants share views and discuss ideas ■ Participants gain insight into pressing concerns ■ Many African cultures rely on small groups for decision making	■ No individual responses since participants influence each other ■ Without a skilled facilitator, some participants may be excluded ■ Bias due to social desirability is extreme
Telephonic interview	■ Cheaper than other interviews ■ Reaches a geographically diverse sample	■ Research assistants need training ■ May introduce sampling bias ■ Many people cannot be reached at all by phone

Key points

1. In both quantitative and qualitative research, the data are collected through observing and questioning the research participants. However, in quantitative studies the researcher selects the technique and instrument of data collection so as to obtain quantifiable data or measurements, whereas in qualitative studies, the content is emphasised through great flexibility in the chosen technique.
2. Each method of data collection has advantages and disadvantages that have to be kept in mind. Some methods are thus more or less appropriate to the aims of particular research projects.
3. The construction of a questionnaire as a source of data collection is a complex excercise demanding a rigorous construct of the entire questionnaire, a precise aim for and an appropriate formulation of each question, an adequate range of answers for multiple-choice questions and clear instructions to the respondent.
4. A questionnaire is only usable when it has been standardised, edited and, if possible, pre-tested through a pilot study. In order to be able to conduct interviews or facilitating focus group discussions well, researchers need to hone their skills and accumulate as much experience as possible. Professionalism and neutrality are essential qualities at all times.

217

Fundamentals of Social Research Methods: An African Perspective

Checklist

Keywords:

Check whether the meanings of the concepts introduced in this chapter is clear to you.

scales of measurements; nominal/ordinal/interval/ratio scales; Likert scale; index; typology; simple and participant observation; non-scheduled interview; non-scheduled semi-structured interview; structured interview; pilot study; experimental method; record method; focus group method ; factual vs opinion questions; open-ended/ranking/contingency/fill-in questions.

Your research:
1. Is the chosen data collection method the most adequate one for your research?
2. Have you checked the quality of your questionnaire according to the given criteria?
3. Have you done a pilot study to ascertain that the instructions and questions are clear?
4. Have you prepared the way you intend to conduct a focus group?

Exercises

1. Using actual examples, distinguish between facts and data. Explain what you understand by primary and secondary data. What are the shortcomings of the latter types of data?
2. Indicate which scales of measurement are used in the following examples:
    a. opinions on the quality of a film expressed freely by a group of teenagers
    b. degree classification of graduating students
    c. brands of toothpaste
    d. income of workers at a car assembly plant
    e. amount of calcium deposit (in milligrams) in the organs of rats that have been subjected to different experimental treatments.
3. A drug was tested on a group of prisoners to observe its effects on human beings. What are the ethical issues raised by this study?
4. Find the flaws in the following questions and suggest improvements.
    a. Have you ever falsified information on your income tax declaration?
    b. How much did your husband spend on clothes last year?
    c. Do you believe that watching television is un-African?
    d. Are you emotionally mature?
    e. Is cancer research feasible in Africa and should one strive for it?
    f. How do you feel about Mercedes-Benz and Peugeot?
    g. Do you consider your working conditions and wages to be excellent … good … fair …?

continued …

CHAPTER 12 Data collection: Basic concepts and techniques

5. Suppose that you would like to find out how much time rural women spend on their various activities, like working in the field, fetching water and wood, cooking, and so on. How would you collect these data? Would it be adequate to use a questionnaire? What method of observation might be suitable?

6. Choose a topic in your field of interest. Suppose that you are to conduct research on the opinions and attitudes of a certain population on the chosen topic. Develop a short questionnaire (10–15 questions) using the types of question presented in this chapter as a guide. Be sure to write a respondent-centred questionnaire, taking into account level of education, language difficulties, emotional barriers and any other factors that arise.

7. Compare and contrast the various techniques of data collection presented in this chapter if you were to investigate the impact of lack of educational facilities in a peri-urban area.

8. The residents of a town are very dissatisfied with the local government. You are responsible for identifying the nature of the complaints as precisely as possible, as well as finding out how the community would like those problems to be resolved. You have chosen to facilitate a series of five focus groups. Construct your instrument (an unstructured questionnaire), identify the composition of each group and prepare yourself to facilitate the discussion. Foresee the possible challenges that you may encounter.

Additional resources

1. Babbie, E R. 2012. *The practice of social research*, 13th ed. Belmont, CA: Wadsworth.

2. Babbie, E & Rubin, A. 2010. *Research methods in social work*, 7th ed. Belmont, CA: Brooks/Cole.

3. Dawson, C. n.d. *How to construct questionnaires*, downloaded from www.howto.co.uk/business/research-methods/how_to_construct_questionnaires/Accessed on 30 November 2012.

4. Krueger, R A. n.d. Focus group onterviewing, downloaded from www.tc.umn.edu/~krueger/focus.html. Accessed on 30 November 2012.

5. Scheuren, F. 2004. *What is a survey?*, downloaded from www.whatisasurvey.info/downloads/pamphlet-current.pdf. Accessed on 30 November 2012.

CHAPTER 13

Ensuring the quality of data

After having identified and formulated a research question, decided on the type of research method to use in terms of planning and design as well as the way in which the data are to be collected, and then having compiled the results, it is time to ask oneself some fundamental questions about the quality of that research and its results. How is 'good' research defined? How does one differentiate between 'good' and 'bad' research? In other words, are there some criteria to keep in mind and apply throughout the research process in order to be able to assess the quality of the findings? And are these criteria the same for all types of research?

The differences in purpose and methodology between quantitative and qualitative research can be expressed as follows: whereas quantitative research aims at giving an explanation, identifying a relationship between variables (as formulated in an hypothesis), expressing a 'social law', and a generalisation of the findings, the aim of qualitative research is to understand a phenomenon in its natural context and extrapolate those findings to other similar situations. Also, whereas quantitative research is based on some standardised instrument with which the 'objective' researcher collects large amounts of measurable data that can then be subjected to statistical analysis, qualitative research relies on less structured interactions between the participants and the researcher who tries to describe and understand their situation in its complexity and uniqueness.

Therefore, different criteria must be used to evaluate the quality of the data collected and analysed in terms of these two approaches: the quality of quantitative research is assessed through its reliability, validity and objectivity, whereas the quality of a qualitative research is evaluated through its trustworthiness, on the basis of credibility, transferability, dependability, triangulation and confirmability.

Because of these important differences, this chapter presents separately the position of quantitative research, in terms of reliability and validity of measurements, and then the situation of qualitative research based on trustworthiness. Thereafter, mixed-method research approaches to data quality are also discussed.

CHAPTER OBJECTIVES

Learners who have completed this chapter will be able to:
- Evaluate the reliability of measurement instruments and techniques.
- Evaluate the validity of measurement instruments and techniques.
- Select measurement strategies that maximise reliability and validity.
- Evaluate the trustworthiness of a qualitative research project.
- Apply verification strategies for ensuring trustworthiness.
- Evaluate the rigour of mixed-methods research.

CHAPTER 13 Ensuring the quality of data

Quantitative research: Reliability and validity of measurements

Once a researcher has identified the constructs or variables that are important to a particular study, it is necessary for them to be operationalised so that they can be measured. The evaluation of such measurement is done in terms of the principles of reliability and validity.

Reliability is the extent to which the observable (or empirical) measures that represent a theoretical concept are accurate and stable over repeated observations. Validity is concerned with just how accurately the observable measures actually represent the concept in question or whether, in fact, they represent something else. Several methods of determining the reliability of observable measures for theoretical concepts are discussed, as well as the different types of validity commonly applied to social science concepts.

As discussed in Chapter 2, social scientists are required to translate the theoretical concepts that they are interested in into observable measures. This is done, in the framework of quantitative research, by choosing an operational definition for each theoretical concept involved in the research. As explained in Chapter 6, an operational definition of a theoretical concept indicates how that concept is to be measured (empirically) by the researcher. Operational definitions do not, however, tell the researcher whether or not the chosen measures are *adequate* measures of the various concepts.

Example

It is hypothesised that factory workers, residing far from their workplace and travelling long distances to reach work, experience greater occupational stress than workers who live close to the factory. In this case, the theoretical constructs of 'travelling time' or 'distance to the workplace' and 'occupational stress' need operational definition.

Note that the way in which these constructs are operationalised greatly influences the value of the research. Is living 'far or close to the factory' to be determined by the distance in kilometres, or by the travelling time independent of mode and availability of transport? The researcher might choose to define workers living far from the factory as those living more than 10 kilometers away. Moreover, if the time factor is considered, can one compare 30 minutes travelling on foot, when the worker is free to leave home at her own convenience, to 30 minutes travelling on a bus, with the stress of catching the bus perhaps two hours early in order to avoid rush hour and the possibility of missing the bus? It should be clear that, by asking how long workers take to get to the factory from home, the researcher may be finding out more about the transport facilities in different areas than about the distances people live from the factory. Here, then, the researcher might define 'living far from the factory' as 'taking more than 30 minutes to reach the factory'. In addition, occupational stress may be defined as the score on a specially constructed stress inventory.

continued ...

> These two definitions suggest how the concepts are to be measured: by finding out how long it takes each person to travel to work from home, and what they score on the stress inventory. Similarly, the measure of occupational stress may give entirely different results depending on whether the workers have a good day at work or not, or how well they slept the night before.

Unfortunately, virtually no measurement technique in social science is perfect. It is therefore important that researchers always evaluate the measures that they use. This is the purpose of reliability and validity.

Reliability

Reliability is concerned with the consistency of measures. An instrument that produces different scores every time it is used to measure an unchanging value has low reliability. It cannot be depended upon to produce an accurate measurement. On the other hand, an instrument that always gives the same score when used to measure an unchanging value can be trusted to give an accurate measurement and is said to have high reliability. In most cases, the **reliability** of measurement is the degree to which that instrument produces equivalent results for repeated trials.

In order to be meaningful, scores on a measure need to vary among the research participants. This measurement is of no use if scores are all the same for all participants. When one person scores more than another it reflects how they differ. This variability between scores is called variance. Participants who possess more of the construct will have a higher score, and those with less of the construct will have a lower score.

However, there may also be error in the measurement of constructs. A measure is similar to a ruler, but because the concepts are a bit more nebulous than length, breadth or height, the measurement is less precise. It's almost like having a scale that is only 80% accurate, or a ruler that is a little bit elastic, and you therefore get an imprecise measurement of the true dimension.

The reliability of a set of scores is the degree to which the variance in scores is due to systematic rather than chance factors. Reliability measures the proportion of variance that is due to true differences between subjects' scores rather than differences due to chance. True differences refer to actual differences rather than measured differences. Therefore when measuring nutrition values in people with HIV, some differences in scores will be due to true differences in nutrition and some will be due to error. If 90% of the variance is due to systematic factors, the reliability is 0,90 (or 90%), and 10% of the variance is due to random factors or chance.

Since reliability is concerned with the stability of scores, a reliable measure is one in which the scores remain the same over several measurement points. This is called test–retest reliability and the greater the consistency of the results, the greater the reliability of the measuring procedure. Unfortunately, very few instruments ever produce entirely consistent results. There are many sources of inconsistency in the social sciences but the adequacy of the method of investigation is often the prime cause.

CHAPTER 13 Ensuring the quality of data

> **Example**
>
> A researcher interested in the health needs of a particular community establishes a list of possible health problems and asks community members to tick off the problems that they think are most important on that list. A week later she repeats the exercise with the same sample of community members and discovers that they tick off a different set of health issues. The checklist approach is not producing consistent results. In this case, the checklist is an unreliable method for assessing the community's health needs. Next, the researcher uses exploratory interviews for the same purpose and finds that these do produce consistent results. The exploratory interview is therefore a reliable instrument. It is possible to speculate that people's immediate needs vary from day to day and thus the checklist approach does not produce consistent data. More careful probing, however, reveals a few basic needs from which all others arise.

But the reasons for lack of reliability can be quite diverse and complex, as shown in the next example.

> **Example**
>
> A worker who is interviewed about a factory's working conditions after a long day at work or after being refused a day's leave may feel that conditions are very poor. The same worker interviewed during a tea break may give an entirely different response to the same question. Similarly, a group of individuals who are being asked a second time to rate a company's public image may rate it the same as they did the first time, despite changes, just to appear consistent. Equally they may change their ratings merely to 'fool' the interviewer, or for other motives not related to the subject of the interview.

It is worth emphasising that in the social sciences there is always concern about establishing *regularities* of perceptions, opinions, behaviours, etc. If some regularity is observed in a phenomenon, it is more likely that something meaningful is being measured. Nevertheless, some instruments are more accurate than others and the social researcher must be able to distinguish the reliable from the unreliable in order to achieve the best results. Without going into the mathematical procedures needed to estimate reliability, the following sections provide a description of the various techniques commonly used. These are: test–retest reliability, equivalent form reliability, inter-rater-reliability, and internal consistency of measures.

Test–retest reliability

To assess test–retest reliability, the same measurement procedure is applied to the same group of people on two or more occasions. A procedure with high test–retest reliability ought to produce very similar results at each testing. The results of a procedure with low test–retest reliability will vary widely. Provided that a researcher can obtain the same people twice to test the procedure, the method is simple. There are, however,

223

several potential problems and one must be careful when interpreting differences in the test and retest results as they may be due to factors such as history, maturation or reactivity rather than lack of reliability of the instrument.

One of the other factors which may have influenced the participants between the two testings may be due to the effects of **_history_** (which was discussed in Chapter 10).

Example

A test is developed to measure the extent of racist stereotypes among school children. This test is administered to the same group of participants twice. The second testing falls six months after the first. In the intervening period, however, the country's education policy is changed and schools become racially integrated. In this case, the second testing may produce results very different from the first. This does not mean, though, that the test is unreliable, only that history has changed the respondents' attitudes.

A similar problem may arise due to **_maturation_** (also discussed in Chapter 10). Maturation refers to changes in the participants that are not due to external events such as those discussed under history.

Example

Suppose that a survey on population issues is conducted and the results show that rural adults in an African country favour having a large number of children. After the survey instrument is administered a second time, it may be found that the results are very different. The change may result from the experience of economic hardship arising from having too many children and not because the instrument is unreliable.

Another potential problem that must be considered by researchers using the test–retest method of determining reliability is reactivity. **Reactivity** occurs when exposure to the first testing influences responses to the second testing. The first time that participants are exposed to a questionnaire they may find it interesting. However, when the researcher presents the same questions some time later, participants may find it boring and even irritating. Also, they may remember the questions from the first testing and then intentionally provide either similar or different responses during the second testing. Here again, there is likely to be disparity between the first and second testing that is not a reflection of the instrument's lack of reliability.

When using the test–retest method, it is important that the researcher finds the most appropriate time interval between the test and the retest. Long intervals make the study more vulnerable to the effects of history and maturation. Too short an interval may increase the effects of reactivity.

CHAPTER 13 Ensuring the quality of data

Equivalent-form reliability

This method of assessing reliability (sometimes called parallel-form reliability) is very similar to the test–retest method but tries to address the problem of reactivity by changing the original test slightly at the second testing. Thus, instead of giving the same test to the same set of subjects on two or more occasions, this method requires the researcher to use an equivalent form of the instrument after the first testing. In the following examples, two equivalent forms of a questionnaire are generated.

Example

A performance potential scale is developed to assess candidates for some middle management post at a bank. The evaluation criteria are: achievement needs, drive to excel, stress-resilience, self-reliance and self-criticism. For each of these criteria, three sets of equivalent questions are developed.

For instance, when testing stress-resilience, equivalent forms could be:
1. When I'm in a difficult situation, I can usually find my way out of it.
2. I can get through difficult times because I've experienced difficulty before.
3. I have a lot of humour.
4. I can usually find something to laugh about.
5. I have self-discipline.
6. I always plan and execute my plans.

By assigning one element of each of these pairs to form a questionnaire, two equivalent scales are composed, one including the even-numbered questions, the other with the odd-numbered questions.

The next example shows how more complex questions related to the same theme can be constructed to generate two equivalent forms for structured interviews (see Chapter 12).

Example

Original questions	Equivalent form
Do the leaders in your community come from a few families or do they originate from a large group of families?	Are there families in your community that play much more of a leadership role than others?
How many community and solidarity actions take place yearly in your village?	In the past year, how often have members of your village come together to address and solve community problems?
People in this village look out mainly for the welfare of their own families and are not much concerned with community welfare.	In this village, individualism and selfishness prevail over feelings of community and solidarity.

225

Although the difficulties caused by history and maturation remain (as for the test–retest method), the problem of reactivity is reduced because subjects are not expected to answer the same questions more than once. The difficulty with the equivalent-forms method, however, remains: whether or not the two versions of the instrument are in actual fact equivalent. However, differences between the first and second testing may be due to subtle differences in the questions and may not mean that the original form has poor reliability. There are always problems associated with the construction of equivalent forms. The process is time-consuming and thus represents a serious drain on resources as literally twice as much work is required for the construction of the research instruments. Moreover, most concepts in social science do not have equivalent concepts that can be used as alternatives in different instruments.

Thus, the equivalent-forms method for determining the reliability of a measuring procedure also has both advantages and disadvantages. The researcher must choose the most appropriate test of reliability for her particular project with great care.

Inter-rater reliability

One of the errors in any research could be that the rater's judgement is influenced by extrinsic factors. In order to avoid this pitfall, the use of more than one rater is recommended. In this case, their respective scores are compared and the consensus of the raters, measured through the agreement or concordance of the scores, is called the inter-rater reliability. If the scores vary largely from rater to rater, it means that the reliability of the scoring system is defective or that the raters need further instruction on the scoring system.

Internal consistency

The various items of an instrument measure the same construct even though there will be some variation between item scores. However, they should vary in the same direction. Someone who has a high level of depression will tend to answer all the items in one direction. Someone who has a low level of depression will tend to answer the questions in the other direction (not depressed). When the scores for the various items are correlated, the internal consistency should be high. Internal consistency is a measure of the homogeneity of the items. When the scores for the various items are inter-correlated, the internal consistency will be high.

CHAPTER 13 Ensuring the quality of data

> ### Example
>
> Imagine the following items on a measuring instrument:
> 1. I enjoy watching cricket.
> 2. I feel sad.
> 3. I get angry quickly.
> 4. My income is greater than R20 000 per month.
> 5. I live with my parents.
>
> These items have very little in common and it is difficult to see what underlying construct they are trying to measure. We might say that there is no internally consistent construct that underlies these items.
>
> Consider the next set of items:
> 1. I feel sad.
> 2. I cry often.
> 3. I do not experience as much pleasure as I used to from the things that I do.
> 4. My appetite is not as good as it used to be.
> 5. I often feel worthless.
>
> In these items there is an underlying construct that informs the way in which people will respond. The construct is 'depressed mood'. Someone who is severely depressed will uniformly endorse all the items in the scoreable direction, while someone with no depression will not. To this extent the items are internally consistent in that they are all driven by a single underlying psychological phenomenon or construct.

We will look at two ways of estimating internal consistency, namely, split-halves reliability and item analysis.

Split-halves reliability

Split-halves reliability is somewhat different to the test–retest and equivalent-forms reliability. Rather than testing the consistency of instruments over multiple testings, the split-halves reliability method is concerned with the internal consistency of instruments. As a result, the problems of history, maturation, reactivity and equivalent forms do not plague this method. Therefore, it is more frequently used by social scientists than any of the other techniques. As the name implies, split-halves reliability involves splitting the test into halves and finding the extent of correspondence or reliability between the halves.

> ### Example
>
> A performance potential scale is developed to assess candidates for some middle management post at a bank. The evaluators are particularly concerned that their candidates should be highly resilient to stress. To assess the candidates they develop a test with 30 items, all addressing some aspect of stress resilience. These 30 items provide a summary picture of overall stress resilience.
>
> Each candidate completes the entire questionnaire. Then the set of 30 items is randomly divided into two sets of 15 items each. By comparing the results of these two sets, the concordance between the results is evaluated and the researchers are able to estimate the overall internal consistency of the 30-item measure.

If the participants respond in a similar way to the two groups of items, high reliability is indicated, that is, the instrument has high internal consistency. Apart from the random approach used above, there are other ways of dividing the test items into halves. Each different split will produce slightly different estimates of the instrument's reliability. Assigning each item to one of the groups on a random basis is most useful when there is some reason to suspect that there are systematic differences between the odd and even items. Dividing the instrument into a first half and a second half is not a good technique. This is because subjects will be less alert and interested in the second half of a test and the items and format will appear strange at the beginning of the test. For these reasons most researchers rely on the odd–even split.

Item analysis

A more detailed method for estimating the internal consistency of an instrument is found in **item analysis**. In this case, the researcher is interested in finding out how well the responses to each item correspond to the responses to the other items, and to the test as a whole. This helps the researcher to identify those items within an instrument which are not providing useful information about the subjects, or which are actually distorting the data. The researcher can then remove these troublesome items from the instrument (replacing them with better items if necessary) and thereby increase the overall reliability of the instrument.

> ### Example
>
> If a researcher was to collect a set of questions all relating to gender prejudice, and put them together, they might form a measuring instrument for gender prejudice . If this instrument was administered to a sample of a male population, which includes people who are more and less prejudiced than others, its internal consistency might be measured.
>
> *continued ...*

CHAPTER 13 Ensuring the quality of data

> If the more prejudiced people tend to respond in a similar way to each item, thus consistently demonstrating high gender prejudice, and the less prejudiced people also tend to respond in similar ways to each item, while consistently demonstrating low gender prejudice, the researcher could argue that the test has high internal consistency. However, if respondents tend to show high prejudice on some items but low prejudice on others, the researcher would be forced to conclude that the items are inconsistent and that the test has low internal consistency and is thus unreliable.
>
> The following two questions illustrate how some items may be useful measures of prejudice and others not.
> 1. How would you feel about having a woman to report to at work?
> 2. How would you feel about working with women?
>
> Item 1 is likely to be a more reliable measure of gender prejudice because of the particular relationship expressed by the words 'report to' which implies a power relationship. Item 2, on the other hand, is ambiguous about the nature of the suggested relationship. Some highly prejudiced men may have no objection to working with women, as long as women are of lower status and have less power than they have.

Often the researcher will measure the degree of match between each item and every other item in the instrument. Those items that give results contradictory to the others must be discarded. An overall test of internal consistency is also carried out often. This is usually done through the use of a statistic called the **coefficient of reliability**. One such coefficient that is commonly used is called Cronbach's alpha. The value of the coefficient of reliability always falls between 0 and 1. An instrument with no reliability will score 0 and an instrument with very high reliability will score close to 1. For the most part social scientists like to use instruments that have been shown to have a coefficient of reliability of at least 0,7.

Validity

Although validity and reliability are both important to the evaluation of an instrument, they are actually entirely different concepts. The term **validity** was used in Chapter 10 where the *internal and external validity of research designs* was discussed. This chapter is concerned with the *validity of data collection procedures and instruments* and, in this context, the term 'validity' has a somewhat different meaning. Where reliability asked the question 'how *accurate* and *consistent* is this instrument?', validity asks questions such as 'what does this instrument actually measure?' and 'what do the results actually mean?' Unless the researcher can be sure that the measurement techniques are actually measuring the things that they are supposed to be measuring, the results are difficult to interpret. For example, one would not use a thermometer to measure how tall someone is: a tape measure would be much more appropriate. A thermometer is an invalid measure of height, while a tape measure is a valid measure. An instrument with very high reliability is useless if it has poor validity.

229

Example

A school principal is concerned about the standard of teaching in her school. She constructs a spelling test and administers it to all the children in the school. To her surprise the pupils do far better than she had thought they would. A little confused, the principal goes back to her office to think. She begins to wonder if the pupils' spelling ability is really a good measure of teaching standards. It may be that even very poor teachers can teach spelling (especially to children with many opportunities for reading). To further investigate the teaching standards, the principal decides to sit in on a sample of classes every day and observe the teachers in action. After a very few days it becomes apparent that many of the teachers are relying on rote learning in the classroom, which may work very well for spelling, but is a very poor teaching method for most other subjects.

In this example, the spelling test was not measuring teaching standards at all, but one particular skill demonstrated by the pupils. As a result, the principal did not find out what she had hoped to. Observation of the teachers' actual practice proved to be a far better measure. In this case the spelling test was not a valid measure of teaching standards, while the observation technique was. The spelling test, however, may have a high reliability, higher even that the observation method (which depends on the observation style of the school principal), in spite of having poor validity.

In Chapter 10, in studying the validity of research design, we distinguished between internal and external validity. When dealing with the quality of measurements, there are also different types of validity. The five most important types of validity studied here are: content validity, criterion-related validity, construct validity, convergent validity, and face validity. Each of these is discussed in more detail below.

Content validity

In many cases, the topics that social scientists are most interested in are very complex and have many different components. In order to measure such complex topics properly, the researcher must find a technique which will provide some information on all of its different components. When one or more components is neglected, the researcher cannot really claim to be measuring whatever it is that he or she is interested in.

Example

A researcher is interested in the interpersonal skills of a group of hospital workers. However, 'interpersonal skills' is a very complex concept and therefore difficult to measure. A good instrument would have to include questions about how the respondents relate to their parents, their children, their friends, their employers, the patients in the hospital and the other staff in the hospital. A questionnaire with high content validity would have to enquire about the participant's behaviour in a wide variety of interpersonal situations. A questionnaire with poor content validity might neglect family relations, even overlooking communication with patients, and focus only upon the interviewees' relationships with their employers and colleagues.

CHAPTER 13 Ensuring the quality of data

Unfortunately, ensuring good content validity is usually far more complex than it sounds. In many cases social scientists cannot agree about what the essential components of any variable are. The next example describes some of the problems relating to research on 'power'.

Example

For the purposes of this research, power is defined as a person's ability to make others do as he or she wants them to do. A full list of the different ways of exerting power might include the use of force, threat, persuasion, influence and reward. However, some theorists would argue that the use of force and threat actually demonstrates an absence of power. Others would suggest that the use of rewards is not a form of power, but that threat and force are. In this case it would be very difficult for the researcher to decide what to include (or exclude) in a measurement procedure.

In the case where there is doubt about the definition of a concept (refer back to Chapter 6 for a discussion of conceptual definitions), it is the researcher's duty to decide upon an operational definition to guide the research and to substantiate that definition (where possible) on the basis of other research or theory. In other words, the researcher in the previous example might choose to define power as incorporating all the components listed above and would then have to explain why such a broad definition was chosen.

This raises the question of how the social scientist goes about measuring the content validity of a new instrument. In most cases this is achieved by referring to literature relating to the researcher's area of study. If the researcher can show that an instrument measures all the various components of the variable in question, he or she can be confident that the instrument has high content validity. In the absence of relevant literature, researchers sometimes ask other social scientists with experience in the relevant research area to evaluate the content validity of their measurement instruments.

Criterion-related validity

One way to test whether an instrument measures what it is expected to measure is to compare it to another measure that is known to be valid. This other measure is then called the **criterion measure**. If the data collected using the instrument in question closely matches the data collected using the criterion measure (which is assumed to be valid), then the researcher may conclude that the new instrument is also valid. Note that the two sets of data must be collected from the same group of subjects. In practice there are two different ways of doing this. When the instrument being tested and the criterion measure are administered at the same time, the term **concurrent validity** is used. When the instrument being tested is used to predict a future criterion, it is called **predictive validity**.

More often than not the researcher is forced to wait for some future event against which to measure an instrument. In the next example, the results of the criterion measure

231

are collected substantially later than the data from the instrument being evaluated. The original data is used to predict the results of the criterion measure.

Example

Using concurrent validity to evaluate a screening device
In communities that have been troubled by civil violence, many young adults (the people most likely to be caught up in conflict) often experience severe trauma and require specialised assistance. Unfortunately, it is quite difficult to identify the individuals most in need of help. To this end, a social scientist puts together a checklist of known symptoms relating to trauma as a screening device. In order to test the validity of this screening instrument, he compares the results of the screening test with the results of time-consuming clinical interviews (which are known to be capable of identifying people in need of help). When the results of the screening test match the results of the clinical interview, he is relieved to have found a valid (and efficient) way of identifying trauma survivors.

In this example, the test in question (the screening device) and the criterion measure (the clinical interview) were administered concurrently. Unfortunately, in most cases it is very difficult to find a suitable criterion that can be administered concurrently. Another, perhaps more common, way of dealing with the same problem is to compare the results of the screening test with an established test with proven reliability and validity.

Example

A researcher in the education sector has evidence that students' motivation is directly related to their final marks. She develops a questionnaire to measure motivation and administers it to a large group of students. On the basis of her results she is able to predict which students will do well and which will do badly in the final exams. At the end of the year the students write their final exams and the researcher is able to determine the accuracy of her predictions derived from a measure of their motivation at the beginning of the year.

The most important difficulty with this approach is that, in most cases, the criterion measure may have resulted from a wide range of variables, other than the specific one that the researcher is trying to test. In this case, students who could afford better textbooks or who had parents who demanded three hours of homework a day might do better than others who lack those advantages. Oversimplification of the relationships between variables can result in highly misleading results. Predictive validity should therefore only be used when the researcher is strongly convinced that the variable in question has a clear criterion measure against which a new instrument can be compared.

CHAPTER 13 Ensuring the quality of data

Construct validity

Construct validity is the extent to which scores on an instrument reflect the desired construct rather than some other construct. Unreliable scores cannot have any construct validity because they are mostly due to random error. However, reliable scores can reflect a construct other than the one that is being measured, for example, depression and social skills are correlated with one another, thus one could mistakenly use a measure of social skills to measure depression and think one was measuring depression. This would obviously be wrong.

Construct validity is the most important and most often used of the various forms of validity test discussed in this chapter. It is important that a measurement technique be closely linked with known theory in the area of research and with other related concepts. Where such close links can be demonstrated, the instrument is said to have high construct validity. When the links between the instrument and the related theory are very weak or non-existent, the instrument has low construct validity.

Chapter 12 of this text covers recommended procedures for the construction of questionnaires and interview schedules. The point was made that the researcher who begins by drafting questions is unlikely to create a useful instrument. Rather, the researcher should begin by making a list of the different pieces of information that the instrument is required to uncover and then design questions to acquire that information. By following this process, the researcher begins to link the items (and thus the instrument as a whole) to the theoretical components of the research topic, thereby contributing to construct validity.

Example

Consider the example, used earlier in this chapter, of youths traumatised by civil violence. Trauma of this kind is theoretically and logically linked to a range of other variables. One would expect highly traumatised youths to have been involved in more traumatic events than less traumatised youths. Also, school performance may drop as a result of the trauma. If the researcher can show that what his instrument measures (level of trauma) relates, as expected, to traumatic events in the person's history and to changes in school performance, he has begun to demonstrate that his instrument has construct validity.

The following three steps are necessary in order to establish construct validity.

1. Identify all of the variables that are strongly related to the variable that the test is designed to measure. This is done on the basis of theory, past research and logical deduction.
2. Measure all the variables involved and determine the relationships between them through the use of statistical tests.
3. Interpret and explain these relationships and develop an argument to demonstrate the construct validity (or lack thereof) of the instrument. The more variables, other than the one under study that can be shown to interrelate meaningfully, the better the construct validity.

233

Convergent validity

One way to establish construct validity is to determine whether the test has any convergent validity with other measures. **Convergent validity** is the relationship between the scale used and other scales that are intended to measure the same construct. There should obviously be a high correlation between instruments assessing the same construct. If this is the case there is said to be high convergent validity. Thus a measure of poverty might be correlated with a measure of literacy, as literacy is related to unemployment. Measures of constructs that are opposite in nature should be negatively correlated with each other. If there is indeed a negative correlation, then there is said to be discriminant validity. Thus scores on a measure of depression should be negatively correlated with scores of a measure of, for example, happiness.

Face validity

Face validity is somewhat different from the other four forms of validity discussed so far. Face validity is concerned with the way the instrument appears to the participant. It is important that an instrument be tailored to the needs of the participants for whom it is intended. Sometimes instruments may appear insultingly simplistic and, as a result, some participants will not take the social scientist or the research seriously. Other instruments may appear far too difficult to the participants, resulting in their giving up before they begin.

Example

A researcher interested in literacy wants to investigate the reading skills of people of different ages in a particular community. To do this he selects a Grade 8 textbook, fully expecting younger children to find it more difficult and adults to find it very easy. When he presents this text to younger children who find it very difficult, they give up without really trying and he cannot get a meaningful measurement of their reading skill. Similarly, he discovers that adults find the content of the reading matter childish and boring and feel insulted. Again, he cannot find a valid measure of reading skill. This approach obviously has very low face validity. After some careful thought, the researcher tries a different approach. He gathers a selection of reading matter suited to a wide range of reading skills. He then gives each age group a reading test that is comparable to their skill. In this way he gains data about the reading skills of people of all ages in the community.

There are many factors apart from the level of complexity that influence an instrument's face validity. Some personality tests tend to ask the same questions in different ways in order to check that the subject is not responding arbitrarily. If this is not done in a very subtle way, subjects may begin to think that the researcher is checking up on them and again react negatively to the instrument.

CHAPTER 13 Ensuring the quality of data

Balancing reliability with validity

Both reliability and validity are important for every instrument. It does not help the researcher to use a highly reliable instrument that has no validity. What is the use of an extremely accurate and consistent technique when one does not know what it is measuring or if it is measuring an (for this research) irrelevant concept? Similarly, an instrument with high validity is useless unless it can be shown to be also reliable. What does it help to measure something when the measurements are not consistent? It is possible for an instrument to have high reliability and low validity. However, it is not possible for an instrument to have low reliability and high validity.

> ### Example
>
> Two researchers set out to measure the quality of hospital care in Lagos. Researcher A measures the quality of each hospital's service by calculating the average number of patients discharged in a day. Researcher B interviews one nurse and one patient at random from each hospital about the quality of healthcare at that hospital. The results that the two researchers come up with are very different, even though they intend to measure the same thing. Obviously something is wrong in the way the researchers are measuring healthcare.
>
> In this example researcher A has chosen to focus on reliability at the expense of validity. Although she is likely to find very consistent results, the number of patients discharged daily is a very poor measure of hospital care. Some hospitals can treat more patients because of better equipment and management but it might also simply be because each patient gets less attention than they would in other hospitals. Researcher B has made the opposite mistake. He has focused on validity at the expense of reliability. Although the perceptions of nurses and patients are probably a valid measure of healthcare, the results depend heavily upon which nurse and patient are chosen, what kind of day they have had and various other variables.

Unfortunately, social scientists often find that reliability drops as validity increases. For example, exploratory interviews are generally considered to be highly valid because they allow the researcher to discuss issues with the respondents in greater depth. However, exploratory interviews require a good deal of subjective interpretation of the interviewees' responses on the part of the researcher and this reduces their reliability (another researcher may interpret the same responses differently or even get different responses from the participants). A set of rating scales put together in a questionnaire would be far more reliable (rating scales require no interpretation). However, this is likely to be far less valid since the researcher would not able to check that the respondents understand the questions in the same way as they are intended, and would also be unable to follow up on interesting responses.

The real skill in designing good measurement techniques involves finding a technique that is adequate in terms of both reliability and validity. No technique is perfectly reliable or valid but, unless an instrument can be shown to be well constructed in terms of both these principles, it should not be used in social research.

235

Qualitative research: Ensuring trustworthiness

Why are the concepts of reliability and validity not suitable for evaluating the quality of qualitative research?

In quantitative research, the reality under observation is viewed as a composite of the elements to be 'measured', and thus it is necessary to develop a measuring instrument. The first concern refers thus to the quality of that instrument: does it measure 'correctly', giving the same result in a constant way (its reliability) and does it really measure what it is expected to measure, as determined by the expectations and definitions expressed in a hypothesis, for instance (its validity)? The situation is quite different in qualitative research, where there is no hypothesis to be tested and the emphasis is on the understanding of a certain phenomenon within the complexity of its natural context. The methodology of the investigation is a more flexible one and does not demand measurement. Moreover, qualitative research seldom begins with *a priori* operational definitions. As such the concepts of reliability and validity, as used in quantitative research, lose their meaning when applied to qualitative research.

Another major difference between quantitative and qualitative research is the role of the researcher. In the former, objectivity and detachment are essential, since results must be independent of the researcher. In the latter, the researcher, as a self-critical, thoughtful, curious and trustworthy human being, is the instrument through which the world is studied. The depth and quality of the research depend on the skills and sensitivity of the researcher. Detachment and objectivity are neither possible, nor desirable.

Trustworthiness

Obviously, this does not absolve the qualitative researcher of the need to evaluate the quality of the research, but in qualitative research this is done in terms of how much trust can be given to the research process and the findings. Thus we speak of **trustworthiness**. Note that social scientists are still divided on terminology related to the quality of research, and one might find different versions of the basic principles outlined here in other texts. The concept of trustworthiness evaluates the quality of quantitative research on the basis of four concepts: credibility, dependability, transferability and confirmability.

Credibility

Credibility corresponds to the concept of internal validity, since it seeks to convince that the findings depict the truth of the reality under study, or, in other words, that they make sense. Studies with high credibility are those in which the researcher has convincingly demonstrated the appropriateness and overall internal logic of the research questions, the study design, the data collection method and the approach to data analysis used. The

CHAPTER 13 Ensuring the quality of data

researcher must be able to defend the design and methodology choices made in terms of current theory and knowledge about the field. For example, a study that uses a broad descriptive methodology but is then published as a test of a specific theory might be criticised on the basis of credibility. It is not reasonable to test a particular theory on the basis of a broad description. Similarly, a study that is designed around the conceptual framework of a very specific theory but then claims to describe the real-life experience of a group of people would be criticised on the same grounds. You cannot describe the real-life experience of people when you have already assumed a particular theoretical framework.

Dependability

Dependability as a concept is similar to, but not the same as, reliability. Dependability demands that the researcher thoroughly describes and precisely follows a clear and thoughtful research strategy. The researcher must show that each step has been completed thoroughly and carefully. Thus, when a researcher fails to describe the method of sampling in detail, even if he shows that the method was properly applied, the critical reviewer will have less trust in the results derived from that sample. On the other hand, when a researcher describes exactly how data was collected, recorded, coded and analysed, and can present good examples to illustrate this process, one starts to trust that the results are in fact dependable.

Transferability

Transferability can be compared to external validity since it refers to the extent to which results apply to other, similar, situations. It requires the researcher to provide detailed descriptions of the context in which the data was collected, about the researcher as a person, and about her relationships with the participants, etc. This information allows other researchers to compare and assess the similarities between that given situation and other settings or contexts, that is, on the transferability of the findings. When we understand the context from which the findings emerge deeply and can imagine several other contexts where such findings might be meaningful, we can speak of a study having high transferability.

Confirmability

Confirmability, which is similar to replicability, requires that other researchers or observers be able to obtain similar findings by following a similar research process in a similar context. The researcher is also expected to present a critical evaluation of the methodology used. When another researcher understands precisely what you did, why you did it, and in what context you did it, he or she should be able to replicate your work in another context and predict if, and how, the results might be different. The

237

broader endeavour that is social science depends upon the possibility of new studies repeating, elaborating, challenging and even defeating old studies. Confirmability makes this possible.

When credibility, dependability, transferability and confirmability are all high we can speak of the research being highly trustworthy, or having high quality. Bear in mind that the rigour of the way in which qualitative data is analysed is also important. We will return to this topic in Chapter 15.

Tools for increasing research trustworthiness

Adequate description of context: Because qualitative research emphasises the context in which the study takes place, detailed descriptions of the researcher, the participants, their relationship, and the context in which they find themselves are essential.

Adequate description of the sample and the sampling procedure: As in quantitative research it is imperative that the researcher adequately describes the sampling procedure used and the sample that actually participated in the research. This includes describing the criteria of inclusion and exclusion and the sampling strategy used.

Concurrent data collection and analysis: By analysing data as it is being collected, the researcher can refine the data collection approach in relation to the emerging results. For example, the analysis of initial results might highlight a particular aspect of the investigation that the researcher was not previously aware of. In this case the researcher might include that aspect in future data collection procedures. This might mean, for example, adding a question to an interview schedule, or even interviewing a different type of person.

Triangulation: Triangulation is the method most frequently used to verify and increase the trustworthiness of qualitative research. It involves combining several different research methodologies to investigate the same phenomenon. The purpose of doing this is to show that the results obtained are independent of the methodology used. If a researcher develops two or three separate data sets in response to a particular research question, and the analysis of these various data sets reveals very different sets of results, the researcher must confront the problem that the method of data collection seems to have a great influence on the results and so the trustworthiness of those results must be low. However, if the results are complementary, the researcher can be much more confident in the trustworthiness of his research. There are several different types of triangulation. *Methodological triangulation* requires that different methods of data collection are used. For example, data from in-depth interviews might be compared with data from direct observation. *Theoretical triangulation* implies the use of different theoretical perspectives in the interpretation of data. For example, how do the results of a thematic content analysis differ from the results of a narrative analysis. (We discuss

CHAPTER 13 Ensuring the quality of data

the analysis of qualitative data further in Chapter 15.) *Data triangulation* is used when the researcher applies the same method of data collection and analysis to different research participants. For example, the researcher might collect most of the data from university students but show that the results are transferable to young people in the working world by collecting data from a small group of young working people and showing that the pattern of findings is essentially the same. Finally, using a variety of researchers leads to *investigator triangulation*, which brings great diversity in the gathering as well as the interpreting of data.

Methodological verification: This is the process of having other experienced researchers verifying the logic and implementation of each step of the methodology. Because qualitative research is more flexible, it often happens that important changes take place after the study has begun. Decisions about such changes must be made with great care and in consultation with other researchers. In this way the individual researcher can justify and explain the methodological choices that have been made.

Ensuring data saturation: While qualitative research is not concerned with representative samples in the statistical sense, the researcher must be able to show that enough data has been collected to reflect the full range and depth of the topic of the research. This is achieved by the researcher demonstrating that the addition of further data is adding virtually no new information to what has already been learnt so far. When this occurs the researcher has some evidence for believing the topic has been exhausted.

Respondent validation: Respondent validation (sometimes called member checking or informant feedback) is a process whereby the researcher presents the results of a study to the people who provided the original data and asks for their feedback. The researcher is interested in whether the participants feel that the results and conclusions drawn correctly reflect the experience of the participants. In the case where participants' feedback shows that the researcher hasn't really understood part or all of their experience, the researcher would need to look more closely at the differences discussed. This might entail a different focus in the analysis, or it might mean collecting more data, or even introducing a change of methodology.

Use of sufficient verbatim quotations: By including many direct quotations from the original data in research reports, the researcher allows the reader to hear exactly what respondents said and how the researcher interpreted that information. In so doing the researcher amplifies the voices of respondents and illustrates some details of the process of data analysis. This is another important characteristic of rigorous qualitative research.

The following example illustrates the use of some of these tools.

Example

In research into the support systems needed by alcoholics following a detox and rehabilitation programme, the researcher begins by interviewing alcoholics while they are still working through the programme inside the rehabilitation centre. After interviewing a few people with semi-structured questionnaires and analysing the data, the interviewer realises that the data is very quickly reaching saturation (that is, nothing new is emerging) and wonders whether a different approach to data collection might not be valuable. She discusses this problem with several of her colleagues who are skilled and experienced in qualitative research. With their advice and support (methodological verification) she decides to ask alcoholics to relate stories about when support did and did not help them to beat their addiction. (This is a different approach to data collection called narrative interviewing.) This approach proves much more useful and the data is rich and interesting. Again, after a time the researcher begins to feel that very little new is emerging from the data (saturation). At this point she begins to interview staff at the rehabilitation centre about their thoughts on alcoholics' need for support (data triangulation). The staff makes some points that have not been mentioned by the recovering alcoholics themselves. To explore this difference more she organises a focus group involving both recovering alcoholics and staff who work at the centre (methodological triangulation). She asks a colleague to facilitate this focus group (investigator triangulation) as she feels that fresh eyes on the project might be help.

When our researcher feels that she has collected sufficient data, she sits down to analyse her various data sets. Based on her analysis she comes back to the rehabilitation centre to report back to all the people who participated in her study. A lengthy discussion follows and her respondents mention many points of agreement, but also correct some details in her understanding (respondent validation).

Finally, when the researcher writes up her research report she makes sure that she describes every detail of her methodology and sample. She also describes the centre in detail, and writes about her relationship with both the recovering alcoholics and the staff. In presenting her results she uses many direct quotes from her interviews and focus group, and even quotes from the respondent validation meeting (verbatim quotation).

Scientific rigour in mixed-methods research

The mixed-methods researcher employs both quantitative and qualitative research methods in the same study. As such, methodological triangulation is built into every mixed-method study by definition. This is an important strength of mixed-methods research.

However, the mixed-methods researcher is still required to demonstrate the rigour of both the quantitative and qualitative aspects of the research as well. Thus the quality of the quantitative parts of a study is evaluated in terms of the different forms of reliability and validity discussed earlier in this chapter. Similarly, the quality of the qualitative parts of a study is evaluated in terms of the various dimensions of trustworthiness. In addition, the researcher using mixed-methods must explain the reasons, timing and

CHAPTER 13 Ensuring the quality of data

methods used to combine qualitative and quantitative research. In other words, the researcher must discuss the process of mixing.

Example

The Department of Arts and Culture, in collaboration with the Ministry of Basic Education, is interested in the conservation of cultural values and their propagation to the young. They intend investigating the role and attitude of primary school teachers regarding the teaching of cultural values at school. The understanding that teachers have of their responsibilities as culture transmitters, as well as the impact it has on children, is to be explored.

The researchers decide to utilise a variety of methods to clarify concepts, such as 'cultural values', and gather the required information. They have one-on-one interviews with some teachers, they organise some focus groups of teachers from various grades and schools, they interview some of the parents of the school governing body, as well as some members of the older (the grandparents') generation within the community. They then expend their research through the participation of the school children themselves, using story-telling methods to assess the actual cultural knowledge of the children. As such, they use a diversification of sampling procedures and samples. Moreover, many well-trained investigators are involved in the gathering and interpretation of the information in order to increase the breadth of the analysis.

The essential advantage of the mixed-method here is the enhancement of credibility of the research where convergence of the findings is evident. Clearly, when findings do no correspond, this information allows the researchers to question and improve the research in all its aspects.

Example

Coming back to the previous example of the research by the Department of Arts and Culture, an additional request has been expressed: quantitative data and a statistical analysis have to be provided on the position of teachers and parents regarding the responsibility of the school system as a transmitter of cultural values. The researchers therefore develop a questionnaire based on some of the information gathered through focus groups, such as the concepts and expectations around cultural values, which they then test for reliability and validity before presenting the questionnaire to a representative sample of teachers and parents in the context of a structured interview. Finally, the researchers express, in terms of percentages, the position of teachers who see themselves as transmitters of cultural norms, and those who do not see this as a part of their responsibilities. The attitudes and expectations of the parents about the role of schools as transmitters of cultural values are also expressed in terms of statistics. This expanded triangulation method reinforces the data gathered through qualitative methods.

In conclusion, when investigating and aiming at understanding reality, the necessity of ensuring the quality of data often results in the researcher adopting a mixed-method type of research. In so doing, she is able to bring the strength and advantages of both the rigour of quantitative research and the exploratory power of qualitative research to the project at hand.

Key points

1. Due to the nature and aims of quantitative and qualitative research, the definitions, methods and instruments related to the quality of the data are different.
2. Whereas in quantitative research the establishment and measurement of the reliability and validity of measurement occur at a early stage, ensuring the trustworthiness and quality of the data is an on-going process when using qualitative methodology.
3. In both cases many criteria and instruments are available to ensure quality as well as to identify dangers and pitfalls.
4. One powerful method of increasing the quality of data that can be utilised within both quantitative research and qualitative research, as well as when using a combination of the two methods, is called triangulation. It consists of studying a phenomenon by adopting different angles or perspectives and applying various methods of investigation to the process.
5. One of the major differences between quantitative and qualitative research is the role of the researcher: in the former case, objectivity and detachment are essential since results must be replicable, that is, independent of the researcher, in the latter instance, the researcher is the instrument' and the depth and quality of the findings depend on the skills and sensitivity of the interviewer.
6. Moreover, as it is possible in quantitative research to assess the quality of the entire process and in particular that of the instrument to be used for data collection at the beginning of the study, the pursuit of quality in qualitative research is a continuous process.
7. In quantitative research, the several types of reliability include test–retest reliability, equivalent form reliability, inter-rater reliability and internal consistency. The several types of validity considered are content validity, criterion-related validity, construct validity, convergent validity and face validity. Balancing reliability with validity is essential.
8. In qualitative research, trustworthiness is based on credibility, dependability, transferability and confirmability, and there are specific tools to ensure the trustworthiness of research.
9. In mixed-methods research, the methods and instruments of both quantitative and qualitative research are used.

CHAPTER 13 Ensuring the quality of data

Checklist

Keywords:

Check whether the meaning of these concepts introduced in this chapter is clear to you.

reliability: test–retest, equivalent-for, split-halves reliability, item analysis, internal consistency; validity: content, criterion-related, construct, convergent, face validity; trustworthiness: credibility, transferability, dependability, confirmability; triangulation.

Your research:
1. Ensure that any quantitative measures that you have selected or developed have acceptable levels of reliability and validity.
2. In qualitative research, check that you have used as many of the tools for increasing trustworthiness as possible.
3. Check that you have fully described your research instruments' validity, reliability or trustworthiness in any proposals, reports or articles.

Exercises

1. Explain why the criteria and methods to ensure quality of data are different in the case of quantitative and qualitative research.
2. Try to think of different ways of measuring each of the following variables, then evaluate each technique that you have thought of in terms of its reliability and validity. For each variable choose the technique which you think would be the best:
   a. the income of families
   b. a person's employment potential
   c. child's social support.
3. What do you understand by the terms 'reliability' and validity'? Is a valid measure always reliable? Explain your answer.
4. Do an internet search to find a scale of time management and develop an equivalent form.
   Using the first example presented in this chapter on travelling from home to the factory, if one of the variables to measure (in the frame of a quantitative research) is the fatigue occasioned by travelling as experienced by the workers, develop three questions to ask them. Then analyse the adequacy of the questions in terms of reliability and validity of the type of answers.
5. Using the same example, how could the fatigue experienced be measured using a qualitative research method, and how could one assess the quality of the result?
6. Using the same example, how could one use triangulation to ensure the quality of the data?
7. Select a (quantitative or qualitative) research article and discuss the reliability and validity of the measures of the variables used in it.

243

Additional resources

1. Golafshani, N. 2003. 'Understanding Reliability and Validity in Qualitative Research', *The Qualitative report*, 4, 597–607.
2. Olsen, W K. 2004. Triangulation in Social Research: Quantitative and Qualitative Methods Can Really Be Mixed, in M. Holborn and Haralambos (Eds) *Developments in Sociology*, London: Causeway Press.
3. Onu, J I. 2002. *Report of Social Capital Household Survey Pilot in Adamawa State, Nigeria*, downloaded from http://siteresources.worldbank.org/INTSOCIALCAPITAL/Resources/Social-Capital-Integrated-Questionnaire/AdamawaStatePilotRptShortVersionAug02.pdf. Accessed on 1 December 2012.
4. Patton, M Q. 2001. *Qualitative Research and Evaluation Methods*. Thousand Oaks, CA: Sage.
5. Worldbank. *Instruments of the Social Capital Assessment Tool*, downloaded from http://siteresources.worldbank.org/INTSOCIALCAPITAL/Resources/Social-Capital-Assessment-Tool--SOCAT-/annex1.pdf . Accessed on 1 December 2012.

Quantitative data analysis and interpretation

CHAPTER 14

The distinction between quantitative and qualitative research has been introduced and systematically presented from the beginning of this book. This chapter addresses the understanding of and techniques specific to quantitative research. It thus concentrates on one of the most important basis of quantitative methodology: the testing of hypotheses. Due to its nature, the topic requires a certain use of statistics, but only at an elementary level. Statistical computations are left to the use of statistical software programmes and are thus beyond the scope of this chapter. Quantitative analysis leads to the interpretation of the outcomes by rejecting, or not, the null hypothesis based of how statistically significant the results are.

> **CHAPTER OBJECTIVES**
>
> Learners who have completed this chapter will be able to:
> - Represent the collected data through tables, graphs and charts.
> - Describe their data using measures of central tendencies and dispersion.
> - Understand and put to use hypothesis testing procedures.
> - Differentiate between different statistical tests and select the most appropriate one according to the characteristics of the research in question.
> - Differentiate between causal and correlational situations and, in both cases, test the significance of the results.
> - Apply correlation and regression analysis.

PART I: DESCRIPTIVE STATISTICS

Data representation: Frequency distributions and tables

The purpose of this section is to show how a set of information collected, the raw data, can be organised in a meaningful way and presented so as to reveal or enhance its fundamental properties. The first step is to reorganise the raw data in the form of a frequency distribution, of which various types exist. Often, it is also useful to present the data in a contingency table subdivided into many categories where the data is grouped according to specific criteria.

The presentation done in this book presumes that students will use statistical software for computations. Thus no formulae will be given and the aim of the presentation is to deepen the understanding of the process, facilitate the selection of the most appropriate test(s), and assist in the correct interpretation of the results.

Let us illustrate the process of data representation using research investigating the level of job satisfaction of nurses. The instrument of measurement is a questionnaire where the respondent has to indicate her level of satisfaction for a range of issues, on a scale varying from very unsatisfied to very satisfied. These scores are then combined into an index where 1 indicates a total dissatisfaction and 10 a total satisfaction with the job. The sample of 200 respondents includes three professional levels (matron, qualified nurse, assistant nurse) and is conducted in four government hospitals. The researcher thus obtains 200 figures varying from 1 to 10. These results, recorded as they are, are called the **raw data**.

The challenge is to present these data in a meaningful way in order to address the aim of the research. This is shown in Table 14.1 below: First, all the scores are recorded in order (1st column) as well as the number of times each one appears (2nd column). This number is called the **frequency** (f) of the scores.

However, in order to compare results, it is better to express the frequencies as percentages. The percentages expressed in terms of the 200 items of data are indicated in the 3rd column: one can read that 23% of the respondents (46 out of the 200) have a score of 6 points. The 4th column $c\%$ indicates the cumulative percentages, that is, for example, that the majority (65%) of the respondents do not score more than 5.

The next step is to take one of the variables of the research, in this case, the different professional levels of the nurses, and classify, in the same way, their scores and frequencies. Again, since the sample sizes of these groups are not the same, it is very useful to express all the results as percentages. The data organised by professional levels indicate that 36% of all matrons but only 14% of the assistant nurses have a score of 6 and that no assistant nurse scores above 7.

Table 14.1 *Job satisfaction among nurses by professional level*						
Scores	Total			Professional level		
	f	%	$c\%$	Matron	Qualified nurse	Assistant nurse
1	4	2	2	0 (0%)	1 (1%)	3 (4,5%)
2	14	7	9	0 (0%)	4 (4%)	10 (14%)
3	20	10	19	1 (3%)	5 (5%)	14 (20%)
4	48	24	43	2 (7%)	25 (25%)	21 (30%)
5	44	22	65	2 (7%)	32 (32%)	10 (14%)
6	46	23	88	11 (36%)	25 (25%)	10 (14%)
7	16	8	96	8 (27%)	6 (6%)	2 (3,5%)
8	4	2	98	3 (10%)	1 (1%)	0 (0%)
9	3	1,5	99,5	2 (7%)	1 (1%)	0 (0%)
10	1	0,5	100	1 (3%)	0 (0%)	0 (0%)
TOTAL	200	100	100	30 (100%)	100 (100%)	70 (100%)

CHAPTER 14 Quantitative data analysis and interpretation

Taking the other variable of the research, the four government hospitals where the interviewed nurses work, the same process gives rise to the following table.

Table 14.2 *Job satisfaction among nurses by place of work*

Scores	Total	Hospitals			
	f (%)	A	B	C	D
1	4 (2%)	0 (0%)	0 (0%)	1 (2%)	3 (6%)
2	14 (7%)	1 (2%)	4 (8%)	4 (7%)	5 (10%)
3	20 (10%)	2 (4%)	5 (11%)	6 (11%)	7 (14%)
4	48 (24 %)	4 (8%)	12 (26%)	14 (25%)	18 (36%)
5	44 (22%)	4 (8%)	11 (23%)	20 (36%)	9 (18%)
6	46 (23%)	24 (50%)	10 (21%)	6 (11%)	6 (12%)
7	16 (8%)	8 (16%)	3 (6%)	3 (5%)	2 (4%)
8	4 (2%)	2 (4%)	1 (2%)	1 (2%)	0 (0%)
9	3 (1,5%)	2 (4%)	1 (2%)	0 (0%)	0 (0%)
10	1 (0,5%)	1 (2%)	0 (0%)	0 (0%)	0 (0%)
TOTAL	200 (100%)	48	47	55	50

In this case one can observe some difference between the four hospitals. The nurses from Hospital A score higher for job satisfaction than those working at Hospital D.

Once a frequency distribution of a set of data has been performed, the next step is to find the simplest and most adequate way to present it according to the type of data and the aim of the study. This is called a **contingency table**.

A more complex table than the two presented above could be constructed, taking into account and combining all the variables. For instance, one might include the professional level of the nurses within the different hospitals and variables, such as age and gender, where each cell contains the frequency of this category. In Table 14.3, an extract is presented as an example: only the professional levels and the hospitals are considered.

247

Fundamentals of Social Research Methods: An African Perspective

Table 14.3 *Contingency table: Job satisfaction among nurses by professional level in different hospitals*

Scores	Total		Professional level										
	f	%	Matron				Qualified nurse				Assistant nurse		
			A	B	C	D	A	B	C	D	A	B	C	D
1														
2														
3														

The purpose of contingency tables is to clearly present, in a comprehensive and orderly manner, the data that are classified by different criteria. The actual frequency of each category as well as its percentage should be given. Often, it is easier to compare percentages rather than frequencies. This is especially true when the various samples are not of the same size. For instance, Table 14.2 shows the results of the samples drawn from the four hospitals by percentage. These samples are of different sizes and their composition in terms of the percentage of matrons, nurses and assistant nurses might differ.

Often, when the data are very large and scattered, it is useful to group them into '**class-intervals**'. This would be the case if, instead of scores varying from 1 to 10, the scores of the nurses' job satisfaction were an agglomerate of different scales, that is, an index (see Chapter 12) with scores varying from 0 to 100. A simplified version of Table 14.1 for the sample of matrons, might then look like Table 14.4 below.

Table 14.4 *Job satisfaction among nurses using class-intervals*

Class-intervals	Total frequencies	Frequencies for matrons
0–10	4	0
11–20	14	0
21–30	20	1
31–40	48	2
41- 50	44	2
51–60	46	11
61–70	16	8
71–80	4	3
81–90	3	2
91–100	1	1
	Total 200	Total 30

Here, the 48 scores which are in the interval 31–40 can be any figure between 31 and 40. The intervals are represented by their **interval-midpoint** and one distinguishes between the **stated interval limits** and the **real interval limits**. Clearly, the stated limits are the ones indicated on the table: 31 and 40 for the 4th interval, but which interval does the space between two consecutive intervals, for instance, the space between 30 and 31 or between 40 and 41, belong to? This introduces the notion of 'real limits' where consecutive intervals 'touch' each other: 30,5 is the **real lower limit** and 40,5 is the **real upper limit** of that 4th interval. The real limits also allow one to calculate the midpoint of a given interval as the sum of its real limits divided by 2. The midpoint of the 4th interval is thus 35,5. Finally, the real limits allow also us to calculate the **size** of an interval as the difference between the real upper limit and the real lower limit.

It is important to note that some precautions must be taken to ensure clarity of presentation. The contingency table must be given a comprehensive, explanatory title. The headings of the columns and rows must be unambiguous and the groups must be independent, that is, the categories must be mutually exclusive. In the above tables, the limits of the class-intervals are clearly defined and the intervals do not overlap. This ensures that each result can be classified in one, and only one, category. The totals for each category and subcategory (grand total and subtotals) must be indicated at the end of each row and each column. The units of the data should be stated, whether they are frequencies, percentages, etc. In the case of secondary data, the source of the data must be indicated.

Graphical representation of data

Once raw data has been organised into a frequency distribution it can be visually represented by various types of graphs and charts (bars, pies and other pictorial representations). Graphical representations have the great advantage of allowing one to grasp the main characteristics of the information immediately. Through these representations, comparison of the different components or fluctuations in numbers or percentages over time (like the annual fluctuations of production or investment in a certain industry over a period of 10 years) is clearly visible without the use of numbers.

Although a frequency distribution describes a set of data, it still remains a list of figures, which has to be studied carefully to get information, for instance, on the variations in the data. There are ways of depicting a frequency distribution in order to allow an immediate grasp of its characteristics. These are based on *visual* representation, where numerical relationships are expressed as spatial relationships. Directly related to frequency distributions are frequency polygons and histograms, and other types of graphs, diagrams and charts are often useful as well. All of these visual representations communicate data in much the same way that a photograph of a person tells you about that person.

249

The main idea underlying visual representations is that a certain value, together with its frequency of occurrence, can be depicted, either by a point within a two-dimensional framework, or by a bar (or other figure), where its height or area is proportional to the frequency and indicates the relative size of the category. Joining the different points into a curve, or placing the various bars near one another, illustrates the fluctuation of the frequency for the different values (be it nominal, ordinal or interval scale) and allows them to be compared easily.

The two categories of graphical representation presented here are *graphs* and *charts*. A **graph** is a graphical representation of data by a continuous line within the framework of two orthogonal axes, the horizontal axis or x-axis, and the vertical or y-axis. This is not necessarily a smooth line (it can be a 'stepped' line, as is the case of histograms or a line 'with corners' such as polygons) but it is nevertheless called a **curve**. Graphs can be used in a general way to illustrate the variations of any two variables x and y, and social scientists tend to use one specific type of graph, where the variable y denotes the frequency of the variable x, that is, **graphs depicting frequency distributions**. Although graphs are easy to construct, there are some *basic rules* which must be observed. Nowadays of course, it often suffices to enter the data into a statistical programme which will automatically produce excellent graphs.

Suppose that the salary received by the nurses in our example is identified as one factor influencing their job satisfaction. One might represent the various salary scales (in any currency) of certified nurses on the horizontal axis and the frequency (number of nurses at each pay grade) on the vertical axis. But, if one is interested in the variation of the average salary of nurses over a period of 10 years, one might indicate the 10 years under study on the horizontal axis and record the corresponding average salary on the vertical axis. The line joining all the points would represent these variations.

A **histogram** or, more precisely, a **frequency histogram**, is used to illustrate a frequency distribution by representing its class-intervals and their respective frequencies in the following way:
1. Two orthogonal axes are used as a frame – the horizontal axis is used to represent the length (or size) of the intervals, whereas the vertical axis refers to the frequencies (f).
2. Corresponding to each interval and its frequency is the surface of a rectangle or *bar*. The length of the interval forms the base of the bar and the bar's height represents the given frequency.

A **frequency polygon** distinguishes itself from the histogram in so far as it is a curve (usually not smooth) obtained by joining the points which represent the frequencies above the midpoint of each interval. However, whereas a histogram starts with the real lower limit of the first interval and stops with the real upper limit of the last interval, a frequency polygon starts at the midpoint of the interval preceding the first one, with a frequency of zero, and stops at the midpoint of the interval following the last interval of the distribution, also with a frequency of zero. This means that the curve joins the *x*-axis at each end and, in so doing, completes the formation of a polygon.

The construction of a frequency polygon is similar to that of a histogram, except that in the first step only the midpoints of the intervals are indicated, including the ones of the two extreme intervals, and that, in the third step, instead of drawing bars, the frequency points above adjacent midpoints are connected by straight lines, as illustrated in Figure 14.1. which combines histogram and frequency polygon representations.

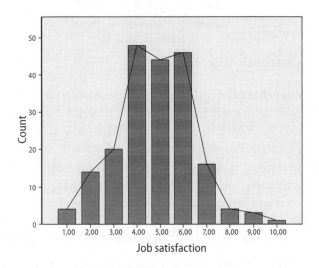

Figure 14.1 *Histogram of nurses' job satisfaction*

Charts refer to any other type of two-dimensional visual representation. Some of them are drawn within an orthogonal framework, like bar charts, but use bars rather than curves. Others use various pictures or geometrical shapes without any frame, like pie charts or pictograms. The basic rules for these are all the same, as those discussed above. There are, however, a few modifications.

Bar charts, whether simple, component or multiple, are not very different from histograms in their construction. They illustrate the magnitude of certain values, measured usually on a discrete nominal scale, whereas histograms usually represent the frequencies of values measured on a continuous interval scale. Therefore, whereas the bars of a histogram have common limits between class-intervals and thus touch one another, the bars of a bar chart are of arbitrary width and separated from one another. Only in the case of a multiple bar chart are they organised into sets, which are spatially separated. Bar charts are very useful for the comparison of categories in terms of their quantities at a certain time, or their variation over time.

Simple bar charts represent data by a series of bars where the height of each bar indicates the size of the figure or value represented, but the width is the same for all bars. This is illustrated in Figure 14.2 that represents the scores of the job satisfaction of nurses according to their professional level.

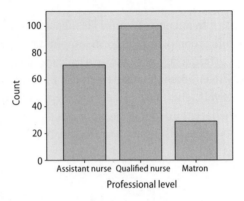

Figure. 14.2 *Simple bar chart of nurses' job satisfaction*

Finally, a **multiple bar chart** allows the representation of many variables simultaneously. It is used when more than one relationship has to be depicted. For instance, if the 'time' factor is considered, by collecting data on job satisfaction at fixed intervals over a period of years, a multiple bar chart would offer the possibility of comparing all the components within a given period, as well as each component for different periods. Using the previous example, one might be interested in studying nurses' job satisfaction as it is spread over various hospitals, or as it fluctuates by professional level for each of those hospitals. Table 14.1. allows us to compare the differences of job satisfaction as it relates to professional levels. Here actual data or percentages can be used.

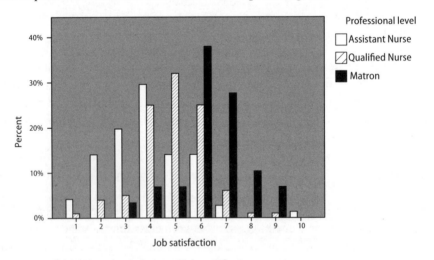

Figure 14.3 *Multiple bar chart of nurses' job satisfaction*

Pie charts are diagrams that do not rely on bars of different heights, but use a circle subdivided into sections by radial lines. Its name comes from the analogy of a pie that is cut into slices. The area of each 'slice' is proportional to the size of the figure represented. It is a very simple method of representing various components and their relationship to the whole.

CHAPTER 14 Quantitative data analysis and interpretation

Using Table 14.1 on page 246 and grouping the data into three categories, one obtains:
1. 0–4: 43% of respondents not satisfied
2. 5–6: 45% of respondents with moderate satisfaction
3. 7–10: 12% respondents very satisfied.

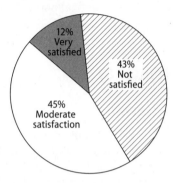

Figure 14.4 *Pie chart of nurses' job satisfaction*

A pictogram is a diagram using pictures to represent data, and is used in particular when addressing a very general readership, since its meaning is conveyed in a very simple way. It uses two techniques: the magnitude of the value is represented either by the number of pictures shown, or by the size of the picture.

Let us represent every 10 infant deaths per 1 000 births by 👶 , a picture of a baby.

Now we can present and compare infant mortality rates for different countries or for different years. Have a look at the following data taken from UNICEF's infant mortality data that compares the number of infant deaths in 2010 for four different South African countries.

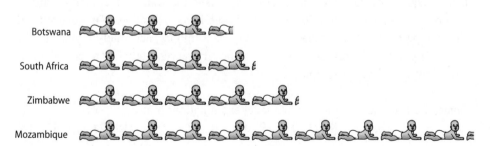

Figure 14.5 *Pictogram of infant mortality in four southern African countries in 2010*

(Unicef, ChildInfo: Monitoring the Situation of Women and Children, downloaded from www.childinfo.org.)

With a quick glance you can tell that the rate of infant deaths in Mozambique is approximately twice that of South Africa. By counting babies you can easily calculate that Mozambique's infant mortality rate is just over 90 deaths per 1 000 births.

The representation is not very accurate. However, pictograms can be a very useful way to communicate information for educational purposes, especially when addressing people with low levels of literacy and numeracy.

Measures of central tendency

Central tendency and its meaning

The term **central tendency of a distribution** describes a value that gives a general description of the bulk of the data, in essence, an idea of the location of all the scores. In everyday life, one can speak of the average income of workers as well as of the opinion of the average citizen on the quality of health services. There usually seems to be a way of representing the majority of the results or facts. A more scientific approach allows us to distinguish between different kinds of measurements of a central value, depending on the criteria chosen. Is one interested in assessing the result occurring most often, or the one dividing the set of scores into two equal parts, or a sort of average? These three possibilities will be examined below.

The mode

At first sight, when looking at a set of data, one is attracted by the value that occurs more often than any other. If one describes the Twa of Congo as people who are short when compared to the Masai people of Kenya, it does not mean that tall Twa or short Masai do not exist, but that they are not in the majority. When one describes a whole population by its most frequently occurring characteristic, we call it the **mode**.

If the majority of the scores in a set of data have the same value, then the mode accurately represents the data. For instance, in the field of fashion, if the majority of youth use a particular style of dress, this style, as a 'mode', accurately represents the fashion in vogue. Yet, in general, the mode is not very representative of a set of data, as is shown in the following example.

The ages of 20 candidates for matric/O-level examinations are:
19, 18, 16, 22, 18, 17, 18, 21, 17, 19, 18, 20, 17, 19, 18, 18, 21, 18, 19, 18.

CHAPTER 14 Quantitative data analysis and interpretation

A quick check indicates that out of these 20, eight candidates are 18 years old, followed by four of 19 and three of 17. Other ages have lower frequencies. The mode is therefore 18 years, which constitutes just over a third of the sample. Note that one should not confuse the highest frequency (here eight) with the **mode**, which is the value corresponding to the highest frequency, in this case 18 years.

One can read the value of the mode directly on a frequency polygon as being the value on the x-axis corresponding to the highest point of the polygon.

When a frequency distribution indicates two values with the same highest frequency, both values are modes and are used together to describe the set of data. Such a distribution is called **bimodal**.

It is easy to determine the mode of a set of ungrouped data. But how does one find the **mode of grouped data**? If the data have been grouped in class-intervals, the interval with the highest frequency contains the mode. Since a class-interval is represented by its midpoint, the mode is defined as the value of the midpoint of the class-interval with the highest frequency. Again, it should not be confused with the value of the highest frequency itself. According to Table 14.4, the mode of the scores of matrons is 11 and lies in the interval 51–60, or more precisely, at its midpoint 55,5, whereas the mode of all nurses is 48 and lies in the interval 31–40, and therefore at its midpoint, 35,5. Note that, in the case of grouped data, more precise methods exist to determine the exact value of the mode.

From the above it becomes clear that the mode is an easy method for determining the central tendency of a set of data. But its usefulness is greatly reduced if the highest frequency is not much higher than the others. This is the case when looking at the distribution of Hospital B (Table 14.2), where the mode, representing 26% of the sample, is followed by two quite similar values of 23% and 21%. As a rule of thumb the mode must constitute at least a third of the total of the data in order to have some representativeness.

The median

An alternative way of describing a set of data is to take the value of the middle of the set as representative. In this case, an equal number of data/scores fall above and below that value, which is called the **median** and is symbolised by Md.

As an illustration, let us consider the following survey published by Ferrinho et al. *Human Resources for Health* 2011, http://www.human-resources-health.com/content/9/1/30. It indicates that the number of inhabitants per registered nurse in the nine provinces of Zambia in 2008 was as follows:

Fundamentals of Social Research Methods: An African Perspective

Table 14.5 Population per registered nurse per province, Zambia, 2008	
Province	Population per registered nurse (in thousands)
Central	12,4
Copperbelt	5,3
Eastern	16,6
Luapula	17,9
Lusaka	4,9
Northern	17,8
North-western	13,0
Southern	10,0
Western	18,8

Arranging these data from the lowest to the highest, one obtains:
4,9; 5,3; 10,0; 12,4; 13,0; 16,6; 17,8; 17,9; 18,8.

The value dividing this set of data into two equal sets of four data is 13,0, which is the median. However, one has to note that the median itself could be an element of the set or it could lie between two scores. For instance, adding a new score, for example, 8,4, to the above set of data, one obtains a median value of 12,7 which does not correspond to one of the scores.

The mean

The best way to estimate the level of job satisfaction for a specific nurse, or the number of people per nurse in a certain province in Zambia, is to compare the results of a particular respondent or province with the results obtained from a sample of nurses or provinces. Here, instead of comparing one by one, it is more useful to compare the particular result with one global value representing all the results, that is, one result which is calculated by taking into account *all* other values. This is the characteristic of the mean as compared to the mode (based only on the frequency) and the median (based only on the position).

The **arithmetic mean** (or **average**) is the sum of all the values or scores divided by the total number of cases and it is symbolised by $\bar{x}$.

Coming back to the previous example and calculating the mean number of people per nurse, one obtains a mean of 12,95 (in thousands) and this mean is the national ratio of population per nurse in Zambia. This value allows one to compare provincial and national data and thus to assess how much better the health services are in Lusaka (4,9 as compared to the national mean of 12,95) and how much lower they are in the Western

CHAPTER 14 Quantitative data analysis and interpretation

Province (18,8 compared to 12,95). Here again, the requested mean, including for data grouped in class-intervals, can be obtained directly through any statistical software.

The combined mean

Suppose a population has been subdivided into groups of different sizes, and the mean of a certain variable has been found for each group. Now, one has to determine the mean for the whole population. If the groups are of the same size, the method would be to average all these means, that is, to add them all and divide the sum by the number of groups. But if the groups are of different sizes, their respective means must be weighted before the average can be computed. This process is called **averaging means** or **weighted means**. It is to be noted that the error of not taking into account the different sizes of the groups when calculating the combined mean is often made by people not familiar with statistics or wanting to misuse data (see the section Use and abuse of statistics further on in this chapter).

Susceptibility of the mean to extreme values

Although the mean is considered the best measure of the central tendency, it has a very important weakness in that it is influenced by extreme values and this can greatly bias the result.

Example

On a public bus which is driving towards a low-income area, a student carries out research on the income of the passengers. Based on the collected data, she computes the means as follows:

Weekly income (in shilling)	Frequency f	fx
500	9	4 500
1 000	20	20 000
10 000	1	10 000

Based on this data, the mean weekly income of the passengers is then calculated to be 1 150 shillings.

This result leaves the researcher puzzled, since 29 out of the 30 passengers have an income of less than or equal to 1 000 shillings! Analysing the data, she finds that if the one extremely wealthy passenger, whose presence in the bus was due to the unexpected breakdown of his Mercedes Benz, is excluded from the sample, the mean of weekly income is 845 shillings, which adequately represents the sample.

Comparison of mean, median and mode, or 'how to choose the appropriate measure of central tendency'

Firstly, the main characteristics of each measure can be summarised as follows:

Mode
- It is the score that occurs most often in a group.
- It does not include all the scores of the distribution.
- It is therefore not affected by extreme values.
- It can only be considered as a good measure of central tendency:
  a. when the occurring frequency is very high compared to all others (at least a third of the total number of scores)
  b. when the distribution is unimodal (has only one mode).
- It can even be applied to scores using nominal scales.
- For grouped data, referring to the calculated values of the median and the mean, the value of the mode can be approximated by the following formula:
  Mode = Mean − 3 (Mean − Median)

Median
- It is the middle value of an ordered set of scores.
- It does not include all the scores of the distribution.
- It is therefore not affected by extreme values.
- It can be applied to scores on an ordinal scale.
- The value of the median might not belong to the set of scores.

Mean
- It makes use of every score of the distribution; it is the most accurate measure of central tendency.
- The value of the mean might be an abstract one (for example: $\bar{x} = 5{,}8$ children).
- It is affected by extreme (low or high) values in the distribution, in which case it is not suitable.
- It changes in the same manner and to the same extent as the scale is changed.

From the above it becomes clear that, except in the case of extreme values, the mean is the best measure for representing a set of data. The median is the best alternative to the mean in case of extreme values, and the mode is useful for giving a rough estimate, in particular when one frequency is much higher than all the others.

Skewness of a distribution

The skewness of a distribution expresses the uneven distribution of scores on both sides of the central tendency. In other words, it reflects the lack of symmetry in the distribution. A distribution can be **positively skewed** or skewed to the right (Figure 14.6a. or it can be **negatively skewed** or skewed to the left (Figure 14.6b.). The **direction of skewness** is reflected in the position of the three measures of central tendency — median, mode and mean, as illustrated in Figure 14.6.

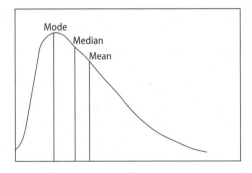
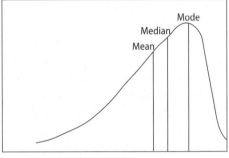

a. Positively skewed distribution   b. Negatively skewed distribution

Figure 14.6 *Skewed distribution and the position of the three measures of central tendency*

Note that the median is always the value between the mean and the mode. In the case of a symmetrical distribution (no skewness), which is called a **normal distribution**, represented by a normal (or Gauss curve) as shown in Figure 14.7, the three central tendencies coincide.

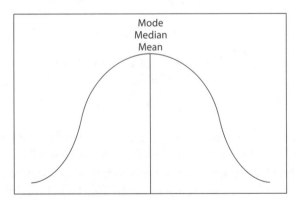

Figure 14.7 *Symmetrical, unskewed distribution*

Finally, the extent to which a distribution is skewed, also called the **magnitude of skewness**, can be measured by the **Pearson's coefficient of skewness** which can be found in more advanced textbooks.

Measures of variability or dispersion

Variability and its meaning

The purpose of this section is to emphasise that the central tendencies discussed in the previous section are not sufficient to give a complete picture of the shape of a distribution. To compute only the measures of central tendency of a distribution can be misleading at times, as will be explained below. Measures of dispersion, also called measures of variability, constitute another type of statistic that summarise a distribution. Just as with the measures of central tendency, there are different methods of measuring variability. The ones presented here are range, standard deviation and variance.

The importance of measuring the variability of the scores in a distribution can be seen from the following example. Imagine that data are collected from 100 female and 100 male students on their ability to perform a given task: the matric examination. This data may show that the mean scores of the two groups (males and females) are almost the same. Yet the scores of one group may show more variability than the scores of the other. As shown in Figure 14.8, the scores of the female students range from 10 to 90 and those of the males from 40 to 60. It becomes clear at once that all the males of the sample are of more or less the same ability and obtain more or less the same scores, while the female students vary markedly in their achievement in that examination, that is, there is more spread in the performance of the females than in that of the males.

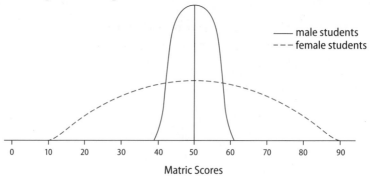

Figure 14.8 *Spread of performance*

This difference in their achievement scores might be of greater interest than the fact that the means of the two groups are more or less the same. Wrong inferences can be drawn by taking into account measures of central tendency only. In most instances, measures of variability are essential to describe a distribution. Researchers may deal with samples or groups of participants that are heterogeneous and therefore have a greater variability than homogenous groups. The reverse of that situation can also be true: one may have two distributions with the same variability but with different averages. In all such instances, variability or spread of scores is an essential item of information. It expresses in quantitative terms how scores in a distribution are scattered. The spread of scores expresses the extent to which scores or data differ from each other in a given distribution.

CHAPTER 14 Quantitative data analysis and interpretation

A very rough estimate of the degree of variation or dispersion of distributions can be found by just looking at the distribution curves or graphic representations. However, estimates based on graphic representation are very inexact – a social scientist needs more accurate measures of dispersion. The ones considered here are:

1. Range
2. Standard deviation and variance.

Range

The **range** can be defined as the difference between the highest and the lowest score in the distribution. The formula for the computation of range depends on whether the data are ungrouped or grouped in class-intervals.

The **range of ungrouped data** is simply:

Range = highest score − lowest score

Let us look again at the example of the ages of 20 candidates for the matric /O-level examination. If the highest age is 22 and the lowest 16, the range is found to be $22–16 = 6$ which means that between the youngest and the oldest student, there is a difference of 6 years.

The **range of grouped data** is defined as the difference between the real upper limit of the highest class-interval and the real lower limit of the lowest class-interval.

Range = real upper limit of the highest interval − real lower limit of lowest interval

Looking again at Table 14.4 on page 248, one can calculate the range of the grouped data obtained by matrons: since all scores are between the intervals 21–30 and 91–100, the range is $100,5–20,5 = 80$, which means that between the score of the matron having the highest job satisfaction and the score of the matron least satisfied with her job, there is a difference of 80 points.

Some properties of the range

The range is an approximate measure of variability. It has the advantage of being easy to calculate, as can be seen from the above examples. It is clear that this measure of variability does not take into account how the intermediate scores are scattered between the extremes, as it is only the two extreme scores that are considered. The use of the range as a measure of variability is therefore restricted to situations where answers are urgently required and the interpretation is not of much importance. Further, it is not recommended when:

261

a. the size of the group is small
b. there are empty class-intervals (with frequency $f = 0$) since this adds to its inaccuracy.

The range is also disproportionately affected by an extreme score, as is the case of the mean, but the frequency of the class-interval does not affect the range. Lastly, the range does not take any account of the form of distribution: a symmetrical or asymmetrical distribution might have the same range.

The standard deviation

The **standard deviation** of a distribution is the mean of the individual deviations or distances of each score from the distribution mean. In other words, after taking into account some mathematical complexities, it expresses the deviations of all the scores through the mean of all these deviations.

For example, let us take the number of grandchildren in five African families. These are 8, 10, 12, 14 and 6, thus the mean number of grandchildren comes to $\bar{x} = \frac{50}{5} = 10$.

Family	Number of grandchildren	$d = x - \bar{x}$
A	8	−2
B	10	0
C	12	+2
D	14	+4
E	6	−4

The third column indicates the difference between each score (or number of grandchildren) and the mean.

Through computations or directly through statistical software, the standard deviation in this example is found to be $s = 3,16$.

Some properties of the standard deviation

Effect of scale changes on the standard deviation

a. **Addition:** If all the scores x of a distribution are changed by adding a (positive or negative) constant number to each of them, then the standard deviation is not affected by the changes. This property has important practical implications for social scientists because it can reduce their computations drastically.

CHAPTER 14 Quantitative data analysis and interpretation

b. **Multiplication:** If all the scores of a distribution are changed by multiplying (or dividing) each of them by a constant number, then the standard deviation of the changed data is equal to the original standard deviation multiplied (or divided) by that constant.

Units of measurement
A very useful property of the standard deviation is that it is expressed in terms of the measuring scale. In other words, the scores, the mean and the standard deviation of a certain distribution can be directly compared to each other as they are all expressed in the same units of measurement: people, hectares, hours, etc.

Comparison between groups
If two groups have the same mean but different standard deviations, these groups can be directly compared in terms of variability. The group with the larger standard deviation is more spread out, with a greater dispersion than the one with a smaller standard deviation. If both means and standard deviations differ, the groups can nevertheless be compared through the coefficient of variation, as explained below.

Coefficient of variation

At times, one needs to compare the variability of different sets of data. These data may or may not be in the same units. One group of results may be expressed in scores or percentages, while the data of another group may be expressed in kilograms, and a third one in hours or days. In such cases, the standard deviation of a group is calculated as a percentage of the mean of that same group. Variability so expressed as a percentage gives some information about the variation within different groups of data, and so allows one to compare these sets. Such variability is called the **coefficient of variation**.

Variance

The average of the squared deviations from the mean of a distribution is called the **variance (s^2)** of that distribution. In fact, the standard deviation (s) of a distribution is the (positive) square root of the variance. The variance (s^2) is zero if and only if all the scores in a distribution do not differ at all from the mean. Otherwise, since the variance depends on the distance of each score from the mean, the more the scores differ, the larger the spread or variance, and the more heterogeneous the group of data. The variance is expressed in squared units of measurement, that is, if the scores are in kilometres, the variance will be in km^2 units. If the scores refer to people or years, the variance will be in square people or years, which might not make a lot of sense. As mentioned earlier, the standard deviation does not have this problem.

263

Comparison of the various measures of variability

All the measures of variability presented in this chapter are frequently used. The choice of which to use depends on the type of data and the purpose of measuring the dispersion of the distribution. When one is interested in having only a rough idea of the dispersion of the scores, the range is used. It is easy to compute but it is not a stable measure owing to extreme scores. Moreover, it does not give any information on the shape or pattern of the distribution. Thus its use as the only measure of variability is not recommended.

The standard deviation is taken to be the most stable and often-used measure of variability, since it takes into account all scores and is expressed in the same units as the scores themselves. Thus, when in doubt, the selection of the standard deviation as a measure of dispersion is recommended.

Descriptive statistics: Concluding remarks

In conclusion, when researchers have collected all the data, they proceed to describe these data by establishing their frequency distribution and often summarising them in a contingency table. They may then want to depict the data through graphical representation, graphs or diagrams. Next they calculate measures of central tendencies as well as measures of dispersion in order to quantify the description of the collected data. Nowadays, these various steps are done with computers. However, in order to correctly interpret the results, it is important to understand the basic concepts and methods of calculation used.

PART II: INFERENTIAL STATISTICS

Distributions

Whereas descriptive statistics are simply procedures for condensing information about a set of measurements, inferential statistics refer to techniques for making statements and decisions on the basis of numerical information relating samples to populations. The present section introduces this particular aspect of statistics by introducing two very crucial and related concepts, with their properties and uses: normal distribution and sampling distribution.

Normal distribution and its properties

At the beginning of this chapter, when looking at the graphical representation of frequency distributions, it was found that polygons can have an infinite variety of shapes. Moreover, when describing frequency distributions through their central tendencies, one special case, called a normal distribution, has already been mentioned and illustrated in Figure 14.7 on page 259.

CHAPTER 14 Quantitative data analysis and interpretation

A normal distribution (see Figure 14.7 on page 259) is a very useful distribution, with the following properties:
a. It is symmetrical, that is, it is represented by a symmetrical unskewed curve.
b. Its mean, median and mode assume the same value.
c. Its curve, given by a mathematical expression (which relates the mean and the variance of that distribution but will not be discussed here), takes the shape of a bell.
d. The two tails, or ends, of the curve are asymptotic, that is, they only reach the horizontal axis at infinity.

Let look at the significance of a normal curve in a more concrete way. One has to return to the concept of *population*, which was introduced in Chapter 11. Suppose the scores for a whole population are represented by a curve. This means that when the *x*-axis (horizontal) shows the scores or measurements and the *y*-axis (vertical) shows the frequencies, the curve is the frequency polygon depicting how many times a certain score has appeared in the population. In other words, the entire set of scores or data constituting the population is represented 'under the curve'. Another way of expressing this is that the area between the curve and the horizontal axis represents 100% of the population. If the curve depicting the frequency distribution of the population is 'normal', that is, satisfies the four properties stated above, much useful information can be inferred.

Properties a. and b. together signify that the mean, because it is also the median, divides the population into two equal parts, each containing 50% of the data. Also, because of this symmetry every property in one half of the curve corresponds to exactly the same property in the other half. In other words, when investigating the properties of the curve, it suffices to consider only one half of the distribution. Through property c. one can infer that normal distributions may differ on account of their mean or their standard deviation but that they will maintain the same shape. Figure 14.9 illustrates this point by depicting in a. two normal distributions with different means and the same standard deviation, and in b. two normal distributions with the same mean but different standard deviations.

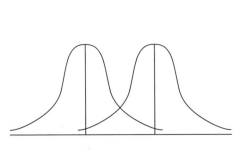 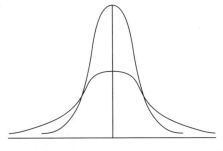

a. With different means and the same standard deviation

b. With the same mean and different standard deviations

Figure 14.9 *Comparison of normal distributions*

This relationship between the mean and the variance (or its square root, the standard deviation) is common to all normal curves, and allows us to express any portion or section of the population under the curve as a percentage of the whole population. In other words, given any two scores or values on the *x*-axis, one can easily determine the percentage of the population situated between these two scores. This issue will become clearer when studying *standard scores*.

The last and most abstract characteristic, property d., reflects the fact that, very often, populations are infinite. Thus there can always be some extreme values of the population that are so far away from the bulk of the data that they are not actually represented on the graph. Their existence is taken into account by not allowing the curve to join the horizontal axis at any particular, finite, value. Note that in practice, when a set of data is given, since the set is finite, this condition is not satisfied.

Finally, there are methods to assess whether a distribution is normal or not. One of them is called the 'goodness of fit test', but it generally suffices to estimate the normality of a distribution by inspecting its shape and whether its measures of central tendency take approximately the same value.

The subdivisions of a normal distribution

As has been shown, a normal distribution can be divided into two equal parts by the score corresponding to its mean, each part containing 50% of the total population. Further, one can expect to find other scores splitting the distribution into 25% and 75%, or 40% and 60%, or any subdivision making up 100%.

Since such subdivisions can be obtained for *any* normal distribution, the dividing scores are best expressed in terms of the main characteristics of a normal distribution: its mean and standard deviation.

Given the mean and standard deviation, any normal distribution can be subdivided, in a unique manner, using its standard deviation as a unit. This is illustrated in Figure 14.10 below.

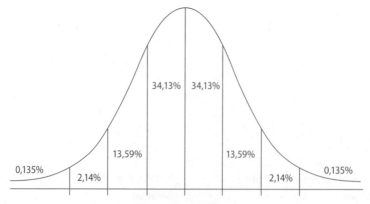

Figure 14.10 *Standard subdivision of a normal distribution*

CHAPTER 14 Quantitative data analysis and interpretation

As can be seen, the distribution is subdivided by three standard deviations on each side of the mean. Due to the shape of the curve, the percentages decrease towards the tails of the curve.

The most useful facts are:
1. The bulk of the data (68,26%) is situated within one standard deviation on both sides of the mean.
2. The near totality of the population (99,73%) is spread within six standard deviations, three on each side of the mean.
3. Less than 5% of all the data are situated further than two standard deviations on both sides of the mean, whereas all the data situated further than three standard deviations on both sides of the mean comprises a mere 2,14% of the whole.

The subdivision of a normal distribution does not solve the problem of determining the scores corresponding to *any* given percentage. To reach this goal, one must first simplify the situation by introducing the *standard normal distribution and its scores*.

Standard normal distribution and normal scores

A very simple normal distribution is the one with a mean equal to 0 and a standard deviation equal to 1. Such a distribution, as represented in Figure 14.10, is called a **standard normal distribution**. In this case, the values of the variable x are called the **standard scores** with symbol z. The transformation of each observed score x to its corresponding standard score z effectively transforms any given normal distribution into a **standard normal distribution** whose values are z-**scores** and which satisfies the condition of a **mean** of zero and a **standard deviation** of one.

In short, the standard score gives information on the deviation of a score from the mean, expressed in standard deviation units.

Application of the normal scores

Suppose that 50 students are asked to sit for two tests, test A on mathematics and test B on geography. The 50 scores on tests A and B constitute two different normal distributions. How can one then compare the results of any student who sat both tests? The problem is similar to comparing the size of the face, the length of the arms and the girth of the waist of two people on the basis of a photograph of them. A direct comparison is easiest if the two photos have been taken from the same distance. If that is not the case, then one has to enlarge one of them, or even transform the format of both of them so that their respective sizes correspond, allowing one to use the same scale of measurement for both.

267

Fundamentals of Social Research Methods: An African Perspective

The same applies when comparing two normal distributions: one needs a method of transforming both distributions in such a way that the same scale of measurement can be used. In other words, the scores of both distributions must be expressed in a standard way, enabling comparison. The solution is to convert the collected scores or data of each distribution into standard scores, taking into account the characteristics of each distribution: the means and standard deviations.

Sampling distributions

In research, data are collected from a sample drawn from a much larger population. On the basis of these data the characteristics or **statistics** of the sample, like measures of central tendency and of variability, can be calculated. However, the corresponding characteristics or **parameters** of the underlying population remain unknown. The major aim of building sampling distributions is to be able to estimate these parameters, that is, mean, median and standard deviation of the population through the characteristics of its samples.

As mentioned in Chapter 11, when doing research, one always draws a distinction between a population, referring to all the objects or units under consideration, and a sample, which is a subset of that population. The data can then be represented by a population distribution or a sample distribution, which may or may not be normal.

At this point another type of distribution, a **sampling distribution**, must be introduced, since it is the basis of many inferential procedures. The unique feature of a sampling distribution, as opposed to population and sample distributions, lies in its scores. Until now the scores of a distribution were the data collected in the process of doing research. The scores of a sampling distribution, however, can be any statistics (mean, median, standard deviations, etc) of the many samples that have been drawn from the population in question. In this section, however, only sampling distributions referring to sample **means** will be considered.

Let us start with an illustration to clarify this new concept and its importance.

A survey is conducted in a rural region of a certain country to assess the consumption of charcoal per person per month. A team of 10 skilled researchers acts jointly: each researcher chooses a random sample of 50 respondents and collects the data in a standardised way. Although there has been no irregularity during the data collection, the mean consumption (in kilograms) of each sample varies as follows:

$$\bar{x}_1 = 6,5; \quad \bar{x}_2 = 6,5; \quad \bar{x}_3 = 5,8; \quad \bar{x}_4 = 6,3 ; \quad \bar{x}_5 = 4,9; \quad \bar{x}_6 = 6,2; \quad \bar{x}_7 = 6,1;$$
$$\bar{x}_8 = 6,0; \quad \bar{x}_9 = 5,7; \quad \bar{x}_{10} = 6,5.$$

Let us assume that the national monthly average per person of charcoal consumption in the rural area is 6 kg. The recorded variation of the sample means is easily understood as a consequence of picking up, by chance, people consuming more or less than the national average. However, the set of all these means, considered now as ordinary

268

CHAPTER 14 Quantitative data analysis and interpretation

scores, itself constitutes a new distribution called the **sampling distribution of means** which shows how much the means of all these samples are spread around the mean of the population.

This example also illustrates the error a researcher can make by using the mean of an arbitrary sample to represent the mean of a population. It should be clear that, whenever the mean (or any other parameter) of the population is unknown, one has to consider the sampling distribution of the corresponding statistics in order to estimate that population mean. In the previous example, only a few samples (all of the same size $n = 50$) were considered. The information is obviously not complete in this case. The distribution is then called an **empirical sampling distribution**, the one occurring most often in research. In the ideal case, the **theoretical sampling distribution** is built on the basis of all possible samples of a certain size that can be drawn from the population. The mean of this new distribution is clearly the mean of all these sample means. Note that the mean of a population distribution and the mean of its theoretical sampling distribution coincide.

Standard error

A sampling distribution, whether empirical or theoretical, is not only described by its mean but also by its standard deviation as a measure of variability. The standard deviation of a sampling distribution, because it measures the sampling error, is called the **standard error**. As before, this parameter refers to the statistic that is under consideration. A standard error of the mean (or of the median, the mode, etc) corresponds to a sampling distribution of means (or medians, modes, etc). Only the standard error of the mean will be discussed here.

Standard error of the mean

It is important to grasp the real meaning of the **standard deviation of a theoretical sampling distribution of means**. Like any standard deviation, it measures the deviation or spread of the scores from the mean. In this particular case, however, since the scores are sample means, it actually measures the deviation of the sample mean from the mean of the population from which these samples have been drawn. For this reason it is called the **standard error of the mean**. In other words, it measures the error made if one uses the mean of a sample instead of the mean of a population, that is, the error of generalising from the statistics of a sample, to the parameters of the underlying population. One can say that the standard error is an index of the sampling error with respect to any given statistic. The more a sample is representative of the population, the smaller the sampling error will be and the smaller the standard error.

In practice social research deals with quite large populations, often of a near infinite size, where means and standard deviations cannot be computed. In this case an estimate of these characteristics must be used, bearing in mind that they can only be approximate

269

values. Generally the statistics of the sample representing the population (that is, on which the research is based) will be chosen for this purpose. Thus, the standard deviation (s) of this sample will be used as an estimate of the standard deviation of the underlying population. The same reasoning will then be used to express the estimate of the standard error.

The *importance of the size* (n) *of the sample* (that is, of the order of the sampling distribution) has to be emphasised: the larger the size of the sample, the smaller the standard error and thus the error of using an estimate for the standard deviation. In other words, the variability of the sampling distribution decreases as the sample size increases. Clearly, very large samples are always more appropriate for representing a population.

Estimating parameters through sampling distributions

As mentioned previously, the accuracy of estimates of the standard deviation of a population using one of its samples depends on how representative and large that sample is. It is therefore necessary to be able to evaluate the degree of accuracy in order to ascertain for example that, with 95% chance, the population mean will be within two given values. There are basically two ways of estimating these parameters.

a.   The attempt to estimate an unknown parameter by finding the best single value to represent it is called a **point estimation**. It is what was done previously by adopting the standard deviation of a given sample as the best estimate of the population standard deviation. Although there are some criteria to measure the accuracy of a point estimate, these are beyond the scope of this book.

b.   The aim of an **interval estimation** is to determine an interval within which the parameter must lie with a predicted probability. This method also allows one to obtain an idea of how accurate a point estimate is.

Coming back to the example on charcoal consumption presented above, for each sample with its mean and standard variation, an interval could be determined with a 95% chance that this interval contains the mean of the population. This is illustrated below, using five samples of charcoal consumers with following statistics:

$\bar{x}_1 = 6,5$ and $s_1 = 2,2$; $\bar{x}_2 = 2,2$ and $s_2 = 1,5$; $\bar{x}_3 = 5,8$ and $s_3 = 1,4$; $\bar{x}_4 = 6,3$ and $s_4 = 1,8$; $\bar{x}_5 = 4,9$ and $s_5 = 4,4$, and remembering that the population mean is 6 kg.

CHAPTER 14 Quantitative data analysis and interpretation

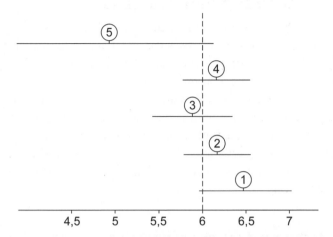

Figure 14.11 *Interval estimates of a population mean on the basis of 5 samples with n = 50*

A few general remarks are necessary to summarise this introduction of sampling distributions.
- First, keep in mind that a sampling distribution is based on random samples, all of the same size *n*. This size determines the order of the distribution.
- The order of the sampling distribution, in turn, determines the shape of the distribution, since a condition for a sampling distribution to be normal is that *n* is large. Moreover, as already mentioned, a large *n* increases the accuracy of the estimates.
- Although the discussions and examples here have been restricted to sampling distribution of the mean, any statistic, median, variance, etc, can be used instead of the mean. Each of these statistics will have its own standard error. The corresponding distribution will then be the sampling distribution of the median, or the sampling distribution of the variance, etc.
- Finally, the characteristics of the different types of distribution are referred to as follows:
  a. population distribution – with mean μ and standard deviation δ
  b. sample distribution – with mean *x* and standard deviation *s*
  c. sampling distribution – with the distinction between the theoretical case, comprising all possible samples, and the empirical case based on only a few selected samples.

Hypothesis testing and statistical tests

The purpose of this section is to introduce the idea of hypothesis testing and the type of reasoning it relies on. It also emphasises the importance of probability in inferential statistics. The understanding of the theory and of the mechanism of hypothesis testing introduced in Chapter 6 is fundamental to the understanding and use of statistical tests. The link between them lies in the notion of statistical significance. The essential function of statistical tests when used to evaluate the correctness of a hypothesis is to assess the significance, or lack of it, of the observed differences between certain characteristics of two or more samples. Here again, it is assumed that the reader will be using some statistical software to provide all information needed to make a decision regarding the hypothesis.

Hypothesis testing and the role of probability

As mentioned before, to infer some properties of a whole population on the basis of the properties of a sample cannot lead to certainty but only to some probability statements. One assumes a certain attribute to exist with sufficient confidence that one is not making an error of judgement. An example should make this clear.

Example

A researcher plans to assess the impact of agricultural extension courses given to small farmers. These courses are aimed at improving the productivity of farmers in growing sunflowers by introducing new methods of production. Productivity is to be measured by weight of sunflower seeds produced per acre. Two groups of 30 farmers have been randomly sampled. These farmers all work under the same conditions with regards to the type of soil, fertiliser, weather, etc. The only obvious difference is that one group, the experimental one, has undergone an agricultural extension course on sunflower growing and is expected to apply the new methods. The other, the control group, will use the traditional methods common to the region.

As predicted, the means of the two groups are not identical, showing higher productivity for the experimental group. Can the researcher conclude that the increase in production is due to the agricultural training and, therefore, that the positive effect of the independent variable, the attendance or not at an agricultural extension course, has been demonstrated? In other words, can the researcher infer from these results that the two groups of farmers belong to essentially different populations of trained and traditional farmers?

continued ...

CHAPTER 14 Quantitative data analysis and interpretation

Two objections can be raised about such an inference. Firstly, the frequency curves of the two samples might strongly overlap so that the mean of one sample could be within one standard deviation from the mean of the other, and so that it is a score with a high probability of appearance. Secondly, in analysing each sample separately, considerable variations in the production of sunflower seeds could be detected for different members of the same group. These variations are called **within-group variations** and they might be as large as the difference between the means of the two groups. As such the difference between the means of these two samples is not enough proof to conclude that the two groups belong to different populations.

Many random factors might play a role in explaining the difference between the groups. Some farmers might be more or less motivated to work, others might be more or less subject to health problems, or a plant disease might even have attacked more of the fields of one group than of the other. All of these 'chance factors', which are due to irrelevant variables, might not have the same impact on the two groups and so might be the cause of small variations.

This analysis shows the difficulty in assessing the importance of observed differences. The problem is thus to find criteria good enough for the researcher to prove beyond reasonable doubt that the observed differences cannot be explained only by the effect of these chance factors. In other words, one has to assess the likelihood of the difference being due to chance only.

If the probability of this difference being caused by chance is high, then the two samples are considered to not be essentially different and they are then taken to belong to the same population. The variable under consideration, the agricultural training, is not effective and the observed difference between the two samples is **not significant**. If, on the other hand, it is very unlikely that chance alone could cause such a disparity, that is, if the probability of this occurring by chance only is too low, one should conclude that the independent variable (the agricultural training) is responsible for the discrepancy between the two groups. This difference between means is then said to be **significant**, that is, it can be explained by the effect of agricultural training, the independent variable, on the dependent variable, the productivity of the farmers.

By stating that the difference between the means of the experimental and control groups is significant (or not), one has rejected (or not rejected) the hypothesis that the difference between the two groups is only due to chance. **Testing a hypothesis** means reaching a conclusion on the significance, or the lack of it, about the difference between groups and rejecting the statement of the hypothesis as being incorrect if it contradicts this conclusion.

The next goal of this section is to define more carefully, and in quantitative terms, the criteria under which a difference is **significant**. This should enable a researcher to reject a hypothesis with sufficient confidence that this decision is correct.

Null hypothesis and alternative hypothesis

In the preceding example, the relationship between the independent variable (agricultural training) and the dependent one (productivity) has been expressed in two different ways:

1. In denying the effect of the independent variable:
   - 'The agricultural training has no impact on productivity.'
   - 'The differences between the two groups are only due to chance.'
   - 'The differences between the two groups are not significant.'
2. In emphasising the importance of the independent variable:
   - 'The agricultural training has an impact on productivity.'
   - 'The two samples do not belong to the same population.'
   - 'The differences between the two groups are significant.'

The first type of hypothesis, since it belittles or even denies the difference between the two groups, is called the **null hypothesis**, with symbol H_0. The second type of hypothesis, since it emphasises the experimental group as being different from the control group, is called the **experimental** or **alternative hypothesis**, as it is an alternative to the null hypothesis with symbol H_1. It will be seen later that both types of hypotheses have a certain specific meaning and role, and thus both have to be stated in any research.

However, the **null hypothesis** is the one that must be directly tested and rejected or not. In other words, in inferential statistics, one always starts from the assumption that the observed differences arise purely because of chance fluctuations of random factors as opposed to the effect of the independent variable. Thus, the samples are taken as being essentially the same, belonging to the same population. If the discrepancies are found to be too significant to be explained by chance factors only, then the null hypothesis is wrong and must be rejected. If, on the contrary, the probability is that the observed differences could be explained by chance factors alone, then the null hypothesis is not rejected, though it is not accepted either. The final statement is simply that 'the null hypothesis is not rejected'.

Why this caution? If the differences are too large to be explained by random factors, other factors that could be the cause have to be identified. Thus, clearly, H_0 is rejected and H_1 *may be true* but *not necessarily* so. H_0 being rejected does not mean that H_1 can be accepted. On the other hand, if the differences could be caused by chance factors alone, it would mean that H_0 *could be* true and that it *could* be *a possible* explanation though not necessarily *the only possible* explanation. In this case, one cannot accept H_0 and exclude all other possible causes. Thus the weaker and more cautious statement is that H_0 is not rejected.

To illustrate this line of reasoning, if a fish is defined as an animal living in water with some additional characteristics, a cat cannot qualify as belonging to the species 'fish' because it doesn't live in water: the null hypothesis can be rejected without hesitation. However, both whales and sharks live in water. Unless one is able to check whether the other characteristics of fish are also present, one might assume that both animals are fish (which would actually be true only for the shark), but one cannot be certain of it and exclude all other possibilities. In this case, if one were to 'accept' the null-hypothesis, one would make the error of considering a whale to be a fish.

Level of significance and confidence intervals

The problem arising at this stage is to find criteria and quantitative values that will help the researcher decide whether a null hypothesis has to be rejected or not. One has to determine limits, called **confidence limits**, within which a decision can be taken with sufficient certainty that it is the correct one. A reasonable decision is that all events or data, which have a very low probability of occurring, should be rejected. It is usually agreed that an event with a probability of ,025 or a 2,5% chance of occurring is too unlikely to take place.

As a first guess, one would assume that this problem is related to z-scores and the standard normal distribution. In fact, the z value corresponding to ,025 of the population at the right extreme of the curve is $z = 1,96$, and $z = -1,96$ for the left tail. In other words, only 2,5% of the scores are situated on each side of the curve beyond the indicated value of z and they will not be considered as belonging to that distribution. Thus these two areas are called the **rejection areas**. By contrast, all the z-values lying between these two z-scores, and which constitute 95% of the population, have a sufficiently high probability of occurring and thus are considered to belonging to the population distribution. Thus, this area or interval $[-1,96 ; +1,96]$ is called the **confidence interval**. Finally, the two z-values themselves that separate the rejection areas from the confidence interval are called the **critical values** or **confidence limits**. These different concepts are illustrated in Figure 14.12 below, where the rejection areas are shadowed.

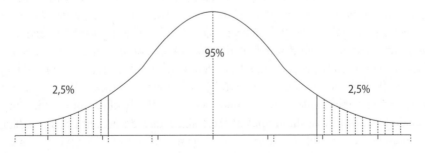

Figure 14.12 *Confidence and rejection areas*

The **significance level** can be described as the probability value that determines the boundary between rejecting or not rejecting H_0. It is symbolised by the Greek letter α called alpha. In Figure 14.13, the level of significance is $\alpha = ,05$, that is, 5% of the scores under the curve have been excluded as too unlikely to occur. In social research, the rejection area varies between 1% (or ,01) and 10% (or ,1) of the population under the normal curve, with the most frequent value being $\alpha = ,05$.

Statistical software normally indicates the **probability value p** which is the chance of occurrence of an event. In this context p represents the probability that the data being compared belong to the same population, or that there are no significant differences between the data. In other words, p expresses the probability of the null-hypothesis H_0 being valid.

If that probability value (p) is larger than the chosen level of significance $\alpha = ,05$ (for instance, $p = ,08$), then the null hypothesis is not rejected. Equally, if p is equal or smaller than α (for instance, $p = ,01$), then H_0 is rejected, since the difference is significant.

Directional versus non-directional tests

The distinction between **non-directional** and **directional** (positive or negative) tests was explained in Chapter 6. The experimental (or alternative) hypothesis H_1 can be formulated in either a directional or a non-directional manner. In the first instance, the type of influence of the independent variable on the dependent one is expressed. The question arises as to how one can take into account the direction indicated in an alternative hypothesis when testing the null hypothesis. The additional information of the effect, positive or negative, of the independent variable must be reflected in the decision rule, since, in this case, rejecting H_0 must be in accordance with the more specific statement of H_1. In other words, rejecting the null hypothesis that two groups are drawn from the same population leads, in the case of a **directional** problem, not only to the conclusion that the two groups are essentially different, but also to *how* they differ. For example, one must specify which group has higher results than the other.

Let us return to the concept of confidence interval and rejection area. In the case of a non-directional hypothesis, the rejection area always comprises two symmetrical areas situated at both ends or 'tails' of the curve. Thus, a non-directional H_1 yields a non-directional or two-tailed test. The observed value leading to the rejection of H_0 could occur at either extreme of the distribution. On the other hand, if H_1 indicates how the independent variable acts on the dependent one (like 'the agricultural training has a positive effect on or raises the productivity of farmers'), it means that the researcher is very confident that some results cannot occur at all. To illustrate this, it would be unrealistic to assume that the output of the trained farmers would be lower than that of the untrained ones. But if it were so, the mean production of the whole population would be greater than the mean production of the trained farmers, and the observed value would be negative. How is such a statement reflected in statistical terms? Stating that this is unrealistic is equivalent to stating that there cannot be a rejection area on the left tail of the curve. The rejection area can only be situated on the right-hand side of the mean in order to decide whether a difference is due to chance or not. For α = ,05, there will be 5% of the population concentrated only on this one tail. In other words, **a directional hypothesis leads to a directional or one-tailed test**. There is only one confidence limit and one rejection area. Statistical software usually indicates the values according the given specification of the alternative hypothesis H_1.

The comparison between the rejection area for a one-tailed and a two-tailed test is shown in Figure 14.13.

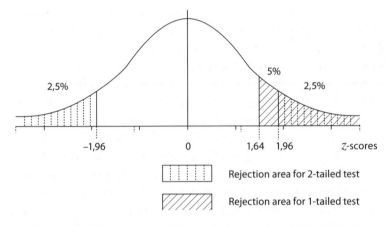

Figure 14.13 *Comparison between the rejection areas for one- and two-tailed tests*

Decision errors

An important question when analysing the process of hypothesis testing concerns the need to use a level of significance and the criteria for its choice. Why is α = .05 a suitable level of significance? Why can it not be much smaller? Why can't researchers decrease or even eliminate the chance of making a wrong decision? The answer is simple: Social scientists are in a dilemma, faced with making two types of decision errors, one being *complementary* to the other. Thus, the chosen level of significance, be it α = ,05 or any another, is a compromise between two evils. Let us analyse these two types of errors, referred to as type I and type II errors.

The **type I error** consists of rejecting the null hypothesis when it is actually true. The obtained result is situated in the rejection area, far from the mean, and its probability of being explained by pure chance factors seems to be unacceptably low to the researcher who therefore concludes that the result exhibits the effect of some non-random variable. In reality, the obtained result, although quite extreme and rare, still belongs to the population and is explained by unfortunate but normal sampling variability or other extraneous variables. It is thus an error to discard H_0.

Concretely, the probability that the output in sunflower seeds of a *randomly* selected sample of farmers is $\bar{x} = 62$ bags per acre is less than 0,0001, thus without doubt very low. It is *not impossible*, it can occur. If such a result does occur, however, the researcher will generally refuse to consider it to be explainable by chance factors alone. The null hypothesis will be rejected and a wrong decision, a type I decision error, will be committed.

A **type I decision error** is made when the null hypothesis H_0 is rejected although it is, in fact, true. The probability of committing this error is given by the level of significance, α.

The **type II error** is the opposite of the previous error. It involves not rejecting the null hypothesis when it is actually false. It occurs when the distribution curves of two populations overlap. In this case, an obtained result lies in the confidence interval of the one population and thus does not lead to a rejection of H_0. However, it actually belongs to the other population and thus should have led to H_0 being rejected!

Assume for instance that a trained group of farmers has only produced $\bar{x} = 57,5$ bags of sunflower seeds per acre. This result, although above the mean of the population, lies within the confidence interval and is quite similar to the result for the untrained farmers. To conclude that the agricultural training had no effect on the productivity of the farmers might be wrong in this particular case. For instance, this same group of trained farmers might have been strongly handicapped by the prolonged illness of some of its members or have experienced storage difficulties due to a fire. Confronted with the same handicaps, non-trained farmers would also have produced far below the population mean. In other words, not to reject the null hypothesis in this instance is an error made because of lack of information.

A **type II decision error** is made when the null hypothesis H_0 is not rejected although it is, in fact, false.

The existence of these type I and II decision errors might shake the trust of a researcher in the use of statistical tests. How can one rely on a decision based on such tests if errors can occur so easily? Clearly, the first requirement of a good test is to lead to a correct decision. It is therefore important to define the **power** of a statistical test as its ability to reject the null hypothesis correctly when H_0 is indeed false.

The procedure of hypothesis testing

When comparing two samples or a sample and a population, the aim of hypothesis testing is to determine whether the observed differences are due to chance factors or sampling variability, or whether they are due to the action of a certain independent variable on a dependent one.

The underlying principle of hypothesis testing is first to establish a certain criterion (based on the level of significance) to assess the likelihood of a certain type of event (for example, a difference between two means) occurring by chance. Then, the probability (p) of the event under investigation occurring by chance (for example, the observed

CHAPTER 14 Quantitative data analysis and interpretation

difference between two given sample means) can be computed and compared with the stated criterion. Finally, if the result does not satisfy the rules, the decision can be made to reject the null hypothesis. Thus the two cornerstones of hypothesis testing are probability of occurrence and sampling distribution.

The procedure of hypothesis testing will now be analysed step by step.

1. *Hypothesis*. The two hypotheses must be stated, first the null hypothesis H_0, and then the alternative hypothesis H_1.

   The statements must be unambiguous and complete, following the principles of hypothesis formulation laid out in Chapter 6. Bear in mind that **the hypothesis to be tested is *always* the null hypothesis H_0, that is, H_0 is the hypothesis, which is tentatively held to be true until it is rejected. The alternative hypothesis, H_1, indicates whether the test is directional or non-directional.**

2. *General characteristics*. Properties of the population distribution, sampling or sample distribution must be explicitly stated. The most common conditions which have to be satisfied in order to use statistical tests are that:

   a. the subjects are independently (or dependently) and randomly sampled

   b. the samples are independent (or dependent) of each other

   c. the population variances are homogeneous

   d. the distributions under consideration are normal

   e. the scale of measurement is interval, ordinal or nominal.

   On the basis of these assumptions, the choice of the most appropriate statistical test can be made.

3. *Decision rules*. These are statements referring to the statistical conditions that should lead to the rejection (or not) of the null hypothesis. The decision rules depend mainly on:

   a. the choice of a level of significance or critical level α

   b. the type of H_1 (directional or non-directional)

   c. the finding of the corresponding probability value p

   d. the formulation of the decision rules based on α, p and H_1.

   The previous four points are explicated as follows:

   a. The **level of significance**, indicated by the letter α, is the chosen probability value that determines the boundary between rejecting or not rejecting H_0. It is the accepted probability of error. For instance, $\alpha = ,05$ (the level of significance usually chosen) implies that if a difference between means has a probability of less than ,05 (or 5%) of being explained by chance factors, H_0 will be rejected even though five times out of 100 the difference will really be due to chance and the rejection of the null hypothesis will be wrong. (Refer back to **decision errors**.)

b. Whether the test is **directional or non-directional** is identified by analysing the formulation of H_1 and this is then selected in the software to determine the (one-tailed or two-tailed) rejection areas.
c. The **probability value p** that is obtained from the statistical software will then be compared to the level of significance in order to make the decision
d. The **formulation of the decision rules** is made in the form of conditions:
- If the probability value p of the test is larger than the level of significance α (that is, if the result is situated within the confidence interval), then H_0 is not rejected.
- If probability value p of the test is equal to or smaller than the level of significance α (that is, if the result is situated in the rejection area), then H_0 is rejected.

4. *Computation*. Once all the relevant information and data are entered into a statistical programme, it will calculate the probability value p.

5. *Decision*. Comparing the obtained probability value p to the decision rules leads directly to the decision either to reject or not reject the null hypothesis.

6. *Conclusions*. This last step really concludes the hypothesis testing process since, once a decision has been taken, the consequence of this decision for the problem at stake must be expressed. Coming back to both hypotheses as stated in the first step, one concludes what the rejection (or not) of the null hypothesis really means for the particular research in terms of the relevance of the independent variable. As such, the conclusions relate more to H_1 than to H_0.

An example of hypothesis testing

The procedure of hypothesis testing will now be applied to the research on the impact of agricultural training on the production of sunflower seeds.

1. *Hypotheses*. Null hypothesis H_0:
a. There is no significant difference between the trained group of small-scale farmers and the small-scale farmer population.
b. The agricultural training course has no effect on the productivity of the farmers

Alternative hypothesis H_1:
a. The trained group of small-scale farmers is significantly different from the population of small-scale farmers.
b. The agricultural training course has an effect on the productivity of the farmers.

CHAPTER 14 Quantitative data analysis and interpretation

Note that the two sets of formulation a. and b. are equivalent, although formulation b. is more explicit. In general, only one formulation for both H_0 and H_1 is made.

2. *General characteristics*
   a. The subjects are independently and randomly sampled.
   b. The samples are independent.
   c. The sampling distribution of the means is normal.
   d. The scale of measurement is interval.

Note that assumptions a. and b. are fulfilled if a sampling procedure for independent, random samples has been used. Assumption c. is also correct because of the relatively large size of the samples. Finally, assumption d. is obvious since the number of bags per acre is recorded.

3. *Decision rules*
   a. Let us choose $\alpha = {,}05$ as a level of significance.
   b. The alternative H_1 is non-directional.

   Thus the **decision rules** are:

   If p is larger than $\alpha = {,}05$, then do not reject H_0.
   If p is equal or smaller than $\alpha = {,}05$, then reject H_0.

4. *Computation.* The obtained probability value, calculated by a statistics programme, is $p = {,}0001$

5. *Decision.* Since $p = {,}0001$ is smaller than $\alpha = {,}05$, H_0 is rejected.

6. *Conclusion.* The agricultural training course does have an effect on the productivity of farmers.

Note that, in order to simplify the example, the trained (experimental) group has been compared directly to the entire population of small-scale farmers. However, this is seldom possible since population values are usually unknown. Generally, one wishes to compare experimental and control groups directly and analyse whether their difference of means can be explained by chance factors only. Tests to achieve this goal will be presented later in this chapter.

Parametric tests versus non-parametric tests

At this point before analysing, in the next sections, different problems and the different statistical tests developed to solve them, two large categories of tests which provide a bridge between the general presentation of the hypothesis testing procedure and more specific tests need to be introduced. This should throw some light on the importance of assumptions and give examples of tests that are more powerful than others.

Parametric tests are statistical tests based on the use *of parameters* (thus their name) such as mean, standard deviation, standard error, etc. They require some assumptions about the population in question.

The three most important **assumptions of parametricity** are:

a. The **normality** of the population distribution, which allows one to use z-scores and evaluate the percentage of the population under the normal curve within any given interval.

b. The **homogeneity of variance** which signifies that the variances of the groups being compared are equal. This condition, also called **homoscedasticity** (a Greek term meaning equal spread) is necessary in order to compare normal distributions. As shown previously, two normal distributions with the same mean and variance are equal. Therefore, in order to test a null hypothesis stating that two population distributions are not significantly different, one has to be sure that they have very similar means and standard deviations.

c. The **interval or ratio scale of measurement** must be used, that is, the data collected must be expressed by figures on at least an interval scale. Clearly, this presentation is essential if one needs to calculate the mean and standard deviation of the distribution. In other words, parametric tests should not be applied when comparing the opinion of different groups of people since those differences are measured on an ordinal or even a nominal scale.

After the hypotheses have been stated, all these preconditions must also be clearly stated, if this kind of test is to be used. In theory a parametric test can be selected only if all such preconditions have been fulfilled. In practice, however, the three preconditions can be weakened without greatly compromising the quality of the test results. If a population distribution is only approximately normal, if the variances are very close to one another without being equal, and if the scale of measurement is an ordinal one, for example, when using a 5- or 7-point attitude scale, the majority of the parametric tests are **robust** enough not to be affected by the violation of the assumptions. There are a number of tests that can be used to assess whether the normality and homoscedasticity preconditions are satisfied, but they are beyond the scope of this book.

Non-parametric tests demand very few preconditions to be stated under 'general characteristics'. Some of these tests rely on an ordinal scale of measurement, some on a nominal one; some require a minimum size of sample, etc. Again, before selecting a particular non-parametric test, these conditions must be known. Note that, since no conditions are made related to some specific properties of the distribution, for instance, normality, non-parametric tests are also called **'distribution-free tests'**. These tests will be discussed in more detail later in this chapter.

As parametric tests seem to be much more demanding, the question of their real usefulness arises. Why not only use non-parametric tests? The main reason is that, although more complex, parametric tests are more powerful and thus more reliable than non-parametric tests. In fact, when their assumptions are satisfied, they are always

CHAPTER 14 Quantitative data analysis and interpretation

to be preferred to non-parametric ones. A more detailed account of the differences between the two kinds of statistical tests, as well as guidelines on how to select the most appropriate ones, follows later in this chapter.

Other characteristics of statistical tests

Bivariate vs. multivariate analysis
When analysing only one sample which is done in descriptive statistics, the process is called **univariate analysis**. **Bivariate analysis** is the analysis of two variables simultaneously and the concurrent analysis of multiple variables is known as **multivariate analysis**. As soon as more than one sample is considered, the analysis aims at determining the relationship between the samples. For example, a frequency distribution of the data collected on the trained workers, which is usually the first step of the process, is a univariate analysis. A statistical test, such as a t-test, applied on the two samples of agricultural workers in order to test a hypothesis and explain the difference, will be a bivariate analysis. More complex techniques, such as *Anova* and *correlations*, are examples of multivariate analysis, which can involve the simultaneous analysis of relationships between three or more samples and variables.

Tests for independent or dependent samples
When choosing the correct test to apply to a particular research project, one of the criteria is whether the samples are independent of each other, such as the two samples used in the agricultural workers of the research mentioned above, or whether the elements of the one sample are related or matched with the corresponding element in the other sample, that is, that the samples are dependent, such as when comparing the agricultural outputs of husbands and wives (see Chapter 11). In general, statistical tests use different formulae for each of these cases (such as t-test of dependent or independent samples) and some tests can only to be used with particular types of samples.

Parametric tests: Comparing means

The student's t-test

When using statistics, a social scientist needs to be confident that these statistics correctly reflect the reality under study. Can the measures describing the central tendency or the dispersion of a distribution be relied upon or trusted? Will inferences based on these statistics be correct? Without this confidence, a researcher cannot draw any inference or conclusion and cannot reach an assured knowledge of a whole population. As has already been mentioned, researchers usually depend on samples drawn from a population. They generalise the results based on the sample statistics in order to answer questions regarding population parameters, that is, they infer properties of the population from information obtained from the samples. Clearly, this refers to populations satisfying parametric conditions and what follows introduces parametric tests.

In this case two types of hypotheses will be considered. The first deals with the question of whether or not a group of data or a sample is really drawn from a given population with known parameters. The second attempts to determine if, given two samples which may or may not be dependent, the difference between the two sample means can be attributed to chance factors and therefore that the two samples belong to the same population, or if the difference is significant and the two samples do belong to different populations. A parametric test, called the student t-test, is then discussed along with its application to the testing of the hypotheses to solve these kinds of problems.

Let us recall the standard process of hypothesis testing (as presented in the previous section) that will be followed in all cases:
1. State the null hypothesis and the alternative hypothesis.
2. Indicate the general characteristics regarding the population normality, whether the groups are independent or related, and the scale of measurement.
3. Indicate the elements that the decision rules depend on: the level of significance chosen, the type of alternative hypothesis (directional or not), and then formulate the decision rules by comparing the probability value p and the level of significance α.
4. Based on the computations of the appropriate statistical test, obtain the probability value p.
5. The decision as to whether or not to reject the null hypothesis is made after comparing the obtained probability value p and the level of significance α, and referring to the decision rules.
6. Draw the conclusion according to the alternative hypothesis and the problem under consideration.

Comparison between the mean of a population and of a single sample

A researcher studying income distribution in rural areas has collected 50 data from a rural community near the capital of the country. However, his concern is that this community might not adequately represent all rural communities in the country. In other words, he questions whether his sample comes from the total rural population, so that he will be able to generalise his findings. Can he use his sample to represent the whole rural population? Could the results or characteristics of that sample be considered as valid for the population? Or is there a sampling bias? Fortunately, the latest national population survey gives the parameters, mean and standard deviation of the income distribution for the total rural population. This allows the researcher to compare the population distribution with his sample distribution by comparing their respective means.

More generally, if one takes a sample and calculates its mean, the question that arises is 'How good or accurate is this sample mean as an estimate of the population mean?' This question is clearly related to but different from the issue studied in the previous

CHAPTER 14 Quantitative data analysis and interpretation

section of determining a point estimation or interval estimation of a population mean based on a sample mean. This is a broader approach since it also allows us to ascertain whether a sample under study has been drawn from a given population or whether the difference between the means is indicative of its belonging to another population. In other words, given a set of data or a sample and a certain population, one can test the null hypothesis that the difference between the means is due to chance factors. This is opposed to the alternative hypothesis that the difference between means is significant, that is, that the given sample is somehow different from that population.

One should always keep in mind that the accuracy of an estimate can only be assessed in terms of probability and as such one can never reach complete certainty.

Example

Let us consider a research project on the size of newborn babies. Suppose a researcher is given a set of 64 measurements of the sizes of newborn babies born to urban, high income parents. The mean size is $x = 55$ cm. The population of all the babies born in the same year in that country, independent of the geographic and economic situation of their parents, has a mean of 50 cm and a standard deviation of 5 cm. The researcher wishes to find out if the given sample was drawn from the population having the above parameters, that is, if the new-born babies of urban, high economic class parents are essentially of the same size at birth as the babies of the whole population.

1. The *null hypothesis* H_0 states that there is no significant difference between the sample mean x and the population mean. The *experimental or alternative hypothesis* H_1 states that the difference between the means cannot be explained by chance factors alone, that is, that the sample was drawn from another population.
2. The *general characteristics* are:
    - The population distribution is normal.
    - The sample distribution is normal.
    - The measurement is at least on an interval scale.
3. To establish the *decision rules*, one first has to determine:
    - the level of significance given as $\alpha = ,01$
    - the type of test: it is a non-directional test
    - the obtained probability value p.
    Finally, the decision rules are:
    - If p is larger than $\alpha = ,01$, then do not reject H_0.
    - If p is equal or smaller than $\alpha = ,01$, then reject H_0.
4. The *computations* of the t-test give a probability value smaller than of $p = ,00001$.
5. As the obtained probability value is smaller than $\alpha = ,01$, the *decision* is to reject the null hypothesis.
6. The *conclusion* is that the sample with a mean $x = 55$ cm was not drawn from the population with the mean of 50 cm. In other words, the relatively large size of the babies of the sample is to be explained by factors unique to the specific population of well-off parents.

285

Comparison between the means of two samples

Quite often researchers are confronted with situations where they need to test a hypothesis regarding the difference between the means of two samples. They may have experimental and control groups randomly chosen from a population or they may try to measure a characteristic under two different conditions. In such situations one is dealing with two statistics, say the mean of a group A and the mean of a group B: the mean of a group of girls compared to the mean of a group of boys, the mean of pre-test scores, and the mean of post-test scores, etc. Such situations are obviously different from those in the last section where only one statistic at a time was involved and compared to a parameter.

Let us first define the underlying problem. A researcher would like to assess the influence or relevance of a given variable (the independent variable), the sex of the subject, for instance, on a certain behaviour or performance (the dependent variable), say 'punctuality at work'. If this characteristic (the sex of the workers, in this case) is essential for the behaviour under study, then one expects that *the female population*, that is, the distribution of the data for all female workers, will be essentially different from the *male population*, that is, the distribution of the data for all male workers. As a consequence any *female sample* will be essentially different from any *male sample*.

On the other hand, if the variable under study, the sex of the workers, has no influence on the behaviour or performance of the subjects, *the female and male populations* will coincide. Their parameters will be the same and they will constitute a single population of workers. In this case the differences observed when comparing a sample of female and a sample of male workers will only be attributable to random factors, such as sampling error.

Based on this reasoning, the difference between the means of two given samples has to be analysed with the aim of assessing whether these samples come from essentially different populations or if they have been drawn from the same population, in other words, whether the property that differentiates the samples has a significant action or influence at the level of the underlying populations. To be very clear, researchers do not compare two samples with a view to making some statements related to those samples only, but prefer to discover properties of the populations from which the samples have been drawn. Accordingly, the null hypothesis will always assume that the two *populations* being compared are identical.

It is important to grasp the whole meaning of such a statement. In the case of parametric tests, populations are assumed to be normally distributed and the criteria for comparison are their *parameters*. As already explained, normal curves are identical if their means and standard deviations or variances coincide. Hence, when testing the significance of the difference between the means of two populations, if their means are equal, one can conclude that the distributions are the same providing that their variances (or standard deviations) are equal. It is thus essential to *assume the homogeneity of the variances as a prerequisite to the test*.

CHAPTER 14 Quantitative data analysis and interpretation

Finally, the two samples or groups whose means are to be compared may be either independent and unrelated, or dependent and correlated (as defined in Chapter 11). If the two samples are taken at random from two populations, they will be independent, but if a group of subjects is used twice under different conditions, the two sets of scores will be dependent.

Comparison between two independent samples

Given two unrelated groups A and B, the issue is to find out whether they are similar or not. If no information on the populations is available, one has to limit the analysis to the given groups and later infer the properties of the populations from the results obtained. The method to be applied in this case is to compare the means of the two groups, more precisely, to analyse their difference under the assumption that the two groups belong to the same population or to two populations with the same mean. In order to achieve this, one needs to refer implicitly to a sampling distribution of the difference between means. One has to check whether the difference between the means of the two groups lies in the confidence interval or in the rejection area of this sampling distribution. In so doing, one tests the null hypothesis that there is no true difference between the two population means.

For the *t*-test to be applied, some *general characteristics* have to be fulfilled. They are:
1. The subjects are independently and randomly sampled within each sample, that is, a probability sampling must have been used.
2. The groups are independent or unrelated.
3. The measurements are made on an interval scale.
4. The sampling distribution of the difference between the means is a normal distribution.
5. The population variances are homogeneous.

(In practice, the truthfulness of assumptions 4 and 5 concerning the populations is rarely checked.)

> ### Example
>
> Let us develop the example on the punctuality of workers. A researcher is interested in finding out whether punctuality is related to the sex of the workers, that is, whether female and male populations differ in respect to punctuality. Suppose a punctuality test has been administered to 75 female workers and to 60 male workers of a certain factory. On the basis of the (fictitious) data collected, the statistics (mean and standard deviation) have been computed for the female sample *F* and the male sample *M*, and the steps of the hypothesis testing are as follows:
>
> *continued ...*

287

1. The *null hypothesis* expresses no significant difference between the punctuality of female and male workers.
   - The *alternative hypothesis* states a significant difference between the two underlying populations, that is, that gender influences punctuality.
2. The *general characteristics* are the five ones stated above.
3. The *decision rules* will depend on:
   a. the level of significance $\alpha = 0{,}01$
   b. the alternative hypothesis is non-directional
   c. the obtained probability value p.
   Thus, the *decision rules* are:
   - If p is larger than $\alpha = 0{,}01$, then do not reject H_0.
   - If p is equal or smaller than $\alpha = 0{,}01$, then reject H_0.
4. The *computations* of the t-test for independent samples lead to the probability value $p = 0{,}15$.
5. The *decision* in this case is not to reject the null hypothesis, since p is larger than 0,01.
6. The *conclusion* is that the punctuality of the workers is not influenced by their sex.

Comparison between two dependent samples

In the example dealing with workers' punctuality, the two samples are clearly independent or unrelated. However, sometimes one test is administered twice on the same group of subjects. For instance, the group of female workers might be tested before and after a substantial improvement in their conditions of service to observe the effect of this change on punctuality (refer to Chapter 10 for a pre-test/post-test design). In such a case, the results of the test and the re-test are dependent on each other and the means of the two sets of scores are said to be correlated. A correlation coefficient (refer to the section on correlation) can therefore be calculated (by statistical software) which will express the strength of the relationship.

Data can sometimes occur in pairs that are matched in such a way that each person or object or event in a group has a match in a second group. The means of such equivalent groups are also correlated. Because of the matching process or the process of using the same subjects twice, related samples always have the same size. In comparing the case of independent and dependant samples, it is important to note that some *general characteristics* are different. Because of the property of the two samples of being dependent on each other or matched, both samples have the same number of elements and the data take the form of pairs of scores that can be numbered from 1 to n (where n is the size of the groups). Instead of calculating the difference of the means of the two samples as is done for independent groups, in this case the difference between the two scores of each pair is taken. Thus assumption 4 of the general assumptions for independent samples now becomes:

4. The sampling distribution of the differences (D) between the pairs of scores is normal.

CHAPTER 14 Quantitative data analysis and interpretation

Of course, assumption 2 must also be altered to reflect that:

2. The two samples are dependent or matched.

An example of an experiment investigating the learning abilities of elderly people will illustrate the usage of this test.

Example

Twelve seniors over 75 years old are asked to learn a series of words by repeating them ten times. A scoring system is used where improvements in both the amount of time taken and the number of words recalled lead to a higher score. The researcher would like to assess whether the improvement from the first to the tenth trial is significant. The observed data are given in Table 14.6.

Table 14.6 *Memory test: Learning scores of the first and tenth trial*			
Participants	1st trial	10th trial	Difference
1	56	68	+ 12
2	42	48	+ 6
3	58	72	+ 14
4	53	50	− 3
5	56	65	+ 9
6	54	62	+ 8
7	40	52	+ 12
8	40	46	+ 6
9	58	54	− 4
10	44	46	+ 2
11	52	58	+ 6
12	60	78	+ 18

1. The *null hypothesis* states that there is no significant difference between the performances of the participants before and after the training programme, and therefore that the means of the two underlying populations will be the same.

   The *alternative hypothesis* states that the training has a positive effect on the performance; that the senior citizens perform better at the last trial than at the first one.

continued ...

289

2. The *general characteristics* are:
   a. The subjects are independently and randomly sampled.
   b. The two groups are related or dependent on each other.
   c. The measurements are made on an interval scale.
   d. The sampling distribution of the differences D between the pairs of scores is normal.
3. The *decision rules* will depend on:
   a. the level of significance $\alpha = 0,05$
   b. the direction of the test given by H_1
   c. the probability value p.
   Thus, the decision rules are:
   If p is larger than $\alpha = 0,05$, then do not reject H_0.
   If p is equal or smaller than $\alpha = 0,05$, then reject H_0.
4. The *computation* of the t-test for dependent samples lead to $p = 0,001$.
5. The *decision* is thus to reject the null hypothesis that the 10 trials have no significant influence on the memory capabilities of the elderly people.
6. The *conclusion* drawn from this experiment is that training improves the memory performance of people over 75 years. This is the case, although in Table 14.6 one can observe that some of the differences between the the first and last trials are negative. In other words, some of the participants struggled more at the last trial than they did at the first one, although this was not true of most participants. The test does, however, allow the researcher to conclude that the general trend shows an improvement at the end of the trials.

Analysis of variance: *Anova*

When a social researcher has to assess the effect of an independent variable by comparing two samples, the use of the student t-test, as discussed above, is most often recommended. However, multivariate cases, situations where more than two samples are involved, are generally dealt with by using the analysis of variance, also called *Anova*. It is not uncommon for a social scientist to be confronted with situations where more than two samples need to be compared in order to test the significance of their differences. Examples of this might be the death rates due to road accidents in three major towns of a country (3 samples), the effectiveness of five methods of teaching a vernacular language to foreigners (5 samples), the impact of four different types of agricultural training on soya beans yields (4 samples), the average production of eight milling factories (8 samples), or the change of attitude towards traditional birth control in ten rural communities (10 samples). Such problems raise the question as to how one can test the significance of the differences between any number of groups, and if the repeated use of the student t-test, taking a pair of groups at a time, would be an adequate method. As it happens the procedure of testing pairs of samples using the student t-test involves many technical problems, most importantly that only two

CHAPTER 14 Quantitative data analysis and interpretation

samples can be taken at a time when using a t-test, and therefore certain type of information cannot be extracted. A researcher who is interested in the interrelationship between all the samples together rather than in the comparison of pairs of samples would need to measure the concomitant influence the different variables have on each other,m which the student-t test cannot do. In this case the best statistical tool is the analysis of variance. Like the t-test it is a parametric test which analyses whether all the samples under consideration have been drawn from the same population or if some of them come from other populations. *Anova* estimates the probability of the sample means differing from one another by sampling error. It answers the question: 'Can the observed differences between samples be attributed to chance or are they indicative of actual differences between the means of the corresponding populations?'

Theoretical considerations

The analysis of variance was first conceived by Ronald A. Fisher, and therefore it is often referred to as the F-test. This statistical tool, though generally considered to be an extension of the t-test, is based on some specific reasoning that needs to be clearly understood. The analysis of variance can be applied to three or more groups of any size. The measure of central tendency used to characterise the samples is the mean, and the measure of variability is the variance, as indicated by the name of the test.

The **null hypothesis** H_0 states that the means of the populations from which the various samples (say k in number) are drawn are all equal. In addition, if the group consisting of all the scores of all the groups (samples) combined is called the **total or combined group**, the **total or grand mean** of its underlying population is also equal to the other population means.

The **alternative hypothesis** states that the population means are not equal, that is that the statement of H_0 is not true. It is important to note that the alternative hypothesis does not indicate which means differ significantly, nor how they differ. It is possible for one mean to differ from all the others, or in an extreme situation for all means to take distinct values. Moreover, since more than two means are being considered, an inequality valid for the whole set of means cannot be expressed, from which one can infer that *Anova* is not a directional test. This is confirmed when looking at the **F-test or *Anova* distribution**.

The most important feature of *Anova* is that the total variability of the scores, that is, their variability or dispersion within the total or combined group, is split into two components. In other words, for each score of the total group, a two-step process is followed. In the first step, the score is looked at as an element of a particular group and hence compared to the mean of this group in order to measure its dispersion from that mean. This leads to the **within-group variation**, which is the average variability of the scores within each group. In the second step, the group containing that element (or, more precisely, its mean) must itself be compared to the other groups, or their means. The variation between these means is called the **between-group variation** and

291

it depends on both the variations of the individual scores within their own group (which determines the means of the groups) and the variations of the means themselves. Thus, the between-group variation is always at least equal to, or larger than, the within-group variation. One can also look at these two variations from another perspective. The within-group variation is indicative of sampling fluctuation or the **sampling error**, which takes place when drawing the samples from their respective populations. The between-group variation, however, reflects the characteristics of each group. If the purpose of testing the significance of the difference between the given groups is to assess the effect of a particular independent variable, each group would be subjected to a different level of that variable, called the **treatment**. In other words, the differences between the means of all the groups will indicate the effect of the treatment.

In short the **total variation**, which is the sum of the between-group variation and the within-group variation, measures the treatment effect and the sampling error. Under the null hypothesis, the treatment effect is not significant and the groups are essentially the same, even though they might be affected by chance factors or sampling error. Thus the two variations (within and between groups) and the corresponding variances or their estimates are identical and constitute the unbiased estimates of the same population variance. One can calculate the ratio of the between-group variance, and the within-group variance. This ratio is called the **F-ratio**: it expresses the equality (or the lack of it) of the two variances. The null hypothesis stating that the populations are the same, that is, that the treatment has no effect, implies that the between and within group variations are nearly the same and hence the F-ratio takes a value very near 1.

Procedure for the *F*-test

1. The *hypotheses* as stated under the theoretical considerations are as follows:
   - The *null hypothesis* H_0 states that all means are equal.
   - The *alternative hypothesis* H_1 is simply that at least two means are different.
2. The *general characteristics* are similar to those of the student *t*-test for independent samples:
   a. The different groups are independent from one another.
   b. The subjects in each group are randomly and independently selected.
   c. The population distributions are normal.
   d. The population variances are homogeneous.
   e. The measurements are made on an interval scale.
   In certain situations, there might be slight departures from assumptions 3 and 4 but *Anova* could still be used, which speaks to the robust nature of this parametric test.

CHAPTER 14 Quantitative data analysis and interpretation

3. The *decision rules* depend on:
   a. The chosen level of significance α.
   b. The obtained probability value p.
   Because of the shape of the F-distribution and because F is a non-directional test, the decision rules are:
   If p is larger than α, then H_0 is not rejected.
   If p is equal or smaller than α, then H_0 is rejected.
4. The *computations* of the F-ratio are quite complex, but statistical software will calculate the probability level p.
5. The *decision* of whether or not to reject the null hypothesis is based on the comparison of the obtained probability value p and the level of significance according to the decision rules.
6. The *conclusion* is drawn from the decision regarding the null and alternative hypothesis.

Example

Example of an *F*-test

The scores of three classes which have been taught under different pedagogical methods are to be examined in order to infer whether or not these three methods are significantly different. The observed scores are given below.

Group I	Group II	Group III
23	8	11
17	12	9
19	15	7
20	10	5
	15	8
	6	

1. The *null hypothesis* of no difference between the three methods states that the means are the same. The *alternative hypothesis* states that the three methods are somehow not the same: in other words, H_1: *At least two means are different.*
2. The *general characteristics* are as given above.
3. The *decision rules depend* on:
   a. *The level* of significance chosen, $\alpha = 0,05$.
   b. The obtained probability value p.
      Finally, the decision rules are:
      If p is larger than α, the H_0 is not rejected.
      If p is equal or smaller than α, then H_0 is rejected.

continued ...

Fundamentals of Social Research Methods: An African Perspective

4. The *computations*, done step by step through the statistical software, give the following results:

Anova					
Score					
	Sum of squares	df	Mean square	F	Sig.
Between groups	324,583	2	162,292	18,244	0,000
Within groups	106,750	12	8,896		
Total	431,333	14			

5. The *decision* is taken to reject the null hypothesis since $p = 0,000$ is smaller than $\alpha = 0,05$. (Note that p is represented in the table above by 'sig.' which stands for statistical significance.)
6. The *conclusion* is then that the three methods of teaching are significantly different, or that the performances of students vary according to the method used, or again, that some methods are more effective than others.

Two-factor or two-way analysis of variance

One-way analysis of variance is applied when the groups of samples are classified by one criterion, only to see if the means of the groups differ significantly or not. However, a researcher might want to compare five groups of baby food of different content in terms of their respective quality. Equally, if she wanted to study the effect of socio-economic status on health conditions in a population, the independent variable might be expressed in terms of monthly income and three groups of low, medium and high income might be compared. In another example, the yield of sunflowers per acre may be the only criterion used to select a specific number of samples. In an earlier example the three different methods of teaching are the variable on the basis of which three groups were formed. However, any of the above illustrations using a one-way *Anova* could in practice be more complex and could involve the study of a second independent variable.

For example, the baby food could be analysed on the basis of its content *and* its retail price. The health conditions of a population could be studied in relation to the socio-economic status of the people *and* their geographic situation (rural or urban). The quality of the seeds *and* of the soil could be the criteria for comparing yields of sunflowers, and one might want to analyse the effect of three methods of teaching and of different kinds of teachers on the performance of pupils. Such instances require a two-factor or two-way analysis of variance. The two-factor *Anova* clearly reveals that the groups of a study are classified by two criteria which are *two independent variables* called **factors**, in this case, factor A and factor B. Each of these two independent variables may have two or more **levels** or values. In a two-way *Anova*, each factor can

294

CHAPTER 14 Quantitative data analysis and interpretation

have any number of levels equal to or larger than two. These various levels may differ qualitatively (for instance, the quality of the baby food or the sex of the teachers), or quantitatively (for instance, the protein content of the food or the age or the school grade of the participants).

Example

In the example of methods of teaching, there may be three or four different methods under consideration, each one representing a level in the variable called the methods of teaching. If the second variable is taken as 'sex of the teacher', this factor would have two levels, male and female. If the significance of three methods of teaching and two categories of teachers, male and female, have to be studied, the two-way *Anova* will give information on a. whether the pupils taught under the three different methods differ in their performance, b. whether the performance of the pupils taught by male teachers differs from those taught by female teachers, and also c. whether there is any interaction between the method of teaching and the sex of teacher in respect of the performance of the subjects. The last aspect relates to the assumption that some of the teaching methods might be more effective when practiced by male than by female teachers, or that the female image and role in society may make it easier for female teachers to successfully adopt methods of teaching which are emotionally laden rather than authoritarian. Equally, it may also be that female teachers are more effective using method A, male teachers using method B and that, for method C, there is no difference in the performance of female and male teachers.

The previous discussion makes it clear that a two-way *Anova* allows one to analyse two types of effect. The **main effects** relate to the separate actions of the two independent variables or factors that constitute the treatment. In the example above this is reflected in points a. and b. The **interaction effect** relates to the combined action of the two factors or how these actions interfere with one another as in point c. above. A more detailed description of this instrument is beyond the scope of this book.

Non-parametric tests

Non-parametric or **distribution-free tests** are statistical tests that analyse data without assumptions about the distribution and can also be used in situations where measurement is made on an ordinal, or even a nominal scale, where data are ranked or belong to various categories. However, because they are distribution-free, that is non-sensitive to any property of distribution, when non-parametric tests compare two (or more) populations, they do not indicate precisely the criteria about which populations are the same (H_0) or are significantly different (H_1). Unlike parametric tests, one cannot infer from the rejection of the null hypothesis that the means of the populations are different or even that the mean of one population is larger than the mean of another. In fact, non-parametric tests only evaluate whether populations are or are not significantly different, while giving no indication of the nature of the difference:

be it central tendency, variability, properties of shape like skewness, or other criteria. This is the major distinction between parametric and non-parametric tests and the way in which they test hypotheses. The main advantage of non-parametric tests is their lack of stringent assumptions, but they do have the disadvantage of not using all the information contained in the data. They are therefore neither as **robust**, nor as **powerful** or **effective** as parametric tests.

These advantages and disadvantages of non-parametric methods over parametric ones often make it difficult to choose between them. There are no concrete guidelines that can be followed regarding the choice, but for any parametric test there is a non-parametric counterpart. In spite of the popularity of non-parametric tests, whenever a situation satisfies the assumptions for parametric tests, the use of those tests is preferable, if only because of their effectiveness and robust nature. In situations where some assumptions cannot be satisfied, the choice of the distribution-free tests is inevitable and they will at least allow one to make inferences or test the significance of difference without assumptions.

A commonly used non-parametric test is called the Chi-square test. Its relevance for social research stems from its very broad usage, based on nominal scale and frequencies, and the fact that it can apply to any number of independent samples. Thereafter, the distinction between the use of independent or dependant samples will determine the choice of other non-parametric tests.

The chi-square test

Definition of concepts and procedure

The chi-square test (or X^2) from the Greek letter X, (pronounced Ki) simply tests whether the observed or actual frequency of a phenomenon corresponds to the frequency which should have been recorded, that is, which is expected if the hypothesis under study was correct. It is thus based on a comparison between **observed frequencies** and **expected frequencies**, that is, between the given facts and the theoretical anticipation, in order to assess whether the facts support those theoretical considerations. Since only the frequencies of events are analysed, the scale of measurement on which the data are recorded is irrelevant: the Chi-square test is very often applied to data recorded in categories only (nominal scale), such as sex, marital status, religious denomination, political affiliation, nationality, area of residence, etc, of respondents. If the data are of an ordinal or interval nature, they are put into independent categories in different rank groups or class-intervals, and the frequencies of those are measured.

The Chi-square test is usually considered a non-directional test whenever there are more than two categories (for reasons similar to those given for *Anova)*, and it does not give any information about the degree of relationship or association between the variables. Since the Chi-square test only analyses frequencies, it can be used in a variety of ways: it can be applied to the study of a single factor with two or more levels

CHAPTER 14 Quantitative data analysis and interpretation

or categories, the **one-way design**, in a study of two factors with any number of levels from two upwards, the **two-way design**, in the study of some characteristics of the frequency distribution, the **median test**, or even in the investigation of whether a given distribution is normal or not, the **goodness of fit** test.

The contingency table for expected and observed frequencies

Contingency tables were introduced when dealing with the presentation of data. Chi-square tables are contingency tables of a simple kind. A table, which has a number of rows (r) and a number of columns (c), is called a $r \times c$ contingency table. Usually, a table has two **entries** indicating the **independent variables** or **factors** studied. Each factor has a certain number **of levels**, each of them recorded in a separate row or column.

What exactly are these expected and observed frequencies? Chance games like tossing a coin or throwing a dice rely on the knowledge that, if the coin or the dice is not biased, the probability of a head or a tail appearing is one out of two, or 50%, and the probability of any one face of the dice appearing is one out of six. In other words, one can expect that when tossing a coin 60 times, the head will appear 30 times, and when throwing a dice 60 times, the three will appear 10 times. These are the **expected frequencies** that have been determined through the null hypothesis of the coin or the dice being homogeneous so that each possibility has the same chance of taking place, the same probability of occurrence.

However, in reality the frequency of appearance of heads on a coin or of face three of a dice during an actual game might be quite different from the expected frequency. One might record heads only 20 times and the three dots 15 times. These are the **observed frequencies** of the study or experiment. For each observed frequency there is an expected frequency.

Although expected frequencies are inferred from the null hypothesis (no significant difference between the frequencies of the various categories), they are seldom as easy to compute as those above.

The one-factor study or $1 \times c$ contingency table

The easiest application of the chi-square test deals with the study of a single variable and its various levels or values. The classical example is the one of the frequency of occurrence of the faces of a dice. There are six possibilities or levels for this variable. Each one constitutes a category, which is entered in a separate column. Thus there will be only one row and six columns leading to a 1×6 contingency table. As mentioned earlier, the chi-square test assesses whether the observed frequencies of each face corresponds to the frequency which is expected for a homogenous dice, that is, if all the categories have the same probability of occurring.

297

In social research, similar problems often occur. For instance, these questions might be asked: 'Do women and men participate equally in trade union meetings? Are the different cinemas in a small town frequented in the same way? Is the sale of movie tickets constant across weekdays? Is the hourly output of an assembly line constant during the working day?'

Obviously, in all these cases, it is not necessary to compute each expected frequency separately. If women and men are expected to participate equally in the trade union meetings, one assumes that there will be 50% of women and 50% of men attending the meetings. If n is the total number of participants, the expected value of each category is $E = \frac{n}{2}$. If the seven cinemas in a small town are frequented in the same way, one can establish a 1×7 contingency table and the expected frequencies of each category will be $E = \frac{n}{7}$, where n is the total number of customers. If the moviegoers visit the cinema evenly across the week, for each of the five days one would expect $E = \frac{n}{5}$ moviegoers to attend the daily performance and the results would form a 1×5 contingency table. Finally, if the daily output of an assembly line is n items, the expected hourly output would be $E = \frac{n}{8}$ for an ordinary eight-hour working day, and that would be recorded in a 1×8 contingency table. It is clear then that whenever all the categories are expected to have the same probability of occurrence, the expected frequencies of a $1 \times c$ contingency table with a total frequency of n are given by $E = \frac{n}{c}$. In the general case, however, the expected frequencies may have to be determined through other criteria, as will be illustrated in the goodness of fit-test, on page 301.

Steps of the chi-square test: the $1 \times c$ contingency table

1. *Hypotheses:*
   - H_0: There is no difference between the observed and expected frequencies of the various categories of data in the population distribution.
   - H_1: There are significant differences between observed and expected frequencies. (This can be true for all or only some of the categories.)

2. *General characteristics:*
   a. The data are randomly and independently sampled.
   b. All categories are mutually exclusive (that is, each observation qualifies for one and only one category).

3. *Decision rules* depend on:
   a. The chosen level of significance α.
   b. The obtained probability value p.
   Thus, the *decision rules* are:
   - If p is larger than α, then H_0 is not rejected.
   - If p is equal or smaller than α, then H_0 is rejected.

CHAPTER 14 Quantitative data analysis and interpretation

4. *Computations:*
The statistical software will compute the probability value p based on the given data.

5. *Decision and conclusions:*
They are inferred directly by comparing the observed probability value p with α, according to the decision rules.

Example

Thirty people were asked to express their opinion regarding the introduction of new legislation on a three-point scale: favourable, indifferent and unfavourable. The results are as follows, where O stands for observed value and E for expected value:

Table 14.7a. *Chi-square contingency table 1×3: Opinion*

Opinion			Total
Favourable	Indifferent	Unfavourable	
$O_1 = 18$ $E_1 = 10$	$O_2 = 8$ $E_2 = 10$	$O_3 = 4$ $E_3 = 10$	$n = 30$

1. The *null hypothesis* is that this new law has equal number of supporters, antagonists and people with no opinion about it.
    The *alternative hypothesis* is that these three categories are not the same.

2. The *general characteristics* are all satisfied, the categories are mutually exclusive and the data are independently and randomly sampled.

3. The *decision rules* are determined for a chosen level of significance $\alpha = ,05$ and the obtained probability value p. Thus the decision rules are:
    a. If p is larger than α, then H_0 is not rejected.
    b. If p is equal or smaller than α, then H_0 is rejected.

4. The *computations* based on the data given in the 1×3 contingency table where the value of the expected frequency is determined by $E = \frac{n}{c} = \frac{30}{3} = 10$ indicates a probability value of $p = 0,006$.

5. The *decision* is hence to reject H_0 and one concludes that at least one opinion is more commonly held than the others.

If, in the same example, the observed frequencies were much closer to the expected ones, for example, 11 favourable opinions, 10 indifferent and 9 unfavourable opinions, the null hypothesis would not have been rejected, since the respondents' opinions would not have shown any major differences.

299

The two-factor study or a (r × c) contingency table

If a researcher intends to examine the effect of two independent variables, each one with different levels, the number of rows of the contingency table will be $r > 1$. For example, the previous investigation could include as a second variable either the sex of the participants (2 × 3 table), or their socio-economic class, or three variables for primary, secondary and tertiary levels of education (3 × 3 table), or four variables to compare the opinions of people towards four different legislation proposals (4 × 3 table). If one wants to assess opinions about the same issue, but on a more differentiated 5-point scale, rather than the 3-point scale used above, one would then use a 4 × 5 table, etc.

The rationale here is similar to the 1 × c-study described above: to test the significance of the differences between the observed and expected frequencies.

Example

A researcher aims at assessing the attitudes of people towards a new law. One hundred people, 60 male and 40 female, are asked to express their opinions regarding the new legislation using a three-point scale: favourable, indifferent and unfavourable. The frequency of each category is recorded in a 2 × 3 contingency table, where O stands for observed value and E for expected value.

The expected values are determined by the frequency of each category (e.g. 40 favourable answers of the 100 respondents) adapted to the size of the group (e.g. 40 females). A figure of 40 out of 100 equates to 16 out of 40. Therefore, the expected number of females giving a favourable response is $E_{11} = 16$.

Table 14.7b. *Chi-square contingency table 2 × 3: Opinion by gender*

Sex of respondents	Opinion			Total
	Favourable	Indifferent	Unfavourable	
Female	$O_{11} = 10$ $E_{11} = 16$	$O_{12} = 15$ $E_{12} = 14$	$O_{13} = 15$ $E_{13} = 10$	$n_1 = 40$
Male	$O_{21} = 30$ $E_{21} = 24$	$O_{22} = 20$ $E_{22} = 21$	$O_{23} = 10$ $E_{23} = 15$	$n_2 = 60$
TOTAL	$C_1 = 40$	$C_2 = 35$	$C_3 = 25$	$n = 100$

In this example, one factor is **gender**, with its two levels or categories, male and female, each in its own column. The other factor is **opinion**, here with three levels or values: favourable, indifferent, unfavourable. The data for each of these levels are recorded in separate rows.

Median test

When a researcher is interested in finding out whether two groups are the same in terms of their median, or whether their medians are significantly different, the chi-square test can easily be adapted to this problem. If the two groups are drawn from the same

CHAPTER 14 Quantitative data analysis and interpretation

population, then it is expected that half of the scores in each group should lie above the *common median*, and half below it. The median test is based on the comparison of samples on the basis of the deviation from the common median of two independent groups that may or may not have the same size.

Test of goodness of fit

As mentioned earlier, the rationale of the chi-square-test is to compare observed and expected frequencies in order to assess whether the observations are near enough to the theoretical evaluations to accept that the differences are due to random factors only. This rationale can also be used to assess whether an **observed frequency distribution** approximates sufficiently well to a particular **theoretical frequency distribution**. In other words, given a set of data and its frequency distribution, one can evaluate how well that distribution fits a normal curve, or any other distribution. Clearly, one is testing the **goodness of fit** of the observed and the theoretical distributions. The importance of such a test is obvious when one remembers that the normality of a distribution is a precondition (or assumption) for the use of parametric tests. Hence, the necessity for having a method to test whether a distribution is normal or not, before deciding which type of test to apply to the problem. Only the goodness of fit test for a **normal distribution** will be considered here.

The general idea for the procedure rests on a $1 \times c$ contingency table related to the class-interval frequency distribution of the observed data. For each class-interval and its frequency there is a corresponding category or column on the contingency table which contains the observed frequency. On the other hand, to each class-interval corresponds an expected frequency, which is determined through the percentage of the *normal* distribution comprised in this interval.

Non-parametric tests for independent samples

This section describes two other non-parametric tests for independent samples – the Mann-Whitney and the Kruskal-Wallis tests. These can be used every time any one parametric condition, such as the normality of the distribution or the use of an interval scale, is not satisfied. The Mann-Whitney test is the non-parametric substitute for the student *t*-test, while the Kruskal-Wallis test is the counterpart of the one-way *Anova*. Fortunately, both have the advantage of being easy to compute.

The Mann-Whitney *U*-test

The Mann-Whitney test, also referred to as the *U*-test, is applied to two separate and uncorrelated groups, which might or might not be of the same size. Using an ordinal scale of measurement, it compares the order or rank of the data in the two groups with the aim of assessing whether any differences in the ranks can be explained by

Fundamentals of Social Research Methods: An African Perspective

chance factors alone. The rationale of the Mann-Whitney test is that if two samples are representative of the populations from which they have been drawn and if, when ranked together, their scores do not essentially differ in their ranking, then one can assume that those two samples have been drawn from the same population.

Example

The managing director of a company feels that there is a difference in production output between workers on the morning and afternoon shifts, all else being equal. In order to test this, the output of 18 workers working on either shift is given a numerical value on the basis of a set of criteria. The Mann-Whitney test is then used to see if the output of the groups is different. The following table includes the ranks of all data put together, that is, ranking done across both groups. The lowest score of 20 is ranked as 1 and the highest score of 68 as 18.

The scores are as follows:

Table 14.8a. *Production output of morning and afternoon shifts*

Group A: Morning shift		Group B: Afternoon shift	
Scores	Ranks	Scores	Ranks
20	1	31	6
24	3	40	11
34	7	68	18
54	16	60	17
39	10	45	14
35	8	30	5
28	4	42	12
21	2	50	15
		44	13
		38	9
$n_1 = 8$	$R_1 = 51$	$n_2 = 10$	$R_2 = 120$

1. The *null hypothesis* states that the production output of the morning and afternoon shifts do not differ significantly.
    The *alternative hypothesis* states that the production output of the workers on the morning and afternoon shifts is not the same.

continued ...

302

CHAPTER 14 Quantitative data analysis and interpretation

2. The *general characteristics* are:
   a. The groups are independent from each other.
   b. The subjects are randomly selected.
   c. The scale of measurement is at least ordinal.

3. The *decision rules* depend on:
   a. The level of significance $\alpha = ,02$.
   b. The alternative hypothesis, which is non-directional.
   c. The obtained probability value p.

   Thus, the *decision rules* are:
   If p is larger than α, then H_0 is not rejected.
   If p is equal or smaller than α, then H_0 is rejected.

4. The *computations* are through the statistical software and identify a probability value $p = 0,027$.

Table 14.8b. *Mann-Whitney U output table*	
Total N	18
Mann-Whitney U	65,000
Wilcoxon W	120,000
Test Statistic	65,000
Standard Error	11,255
Standardized Test Statistic	2,221
Asymptotic Sig (2-sided test)	0,026
Exact Sig (2-sided test)	0,027

5. The *decision* is thus to reject the null hypothesis: the distributions of the output of the morning and afternoon shift workers are different and the *conclusion* will be that the output of the workers is affected by the time of their shift.

Kruskal-Wallis *H*-test

The Kruskal-Wallis test, also called the *H*-test, is a very useful test because of two main characteristics. Firstly, it is considered an extension of the Mann-Whitney test, since it essentially deals with the same type of problems, but for more than two independent groups. Secondly, just as the Mann-Whitney test is the non-parametric equivalent of the student *t*-test for independent samples, so the Kruskal-Wallis test is the non-parametric equivalent of the one-way analysis of variance. It has no restrictive prerequisites concerning population distribution, such as normality or homogeneity of the variances,

Fundamentals of Social Research Methods: An African Perspective

and requires only an ordinal scale of measurement. It is based on the ranking of the scores of a set of k independent groups (where the number k can be three or more) in order to assess whether the ranks are well mixed among these groups, that is, that these groups stem from the same population, or whether the differences between them cannot be explained by chance factors alone. The *alternative hypothesis* assumes that the various independent groups somehow come from different populations. Bear in mind that because there are more than two groups involved, the Kruskal-Wallis test is not a directional test.

Example

Knowing the importance to mentally handicapped children of being accepted in their social environment, a social worker carried out a research project on the attitudes of a community towards these children. Three categories within the community were considered: children between 8 and 14 years, women between 20 and 40 years, and men in the same age group. Three random samples were drawn, one from each category, in an independent way: 5 children (Group I), 8 women (Group II) and 9 men (Group III) were interviewed and their scores were recorded on an ordinal scale. The results are shown in Table 14.9a.

Table 14.9a. *Survey on attitude towards handicapped children*

Group I : Children		Group II : Women		Group III: Men	
Scores	Ranks	Scores	Ranks	Scores	Ranks
4	1,5	4	1,5	8	4,5
25	17,5	6	3	12	7
25	17,5	8	4,5	13	8,5
30	21	10	6	15	10,5
34	22	13	8,5	18	12
		15	10,5	22	13,5
		22	13,5	24	16
		23	15	26	19
				28	20
$n_1 = 5$	$R_1 = 79,5$	$n_2 = 8$	$R_2 = 62,5$	$n_3 = 9$	$R_3 = 111$

1. The *null hypothesis* states that the attitudes of children, women and men towards challenged children are not significantly different. In this case, it means that the sums (R_i) of the ranks of the scores of the three groups are not significantly different.
   The *alternative hypothesis* states that children, women and men do not share the same attitude towards handicapped children.

continued ...

304

CHAPTER 14 Quantitative data analysis and interpretation

2. The *general characteristics* are:
   a. The groups are independent from each other.
   b. The subjects are randomly selected.
   c. The scale of measurement is at least ordinal.

3. The *decision rules* depend on:
   a. The level of significance $\alpha = 0,05$.
   b. The obtained probability value p.

   Thus, the *decision rules* are:
   - If p is larger than α, then H_0 is not rejected.
   - If p is equal or smaller than α, then H_0 is rejected.

4. *Computations:*
   The data, once inserted into the statistical software, will yield a probability value $p = 0,080$.

Table 14.9b. *Kruskal-Wallis H output table*	
Total N	22
Test Statistic	5,041
Degrees of Freedom	2
Asymptotic Sig (2-sided test)	0,080

5. The *decision* is thus not to reject the null hypothesis and the *conclusion* is that there is no significant difference in attitude between children, women and men towards handicapped children.

Non-parametric tests for dependent samples

Having looked at hypothesis testing related to independent samples, in this section we will deal with the same issue in respect of dependent samples. Two tests will be explored, the Wilcoxon test, which is the non-parametric equivalent of the student *t*-test for dependent groups, and the Friedman test, which is the non-parametric equivalent of the one-way *Anova* test for three or more dependent samples.

The Wilcoxon test

The Wilcoxon test can be compared to the *t*-test for dependent groups (which is its parametric counterpart), but it is also the equivalent for dependent groups of the *U*-test since both are non-parametric. However, the Wilcoxon test refers to dependent groups, where the scores of the two groups may be related in any way, as was explained for the *t*-test. The scores are in pairs and the two groups are of the same size. In other words, if a researcher wishes to know whether two dependent groups are drawn from the same population, two alternatives are available: either a *t*-test, or, if the normality conditions or other parametric conditions are not satisfied, the Wilcoxon test. Like the *U*-test, the Wilcoxon is based on ranks rather than the data themselves. The difference between each pair of scores of the two matched groups must therefore be worked out and then these differences are ranked, leading to **positive or negative ranks**, depending on the signs of the differences. In so doing, the test takes into account the **directions** as well as the **sizes of the differences** between the scores. The rationale of the test is that if the null hypothesis is true, that is, if the two population distributions are identical, then the positive and negative differences between the scores of sample A and sample B should be equal except for sampling error. In other words, there should be about the same number of occasions where the scores of group A are larger than those of group B and vice versa, and the sizes of the differences should also be about the same. H_0 states the possibility that the sums of positive and negative ranks are equal. If the scores of sample A and B are quite different and A>B, this will result in more positive differences and positive ranks , while if B>A, there will be more negative ranks. H_1 by contrast expresses the possibility that the sums of the positive and negative ranks are not equal. Finally, as usual, the *null hypothesis* states that the two population distributions are identical. The (non-directional) *alternative hypothesis states* that the population distributions are somehow different.

The *general characteristics* for the Wilcoxon test are the usual ones for non-parametric tests, in particular, an ordinal scale of measurement can be used. The *procedure* consists of finding the **differences between each pair of scores** which are then labelled D and ranked across the groups.

Example

In a marketing survey, two internet service providers are judged by a group of 10 people. In evaluating each service provider, each rater gives numerical scores to both services.

1. The *null hypothesis* states that the evaluations of the service providers are equivalent. The *alternative hypothesis* states that the judgements are different.

2. The *general characteristics* are:
   a. The two groups are related, since each rater gives two judgements.
   b. The pairs of data are independently and randomly selected.
   c. An ordinal and continuous scale of measurement is used.

3. The *decision rules* depend on:
   a. The level of significance, here $\alpha = 0,05$.
   b. The alternative hypothesis is non-directional.

continued . . .

CHAPTER 14 Quantitative data analysis and interpretation

Thus, the *decision rules* are:

a. If p is larger than α, then H_0 is not rejected.
b. If p is equal or smaller than α, then H_0 is rejected.

4. The *computations* regarding the ranking are done directly by statistical software. The presentation below only serves to make the underlying process of the Wilcoxon test in terms of the differences between the scores and their (signed) ranking more concrete. In practice, the obtained probability value p suffices to make a decision.

Table 14.10a. *Evaluation of service providers*

Rater	Service provider A	Service provider B	Difference	Rank	Signed rank
1	16	18	−2	5	−5
2	16	9	+7	9	+9
3	18	16	+2	5	+5
4	14	13	+1	2	+2
5	13	8	+5	8	+8
6	16	18	−2	5	−5
7	15	14	+1	2	+2
8	16	12	+4	7	+7
9	11	11	0	---	---
10	10	11	−1	2	−2

The observed probability value is in this case is $p = 0,210$.
Non-parametric Tests: Related Samples.

Table 14.10b. *Output for Wilcoxon test*

Total N	10
Test Statistic	12,000
Standard Error	8,382
Standardised Test Statistic	−1,253
Asymptotic Sig. (2-sided test)	0,210

5. The *decision* is thus not to reject the null hypothesis since the observed value is larger than the level of significance.

6. The *conclusion* is that the assessments or evaluations of the internet service providers A and B by the 10 people are equivalent, that is, that the peoples' estimations of the two service providers do not differ significantly.

The Friedman test

The Friedman test, also called the Friedman two-way analysis of variance, can be considered as an extension of the Wilcoxon test, as it also applies to dependent samples. However, it allows one to compare more than two samples. Its underlying reasoning is similar to the other non-parametric tests in that it assumes that if the groups being studied do not differ on the basis of the variable in question then the ranked scores will be equally distributed among all the groups. The testing process is based on ranking all the scores and the null hypothesis states that the ranking is evenly distributed, in other words, the differences in rankings between the different groups are not significant, but due to chance. A typical use of the Friedman test is to expand the type of research on the rating of multiple products (as seen above) without the two-group limit of the Wilcoxon test. Instead of rating only two brands, one can have four or five products rated by the same evaluator. Based on dependent samples design, the test allows a repeated-measures design, as well as a matched-subject design, and the process of hypothesis testing is similar to that of the Wilcoxon test described above.

Concluding remarks on statistical tests

Having studied some parametric and non-parametric tests, it should be clear that one of the most important decisions one needs to take while engaged in any research project is that of which type of test to use. There are numerous statistical tests available and each one is best suited to a specific type of problem.

The three main characteristics differentiating the tests are whether:
1. The tests are parametric or non-parametric.
2. The groups are independent or dependent.
3. The number of groups is two or more than two groups.

Only a few of the possible tests have been considered in this book. In order to make the choice easier, their specifications are shown in a summary table below.

Table 14.11 *Summary table of statistical tests*

Design	Parametric test	Non-parametric test
One-sample	Student t-test	
Two-sample *Independent*	Student t-test	Mann-Whitney U-test X^2-test
Two-sample *Dependent*	Student t-test	Wilcoxon test
k–sample *Independent*	*Anova*	Kruskal-Wallis H-test X^2-test
k–sample *Dependent*	*Anova*	Friedman test

Correlations and scatter graphs

Introduction to correlation and regression

The previous sections explored ways of testing alternate hypotheses relating to causal relationships between independent and dependent variables. In this section techniques for analysing the relationship between two variables which are changing simultaneously are presented. This is done in terms of a correlation coefficient, or a regression equation or regression line.

Often, a social scientist is confronted with the need to find out which variables are related to a given one, in the sense of co-variation (concomitant or simultaneous variation), without any need for or interest in specifying the type of relationship (causal or not). **Correlation analysis aims at measuring the discrepancy between the ideal situation** (where the data would exactly satisfy the regression equation with all the points on the regression line), **and the observed situation** (where the points are scattered along the line), as will be explained in more detail later.

The strength of the relationship, that is, the accuracy with which the regression line describes the relationship is then expressed in the form of a **coefficient of correlation** (**r**). This coefficient is then assessed to determine whether the relationship is significant or not. On this basis the researcher can conclude whether the observed relationship is real (significant) or due to chance factors. The **coefficient of determination** allows one to determine the proportion of variability of y that can be attributed to x. It will be explained in more detail later.

Correlations and scatter graphs

Two characteristics or variables often appear to be related to one another without either necessarily being the cause of the other. For example, the height and weight of people seem to be related: people who are tall generally tend to be heavy as well. There might also be some relationship between the income per head and the frequency of illness in a family: the lower the income, the more often family members fall ill. In both examples two sets of data or scores are available, each set describing a certain variable, but each data item of one variable is related to a data item of the other. In the second case, each family becomes a **unit of observation** comprising two values: the annual income and the annual number of people falling ill in this family. Thus a unit of observation represents a joint event, the co-occurrence of a value for each variable, or the simultaneous observation of both variables. In the first example, the unit of observation is a person characterised by both her/his height and weight. In both examples the variables are measured on an interval scale, and therefore each unit can be represented by a point on a two-dimensional graph.

It is important to note that the variables can be expressed by an interval or ordinal scale of measurement, each of which will yield a different coefficient: the product-moment and the rank order correlation coefficient. In addition, the correlation can be simple (considering only two variables), or complex (partial and multiple correlations), when more than two variables are at issue. The latter is beyond the scope of this book.

Once the type of relationship between two variables has been determined, the next goal is to measure the strength of that relationship or the **degree of association**. In the first instance, a mathematical expression, the regression equation, is used to symbolise this relationship. This equation can be represented as a line, the regression line, which shows a perfect relationship between the two variables. In other words, every time a unit of observation is *not* on the line, it shows that the correlation is not perfect. A correlation can be described as the measure of the distance of the different units of observation (or points on the graph) from the perfect relationship (or the regression line). This leads to the computation of a correlation coefficient between the variables which may or may not be linear and can be positive, $r = +1$, negative $r = -1$ or non-existent, $r = 0$. The closer the sets of paired data plotted on the graph can be approximated by a regression line, the higher the degree of correlation. The graphic representation of correlations, called a scattergraph, is illustrated in Figure 14.14. Clearly, each point represents a unit of observation and the line, called the regression line, is the mathematical expression determined from the set of data.

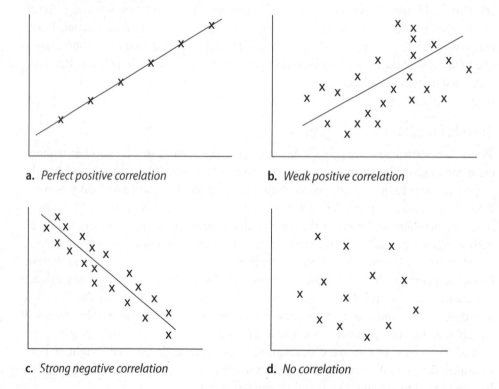

Figure 14.14 *Graphic representation of correlations*

CHAPTER 14 Quantitative data analysis and interpretation

Graphically the strength and the direction of a correlation can be expressed as shown in Figure 14.14 as follows: Figure 14.14a. represents the situation of a **perfect positive correlation**, symbolised by $r = +1$ where all the points are on the regression line and the direction is positive. (Here 'perfectly' means in such a way that, given the value of one variable, the corresponding value of the other variable can be determined *exactly*.) Figure 14.14b. shows a weak positive correlation where the points are widely scattered around the line. Figure 14.14c. indicates a high correlation since the cloud of points is very close to the regression line, but here there is a negative slope which indicates the direction of the correlation. Finally, Figure 14.14d. represents the situation where $r = 0$, and where there is neither correlation nor direction.

The Pearson correlation coefficient

A requirement that occurs very often is assessing the correlation between two variables, x and y, measured on an interval scale. This can be done by using the **Pearson correlation coefficient**. Let us illustrate the process by analysing some (fictitious) research results.

Example

A nurse starts an immunisation campaign against measles in a very small rural community. She calls together all the mothers of small children and explains to them the necessity of vaccinations. She then records the number of children brought to her for vaccination. The record sheet of her first eight immunisation sessions indicates the number x of the session with all the mothers and the number y of vaccinations that took place just after that education session.

Table 14.12 *Data on an immunisation campaign*

No. of sessions	No. of vaccinations
x	*y*
1	1
2	1
3	3
4	2
5	3
6	5
7	4
8	5

continued ...

The points have been plotted in Figure 14.15 below with the obtained the regression equation.

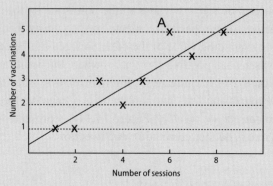

Figure 14.15 *Scattergraph of the immunisation campaign*

If the variables *x* and *y* were perfectly correlated, all the points of the scattergraph would have been on the straight line, which would have described the relationship between the two variables *perfectly*. Since this is clearly not the case in this example, the correlation coefficient will measure the deviation of the points from the line. How can one measure this? Let us take a point not situated on the line, for example A = (6,5). As can be read directly from Figure 14.15 from the regression line (or obtained through the regression equation), the estimated value of *y* (that is, the value *y* should have had for *x* = 6 if point A was on the line) is *y* = 3,9. Obviously, this would have to be repeated for each point on the graph and a less tedious way is to enter the data into statistical software that will calculate the correlation coefficient to be *r* = 0,91.

Interpretation of a correlation coefficient

Once a correlation coefficient has been calculated, one has obtained a measure of the degree of covariation between two variables. However, unless it shows a perfect correlation ($r = \pm 1$), one still has to assess the effect of the one variable on the variation of the other. To be more precise, one determines how much of the variability of the variable *y* can be attributed to *x*, which in turn will lead to finding the significance of the correlation coefficient in order to reject or not reject the null hypothesis.

It is important to realise that *r* = 0,5, for instance, does not mean that 50% of the variance in *y* is associated with the variable *x*. In fact, it can be calculated, through a **coefficient of determination**, that for this value of *r*, only 25% of the variation in *y* can be attributed to the influence of *x* on *y*. This means that a correlation coefficient of *r* = 0,71 would be considered double that of *r* = 0,5, since the percentage of variation of *y* which can be accounted for by the variation of *x* is 50% for *r* = 0,71, but only 25% for *r* = 0,5.

Applying the coefficient of determination to the previous immunisation campaign example, *r* = 0,91, indicates that the variation in the number of vaccinations can be explained by the education sessions in 82,8% of the cases.

CHAPTER 14 Quantitative data analysis and interpretation

Testing the significance of *r*

Correlational research is generally expressed in the form of a hypothesis to be tested. This hypothesis refers to the populations from which the samples have been selected. Hence the task is to assess whether the correlation coefficient obtained indicates a significant correlation and therefore whether or not the populations are correlated.

A null hypothesis denies the existence of a particular relationship between two variables. Therefore, in the case of a correlation problem, the *null hypothesis* H_0 assumes that there is no correlation.

The *alternative hypothesis* H_1 affirms the existence of a correlation that could be positive or negative in a directional test, or non-directional.

Note that the *general characteristics* for linear correlation are:

- The subjects in each group are randomly and independently selected.
- The population distributions for the two variables are normal in form.
- An interval scale of measurement is used.

The last assumption is a precondition for the product moment correlation coefficient, but this condition can be relaxed for some other correlation coefficients, as will be seen when introducing rank-order correlation.

Coming back to the study of hypotheses and the *decision rules*, what exactly does it mean 'to test the significance of a correlation coefficient'? One wants to assess whether the computed value r represents a real correlation or is merely the result of chance factors, that is, 'is the r in question a chance deviation from a population with no correlation?' To put it in the opposite way, one can ask 'what is the probability that the obtained coefficient r is different from what would be expected if there were no relationship between the two variables, that is, if the measured relationship were merely the result of chance?' It is important to note that a correlation coefficient has quite different meanings depending on the amount of data it is based on. For example, $r = 0,8$ seems to show a high correlation, but although it might be highly significant for $n = 50$, if it is computed on only five pairs of data ($n = 5$) it may not be significant at all.

Testing the difference between two correlation coefficients

A common research problem is the one of comparing the parameters of two populations.

Suppose that the immunisation campaign has been performed separately for two groups of women: one made up of married women and the other of single mothers. One might assume that marital status would have no influence on the relationship between the number of counselling sessions attended by the mothers, x, and the number of children vaccinated against measles, y. Therefore one would expect the correlation coefficient of the two populations of married (m) and single (s) mothers respectively to be the same. The hypotheses are therefore:

313

- H_0 assumes that there is no correlation; the *alternative hypothesis* H_1 is non-directional: the populations are somehow different.
- On the other hand, one might be interested in the effect of age on the attitude of the mothers towards measles vaccination. One would then compare the correlation coefficient of a population of young mothers between 15 and 25 to one of a population of women older than 38. Here again the null hypothesis would be that there is no difference between the two populations, whereas the experimental (directional) hypothesis might state that correlation in the young population will be higher than in the other.

Factors influencing the correlation coefficient

Although very useful and frequently used, correlation coefficients can easily lead to incorrect results or conclusions. Some of the most important pitfalls are discussed in the sections below.

The effect of range

The correlation coefficient obtained for a large group might not be same as the one obtained for some sub-groups. This can easily be illustrated with a scattergraph (Figure 14.16).

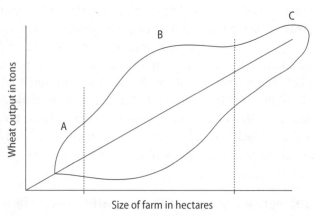

Figure 14.16 *Scattergraph showing different strengths of correlation for the whole and parts of the sample*

This scattergram indicates a positive correlation between the size of a wheat-producing farm in hectares x, and the wheat output in tons per hectare y. One can recognise three parts of the scattergraph: A: the small farms with low wheat output and low dispersion around the regression line, C: the large farms, all with high output and a low dispersion around the regression line, and B: the middle-sized farms with a great variability of output. These distinctions could refer to subsistence farmers (*A*) who occasionally

CHAPTER 14 Quantitative data analysis and interpretation

cultivate some wheat but who lack the necessary equipment and knowledge, the big commercial farmers (C) equipped with irrigation schemes, sophisticated machinery and agricultural know-how, and the middle or emergent farmers (B) who might be less well equipped than those in group C. Although a correlation between the size of a wheat-producing farm and the wheat output per hectare is clearly indicated for the whole sample of wheat producing farms, researchers restricting their studies to a particular type of farm might reach other conclusions. For instance, researchers concentrating on farms between 30 and 60 hectares in size, that is, restricting the range of x to the middle group, might find a very low correlation between x and y. Of course, not being aware of the effect of only having considered an interval within the range of x, the researchers might generalise their findings to the whole population of farmers and conclude the non-existence of a correlation between size and output of wheat-producing farms which is clearly incorrect in terms of the bigger picture.

This type of bias occurs very frequently, and should highlight the importance of broad pilot projects (Chapter 5) to acquire a general view of problems before going into details.

The effect of extreme groups

This effect is almost the opposite of the previous one. If, instead of restricting the study to middle-sized farms, the researchers had concentrated only on commercial farms which constitute an extreme group, they would have found a very high positive correlation, not at all representative of the correlation of the whole population. In fact, selecting extreme groups in respect of one variable always increases the size of the correlation coefficient beyond what it would be in the case of a random sample.

The effect of combining groups

Suppose that the study of wheat-producing farms took into account the households headed by women and that the study showed a weak negative correlation between the size of their farms and wheat output. It might have been found that, if the field is small, the woman are able to look after it well and reach a good output, but as soon as the field reaches a certain size, the lack of labour power has a negative effect on the state of the field, and the output drops. If the result of this study were combined with the results obtained for commercial farmers, the combined result would not depict the situation of the total population at all. This is related to the fact that the two groups differ in other respects, not only in terms of the size of their farms. Such generalisations should always be avoided.

315

The rank-order correlation coefficient

So far, the study of correlations has been devoted to the general principles of correlation analysis, with special emphasis *on product-moment correlation*, related to a simple linear regression. This correlation is indeed the one most widely used and most accurate. However, it has two assumptions referring to the parametric properties of the test which are not always fulfilled: firstly, the normality of the population distribution and, secondly, particularly important in the social sciences, the scale of measurement having to be an interval one. As a result it has been necessary to develop non-parametric alternatives to the product-moment correlation. When only an ordinal scale of measurement is available, the common method used is the **rank-order correlation**. In practice many problems include more than two variables. When the correlation of many variables or the relationship between one variable and a combination of two or more other variables has to be studied, a **multiple correlation coefficient** has to be defined. Equally, one might be interested in analysing the relationship between only some of the variables, keeping others out of the analysis which requires a **partial correlation coefficient**. However, both of these cases are beyond the scope of this book.

Many events or objects cannot be measured on an interval scale, but can be compared with each other and then rated in respect of a particular criterion: comfort levels in hotels, beauty of tourist resorts, fluency in English of air hostesses, etc. The case may then occur that some covariation is suspected between two such variables, or between one variable measured on an ordinal scale and one on an interval scale. In both cases, a product-moment coefficient cannot be used, since means of ranks would be totally inadequate. What would make sense would be to find out whether low ranks in one variable correspond to low ranks in the other, or vice versa. A comparison of ranks would allow one to calculate the magnitude of the differences of the ranks of the two variables. If the ranks measured on the two variables x and y fluctuate in the same way, one could expect the total difference to be small, and if the rank of variable x is exactly the same as that of variable y in all cases, the difference may even be zero. A further advantage of the rank-order correlation is that the assumptions are weaker than those of the product-moment correlation. The condition of normality of distribution need not be fulfilled, which allows the use of the rank-order correlation when the variables exhibit a skew distribution even though they are measured on an interval scale.

CHAPTER 14 Quantitative data analysis and interpretation

Example

In order to illustrate the whole process, the following example uses an interval scale of measurement that has to be transformed into an ordinal scale, on the assumption that the population distribution is not normal.

A study of the loan policy in the northern province of Zambia compares the number of loans given to men and women by the Agricultural Finance Corporation (AFC). The data for seven districts over a period of 15 years are given below. One wishes to find out whether there is a correlation between these two sets of data.

Table 14.13a. *Recipients of AFC finance in the northern province*

District	No. of male recipients	No. of female recipients
Chinsali	2 635	68
Isoka	4 940	504
Kasama	6 646	854
Luwingu/Chilubi	1 341	925
Mbala	4 126	200
Mpika	2 411	289
Mporokoso/Kaputa	2 244	4

[Source: AFC, Kasama Provincial Office, Zambia]

1. *Hypotheses*

   H_0: The *null hypothesis* states that there is no correlation between the number of loans given to men (x) and the number of loans given to women (y) across the seven districts.
   H_1: The *alternative hypothesis* states the existence of such a correlation.

2. *General characteristics*
   a. The groups are related.
   b. The observations are randomly and independently chosen (in this case it means that, for the results of the investigation to be generalised to the whole of the northern province, the chosen districts must be representative of the province. In the present study, these seven districts cover the whole province).
   c. The scale of measurement is at least ordinal.

3. *Decision rules*
   Comparing the probability value p to the level of significance:
   a. If p is larger than α, then H_0 is not rejected.
   b. If p is equal or smaller than α, then H_0 is rejected.

4. *Computations*
   Inserting the data in statistical software gives a probability value $p = 0,513$.

continued ...

317

Fundamentals of Social Research Methods: An African Perspective

Table 14.13b. *Output for Pearson Correlation*			
Correlations			
		male	female
male	Pearson Correlation	1	0,300
	Sig. (2-tailed)		0,513
	N	7	7
female	Pearson Correlation	0,300	1
	Sig. (2-tailed)	0,513	
	N	7	7

5. *Decision*
   H_0 is not rejected. The result indicates a low positive correlation which is not significant, at $\alpha = 0,1$.

6. *Conclusion*
   AFC does not seem to have any policy concerning the distribution of loans to men and women in the northern province.

7. *Discussion of this study*
   Analysing the set of data, one observes a discrepancy in the case of Luwingo/Chilubi which seems to represent an extreme case, with a very high number of female recipients compared to the number of male recipients. This anomaly is reflected in the rank difference which reaches the maximum of six.

   In fact, the researchers note that this anomaly is explained by the very high percentage of households headed by females found in Chilubi (52%), compared to the average for the rest of the province (36%). As it happens, if this district were excluded from the list, and after the new ranking of the y-value, the new correlation coefficient (for $n = 6$) would be $r = 0,83$. In this case, without this extreme case, H_0 would be rejected and one would conclude that there is a correlation between the number of loans distributed by the AFC to men and women in the northern province.

Regression and time series

Regression

Regression analysis relies on the assumption that the relationship between the two variables is a systematic one which can therefore be depicted or approximated mathematically. The simplest form of such a relationship is a linear one, as is the case with the example of the immunisation campaign (Figure 14.15 on page 312) given

CHAPTER 14 Quantitative data analysis and interpretation

when discussing correlations. A **linear regression** is represented graphically by a **straight line**, and mathematically by a **linear equation** called a **regression line**.

Non-linear relations and regressions can be parabolic, hyperbolic, exponential, etc. For instance, the relationship between the time a student spends studying and a corresponding knowledge-test result cannot be described by a straight line since, after a certain number of hours, saturation will take place and the student will be unable to increase her/his knowledge. By persisting further in studying without eating or sleeping, the student might even experience difficulty in concentrating and loss of memory, which can impede the acquisition of knowledge and therefore negatively influence a test result. Such relationships are beyond the scope of this textbook.

Linear regression and regression analysis

If one has two variables x and y, each one with a set of values such that they constitute sets of paired observations or data, the first aim of linear regression is to determine the straight line which will best describe the relationship between these two variables, while the second is to use this mathematical expression for the relationship to predict any value of y corresponding to a given value of x. This is usually done using a statistical programme.

The aim of regression is to allow prediction. As soon as a law more or less accurately describing the relationship between two variables has been determined, this law enables one to predict the variations of one variable based on knowledge of the variation of the other. In fact, the regression line describing the relationship between the two variables, x and y, is expressed such that y is called the **predicted value of y** as opposed to the observed value of the variable y.

However, this prediction procedure also has its weaknesses, and regression analysis is the study of all issues related to the quality or 'goodness' of the regression. This includes any lack of accuracy and its causes, the type and extent of errors of estimate, as well as methods for obtaining points and interval estimates or confidence limits. If, when looking at a scattergraph onto which a mathematically-determined regression line has been added, many points are not on that line and for a certain value of x the estimated value of y is quite different from the observed one, then the degree of accuracy for the regression is clearly low. One can therefore say that **the greater the variability of the points about the regression line, the greater the error in prediction**.

Let us illustrate the use of regression and correlation, as well as their interrelationship, through the following fictitious example.

319

> **Example**
>
> An economist is interested in the relationship between the number of pupils attending a private school and the revenue registered by this school during a seven-year period. The data are presented in Table 14.14 below.
>
> **Table 14.14** *School revenue and number of pupils, 2005–2011*
>
> | Year | No. of pupils | Revenue (in thousands of R) |
> |---|---|---|
> | | *x* | *y* |
> | 2005 | 810 | 276 |
> | 2006 | 887 | 306 |
> | 2007 | 1 048 | 401 |
> | 2008 | 1 011 | 432 |
> | 2009 | 767 | 309 |
> | 2010 | 746 | 315 |
> | 2011 | 1 156 | 385 |
>
> On first inspection it can already be seen that the two variables, school revenue and the number of pupils, are related to one another, and that the revenue appears to increase as the number of pupils increases. A deeper analysis of this set of seven paired data sets (each year corresponds to a specific school revenue and a certain number of pupils) reveals that the relationship can be described by a linear equation, in this case $y = 70{,}92 + 0{,}3\,x$ where *x* represents the number of pupils and *y* the estimated school revenue in thousands of Rand, for the same year. By graphically representing the pairs of data for each year on a scattergraph and adding to that the straight line representing the linear equation describing the problem, one observes that the collected data do not perfectly obey (fit) the mathematical model.
>
>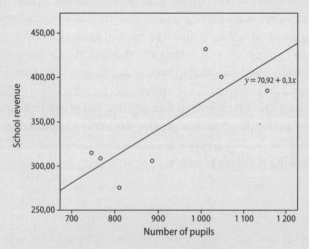
>
> **Figure 14.17** *School revenue and number of pupils, 2005–2011*
>
> *continued …*

CHAPTER 14 Quantitative data analysis and interpretation

Given a certain number of registered pupils, for example, $x = 1\,200$, the regression equation or the line representing it allows one to predict a school revenue of $y = 430{,}92$ (x R1 000). However, this quantity or value y is *only* an expected value, which would only be accurate if the relationship between the revenue and number of pupils followed the regression line exactly. Therefore the regression analysis aims at predicting the average value of one variable in terms of a certain value of the other variable. In this example, a **correlation coefficient** of $r = 0{,}78$ is obtained and using the **coefficient of determination** one can calculate that among all the factors which contribute to the annual variation of school revenue, the number of pupils accounts for only 61,5% of the variation. In other words, the proportion of the 'over the years variation' of school revenue that can be explained by the variation in the number of pupils is about three-fifths. This means that, if the number of pupils had not changed during those years, the revenue of the school would probably still have varied, but not nearly as much.

If a relationship has been incorrectly classified as linear when it is not, any regression line will be a bad approximation of that relationship. One should remember the example at the beginning of this section, of the relationship between the time a student spends studying and his results in knowledge-tests. It might appear that within the first three to five hours the relationship is approximately linear but it would be a mistake to infer the same type of relationship after 18 hours. In other words, if the relationship is established within a given interval (or range) of the variable x, prediction should only be made for values of x of about the same magnitude. In addition, the inability of the observed scores to satisfy the regression equation, that is, the variation of the observed scores about the regression line can be statistically interpreted in a similar way to the variation of the scores of a distribution about the mean.

Often the situation would be improved if one could determine confidence limits and confidence bands related to the regression line. There is thus a similarity between the standard deviation of a distribution and the standard error of estimate for a regression line. As discussed previously, when dealing with a normal distribution, one standard deviation on each side of the mean will determine a confidence interval containing over 68% of the population, whereas two standard deviations on both sides of the mean determine a confidence interval containing over 95% of the whole population. In the case of a regression line one is often interested in predicting a range of values within which 95% of the scores will fall. A very useful method of establishing a confidence band around the regression line by using the standard error of estimate has been developed, which is based on three important assumptions. The first one obviously is that the relationship must be a *linear one*. The second is that the *distribution* of each y must be *normal*. This assumption is necessary in order for standard scores to be meaningful. The final assumption is that the variances of all subdistributions must be comparable, a condition called homoscedasticity, which is beyond the range of this book.

Time series

Time series is a concept often associated with economic issues. However, its usefulness for representing the development over time of various kinds of social phenomena is recognised in all social sciences. More than just giving a description, a time series allows the analysis of the different components of a study over a period of time, which yields a deep understanding of both the past and present. This analysis can then be used for forecasting future developments, which makes it particularly useful in the social sciences. Various methods commonly used to analyse the components of time series are presented here and examples are given to illustrate them.

Time series can be defined as a set of quantitative data arranged in their order of occurrence. It is a series because the order of succession is fixed; it is a time series because the order of succession is of the variable 'time'. In this way, it can be understood as a special regression curve where the 'independent variable', represented on the x-axis, is the time (t), whereas the variable y can be any function of time.

A time series is therefore usually given as a set of values $y_1, y_2, y_3, \ldots$, observed at time $t_1, t_2, t_3, \ldots$ It describes events developing over time and measurements are taken at regular intervals (days, months, years, etc). One might be looking at economic issues: annual variation in agricultural or industrial production, monthly fluctuations of prices for commodities or quarterly changes in the labour market. Sociology and demography might be interested in representing and analysing certain social trends, for example, growth of the urban population, rate of divorce, etc. Psychology might use time series in longitudinal studies.

The **analysis of time series** is the analysis of the variations in the time series in order to discover its regularities. It aims at separating those factors that affect the results periodically from those that affect them randomly. Each of the non-random influences is then studied in isolation, and this should hopefully allow their interaction to be understood.

The purpose of the analysis of time series is therefore twofold. Firstly, it is to understand the past and present through the deconstruction of the time series into its components and evaluating the importance of each of them. Secondly, it aims at forecasting the future on the basis of that analysis.

The different components of a time series

One usually distinguishes three component parts of a time series: secular trend, seasonal variation and random (irregular) variation, although not all will always be present.

The **secular trend** is an overall tendency of the curve to rise or fall, that is it is a long-term movement of the time series, reflecting either continuous growth, stagnation or decline. The secular trend is the result of fundamental forces that shape the long-term development of the series in question. As such, trends are slow and continuous movements, rarely subject to sudden alterations. Therefore the other variations (seasonal and random) are more or less extensive fluctuations around the **trend curve**.

CHAPTER 14 Quantitative data analysis and interpretation

For instance, the world population is steadily growing. The fluctuations due to epidemics, wars or even the introduction of some population control measures do not essentially affect the *long-term* trend of growth, that is, a positive trend. On the other hand, the control of smallpox in the world generally shows a negative trend: although some local epidemics still break out in some regions of the world, the percentage of people affected by smallpox is on the decline.

Seasonal variations are systematic variations occurring within each year which are tied to some properties of the year, as are the seasons. For instance, seasonal variations might be related to climatic factors, as is the higher consumption of cold drinks and ice-cream during the hot season, or the increased rate of road accidents during the rainy season. Moreover, the higher rate of road accidents at weekends, due to heavy drinking, is also referred to as seasonal variation.

A more detailed time series analysis sometimes contains an additional factor called **cyclical variation**, which is a longer-term variation than a seasonal one, that is, over a year or more, and it is thus often associated with the secular trend. However, cyclical variation is a repeating variation which occurs periodically although not necessarily at equal time intervals, and so it is often associated with seasonal variations. A typical illustration of cyclical variation is the business cycle, whose period, it is argued, can vary between seven and about 50 years.

Irregular or random variations include all the variations that are neither related to the trend nor to seasonal or cyclical variations and are generally unpredictable.

The consumption of cold drinks might be temporarily affected by a fire which has destroyed the largest cold drink factory or by a shortage of the raw materials necessary to produce the drinks. Natural catastrophes like droughts, floods, epidemics and earthquakes are often the cause of irregular fluctuations.

Prediction: interpolation and extrapolation

The second aim of time series analysis, that of forecasting, can only be considered after the time series has been deconstructed into its different variations, and each one has been assessed separately.

At this stage, the social scientist should be in a position to predict values in two different ways:

1. **Interpolation** consists of determining a value which lies between two given values, or the extreme points of the given time series. This intermediate value can be read directly from a very accurate scattergraph, or determined through the trend equation. Using the seasonal indices, the influence of season can also be established.
2. **Extrapolation** is the assessment of a value lying outside the given range of the time variation t. As already discussed, it can be quite hazardous to predict the shape of a curve, and any extrapolation of values far from the observed

323

ones has to be considered as dangerous. However, it is acceptable to estimate values situated outside the range of *t* if they are still close to it. In this case one can expect the forecast to be reasonably accurate. This shows the strength and relevance, but also the limits of time series analysis.

Managing missing data

What is missing data and when does it occur? Unfortunately a researcher is often confronted with the situation where participants don't complete some items or questions or fail to provide certain information that is needed for the research. This is particularly common when participants are requested to complete questionnaires by themselves, but even in interviews some respondents might refuse to divulge certain information that they consider too personal or compromising, such as their income. No matter the reason, if the collection of data is not complete, the research may be compromised. If the amount of missing information is large, it may have a negative impact on the quality of the research. Suppose that, out of 50 participants, 20 refuse or forget to divulge their monthly salary: if the statistical analysis for the research is based only on the 30 available data sets, this will bias the results considerably since the missing data might relate to some characteristics of the respondents.

Although very little can be done to replace the missing data, there are quite sophisticated techniques (beyond the scope of this book) which can reduce that impact of missing data on the quality of research. However, missing data must never be considered (or entered into statistical software) as 'null' or zero answers. They must be registered as 'missing' data and their number or extent should be mentioned in the research report.

Use and abuse of statistics

The second half of the 20th century has been designated 'the age of statistics' Since World War II statistical procedures, which were formerly the preserve of actuaries in insurance companies and the practitioners of some branches of the physical sciences, have been used more and more in the analysis of quantitative data from all of the sciences, especially sociology, economics and biology. Fifty years ago, statistics were compiled and then calculated manually without the benefit of any of the statistical software available to the researcher today. It should be obvious that a good grasp of statistics is essential for anybody wishing to understand a modern research paper or even a well-documented magazine article. For those wishing to carry out a research project that produces quantitative results, a familiarity with the proper use of statistics is essential.

Despite what is about to be said about the abuse of statistics, it is important to stress that one *should use statistics* and not be frightened either by the possibility of misusing them or by the mathematical manipulations involved. If one wishes a quantitative

CHAPTER 14 Quantitative data analysis and interpretation

research to be taken seriously, one should make sure that the research is designed with the final analyses and statistical procedures clearly in mind. Bringing a mass of data to a statistician and hoping that he or she will be able, by some mysterious process, to extract some meaning from it, is unrealistic and will lead to frustration for the statistician and disappointment for the researcher.

Nowadays, the use of statistical software is so widespread that the testing of hypotheses has become a mechanical process: one enters the data on a computer, selects the appropriate items from a drop down menu, and in moments the computer provides the final results! Most often, the underlying reasoning and the mathematical processes that produce these results are unknown to the researcher, but thanks to the sophistication of the computer technology, if the correct statistical test has been selected, one can be assured of a correct result.

The term **'abuse of statistics'** seems to connote conscious distortion of statistical data in order to mislead people. It must be admitted that this is sometimes done by commercial advertisers for motives of profit, or by politicians in order to win votes or stay in power by other means. One of the advantages of studying statistics is that one will be able to recognise such attempts at deception. There are a number of well-written books and articles dedicated to this issue which can help one to unmask such deliberate manipulation.

Presumably, readers of this book will not be interested in statistically distorting their data for dishonest ends, but they will need to guard against not so much the *abuse* as the *misuse* of statistics through inexperience or carelessness.

One of the greatest pitfalls in research is the inappropriate use of particular significance tests. When reporting the results of a piece of research to a general audience (for example, in a newspaper article), it is often difficult to explain the meaning of significance levels in statistical tests to people with no statistical background. When the critical value associated with the chosen significance level is close to the observed value, one must make every effort to convey to the reader that the findings are neither definite nor absolute. A newspaper reporter will want clear, dogmatic statements about the findings, but she must be made to understand that there is, for instance, a one in 20 chance of the conclusions being wrong. The popular view of science is that it can make definite, clear-cut, reliable statements, but in truth, all that one has at the end of a research project is the **probability** that certain things fit a hypothesis, and one should not be ashamed of not being 100% certain, either in public or amongst colleagues!

Examples of biases often occur when estimations of unemployment are given: depending on the approach taken (the inclusion or exclusion of casual employment or informal sector activities), the percentage might vary from 12% to 36%. Equally, the size of the group is essential to qualify the changes clearly: if the passing rate for an exam has doubled from 20% to 40%, this might seem an excellent result. However, if the size of the group under study is 20 candidates, those numbers actually reflect that the number of passes has increased from four to eight candidates out of the 20, and in fact only four more candidates have managed to pass the exam! When analysing correlations, one must also be aware that a coefficient of $r = ,5$ does not mean that 50% of variations are explained by this correlation.

The choice of the appropriate tests has been dealt with quite systematically throughout this chapter and the pitfalls or possible sources of errors or factors influencing the results (such as the effect of extreme values in the calculation of means or correlations) have also been mentioned wherever they might occur. Choosing the correct test in particular circumstances becomes easier with experience, but even then it is always worth consulting a textbook or somebody with wide experience in the use of statistics before choosing which procedures to use.

This book does not deal in detail with the use of computers in social statistics. This was a decision based on the understanding that a foundation text on social statistics should introduce the reader to the content and reasoning of statistical analysis rather than the mathematics. However, those who have acquired the skills for using computers and statistical packages should be cautioned about possible pitfalls and abuses. Computer processing of data has taken most of the tedium out of statistics. Once the data has been entered and thoroughly checked for accuracy, no further human error can enter the process if one is using reputable and well-programmed software. With commercial packages one can assume that the programs have been well written and fully debugged, but the danger is always that users will input data and draw results without having any idea of the process that makes those results possible. It is for that reason that this chapter has been so detailed. In spite of the possibility of distorting statistics either deliberately, unconsciously or due to lack of mastery, their use in research remains vital in helping to understand the complexities of today's world.

Key points

1. The function of descriptive statistics is to condense information about a set of measurements, to organise this information or the raw data in a meaningful way, and present the collected data so as to reveal or enhance their fundamental properties.
2. Inferential statistics enable the researcher to make statements about a population based on quantitative data collected from a sample.
3. Inferential tests allow for the calculation of p, the probability of occurrence for the null hypothesis not to be rejected (that is, to be true).
4. By convention, a null hypothesis is rejected when $p < 0,05$ (or $p < 0,01$).
5. Parametric tests are statistical tests based on the use *of parameters* such as the mean, the standard deviation, standard error. They necessitate some assumptions about the population and the data at stake, in particular, the normal distribution and the use of an interval scale of measurement

continued ...

CHAPTER 14 Quantitative data analysis and interpretation

6. Non-parametric tests, also called distribution-free tests, analyse the data without assumptions about the distribution of the data and can be used for all types of measurement. This makes them more flexible. However, they are less powerful than the parametric tests and less effective.
7. For the use of parametric as well as non-parametric tests, one must differentiate between independent and dependant samples.
8. Some statistical tests also allow the comparison of more than two samples.
9. Correlation analyses variables only partly influence each other, but vary concomitantly.
10. Regression and time series allow one to estimate the value of one variable, knowing the value of the other.
11. Statistical analysis can be easily distorted by missing data, thus one has to be aware of the reason for missing data and how to deal with it.
12. When dealing with statistical analysis, one has to be very aware of the misrepresentation of data and thus the misuse of statistics.

Checklist

Check whether the meaning of these concepts introduced in this chapter is clear to you.
- the characteristics of descriptive versus inferential statistics
- the different ways of presenting data: through graphics, tables, central tendencies and dispersions
- the main features of distributions, and the logic and procedures of hypothesis testing
- the main differences between tests: parametric or non-parametric, independent or dependent samples, and number of samples
- the various statistical tests presented, their characteristics, uses and procedures
- correlation and regression for non-causal relationships.

Exercises

Note: Some of the following exercises require the learner to have access to a computer and statistical software or an advanced spreadsheet programme.

1. Given the 30 data:

54	81	18	63	67	60
91	47	75	87	49	86
26	41	90	13	31	68
29	70	22	50	42	27
42	38	69	31	45	51

continued ...

Fundamentals of Social Research Methods: An African Perspective

Construct a frequency distribution and identify the real limits, midpoints of intervals as indicated below. Identify the interval size and calculate the measures of central tendencies. Which one is best in this case?

Class interval	Real limits	Midpoint	Frequency f	Cumulative f
11–20	10,5–20,5			

2. The following data are the time in minutes needed by 80 workers to perform a certain task:

```
42  42  52  31  30  53  38  34  42  30
27  49  39  42  49  33  48  39  32  51
36  34  36  49  33  48  43  50  42  39
37  39  51  39  21  29  27  36  45  48
39  45  25  44  35  49  45  42  38  27
24  57  48  30  36  30  30  39  27  38
44  27  45  21  25  41  35  39  42  49
42  33  39  49  33  48  39  57  36  39
```

a. Determine the time needed by the five fastest workers. How long did the slowest worker take to perform the task?

b. Construct a frequency distribution using $i = 5$ and indicate the midpoints of the intervals. Is it a normal distribution? Is the distribution skewed?

c. Convert the obtained distribution into a relative frequency distribution.

d. Draw an histogram using these data.

e. Find the cumulative frequencies of the above data.

f. Calculate the mode, median and mean of this distribution.

3. In 2010, the enrolment of students in four African universities labelled A, B, C and D was as follows:

- In University A, 1 800 students were registered for Humanities and Social Sciences and 1 200 for Natural Sciences. Out of the 1 200, 900 were males, and out of the 1 800, 1 400 were females.

- In University B, the total number of students registered was 3 500, out of which 2 100 were registered for Natural Sciences. The number of females registered for Humanities courses was 1 300, which was 700 more than the number of females registered for the Natural Sciences stream.

- In University C, the total number of females registered was 450, out of which 300 were in the Humanities. 1 700 in all were in the Natural Sciences stream and 500 in all were in the Humanities and Social Sciences stream.

- In University D, 2% of the total intake of 4 000 were in the Humanities and Social Sciences, out of which only seven were females, whereas the female population of the other faculties represented 15%.

continued ...

328

CHAPTER 14 Quantitative data analysis and interpretation

Use a contingency table to present the data above, providing a suitable heading to the table.

4. Draw a multiple bar chart to show the crime rate of three cities A, B and C, from 2007 to 2009. Then draw a pie chart to represent the year 2009.

City	2007	2008	2009
A	2,0	3,5	6,0
B	1,0	4,5	8,0
C	1,5	2,0	4,0

5. In a series of 20 'spot checks', the following number of passengers were seen at a certain bus stop:

37   36   35   36   35   35   37   38   36   37
36   36   38   37   36   37   36   36   38   35

Based on these figures, determine the following:
a. The mean number of passengers, the median and the mode.
b. It was later discovered that the last observation done on a Sunday was incorrectly recorded. It should have been five instead of 35. Recompute the three measures of central tendencies. What features of these central measures do the revised figures bring out?

6. A distribution of the wages paid to foremen showed that, although a few reach very high levels, most foremen are at the lower levels of the wage distribution.
a. If you were an employer resisting foremen's wage claims, which measure of central tendency would suit you best?
b. If you were the foremen's representative, which measure of central tendency would you select?
c. If you were contemplating a career as a foreman, on which measure of central tendency would you rely?
Give reasons for each of your answers.

7. Which measure of central tendency is the most suitable for each of the following sets of scores? Calculate the measure of your choice.

A	35 34 32 29 37 36 8 38 33 30
B	10 15 14 11 12 16 13
C	3 4 7 8 9 6 8 7 4 8 18 10 8 9 8

continued ...

329

Fundamentals of Social Research Methods: An African Perspective

8. The data below gives the efficiency scores of workers at two factories, A and B.

Efficiency scores	Frequencies	
Class-intervals	Factory A	Factory B
0–14	15	43
15–29	25	99
30–44	40	54
45–59	108	40
60–74	92	14
75–89	20	0
	300	250

   a. Compute and compare the measures of central tendencies of these two distributions.
   b. Compute the standard deviation of these distributions and state which one has the greatest variability by comparing their coefficients of variation.
   c. Draw the two frequency distributions on the same diagram.

9. A criminal trial can be thought of as a decision problem, the two possible decisions being 'guilty' and 'not guilty'. The null hypothesis in a criminal trial is that the judge will continue to hold a viewpoint until he or she has strong evidence against it. Therefore, criminal trials are similar to hypothesis testing.
   a. Identify the null hypothesis $H0$ and the alternative hypothesis H_1 as stated below, each one in two different ways:
      i. The accused is guilty.
      ii. The accused is innocent.
      iii. The evidence against the accused can be attributed to random factors.
      iv. The evidence against the accused cannot be attributed to random factors.
   b. Identify the type I and the type II errors, if there is any error:
      i. convicting an innocent person
      ii. convicting a guilty person
      iii. acquitting an innocent person
      iv. acquitting a guilty person.

10. Explain the meaning of the expressions:
   - 'significant difference'
   - '90 per cent confidence level'.

continued ...

330

CHAPTER 14 Quantitative data analysis and interpretation

11. Are the following problems directional or not? State the null and alternative hypothesis in each case.
    a. A scientist wants to test the efficacy of a new painkiller. The hypothesis is that the new drug is much more effective than the old one.
    b. A teacher is interested in finding out whether school television has any stimulating effect on Grade 7 pupils.
    c. It is hypothesised that smoking has a negative effect on appetite.
    d. A teacher assumes that a coaching programme helps pupils with language difficulties.
    e. A managing director wishes to know if the mechanical ability of the specialised workers at two different workshops is different.

12. In a pain tolerance test, five girls and five boys obtained the following scores out of a total of 10 points:
    - **Girls:** 8 3 5 7 7
    - **Boys:** 4 5 6 7 6
    Do the results reveal a significant difference between sexes at a level of significance of 0,1?

13. Two drugs tested on diabetic patients are expected to have some sedative side-effects. More precisely, drug B is expected to affect the reaction time of the patients less than drug A. In other words, the hypothesis of the experimenter is that the reaction times of a small group of patients under drug A will be longer than the ones of an independent group of patients under drug B. Is this hypothesis confirmed at $\alpha = 0,05$ by the following reaction times measured in seconds?
    Drug A: 6 8 7 9 8
    Drug B: 4 7 5 4 5 6 4

14. In a personnel management meeting, the average time taken by the workers to reach the factory every morning was said to be 41,3 minutes. Can this figure be substantiated by the result of a survey on 60 workers of that factory who took an average of 39,7 minutes to get to work, with a standard deviation of 8,2 minutes? ($\alpha = 0,01$)

15. At the end of their first year at school the children of a particular city all sit for a standardised general test. The mean score obtained is 75 points. A sample of 26 children, all having attended one year of pre-school, obtains a mean of 81 on the same test. The population standard deviation is not known but the standard deviation of the sample turns out to be 16 points. Has the pre-school education had a positive effect on the children? ($\alpha = 0,01$)

continued ...

Fundamentals of Social Research Methods: An African Perspective

16. The following are the number of mistakes made on five successive days by three workers on an assembly line:

Worker A	Worker B	Worker C
8	8	15
5	10	10
2	4	7
3	12	10
2	11	13

Test the null hypothesis at the level of significance $\alpha = 0,05$, using the analysis of variance.

17. A social scientist is interested in finding out the views of students from different institutions regarding left-oriented versus right-oriented parties in their government. His data are given below. Using a chi-square test, decide if the views of the students in the various institutions coincide at $\alpha = 0,05$ level of significance.

	Institutions			
Opinion	A	B	C	D
Pro left-oriented party	30	20	40	10
No opinion	60	10	20	10
Pro right-oriented party	50	20	20	20

18. The following data reflect attendance at government health centres, private doctors and traditional healers by highly skilled, semi-skilled and unskilled workers in percentages. On the assumption that these data are derived from random samples, using a non-parametric test, test the hypothesis that there is no difference between the three groups with regard to the proportion of them attending health services offered by the government and private or traditional doctors.

Type of doctors	Type of workers		
	highly skilled	semi-skilled	unskilled
Government	62	51	32
Private	25	5	2
Traditional	13	44	66

continued ...

332

CHAPTER 14 Quantitative data analysis and interpretation

19. The results of the 2011 Grade 11 examination were compared for two samples of pupils from Lusaka and the Copperbelt. Use the Mann-Whitney U-test to determine whether the populations from which the two samples were drawn are identical at both the 0,01 and 0,05 levels of significance.

    Lusaka: 46   47   46   80   53   55   10   61

    Copperbelt: 30   90   80   79   55   55   55

20. Using an ordinal scale (1 = low to 10 = high), a group of men and a group of women grade their emotional reaction towards violence in films. The sampling is done randomly and the two groups are independent. Test the null hypothesis at the 0,05 level of significance that the two samples come from the same population against the alternative hypothesis that women react more strongly to violence in films than men do.

    Men scores: 5   2   8   3   6   2

    Women scores: 4   9   6   8   9   6   7   10

21. University students in different years of study were given a questionnaire to assess their interest in current political affairs. The following results were obtained:

    First year of study: 65   45   64   80   50   77

    Second year of study: 78   40   72   72   66

    Third year of study: 72   72   60   29   61

    Fourth year of study: 77   64   64   40   44

    a. Using a non-parametric test to compare these four independent groups, can one conclude that the year of study does not influence the students' interest in current political affairs?

    b. It is claimed that the students' interest in current affairs increases with each year of study. In order to test this hypothesis, the results of only the first and the fourth year students are compared. What conclusion can be drawn at $\alpha = 0,1$?

22. What are the differences in the assumptions for:

    a. the U-test and the Wilcoxon test

    b. the U-test and the Kruskal-Wallis test

    c. the t-test for independent samples and *Anova*

    d. the t-test for dependent samples and the Wilcoxon test?

continued ...

333

Fundamentals of Social Research Methods: An African Perspective

23. The following data give the annual income in thousands of local currency of 10 husband and wife pairs randomly sampled. Using the Wilcoxon, test the hypothesis that a husband earns more than his wife at α = 0,05.

Husband's income	Wife's income
9	14
14	10
16	8
16	14
18	13
19	16
22	12
23	40
25	13
78	24

24. For each of the situations below, indicate whether you expect a positive (+), a negative (−) or no (0) correlation:
   a. the number of cars on the highway and the number of accidents
   b. the birth rate and the socio-economic level of the community
   c. the length of the sides of a square and the length of its diagonals
   d. male students' financial situation and their number of 'dates'
   e. the age of people and their number of permanent teeth
   f. the age of cars and their trade-in value
   g. students' age and their IQ
   h. the horse power of engines and their fuel consumption.

25. Indicate if the following statements are TRUE or FALSE:
   a. The existence of a correlation between two variables A and B means that A causes B.
   b. The best-fit or regression line represents a scattergraph of correlational data in the same sense that the mean represents a set of scores.
   c. The regression analysis is very useful for prediction purposes.
   d. Correlation literally means related or simultaneous movement between variables, and regression literally means return to the normal which is true on account of the known relationship.

continued ...

CHAPTER 14 Quantitative data analysis and interpretation

26. A study of peer ratings and students of the performance of college teachers reports a correlation of $r = -1,21$. Check the correct conclusion which can be drawn from it.
    a. Peers and students tend to disagree on who is a good teacher.
    b. Peers and students tend to agree on who is a good teacher.
    c. There is little relationship between peer and student ratings of teachers.
    d. A mistake in computation has been made.
    e. There is a perfect negative correlation.

27. The personnel manager interested in comparing the number of years in service and the monthly income decides to calculate a correlation coefficient on the six data collected and to assess its significance at $\alpha = 0,05$.
    a. Because of lack of time, he first decides to compute a rank order correlation coefficient.
    b. Later, having some doubts that the results are accurate enough, he assesses the relationship using a product-moment correlation coefficient.
    Comparing the results, what will his conclusions be?

28. A health clinic has recorded the monthly cases of malaria X and of measles Y. A medical assistant presumes that there is some relationship between the occurrences of these two diseases in his community.

    Based on the collected data:
    a. He establishes the regression equation.
    b. He plots the data and draws the regression line on a scattergraph.
    c. He estimates the number of cases of measles to expect in a month when 15 cases of malaria are recorded.
    d. With the help of the second regression equation, he estimates the number of cases of malaria in a month when 25 cases of measles are recorded.

    What results does he obtain and would you support his assumption of a relationship between the occurrences of the two diseases as based on the following data?

Month	Cases of malaria	Cases of measles
January	14	19
February	66	11
March	12	7
April	8	18
May	10	5
June	3	24
July	5	16
August	6	22

continued ...

335

Later on, when presenting his assumption of a relationship between the occurrence of malaria and measles, the medical assistant was confronted with great skepticism on the part of the medical doctor in charge of the clinic. He was thus requested to provide a correlation coefficient and to test his hypothesis at $\alpha = 0{,}01$ in order to substantiate his assumptions. Do the conclusions correspond to your expectations?

29. Twelve culturally deprived children are given an intensive pre-school enrichment programme in an attempt to raise their IQ. The IQs of the children before and after the programme are given below.

X: Initial IQ	Y: Post-training IQ
89	103
95	97
82	100
101	98
91	96
85	88
96	97
93	105
86	99
99	110
90	107
84	86

a. Plot the points and draw an (approximate) regression line.
b. According to your regression line, what IQ can one expect after training from a child with an initial IQ of 80, and an initial IQ of 90?
c. The team of community workers, educationalists and psychologists involved in this pre-school enrichment programme have to prove that their programme has a favourable effect on the children and that there exists a significant positive correlation between the initial and the post-training IQ of the children. Do the collected data support their hypothesis?

continued ...

CHAPTER 14 Quantitative data analysis and interpretation

30. With which characteristic movement of a time series, would you mainly associate each of the following:
    a. a country's failure to export its minerals due to war in the neighbouring country
    b. the need for increased maize production due to a constant increase in the urban population
    c. the high volume of sales in clothing shops during the month of December every year
    d. a period of high unemployment
    e. the monthly number of millimetres of rainfall in Maputo over a 20-year period
    f. high and low bank deposits at the beginning and towards the end of the month respectively
    g. the growth of Zimbabwe's population
    h. the higher rate of road accidents during the weekends and month ends due to high consumption of alcohol
    i. the sale of raincoats and umbrellas in a large and popular shop
    j. a drop in the agricultural production and employment due to flood or drought in a particular year.

Additional resources

1. How2stats blogspot at http://how2stats.blogspot.com/p/home.html

Qualitative data analysis and interpretation

CHAPTER 15

This chapter provides an overview of qualitative data analysis. Included in the chapter are discussions of how qualitative data should be recorded, stored and prepared for analysis. Although many different forms of qualitative analysis exist, it is possible to identify some broad steps in the analytic process. These are discussed in some detail in relation to the analysis of interview data. The advantages and disadvantages of using computers and automated analytic tools are also described. Thereafter the chapter lays out the principles and techniques of thematic content analysis, a commonly used form of qualitative analysis. The defining characteristics of analytic approaches are presented in comparison to thematic content analysis. Finally, the question of scientific rigour in qualitative data analysis is debated.

> **CHAPTER OBJECTIVES**
>
> Learners who have completed this chapter will be able to:
> - List the key characteristics of qualitative data.
> - Record, store and prepare qualitative data for analysis.
> - Describe the basic steps of qualitative analysis.
> - Conduct a simple thematic content analysis.
> - Differentiate other types of qualitative analysis.
> - Evaluate the scientific rigour of qualitative analysis.

Fundamental themes in qualitative analysis

Qualitative research designs and data collection methods create qualitative data sets which present interesting challenges and opportunities to the researcher. Typically qualitative researchers are interested in the lived experience of the individuals, groups and communities that they study. This means that these researchers are interested in how people experience themselves, their relationships and their worlds. While a quantitative researcher might measure the times of world champion runners, the qualitative researcher is interested in how it feels to run, or to beat one's competitors, or to better one's previous time. Where a quantitative researcher might measure self-confidence, the qualitative researcher will ask what it feels like to be confident. Qualitative researchers argue that numerical scores cannot capture the essence of human experience. Instead these researchers use words and sometimes images to investigate people's real-life experiences.

CHAPTER 15 Qualitative data analysis and interpretation

It is important to note that qualitative researchers do not accept that what respondents say, in interviews for example, is necessarily 'true' in the absolute sense of the word. Instead, qualitative researchers argue that human beings construct meaning about their lives and the worlds in which they live. In other words, qualitative researchers are interested in the stories that people tell to themselves about themselves. Whether the story is 'true' or not is less important than whether it captures a person's experience of their life and world. So to qualitative researchers 'truth' is always understood in relative or personal terms. Each person has their own unique perspective on the world.

The uniqueness of individual perspectives on the world leads to two further important themes in qualitative research and analysis. Every respondent is understood to have their own unique view on the topic of the research, and so very often the researcher aims to describe the range and diversity of experience within the sample. Whereas quantitative researchers usually focus on the commonalities and middle ground of respondents' experiences, qualitative researchers are often more interested in multiple, unique perspectives. Often it is the unusual perspectives that provide the most new information about the topic.

Also, it is very important to qualitative researchers that respondents' experiences are authentically transmitted and communicated through the results of the research. For this reason qualitative researchers constantly ask themselves whether they are imposing their own interpretation on to the respondents' words, thereby changing their meaning. To prevent this from happening, qualitative researchers nearly always include many lengthy quotations from the data in the research report. Put another way, qualitative researchers seek to amplify the voices of the people who participate in their research.

Finally, qualitative researchers are also very interested in context, believing that one cannot understand people without understanding the context in which they live. Context is an extremely broad concept and includes the geographical place in which people exist, the family structures around them, their occupations, the economic and political worlds in which they live, their religious context, and so on. It is impossible to describe every detail of even a single person's context because it is so complex and constantly changing. However, qualitative researchers argue that unless one knows something about their world, our understanding of people will always be severely limited. Think how different the experience of winning will be for an athlete whose father was a previous champion, as compared with an athlete who is the first person to achieve public success in their family. Their personal experience will be completely different, and the reason for that difference lies largely in their family contexts. How does it feel to be confident when you come from a very poor community with few opportunities for education and employment? How is that experience of confidence different for a person who has always had many opportunities?

A summary of the previous paragraphs provides a list of themes which are central to all qualitative research and underpin the way qualitative analysis is conducted. Qualitative analysis aims to:

1. Describe and understand respondents' lived experience.
2. Examine the way respondents construct personal meaning in the lives.
3. Describe the range and diversity of respondents' experience.
4. Amplify respondents' voices.
5. Study people in their natural context.

While analysing qualitative data the researcher is constantly questioning the extent to which these aims are being achieved.

High quality qualitative data

While images (such as those found in art work, photographs, and film) can be analysed qualitatively, most qualitative data takes the form of words, either spoken or written. In this book we will focus mainly on the analysis of words. The capacity for language is one of the defining features of human beings as a species. Words fill almost every part of our lives and provide a fascinating window into how people think, how they relate to each other and how societies function. For the social researcher, words are data and they come from interviews, focus group discussions, the responses to open-ended questions in questionnaires, people's diaries, the letters that they write to one another, the media that they read, and, of course, the poems, plays, stories and novels that they produce. The same principles of qualitative analysis apply to all these kinds of words. However, in this chapter we will focus on the words that come from interviews and focus groups, and how to record these words accurately and generate high quality data in preparation for analysis.

Qualitative interviews and focus groups are nearly always semi-structured or unstructured (see Chapter 12) because these formats encourage respondents to describe their experience with the least interference and influence from others. While data is sometimes recorded as detailed notes by the interviewer or an assistant, it is preferable to record interviews. Modern digital recorders are very easy to come by and some mobile phones offer excellent built-in voice recorders. Older tape recorders are perfectly adequate, but the process of changing tapes and rewinding can disturb the interview process and be inconvenient during transcription. Make sure that you are absolutely sure how to operate your digital recorder before starting an interview. Also check that you know what the maximum recording time is, and how and where the recording will be saved. It is costly and disrespectful to lose respondents' interviews through a preventable mistake. Make sure that recordings are clearly marked and stored in a safe place. Because qualitative data almost always includes information that might be used to identify your respondents, keeping the data safe means protecting it from being read by unauthorised persons. Typically this means keeping the original audio files plus back-up copies in a password protected place on a hard drive or similar memory device, and any notes in a locked filing cabinet.

When recording, try to ensure that the interview is conducted in a private and very quiet room. Remember that the human mind is very skilled at filtering out background noise during an interview. Unfortunately, those background sounds are not filtered out on a recording and poor recordings can make transcription extremely difficult. It is common practice to take notes of facial expression, gestures and so forth while recording interviews. For example, an assault victim points to parts of their body which were injured. This information might be important but would not be captured on the recording.

Transcription is an extremely time-consuming but very important task. Specialised transcription technologies are available to assist with both tape and digital recordings. These technologies take a great deal of the inconvenience out of the work but it still requires a great deal of time and patience. It is possible to hire external people to transcribe recordings although this can be very expensive. In this case it is very important to ensure that the transcriber understands all the steps that the researcher has put in place to protect data and maintain confidentiality. Transcriptions also need to be cleaned. In the case of qualitative data this typically means removing any information that can be used to identify the respondent. The removal of names and addresses is somewhat obvious. However, with very particular populations it may be possible to identify someone from other kinds of information. For example, a respondent might say something like 'I'm in the human resources department but my office is on the third floor'. In a company in which only one person from that department has an office on the third floor, this respondent would be recognisable by anyone from the company. It is the researcher's responsibility to ensure that all potentially identifying information is removed from the transcript.

When the cleaned transcripts have been completed, the original recordings should either be stored in a very secure place or destroyed. When doing this, make sure that all copies are removed from external transcribers' or research assistants' computers. Bear in mind that the nature of qualitative data is such that it is often much more compromising of respondents than quantitative data. At this point the data is ready for analysis.

Qualitative analysis of unstructured data

In previous chapters, the process of qualitative research was described as flexible and at times iterative. In other words, some data analysis is likely to take place while data is still being collected. Depending on the results of this initial period of analysis, many aspects of the data collection might change. The researcher might opt to alter the data collection instrument, might employ a different sampling strategy or could conceivably even modify the research question. This flexibility is one of the characteristics and strengths of qualitative research. Just as the broader qualitative research process is

Fundamentals of Social Research Methods: An African Perspective

flexible and iterative, so is the more particular process of qualitative data analysis. Of course, this does not mean that the qualitative researcher merely does as he or she pleases from moment to moment. Each decision point must be carefully thought out and documented so that in the final presentation of the completed research, the researcher is able to explain exactly what was done, and why it was done that way. (Refer to Chapters 2 and 13 for more information about qualitative research processes and rigour.)

Much of qualitative data is unstructured, that is, respondents are free to talk or write about whatever they choose, and in whatever order they choose. Unstructured text of this kind is produced by unstructured interviews and focus groups, as well as through the analysis of letters, speeches, and so on. (Structured text is produced when respondents are answering very particular questions in order, such as in a structured interview or questionnaire with open-ended questions.)

Bearing in mind the flexible nature of qualitative data analysis, it is nevertheless possible to outline some broad steps.

1. *Immersion in the data.* The foundational step in qualitative data analysis is the process by which the researcher reads and rereads the data collected up to that point. Good qualitative data is rich, complex and typically covers many pages. By repeatedly reading the material collected, the researcher creates a mental picture of the entire data set. He or she knows broadly what is contained within that data set, and what important information might be missing. Furthermore, some ideas about how to categorise the data should be starting to emerge. Most qualitative researchers keep a notebook close at hand in which they record ideas and questions that occur to them during the immersion phase of the research.

   There is an important link here to the concept of saturation, which was explained in Chapter 13. A qualitative researcher is unable to judge when the data set is approaching saturation if he or she does not have a clear idea of the content of the data collected so far. When a researcher is immersed in the data, it immediately becomes clear when no new information is being added. Some researchers find that the process of transcription is an important part of this immersion phase and thus prefer to transcribe their own data.

2. *Preliminary coding.* A core component of qualitative analysis is the process of **coding**. This is where the text is broken into fragments which share some common characteristic. Thus '**codes**' can be thought of as categories, and the process of '**coding**' involves breaking up the original transcripts and classifying all the fragments into these various categories. Very often qualitative researchers develop the codes by looking for themes and patterns within the data itself. One way of starting this process is by writing notes with possible codes alongside the original text.

CHAPTER 15 Qualitative data analysis and interpretation

Example

Below is an extract from Thabo Mbeki's speech, 'I am an African!' given on 8 May 1996 to the South African Parliament (http://www.anc.org.za/show.php?id=4322).

Table 15.1 *Pre-coding of unstructured text*

TRANSCRIPTION	Comments and possible codes
'But it seems to have happened that we looked at ourselves and said the time had come that we make a super-human effort to be other than human, to respond to the call to create for ourselves a glorious future, to remind ourselves of the Latin saying: *Gloria est consequenda* – Glory must be sought after! Today it feels good to be an African...	Possible code for 'Super-human efforts'?
I am born of the peoples of the continent of Africa. The pain of the violent conflict that the peoples of Liberia, Somalia, the Sudan, Burundi and Algeria is a pain I also bear. The	CODE: War in Africa
dismal shame of poverty, suffering and human degradation of my continent is a blight that we share. The blight on our happiness that derives from this and from our drift to the periphery of the ordering of human affairs leaves us in a persistent shadow of despair. This is a savage road to which nobody should be condemned. This thing that we have done today, in this small corner of a great continent that has contributed so decisively to the evolution of humanity says that Africa reaffirms that she is continuing her rise from the ashes...	CODE: Poverty in Africa CODE: Recovery metaphors?
Whatever the difficulties, Africa shall be at peace! However improbable it may sound to the sceptics, Africa will prosper!	CODE: International scepticism
Whoever we may be, whatever our immediate interest, however much we carry baggage from our past, however much we have been caught by the fashion of cynicism and loss of faith in the capacity of the people, let us err today and say – nothing can stop us now!	CODE: Calls to action. (Perhaps combine with super-human efforts?)

As the researcher writes more and more notes and tries out different combinations of codes, the beginnings of a coding system start to emerge. Some of the preliminary coding ideas will be refined and developed, others will be discarded. Again, this process might take several cycles through the entire available data set at that time. As more data gets added to the data set, it may be necessary to add new codes or refine existing ones.

Eventually, as the data set reaches saturation, the researcher should be able to find a set of codes that fits the data well, and that addresses the research question appropriately. At this point, the researcher moves on to the next step in the process.

3. *Coding definitions*. At this point the researcher is ready to start defining the codes. Each code must be clearly defined so that the researcher can code consistently, and also explain the coding system to others. A **code definition** should include at least a title and a description of what kind of data is to be categorised under that code. Sometimes researchers will also mention kinds of data that are *not* included under that code and even give typical examples of that code.

Example

Code title: Positive expressions about African identity

Definition: Any reference to feeling proud, happy, confident, connected and socially supported that is linked to being African. In this context African implies any person who describes themselves as African. A typical example would be *'I am happy when I meet my African brothers and sisters. I know we are one!'* Note that country specific references such as *'I am proud to be a South African!'* are not included here.

Very often codes are organised hierarchically. In this case, there are some high level codes which are somewhat broad in scope. These high level codes are then broken down or disaggregated into lower level codes of narrower scope. Typically, qualitative researchers begin with broader codes and gradually break these down into narrower, more specific codes as the analysis becomes more detailed. This is illustrated in the following example.

Example

High level code: Positive expressions about African identify

Lower level codes: Pride in African cultural beliefs and practices
Pride in developmental achievements of African countries
Identification with African celebrities
Enjoyment of African sense of humour

4. *Coding*. Once the coding system has been finalised, the researcher is ready to recode the entire data set. This is done by working through the transcripts and breaking up the text into fragments which are then allocated to particular codes.

CHAPTER 15 Qualitative data analysis and interpretation

Example

Table 15.2 *Coding of unstructured text*

TRANSCRIPTION	CODING
'But it seems to have happened that we looked at ourselves and said the time had come that we make a super-human effort to be other than human, to respond to the call to create for ourselves a glorious future, to remind ourselves of the Latin saying: *Gloria est consequenda* – Glory must be sought after! Today it feels good to be an African… I am born of the peoples of the continent of Africa. The pain of the violent conflict that the peoples of Liberia, Somalia, the Sudan, Burundi and Algeria is a pain I also bear. The dismal shame of poverty, suffering and human degradation of my continent is a blight that we share. The blight on our happiness that derives from this and from our drift to the periphery of the ordering of human affairs leaves us in a persistent shadow of despair. This is a savage road to which nobody should be condemned. This thing that we have done today, in this small corner of a great continent that has contributed so decisively to the evolution of humanity says that Africa reaffirms that she is continuing her rise from the ashes… Whatever the difficulties, Africa shall be at peace! However improbable it may sound to the sceptics, Africa will prosper! Whoever we may be, whatever our immediate interest, however much we carry baggage from our past, however much we have been caught by the fashion of cynicism and loss of faith in the capacity of the people, let us err today and say – nothing can stop us now!	*CODE: Positive expressions about African identity* Today it feels good to be an African… I am born of the peoples of the continent of Africa. Whatever the difficulties, Africa shall be at peace! However improbable it may sound to the sceptics, Africa will prosper! *CODE: References to conflict in Africa* The pain of the violent conflict that the peoples of Liberia, Somalia, the Sudan, Burundi and Algeria is a pain I also bear. *CODE: References to poverty* The dismal shame of poverty, suffering and human degradation of my continent is a blight that we share. The blight on our happiness that derives from this and from our drift to the periphery of the ordering of human affairs leaves us in a persistent shadow of despair. This is a savage road to which nobody should be condemned. *CODE: Calls to act to develop the continent* But it seems to have happened that we looked at ourselves and said the time had come that we make a super-human effort to be other than human, to respond to the call to create for ourselves a glorious future, to remind ourselves of the Latin saying: *Gloria est consequenda* – Glory must be sought after! This thing that we have done today, in this small corner of a great continent that has contributed so decisively to the evolution of humanity says that Africa reaffirms that she is continuing her rise from the ashes… Whoever we may be, whatever our immediate interest, however much we carry baggage from our past, however much we have been caught by the fashion of cynicism and loss of faith in the capacity of the people, let us err today and say – nothing can stop us now!

This example (http://www.anc.org.za/show.php?id=4322) illustrates some simple coding of a fragment of a much longer speech. If the researcher were to collect a sample of significant speeches delivered by African leaders during the past 20 years, more and more fragments from many different speeches could be added to the four codes selected here. The researcher could then focus in on the code for 'References to poverty' and start to describe and analyse the various comments made about poverty by various African leaders in the past two decades.

Different qualitative researchers have different approaches to the actual work of coding. Some prefer to work with the data physically and so will literally cut up printouts of transcripts and write on them with coloured highlighters and pens so as to show the different coding categories. The 'cut and paste' function on modern word processors and spreadsheet programmes is also a very useful tool for the qualitative researcher since large extracts can be moved freely from place to place, and from document to document.

A number of software packages are also available to the qualitative researcher. These packages allow the researcher to import a large data set, build a coding system, and code, all within a single programme. These programmes can then print out reports on the coded data. These packages also include an option for automated coding. To use automated coding, the researcher must associate particular codes with specific words or phrases in the transcripts. The computer then searches through the data and any text associated with the chosen words or phrases is automatically categorised under the associated code. While automatic coding can be an extremely powerful tool in the hands of experienced researchers working with large data sets, it should be used with care. Words often take on different meanings in different contexts and, as a result, important data can be missed when using automatic coding.

5. *Inter-coder reliability*. One key aspect of the dependability of a qualitative
    analysis (see Chapter 13) is the question of inter-coder reliability. Would a
    different coder have assigned the same fragments of text to the same codes,
    or would it have come out differently? This question can be answered with an
    inter-coder reliability check. The researcher trains a colleague how to code
    the data, using the coding definitions previously developed. Then that colleague
    codes part of the data set independently of the researcher and the results are
    compared. The degree of agreement between the two codings represents the
    inter-coder reliability. An inter-coder reliability coefficient of 0 means that there
    is no similarity between the two codings (a very poor result), while a coefficient
    of 1 means that the two codings are identical. Qualitative researchers aim to
    have an inter-coder reliability of at least 0,8. Several different formulae exist
    for calculating inter-coder reliabilities, but these are beyond the scope of this
    textbook. These statistics are calculated automatically by qualitative analysis
    software packages.

CHAPTER 15 Qualitative data analysis and interpretation

6. *Interpretation of results*. Having completed a careful coding of the entire data, the researcher can begin to interpret the results. How this is done depends on the objectives of the research, and the particular research question. In an exploratory or descriptive study, the researcher is likely to describe the material contained within each of the codes. The range of responses recorded under that code would be described, and the researcher would point out areas of agreement and disagreement between respondents. In correlational and explanatory research, the researcher will attempt to link different concepts or variables. For example, it could be that two codes consistently appear together in the text. When this happens it suggests that the two concepts represented by those codes are somehow linked. Similarly, different groups of transcripts might differ with respect to particular codes. For example, transcripts from male and female respondents might vary with respect to their comments on the quality of public transport in a community. In this case, respondents' gender appears to be related to perceptions of public transport.

Example

It is possible to explore many research questions using data from the African leaders' speeches example introduced on page 345. A researcher conducting an *exploratory* study might ask, 'Which themes are mentioned more frequently in the speeches of African leaders?' A researcher conducting a *descriptive* study might ask, 'What is the range of comments that African leaders make about poverty in their speeches?' A researcher conducting a *correlational* study might ask, 'Do speeches from the period 1990–1999 and the period 2000–2009 differ with respect to comments on poverty?' or stated another way, 'Have African leaders' comments on poverty changed over the past two decades?' A researcher conducting an *explanatory* study might ask, 'Does the popularity of a leader at the time of the speech influence the way poverty is described in the speech?'

Qualitative analysis of structured data

Qualitative data analysis can also be applied to more structured data, such as the kind produced by structured interviews, focus groups and questionnaires containing open-ended questions. Here the researcher might have many more cases. However, the text is more highly structured and typically shorter and simpler than that produced by in-depth interviews and focus groups.

Fundamentals of Social Research Methods: An African Perspective

> ### Example
>
> A local municipality conducts a survey to evaluate rate-payers' satisfaction with the quality of services provided. Interviewers visit a simple random sample of 7 500 ratepayers in the community. Using a structured interview, the interviewers ask each respondent to rate their satisfaction with different services provided by the municipality. They also ask respondents to explain the reasons for their rating. These reasons are recorded verbatim. One question out of this interview reads as follows:
>
> *How satisfied are you with the ways in which local roads and footpaths are maintained? Please explain.*
>
> Responses to this question vary enormously. Some people use only a few words, such as 'Everything's fine' and 'No problems'. Others make short comments such as 'Generally I'm happy, but I do notice that lately there has been a lot of litter on the road into town', or 'There's a pothole outside my home. I've reported it several times but nobody ever does anything about it'. Some people give much longer answers, comparing the situation in different parts of the town. All of these responses, long and short, are carefully noted down.

To analyse this kind of data, the researcher will follow a similar set of steps to those outlined for less structured data above.

1. *Immersion in the data.* Since there is likely to be much more repetition in this kind of data, the researcher is more likely to sample a part of the data in order to get a broad idea of what is contained within the data.

2. *Preliminary coding.* Based on the initial examination of a subset of the sample, the researcher will make a list of the types of responses in the data set.

3. *Coding definitions.* The types of responses can be given names and definitions as before.

4. *Coding.* The coding phase is much simpler for this data. Instead of breaking up the text into fragments and then attaching different codes to the fragments, the researcher would treat one respondent's entire response as a whole and attach it to a single code. In other words, each survey participant's response is placed into one of the categories created during the preliminary coding phase. The researcher then counts the number of responses (or the percentage of total responses) that fall into a particular code. Note that by doing this, the researcher has actually created quantitative data out of qualitative data. While simple, descriptive statistics can be performed on such data, the researcher should be very cautious about using any inferential statistical tests. It is very unlikely that this data meets the assumptions demanded by inferential statistics. (Descriptive and inferential statistics were explained in Chapter 14.)

CHAPTER 15 Qualitative data analysis and interpretation

5. *Inter-coder reliability*. Inter-coder reliability can be checked in precisely the same way as previously described. A subset of responses are sampled and coded by an additional trained researcher. The two codings are then compared and an estimate of inter-coder reliability is calculated.

6. *Interpretation of results*. Data of this type is typically presented as a list of different response categories (the codes), together with the number and percentage of responses that were placed within that category. Results of this kind show which categories were most commonly mentioned by survey respondents and which were not mentioned very often. Such data can often be presented very clearly using pie and bar charts (see Chapter 14). More complex descriptive and correlation questions can be answered by comparing the response patterns of different groups of respondents. This process is illustrated with the example of the municipal satisfaction survey.

Example

The researcher collects all 7 500 responses to the question about the maintenance of local roads and footpaths. In order to have a good idea of what is included in the data (*immersion*), the researcher randomly samples 1 500 responses (20% of the total) and reads through these carefully. While reading through this subset, the researcher starts to create categories of response (*pre-coding*) until a point is reached where virtually all the responses can be easily categorised under one of the new codes. The researcher then formally names each new code and writes a short description of what kinds of responses should be categorised under that code (*coding definitions*).

No response – Left blank, or where the respondent refuses to answer for any reason.

Satisfied – The respondent indicates satisfaction with the services, or doesn't mention any problems.

Improvement on past performance – The respondent reports that the maintenance of roads and pathways has improved in recent years or months.

Grass not cut: untidy – Complaints about grass not being cut, which is related to the look of the neighbourhood, property prices and tidiness.

Grass not cut: criminal danger – Complains about grass not being cut, which is related to offering hiding places to criminal elements within the community.

Litter – Any reports of litter not being cleaned up.

Traffic lights not working – Any reports of broken traffic lights not repaired over more than a week or after being reported.

Potholes – Any reports of potholes not repaired more than a month after being reported.

Other – Any reports not fitting into any of the previous categories.

continued ...

349

Fundamentals of Social Research Methods: An African Perspective

Thereafter, the researcher works through the entire data set again (7 500 responses) and places each response into one of the codes (*coding*). The researcher also trains a colleague to code the responses. They each code the same random sample of 750 responses, compare their results and calculate a reliability coefficient (*inter-coder reliability*).

Table 15.3 *Inter-coder reliability*

Code	Coder 1	Coder 2
No response	52	52
Satisfied	65	63
Improvement on past performance	15	18
Grass not cut: untidy	148	140
Grass not cut: criminal danger	189	201
Litter	29	10
Traffic lights not working	68	72
Potholes	160	180
Other	24	14
Total	750	750

Based on these results, the inter-coder reliability is 0,87, a satisfactory result.

Once all 7 500 responses have been coded and counted up, the researcher presents a table showing the relative frequency of all responses to the town council. The council is interested in whether the responses of older and younger ratepayers are different and so the following table and chart are prepared.

Table 15.4 *Qualitative survey data results*

Code	Total Sample (n=7,500)	18-35 years (n=3,245)	36 + years (n=4,255)
No response	544 (7%)	63 (2%)	481 (11%)
Satisfied	529 (7%)	112 (3%)	417 (10%)
Improvement on past performance	132 (2%)	83 (3%)	49 (1%)
Grass not cut: untidy	1 492 (20%)	870 (27%)	622 (15%)
Grass not cut: criminal danger	1 865 (25%)	1 292 (40%)	573 (13%)
Litter	287 (4%)	72 (2%)	215 (5%)
Traffic lights not working	694 (9%)	108 (3%)	586 (14%)
Potholes	1 698 (23%)	503 (16%)	1 195 (28%)
Other	259 (3%)	142 (4%)	117 (3%)
Total	7 500 (100%)	3 245 (100%)	4 255 (100%)

continued ...

CHAPTER 15 Qualitative data analysis and interpretation

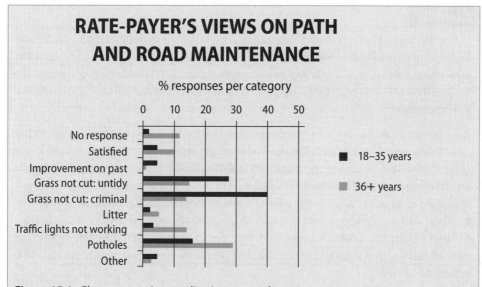

Figure 15.1 *Chart presenting qualitative survey data*

A quick glance at this chart shows that younger respondents are much more likely to mention problems with the grass not being cut, while older respondents are more concerned with traffic lights not working and potholes. Also, older respondents were more likely to give no response or say that they were satisfied with the services.

Coding from theory

In the examples above, the researcher has always drawn the codes from the qualitative data itself. While this approach is commonly used, it is not the only possibility. It is possible to create a coding system independently of the data by drawing the codes directly from theory. The advantage of drawing codes directly from the data is that the researcher knows that the codes used in the analysis will be directly relevant to the characteristics of the data. However, the researcher has no way of guessing how well those codes will fit with existing theory in the field. The advantage of drawing codes from theory is that the researcher knows that the codes will be directly comparable with the theory and with other research that draws on that theory. However, the researcher cannot know whether the coding system will really be relevant to the data she has collected for her study. When a researcher wishes to explore or describe a population or phenomenon, it is more appropriate to draw the codes directly from the data as described above. However, when a researcher wishes to test the applicability of an existing theory to a particular population, it may be more appropriate to draw the codes from theory. The use of codes drawn from theory is illustrated in the following example.

> ### Example
>
> In his 1954 book, *Motivation and Personality*, Abraham Maslow published his now famous hierarchy of needs. Maslow argues that human needs exist at different levels, and that higher level needs only become important to people after lower level needs have been met. The five levels that Maslow proposed were physiological, safety, love and belonging, esteem, and self-actualisation.
>
> It is conceivable that a researcher might use Maslow's theory when conducting a qualitative community needs assessment. The researcher might interview a range of people in the community and then analyse the transcripts in terms of the five levels of Maslow's theory. In this case, Maslow's levels become the foundation of the coding system and thus the analysis. A person's comments that 'there is a lot of crime in the community' would be classified as a *safety need*, as would a remark that cars often speed through the town and children are sometimes knocked down. A suggestion that the community would benefit from more football fields so that children can develop their talents further would be classified as a *self-actualisation need*.
>
> Note that the coding system reflects the theory and did not emerge from the data itself.

More advanced forms of qualitative research

All the examples mentioned thus far in this chapter have discussed coding based on the content respondents', words, the concepts that they are talking about. In the analysis of Thabo Mbeki's speech the codes related to war, poverty and pride in African identity because these were concepts that he was discussing. In the survey example, the codes related to the problems of maintenance that rate-payers were concerned about. Finally, in the example using Maslow's theory, the codes relate to the type of needs mentioned by community members. In all cases, it is the content of the material that is being coded. Thus these would all be examples of content analysis.

Content analysis is a research methodology used to systematically analyse the meaning of communications. Of central interest are the core themes that speakers refer to, the information or message that they want to pass on to their audience. When conducting content analysis, the researcher constantly asks, 'What is this respondent intending to communicate?'

Content analysis dates back to the 1930s and served as the starting point for much of modern-day qualitative analysis. In the 1960s Glaser and Strauss developed **grounded theory**. Grounded theory is a methodology for developing theory from data, nearly always qualitative. The codes used in a grounded theory analysis are always drawn directly from the data, never from theory. Researchers using this approach try to ensure that they make no assumptions about the data based on past experience or theoretical knowledge. Rather, the data is understood to be the sole source of information and all analysis is based on repeated themes and patterns contained therein.

CHAPTER 15 Qualitative data analysis and interpretation

Another approach to qualitative research in which researchers avoid imposing their own preconceptions or assumptions on to the data is **phenomenological analysis**. A researcher using the phenomenological approach is concerned with describing respondents' lived experience of a particular aspect of their lives. In other words, phenomenological researchers attempt to describe the phenomenon under investigation as experienced by, or through the eyes of, their respondents.

Narrative analysis represents a more recent innovation in the development of qualitative analysis methodology. Narrative researchers argue that one way to understand people better is to analyse the stories, or narratives, about themselves, their lives and their world. Researchers using this methodology break transcripts up into narrative sections which often have a beginning, middle and end. They pay attention to what moments in their lives people construct narratives about, and which moments are not included. They note the characters in the story, as well as the actions carried out by those characters. They also notice events in the stories and the causal links between actions and events.

Discourse analysis is a form of qualitative analysis that has its roots in linguistics, the study of language. Researchers working in discourse analysis argue that our perception of ourselves and our world is created through interaction and conversation between people. Thus, by looking deeply into the way people interact we can understand much more about how they see the world. Discourse analysis looks at the relationships between people, the things that can (and cannot) be said in different relationships and contexts, the types of language, as well as the choice of words that people use.

Ethnography is an approach to qualitative research designed for the exploration of cultural phenomena. Data is often collected through participation observation during which the ethnographer takes detailed field notes of what is observed within a particular cultural setting. These field notes, together with other artifacts such as stories, songs and poems of the culture being observed, become the data that is recorded and analysed using qualitative methods similar to those described above.

Final comments on the quality of qualitative analysis

Chapter 13 deals with ensuring the scientific rigour of research designs, including qualitative designs. Because data collection and analysis are so closely interconnected in qualitative research, all of the points mentioned in that chapter apply here. During analysis the researcher must ensure that adequate attention is being paid to the context in which the data was collected, the way the sample was selected, triangulation between different sets of data and processes of respondent validation. As described above, it is necessary to calculate the inter-coder reliability and to ensure that any results are strongly supported by verbatim quotations. Most importantly, the researcher must explain each step of the data analysis process in detail.

Novice researchers who wish to avoid the mathematics required by inferential statistics sometimes select qualitative research as a seemingly easier option. In fact, high quality qualitative research often demands much more time and effort than quantitative research. Ultimately, the research question should dictate the approach used. Using qualitative research methods and analysis to answer a question that is essentially quantitative will never produce exciting results.

Key points

1. Qualitative analysis is appropriate for the analysis of spoken or written language.
2. Data should be carefully transcribed verbatim wherever possible.
3. Broad steps in the analysis process are (i) immersion, (ii) preliminary coding, (iii) coding definitions, (iv) coding, (v) inter-coder reliability check, and (vi) interpretation of results.
4. Qualitative research can be used to analyse large databases such as survey data. In this case qualitative data is often converted into quantitative data, and presented as such.
5. Codes can emerge from the data itself or from relevant theory.
6. Many different forms of qualitative analysis exist. These include content analysis, grounded theory, phenomenological analysis, narrative analysis, discourse analysis and ethnographic research.

Checklist

Keywords:

Check whether the meaning of these concepts introduced in this chapter is clear to you.

transcription; immersion; preliminary coding; coding; inter-coder reliability; content analysis; grounded theory; phenomenological analysis; narrative analysis; discourse analysis; ethnography.

Your research:
1. Make sure that your qualitative data is carefully recorded, transcribed, cleaned and stored.
2. Start your analysis while you are still collecting data.
3. Modify your data collection if the preliminary data analysis suggests that this would improve the study.
4. Use an iterative process to refine your coding system until it adequately covers the breadth of your data.
5. Code carefully, and always calculate an inter-coder reliability coefficient.
6. Report your methodology in detail and quote your respondents liberally in support of your results.

CHAPTER 15 Qualitative data analysis and interpretation

Exercises

1. Purchase three different newspapers published on the same day and conduct a simple content analysis of the stories included on the front page.
   a. Describe the themes most commonly reported in the newspapers.
   b. Do different papers focus on different themes? Explain your answers.
   c. Pick the most common overall theme. Is this theme handled differently by different papers?
   d. What conclusions can you draw about the newspapers from this analysis?
2. Describe in detail the steps of your analysis of the newspapers.
3. Consider the following quotation from a woman giving her opinions on a visit to the local clinic.

   I like to visit this clinic. The sisters are always friendly to me. Sometimes we sit and have tea together and they tell me about their work. They get very angry when the young girls from the slum come here looking for abortion. They should go to their own clinic and not come here. I don't know why they come here. Yesterday two girls came asking for abortion. The head sister shouted at them. She told them that she was a Christian and that she wouldn't give them what they were asking for. People were looking but she didn't care. She told those girls! Those girls looked so ashamed when they left. She did them a favour. They don't know it now but one day they will be grateful to her. Who else is going to teach these girls how to behave?

   Think of a research question relating to this abstract which would be most appropriately answered using:
   a. Content analysis
   b. Phenomenological analysis
   c. Narrative analysis.

Additional resources

1. Denzin, N K & Lincoln, Y S. (eds) 2011. *The Sage handbook of qualitative research*, 4th ed. Thousand Oaks, CA: Sage.
2. *Qualitative Health Research:* http://qhr.sagepub.com/
3. *Qualitative Inquiry:* http://qix.sagepub.com/

Research findings and dissemination

CHAPTER 16

The purpose of this chapter is twofold. Firstly, it discusses how the researcher should check for inconsistencies, bias and error in the interpretation of results. Only when that is complete can the researcher decide how generalisable the research results are to the broader population or similar contexts, and draw general conclusions. At this point the researcher is able to compare the study results with existing knowledge relating to the research question. The researcher is also in a position to make recommendations for practice, policy and/or further research in the area. The second part of this chapter provides some guidelines on how to disseminate the research to different audiences, and how to write a research report.

> **CHAPTER OBJECTIVES**
>
> Learners who have completed this chapter will be able to:
> - Interpret the results of the data analysis process.
> - Identify possible sources of error and bias in a study.
> - Draw appropriate conclusions from the findings.
> - Present research findings in an appropriate manner.
> - Disseminate research findings in a variety of ways.

Interpreting the findings: Detection of possible errors

In quantitative studies, research results typically comprise tables of descriptive statistics representing the sample, and the results of inferential statistics demonstrating differences between different parts of the data. Qualitative data typically comprises descriptions of key themes and accounts of differences between those themes or between groups of respondents. Mixed methods include a combination of the two.

These findings, as well as the whole process which generates them, must be thoroughly and critically reviewed to detect any errors, mistakes or bias in sampling, data collection, measurement or analysis that might have distorted the report description of the aspect of social reality under study.

When carrying out a research project, it is essential to recognise that observations of any kind can never be made without some error or bias. Our methods of observation are not perfect, and researchers, as human beings, have their own built-in assumptions and biases. However, recognition of error and bias does not mean that one should passively accept them. On the contrary, every effort should be made to identify, reduce and compensate for error and bias. This is only feasible if all possible sources and types of errors are identified and investigated.

CHAPTER 16 Research findings and dissemination

Types of error and mistakes

Many sources of error exist. First of all, there are *measurement* and *classification* errors. **Measurement errors** refer to data that is wrong or inaccurate, whether it pertains to the income of families, the age of children or respondents' true feeling about a particular political candidate. Such errors occur when the research design or data collection does not produce an accurate measurement or description of the phenomenon being investigated. For example, a quantitative measure, such as a school examination in which second language students are disadvantaged, would not produce an accurate measure of those students' knowledge. Similarly a qualitative interview conducted in the respondents' second language might result in them not being able to express certain concepts, thereby changing the data they might otherwise have provided. **Classification errors** are made when data is wrongly identified and put in an inappropriate class. Common examples include the identification of refugees living in a certain country as nationals of that country, and the classification of all children living in a certain house as the offspring of the house-owner. Poor coding in qualitative research would also be an example of classification error. Both measurement and classification errors can be reduced or eliminated by careful and precise handling of the data and by asking more precise questions.

A second group of errors consists of *constant* and *random errors*. **Constant errors** are systematic, repeated errors throughout the research which can introduce significant biases. An evaluator might systematically underestimate the number of people attending events, or an interviewer might repeatedly avoid a particular aspect of the interview schedule. A **random error**, on the other hand, occurs on some occasions but not on others; it is thus non-systematic and unpredictable. It may be an overestimation of the number of participants on one day, an underestimation on a second day, then a correct count on the third, so that, on average, random errors compensate for one another within large numbers of data. As such, random errors are not considered to be very serious, but constant errors do create serious bias and must therefore be identified and eliminated wherever possible. It is important to remember that in quantitative research it is often possible to use statistical methods to estimate and allow for random error (see Chapter 14).

Finally, we must also distinguish between *errors* and *mistakes*. Although considered as equivalents in everyday language, these two words have different meanings in research. **Errors**, as those mentioned above, introduce bias and inaccuracies in measurement, but their sources can be detected, their seriousness evaluated and their effects ameliorated. The biased formulation of research problems, difficulties in the way the researcher approaches respondents, or when the analysis is skewed by the researcher's own assumptions and opinions, are examples of error. **Mistakes or blunders** on the part of the researcher are, on the other hand, generally neither predictable, nor detectable in a way which permits their systematic analysis and correction. Since these are very often related to the inexperience or incompetence of the researcher, they should and could be avoided through sound training and support from more experienced researchers.

357

Sources of error

Errors can be introduced at all levels of the research process. Thus, it suffices to analyse each step in order to identify possible sources of bias. The list presented below is not exhaustive, and is in many aspects a summary of what has been presented in previous chapters.

1. *Vagueness of definitions and inaccuracy of hypotheses or research questions.* If the research question or problem is vaguely stated, this may introduce a situation where the researcher conducts a study to confirm his own biases. A clearly stated and isolated research problem will lead the researcher towards relevant literature as well as an appropriate theoretical framework. This will eventually make the researcher's work much easier. Similarly, the lack of adequate operational definitions can lead to an inaccurate description of the population, and of the types of information to be collected.

2. *Inadequacy of design and planning of research.* This source of error arises from a failure to identify all important variables, having too many uncontrolled variables, or having too many sources of error that have escaped detection. Every study comprises many different aspects, any of which might have been overlooked. Thus, all studies must be properly planned and have a clear research design.

3. *Sampling errors and other errors.* In quantitative research, sampling errors affect the representativeness of the sample. A discrepancy may exist between the actual population from which the sample was drawn and the target population to which inferences are to be applied. This may be due to the inadequacy of the sampling frame or a high number of non-responses. The sample may also not be representative of the population because of the choice of an inappropriate sampling method (see Chapter 11), a very small sample size or no estimate of sampling error. Qualitative researchers, who ignore the principle of saturation, preferring instead to work on a percentage or formula of representativeness, might fail to collect information about some aspects of the issue under study. Often, even though the correct sampling method has been chosen, it is not implemented correctly because of the inexperience of the interviewer or other unexpected difficulties. Sometimes researchers might even fail to properly observe sample inclusion and exclusion criteria and so include inappropriate respondents in the sample.

4. *Imperfection in the research instrument.* In experiments, laboratory equipment may be deficient or not properly adjusted to particular conditions. In the case of interviews and questionnaires, many more errors are often introduced relating to the length of the questionnaire, the venue, the order of presentation of the questions, the type of questions, and the content. For instance, leading questions, double-barrelled questions, or questions with incomplete choices of answer or

CHAPTER 16 Research findings and dissemination

with unfamiliar vocabulary are particularly likely to produce error. Data collected under unfavourable conditions, for example, recordings taken against background noise which prevents accurate transcription, also produce errors. Finally, it is also not unusual to come across interview guides that bear little resemblance to the research question. This problem leads to the researcher being unable to test the study hypotheses or answer the research questions.

5. *Bias*. Bias is the systematic introduction of extraneous variables that may distort or disguise the relationships among the experimental variables. In order to better understand the differences between error and bias, consider the following examples. Someone reads a book written in Spanish. This person has a fair knowledge of Spanish but may struggle to understand the exact meaning of some words. She can prevent the **errors** of misinterpretation by consulting a dictionary, because she is aware of specific problematic words. She might also prefer to read an English translation of that book if English is her mother tongue. However, in that case, she would be at the mercy of any **bias** introduced by the translator, who would have had his own understanding of the original text. Similar challenges face the researcher who works with an interpreter when collecting data in the field. It is difficult to know how accurately the interpreter is transmitting the actual sense of what the respondents are saying. The translator's interpretation might not be incorrect, but the meaning might have been slightly but systematically different had the researcher and the respondents been speaking the same language.

There are several sources of bias.

a. *Interviewer bias*

The interviewer can affect the answers of the respondents through the way in which he relates to them, such as by being too lenient, aggressive, impatient or partial. In truth, even the interviewer's demographic characteristics could influence the results. For example, a man interviewing female victims of spousal abuse is likely to collect data that is systematically different from data collected by a female researcher. The interviewer can also bias the information by recording it inaccurately, either by translating the ideas of the respondent into the interviewer's own words and thus interpreting the answers according to her own views, or by writing down only a summary or part of an answer. Unscrupulous interviewers may falsify the answers so as to reflect their own convictions, or even fill in questionnaires without actually interviewing anybody.

b. *Respondent bias*

These are biases introduced by unresponsive participants, or uncooperative ones who only answer at random, as well as by respondents who purposefully give false information because of mistrust, fear and desire to conform or because of social pressures. This category of bias also includes responses based on

359

the misunderstanding of a question or a word, and difficulties experienced by respondents in expressing themselves. Pilot testing every new data collection instrument is one way of addressing these problems.

c. *Analyst bias*

These are all the errors introduced at the level of processing, coding and analysing the data. In quantitative data, misinterpretation of responses to open-ended questions often leads to incorrect classification. Similarly, the statistical treatment of quantitative data may be distorted by the choice of an inadequate test or because of computation errors. Moreover, analysts have many ways of projecting their own expectations and prejudices on to computations, comparisons and the presentation of results.

d. *Researcher bias*

Throughout the research process the philosophical, political and religious beliefs of the researchers, as well as their racial attitudes and other convictions, all play an underlying role. As human beings, researchers can never be completely objective, particularly when dealing with social phenomena. They have expectations not only on the basis of scientific considerations but also on the basis of their personal views. These views surface in their interest in and choice of research topic, as well as in many other steps within a research project. They may intentionally choose a particular population, isolate a certain sample, ask (or refrain from asking) some specific questions, and deliberately omit to take into consideration some theories or research findings that contradict or question the validity of their approach.

An exuberant researcher may subtly (or not so subtly) promote the effectiveness of one intervention over others. Investigators who use newly developed treatments are often more enthusiastic about them than those who use old treatments, and this enthusiasm can be communicated to the participants. If an experimenter is not sufficiently motivated, this can also be communicated to the participants and they may not be as keen to enrol in the study as they might otherwise be. One possible consequence of this would be large amounts of missing data.

Some solutions to the problems of bias include:

- Make sure that all research staff are aware of, and trained, in the issues of bias.
- Where possible in quantitative research, keep the research staff who are responsible for data collection unaware (that is, blind) of the research hypotheses.
- Where possible in experimental research, keep the research staff who are responsible for data collection unaware (that is, blind) of the identity of each group (experimental, comparison or control).
- Design your data collection tools carefully, using simple and accessible language, avoiding double barrelled questions, etc.
- Test data collection tools in a pilot study.
- Provide adequate training to research assistants responsible for collecting, entering and coding data.
- Keep issues of bias in mind at all times when conducting research.

CHAPTER 16 Research findings and dissemination

6. *Poor research procedures.* There are many procedures involved in the conduct of any research study: recruiting participants, greeting participants, obtaining informed consent, providing a rationale for the study, allocating respondents to groups, giving instructions, administering interventions, recording data, reminding respondents about returning questionnaires, interviewing respondents, entering data into computers, cleaning and coding data, and so on. One problem here can be procedural imprecision, which is when the researcher treats respondents differently because he or she has no specific instructions about how to behave or what to say. Such differential treatment could be a potential source of bias.

Researcher fatigue is an important factor when interviewing a large number of respondents in a short space of time. If participants feel that the interviewer is not that interested in them they might give short answers rather than the more detailed answers that other people gave earlier in the day. If the researcher behaves differently from one respondent to the next this can add another variable to the study, eg, if the researcher flirts with one participant but not with the rest, that respondent will probably behave differently.

If there is procedural variation, the researcher may not know exactly how this affected the study and the resultant data. The data may have been influenced by any number of things related to the research procedures which is a serious threat to internal validity.

Some solutions to the problems of procedural imprecision

The most important remedy for **procedural imprecision** is to make every procedure explicit in the finest detail. The more complex a study, the more procedures there are, and more important procedural precision becomes. If the researcher is expected to make certain statements to participants during data collection, it is often best that those statements are scripted so that each person hears exactly the same statements in the same way. If different groups within the sample are to receive different interventions, it is critical that those interventions are carefully standardised so that all participants in a particular group experience exactly the same intervention. In this way the researcher can be sure of exactly what it is that is being tested.

Of course, merely writing down the procedures is not sufficient. It is also important that the researcher train every person involved in the research in the implementation of those procedures. This may involve explaining exactly what the procedures mean, practicing certain tasks and role playing them to demonstrate competence. It is also a good idea for the researcher to stay close to all research activities so as to ensure that the procedures are being correctly followed, and to address any deviations immediately they arise.

Once all the sources of error have been investigated and the extent and type of possible bias has been estimated, the findings can be interpreted. On the basis of a critical study of the procedure, the researcher should be able to explain any inconsistencies in the research results, and between these results and the findings of other researchers. The scientist should also be in a position to state the shortcomings and limitations of the research, and be able to take these into account in her evaluation of the findings.

Drawing conclusions

After interpreting the findings it is useful to summarise the aims of the research and to compare them with the findings, thereby drawing conclusions as to how much and in what manner the aims of the research have been achieved. In quantitative research the researcher should pay attention to the extent to which hypotheses have been confirmed, and whether it has been possible to infer causal or correlational relationships between variables. In qualitative research the researcher should pay attention to the extent to which new information about the research question has been gathered and presented, and also examine possible causal or correlational relationships between key concepts.

Generalising research findings

Once conclusions reflecting some properties of the target population have been drawn, one can estimate how far these findings can be generalised to a larger population, and suggest modifications that should be taken into consideration when making such a generalisation. For instance, one might be interested in estimating how far results obtained on a target population of university students could be generalised to the broader population of students in tertiary educational institutions.

Even more important is the integration of research results with previous research findings and with the theoretical framework used in the research. The first point refers to the comparison of the findings of the present research with the ones of investigations that were considered in the literature review. Are the present empirical results in accordance with the others in literature? Do they contradict some of them? How does one explain the differences? This critical analysis may help to discover important flaws, misinterpretations or relevant variables that have been overlooked by either the present or previous researchers. Unexpected similarities might also help to uncover an important common factor. For instance, many investigations have aimed at assessing whether, and how, the viewing of violence in films affects the behaviour of young children. Seemingly contradictory results have been found: heightened levels of aggression in some cases and a cathartic effect that decreases the level of aggression in others. These opposite findings lead to a deeper analysis posing such questions as: In what circumstances, and for what type of children (age, sex, social class), is the effect soothing? What kinds of films produce what reactions?

The researcher should also try to integrate her final conclusions within a theoretical framework. Do the findings support a certain theory? Do they, on the other hand, raise questions about any accepted principles? Do they add new perspectives or answer old questions? Do they constitute a 'missing link' between theories?

CHAPTER 16 Research findings and dissemination

Suggestions and recommendations

Research is mainly relevant due to its implications for the improvement of the human condition. As such, the practical aspects of the findings must be analysed as well. On the basis of the results, suggestions may be made for further investigations to clarify certain aspects, to generalise some findings, or to check the importance of some variables and, perhaps, to avoid various pitfalls. One might also mention the possible application of the results to other fields: for example, some investigations on emotions could have relevance to the medical profession, in industrial relations or in education. Lastly, recommendations should be made on how programmes or policies might be altered. These recommendations should be both detailed and practical, such as types of rewards and incentives for use in schools to increase motivation and achieve optimal learning.

In action-research, recommendations and suggestions are central to the research process. Concrete plans for the implementation of such suggestions should be formulated by the research *participants*. These become the action of the action-research process.

Ways of disseminating findings

The dissemination of research findings takes many forms, depending on the researcher's aims and the intended audience. The form of presentation, completeness and length, emphasis on one or other aspect, and the level of scientific rigour can vary widely. Several different dissemination platforms are discussed here.

Reports at research sites and to research participants

Much of the research discussed in this book involves applied and community-based studies where the community itself is the most important consumer. Researchers presenting the results of their work to community representatives and research participants must summarise the information in a way that is easily accessible and stimulates questions and discussions.

Presentations to close colleagues

It is sometimes very helpful for inexperienced researchers to begin the process of dissemination by presenting their results to a group of colleagues or peer researchers. This allows the researcher to present new ideas for friendly discussion and critique.

Organisational or departmental seminars

More formal seminars within one's department or organisation can serve the same process. The researcher has a chance to practise presenting the research in a clear and concise manner, and discussions with colleagues often lead to ideas being refined and elaborated.

363

Professional conferences

Professional conferences provide another platform at which researchers can present their work. Professional associations and conferences differ greatly in their aims and the kind of presentations that are expected. It is a good idea to read the conference invitation carefully and to speak to people who have more experience of that particular organisation before proceeding.

Reports and presentations to clients

Much research is contracted and paid for by governments, private companies, and both local and international non-governmental organisations and funding agencies. Very often researchers are called upon to present the results of the work to their clients. In such cases the emphasis is usually on the results and implications of the research, although a summary of the method to explain exactly how funds were used is also always required.

Research in the mass media

One of the more difficult challenges for a scientist is to present research through the mass media in a responsible way. Radio, television, newspapers and magazines all want very short explanations of the research findings and sometimes try to overinterpret or sensationalise results. Usually research findings are complex and need to be considered within the context and limitations of any particular study. The advantage of using the mass media is that the findings can be broadcast to very large populations very quickly. The researcher using the mass media should think carefully about how to communicate the research findings in a very brief but nevertheless responsible way.

Scientific journals

Publication of research in a peer-reviewed scientific journal is the most demanding of the various platforms available to the researcher. This is because the process of peer review, by which the scientific community ensures a high minimum standard of research, can be extremely challenging. **Peer review** is conducted anonymously, and articles submitted for review are typically reviewed independently by at least two suitably experienced and knowledgeable reviewers. While reviewers are always encouraged to be respectful and constructive in their criticism, this is not always the case. Inexperienced researchers should try not to be put off by the harsh criticism that is sometimes forthcoming from reviewers.

CHAPTER 16 Research findings and dissemination

Organisation of a research report

The most detailed, complete and scientific report for research-funding institutions and archives should present all the different steps of the research in detail, but it is also possible to have less complete reports for specific purposes. A report written for publication in a scientific journal will have to show a high level of scientific quality condensed into a few pages, one written for an agency particularly interested in conclusions and practical consequences might cut short the technical aspects of the research and emphasise the discussion of findings and their implications, while one that needs to be understood by the average educated readership of a magazine may present findings in more general terms, avoiding scientific vocabulary. In other words, different reports stress one or the other aspect of the complete research report. Thus, it is sufficient here to present the format of such a complete report from which other reports may be extracted.

Although no strict rules exist on the structure of a research report, logic and consistency impose a certain order. The guidelines presented below constitute only one possibility. Within each of the main sections the order of the different subsections may vary to suit and some sections may even be omitted altogether. On the whole, the guidelines follow the presentation sequence of this book and each subsection refers to a related subsection of the book. Writing a research report may be considered the culmination of the research process and the main sections of a research report are: introduction, methods, results, discussion, conclusion, recommendations, and references. However, funding or sponsoring organisations may expect the researchers' format to be in line with their organisations' preferences.

Title

The title of the study or article should describe the essence of the research. It should catch potential readers' attention while at the same time letting them know exactly what the study is about.

Abstract or executive summary

Abstracts are required for journal articles and also for some other types of reports. Abstracts are usually between 100 and 200 words long, briefly describing the four main sections, namely: research question, method, results, and conclusions. Emphasis should be placed on the results and their significance, but information on the design and the characteristics and size of the sample is also important. The reader should be in a position to grasp the essence of the whole study by reading the abstract.

Executive summaries are longer and contain all the key points of all the sections of the research report. Executive summaries are usually several pages long.

365

Acknowledgements

It is appropriate (and an ethical requirement for researchers) to acknowledge the people and organisations who have contributed in different ways to the research. Contributors might include funding agencies, other experienced researchers who have given advice and support, academic institutions, government departments, private companies and civil society organisations that supported the research in different ways. Funding organisations may expect acknowledgement of their sponsorship as well as their company name and logo on the covering page of the report. There are no hard and fast rules as to how acknowledgments should be made. However, it is essential that acknowledging that research is not a value-free exercise. Potential consumers of the research might wonder to what extent the organisations that supported and paid for the research might in fact have swayed the conclusions. For this reason it is essential that researchers acknowledge all sources of funding and other kinds of support.

Introduction

1. *Identification of the research question.* The question to be dealt with is introduced and the area within which it is situated is identified. Authoritative sources, including other scientists, are quoted to clarify what is known about the particular issue and what is still unclear and needs further investigation, as well as the relevance of such investigations.

2. *Significance of the study.* The relevance of the problem is highlighted in terms of both its theoretical and practical implications. How will this study contribute to general knowledge? And, how will the findings contribute to improving people's lives?

Literature review

1. *Literature review.* Only the relevant articles are cited and commented upon. Often it is useful to group the articles into different categories related to particular variables or other conditions considered relevant. Subheadings can be useful. Other types of background information should also be presented.

Method

1. *Statement of the problem.* The statement of the problem refers to the first two points referred to in the introduction, but contains a more precise approach to the issue and clarifies the purpose of the study. It should be very short and identify the main variables, which should be defined conceptually at this stage.

CHAPTER 16 Research findings and dissemination

2. *Statement and rationale of the hypotheses or research question.* In quantitative research the hypotheses should be clearly and concisely stated in terms of the conceptual definitions of the variables. This section should provide logical arguments to show that each hypothesis is reasonable and sound. It should also provide empirical evidence to justify the hypotheses. In other words, the reader should be convinced that there are good grounds for stating these hypotheses. In qualitative research, more particular research questions are often included at this point. Again, such questions are stated in terms of the conceptual definitions of the key variables.

3. *Operational definitions of the variables and hypotheses.* Of greater importance to quantitative research is the question of providing operational definitions of all variables and, where necessary, restating the hypotheses in these terms. Here the researcher includes information about how specific variables will be measured.

4. *Research type and design.* In this subsection the researcher must describe the kind of research that is being written about and the research design being used.

5. *The sample.* Here all issues and information concerning the research participants are examined. Among these are the characteristics of the target population and of the sample, the sampling procedure and the size of the sample.

6. *Data collection instruments.* Any instruments or systems for collecting data should be described in this section. This would include explaining how instruments were developed or selected, whether or not they have been previously tested with the population in question, as well as information about the reliability, validity or trustworthiness of these instruments.

7. *Procedures.* The researcher should explain in a step-by-step fashion all the steps of the research. This should be done in enough detail that another researcher would be able to repeat the study exactly, and hopefully produce similar results.

8. *Data analysis.* The process of data analysis must be described in detail. These processes will depend on the nature of the research question and the type of data.

9. *Ethical provisions.* The final subsection of the methods part of a research report should explain the ethical provisions of the research method, as well as the process whereby the researcher gained ethical approval for the project from an independent body.

367

Results

Typically, this section involves two steps.

1. *Summary of the findings*. The main findings following from the data analysis are presented here. Tables, graphs and diagrams are particularly effective in quantitative research and should be used to help the reader understand the data. In qualitative studies, a summary of the results should include descriptions of the key themes illustrated with verbatim quotations from respondents.

2. *Analysis of the hypotheses or research question*. In quantitative research each hypothesis is analysed in the light of the research results and decisions to reject or retain each hypothesis are made. Similarly, qualitative research questions are discussed in the light of qualitative findings. The researcher should analyse the extent to which the research questions have been answered and the trustworthiness of those answers.

Discussion and conclusions

This section is in many ways the most important part of the report where the researcher provides:

1. an interpretation of the findings
2. a discussion of the significance of the findings for knowledge of the research topic
3. a discussion of the significance of the findings for the betterment of society
4. a discussion of the limitations and weaknesses of the current study
5. recommendations for policy and practice arising from the study findings
6. recommendations for further research in the field.

Metaphorically, research can be compared to a relay race where each participating athlete is expected to pass the baton to the next member of the team in order to complete the race. Although there have been some groundbreaking research studies, the vast majority of scientific knowledge is accumulated through the small contributions of many researchers. The final sections of a research report in which the researcher critiques her own work and makes recommendations for future work is represented by the act of passing the baton to the next runner.

References and bibliography

A reference list is a list of all the materials that have been cited in the report or paper. A bibliography refers to all the works or sources that have been consulted during the research, some of which have been cited in the text. The list is usually presented in alphabetical order by the names of authors, and includes all information required to find each reference. Typically this includes the name of the author(s), the year of publication,

CHAPTER 16 Research findings and dissemination

the title of the book or article in italics, the place of publication, the publisher's name and the relevant page numbers. Examples are:

- Mpofu, E. (Ed.) 2011. *Counseling people of African Ancestry*, *New York*, NY: Cambridge University Press.
- Creswell, J W. 2010. Mapping the developing landscape of mixed methods research, in A. Tashakkori and C. Teddlie (eds). *SAGE Handbook of Mixed Methods in Social and Behavioral Research*, 2nd ed. Thousand Oaks: Sage.

Journal articles are referenced by indicating the name of the journal in italics after the title of the article, as well as by indicating the volume and the number of the issue before the page number:

- Sideris, T. 2003. War, gender and culture: Mozambican women refugess. *Social Science and Medicine*, 56 (4), 713–724.

Appendices

Appendices usually contain summarised data and the results of the data analysis, both often presented as tables. It is essential to give a number and title to each appendix in line with how they are referred to in the text. Where the instrument of measurement is a questionnaire or any material that can be printed, it may also be added as a separate appendix. In qualitative research, coding definitions should also be included in an appendix.

Guidelines for writing

Scientific writing, much like creative writing, is an idiosyncratic exercise. Each person presents information and data according to their own style. However, academic writing is governed by more guidelines, conventions and rules. Although some writers find these guidelines restricting, most find them very helpful in providing structure to an otherwise somewhat daunting task. The following guidelines should assist researchers in producing high quality material in line with the expectations of the scientific community.

Know your audience. The results of research reports are read by many different kinds of people. It is important that you keep in mind a clear picture of your audience when you are writing. What format is your audience accustomed to reading? What information is most interesting to them? What are they less interested in? How accustomed are they to reading complex charts and tables? What is the general level of literacy likely to be? For example, writing a research report on a needs assessment for an urban neighbourhood would require that the researcher describe the methodology somewhat briefly, to get quickly to the core needs of the community, and a list of recommendations for action which is what that audience is interested in. Charts and tables should be relatively simple and carefully explained. By contrast, when the researcher is writing for a scientific

369

journal, the audience is much more interested in methodological details, the results of the study and the extent to which they are generalisable to various communities with similar challenges. In this case, the researcher can assume that the audience will know how to read more complex charts and tables.

In scientific writing, institutions and journals often have their own style and formatting guides, and these are almost always found online. Make sure that you download and carefully read all instructions for authors before writing up your research.

Know your theme. Too often novice researchers begin writing before they know exactly what it is that they want to say. When the theme of the paper or report is not clear the researcher often gets lost in digressions and arguments that end up being circular or leading nowhere. In this regard the structure of the research report outlined above is a very useful tool to keep the researcher on track while writing. Even more important is to plan a paper in a great deal of detail before writing. The more thought the researcher puts into the planning process, the easier the writing process will be and the better the final product.

Use simple language. Modern scientific writing emphasises the importance of clarity. Clarity in writing comes from avoiding jargon, excessively metaphorical or flowery language, phrases in foreign languages, and rhetorical devices such as repetition and unanswerable questions. Some simple grammatical and stylistic rules to keep in mind are:

- *Write as much as possible in the active voice.* Instead of writing 'Ten respondents were interviewed', write 'I interviewed 10 respondents'. Sentences in the passive voice tend to be more difficult to understand and remove the researcher from the equation. This suggests that research is a purely objective, value-free enterprise, which, as we have discussed, it is not.
- *Write as much as possible in the first person.* Instead of writing 'The researcher interviewed 10 respondents', write 'I (or we) interviewed 10 respondents'.
- *Write mainly in the past tense.* Since a research report is a description of events that have already occurred, it should be written mainly in the past tense.
- *Avoid being verbose.* Try to write in short sentences and avoid unnecessary words and phrases. Make sure that every phrase adds something new to the overall message. Make sure that any long sentences are not ambiguous, that is, they cannot be understood in more than one way.
- *Use simple words.* While technical language is an unavoidable part of scientific writing, extremely technical language should never be used merely to appear more intellectual or academic. If there is a simpler way of saying something, it is almost always better to do so. Research reports often contain a list of abbreviations and acronyms, or a glossary to assist readers with technical language. Nevertheless, all abbreviations and acronyms should be written out in full on first usage in a paper or report.

CHAPTER 16 Research findings and dissemination

- *Avoid any kind of discriminatory or pejorative language.* Regardless of any researcher's personal prejudices and bias, scientific writing holds every human being to be equal and worthy of respect. Language used in scientific writing should avoid perpetuating any stereotypes or prejudices. This means that language that is sexist, racist, xenophobic, homophobic or discriminates against people on cultural, ethnic, religious or economic grounds must be avoided.

- *Do not plagiarise.* This is an important ethical issue covered in Chapter 3. However, much plagiarism is committed unknowingly by inexperienced writers. This is partly due to the easy availability of electronic literature which can be 'cut and pasted'. Many cases of plagiarism occur when inexperienced researchers drop material from another source into a paper that they are working on and then forget that that material is not in fact their own. Even when such researchers translate the ideas into their own words, the ideas may still be plagiarised. Avoid putting lots of material into a document before you start writing as a means of getting started. While it may feel good to have lots of words on the page, those are not in fact your words. Make sure that all sources are cited both in the text and in the reference section at the end of the report.

  Today it is possible and affordable to check your work for any inadvertent plagiarism. An internet search will reveal several sites that will review your work for plagiarism for a small fee. Two such websites are included in the additional resources to this chapter.

- *Edit and check your work.* No researcher writes without making mistakes. It is important that you read and reread your work to ensure that what you have written is of the highest quality and contains no errors. Use the spellcheck on your word processor to make sure that all spelling and typing mistakes have been corrected. While some universities have language departments that provide editing facilities for a small fee, most researchers ask friends or colleagues to help them with this process, or do it themselves.

In conclusion, the difficulty of writing, regardless of whether you are a first or second language speaker, is often underestimated. In fact, writing well is one of the most important skills that the novice researcher must master. Give yourself lots of time to write, get lots of support from colleagues, friends and teachers, and do not give up. It takes time to learn this skill and even though your first attempt might fall short of the mark, your next attempt will be better. There are also some excellent writing support programmes available over the internet, one of which is listed under additional resources.

Fundamentals of Social Research Methods: An African Perspective

Key points

1. The interpretation of results is the culmination of the research process and must be done thoroughly.
2. Researchers should be mindful of all possible sources of bias and error that might have influenced the results.
3. Dissemination of findings may take many forms, each of which makes different demands on the researcher in terms of style, content and scientific rigour in presentation.
4. The researcher must always pay careful attention to the particular characteristics of the target audience.
5. Many institutions and publications have very particular style and format requirements to which the researcher must adhere.
6. Scientific writing should be clear, concise, detailed and respectful.
7. Scientific writing is a skill that can only be mastered with time and practice.

Checklist

Keywords:

Check whether the meaning of these concepts introduced in this chapter is clear to you.

error; mistake; bias; constant error; random error; abstract; peer review.

Your research:
1. Make sure that you consider all possible sources of error when interpreting the results of your research.
2. Make sure you discuss all limitations of your study and make recommendations for further research on the topic.
3. Make sure you consider multiple platforms for dissemination of your results.
4. Be clear about your audience and your message before you start writing.
5. Make sure that you have read the style and format guidelines for your target publication before writing.
6. Check that your writing is in line with the guidelines listed in this chapter.
7. Check that you have not inadvertently plagiarised another author.
8. Edit and proofread your writing before submission.
9. Try to learn from peer review, no matter how critical and unfair it seems.
10. Take time to practice the skill of scientific writing.

CHAPTER 16 Research findings and dissemination

Exercises

1. A researcher measures the attitude of farmers in a rural district towards family planning. The results indicate a clearly negative attitude. Using the same questionnaire, another scientist replicates this study on an equivalent sample of farmers. The new results show a slightly positive attitude towards family planning.
   a. Which sources of error or bias could explain this difference?
   b. What can be said about the scientific rigour of this research?
   c. What further steps would you propose to these researchers?
2. Explain how a researcher might inadvertently influence an investigation during each of the following steps:
   a. selection of a problem for research
   b. selection of the sample
   c. design of the research
   d. construction of the tools of measurement
   e. data collection
   f. analysis and interpretation of results.
3. How might the problems listed in your answer to the previous question be avoided?
4. Locate the website for a journal called *Social Science and Medicine* and download the guide for authors. Make a list of 10 important points that you would need to remember if you were preparing a manuscript for this journal.

Additional resources

1. Checking for plagiarism: https://www.writecheck.com
2. Online writing guide: http://owl.english.purdue.edu/owl/
3. Online writing support: http://www.eseo.cl/eng

CHAPTER 17

Research management

Since all human beings are the product of their social environment, they are socialised into and act according to certain cultural values and beliefs of which they may only be vaguely aware. It is therefore important to discuss the relationship between the neutrality demanded by science and every individual's system of values. Moreover, since research is supported by a society, the nature and the consequences of this support call for analysis. This entails an examination of the role of research-funding institutions, as well as the management of self-initiated and funded research projects. Finally, in order to access resources necessary for research, a research proposal must be developed on the basis of thorough planning of the research and how it will be managed.

CHAPTER OBJECTIVES

Learners who have completed this chapter will be able to:
- Critically discuss the relationship between individual values and the social sciences.
- Analyse and manage the various interpersonal and interorganisational relationships that are part of most social research projects.
- Plan, execute and manage research projects.

The research world

Because introductory texts in research methodology strive to be as clear as possible, they sometimes do not prepare the inexperienced researcher for the complex world of research. Researchers do not work alone. In nearly all cases a range of different people have some kind of stake in the research process. These people include participants in the research, other researchers, research-funding institutions, various administrations that control access to particular target populations, tertiary education institutions, and publishers. One of the challenges facing the researcher is to develop productive working relationships with all of these different groups so that the research can proceed as smoothly as possible.

CHAPTER 17 Research management

> ### Example
>
> The parent–teacher association of a school is concerned about the increase in teenage pregnancy at their school. In particular, they want to know whether this is a local trend or whether it is also happening in other schools in their district. Finally, they want to identify the best strategy for reducing the number of teenagers falling pregnant. They call in a social researcher for advice and together plan a survey of schools in the area, and an investigation of other attempts to prevent teenage pregnancy. As the study will be quite expensive, they put together a funding proposal and submit it to a research donor operating in their area. Having accessed the necessary funds, they find that they must get permission from the Minister of Education in order to conduct research in schools.
>
> Having done all this they now also have to explain the project to the headmasters of the schools in which the research is going to be conducted. The researcher also identifies three teenage pregnancy prevention projects in the region, and liaises with the people in charge of each, in order to discover which strategies they have found to be the most successful.

Furthermore, one notes that many research projects involve more than a single researcher. Because many social research topics are extremely complex and difficult to investigate in their entirety, it is often necessary to break topics down into a series of smaller questions (see Chapter 4). Often social scientists embark upon linked research projects, each contributing to a more general topic in a specific way. This is an effective technique, which can produce excellent results as long as one common pitfall is avoided – frequently the links between the various research topics fall away, and when the various results emerge, they do not relate to each other in any meaningful way. Thus, although five researchers have all studied the same topic, if they have defined their research questions and variables in very different ways the results may not be comparable. It is crucial that all research questions that relate to the topic are derived together and that conceptual and operational definitions of all variables that have relevance to the broader study are mutually agreed upon before the research begins.

With the ongoing development of the various social science disciplines, areas of overlap are becoming more and more significant. Analysing social reality in terms of varying perspectives is very rewarding but may be complicated. When a team of researchers from different disciplines cooperate on a single research question, the term **multidisciplinary research** is used.

The chief value of this form of research is that it helps social scientists to overcome the somewhat arbitrary boundaries that exist between bodies of knowledge within the social sciences. When sociologists, economists and political scientists (for example) work together on a project they bring a broader range of experience, expertise and theory than any group of people from a single discipline could do. In multidisciplinary research, strict attention to the way in which questions are asked and variables are defined is even more crucial if the problems mentioned above are to be avoided. This is because the various disciplines tend to conceptualise research questions and social concepts in different ways. It is important that social researchers from different

375

disciplines are speaking a 'common language' before they embark on a joint research project.

Role players in research projects all have their own expectations of what the project might produce, and they will therefore exert influence in different ways. The researcher must be aware of all the different expectations and concerns of this group of people and make sure that their influence on the outcome of the research is minimised.

Science and values

Even now some scientists, among other people, believe that science is empirical and therefore value-free and detached from culture, ideology and politics. Their belief is that science is purely objective and neutral. This myth must be discarded and the various ways in which culture, ideology and politics impact upon scientific research needs to be analysed.

For social scientists, and all the other participants in research projects, culture and ideology play an important role. In fact they influence every step of the research process, from the choice of the research topic and the formulation of hypotheses or research questions, to the final interpretation of results. Culture, ideology and politics create implicit and explicit expectations of outcomes that permeate the research. Although it is expected that scientists should set aside their personal values, or at least clearly acknowledge them and take them into account when carrying out research, practice has shown that this expectation is not always easily met.

Example

A study on work motivation in industry could be undertaken in accordance with the interests of an employer who wishes to avoid industrial action which would curb production and profits. Equally, the same study could be undertaken with the interests of the workers, their well-being and their dignity as human beings, as its focus. Depending on the approach chosen and the type of data collected, the conclusions would be very different, even if, *officially*, the adopted interest is that of the firm or industry as a whole.

To understand the extent to which research is tied to social politics, one must appreciate the interrelationship between research and society. As mentioned in Chapter 1, the development of knowledge and of research in particular is a direct function of the needs of society. Moreover, the emphasis given to different problems, and thus the effort to solve them, is determined by the people in decision-making positions. Research can very easily become a tool in the hands of the most powerful people in society and may be used, either consciously or unconsciously, to promote the needs of those people, at the expense of the needs of less powerful people.

Control over research by the most powerful people in a society is maintained in two ways. Firstly, the resources necessary to conduct social research may be controlled by a particular group. Secondly, the skills necessary to conduct social research may be

CHAPTER 17 Research management

found only in a particular group. South Africa provides a good historical example of this situation but almost every country in the world has at some time or another faced similar problems. In South Africa, research funds were for many years controlled by the relatively wealthy white population (both English and Afrikaans speaking). This group had particular interests and beliefs about the world, and resources were allocated to research that supported that agenda. At that time very few people outside of this group had access to good quality education or the opportunity to develop competent research skills, so control of research was easily maintained.

The impact of politics, ideology and culture on the application or the use of research findings cannot be ignored. As mentioned before, research is not usually conducted for the sake of pure knowledge but mainly in response to the needs of society. The social scientist, on the one hand, and the funding institutions on the other, may have quite different views about the relevance of a research topic and its possible applications. Social scientists may even be unaware of the end purposes of those who fund their investigations. Although some researchers may be strongly opposed to certain uses to which their scientific findings may be put, other scientists may willingly adopt the aims determined by decision-making or funding bodies. For example, some psychologists, either willingly or unknowingly, have been instrumental in developing psychological weapons to boost the morale of invading troops while disempowering and terrorising the civilian population of the invaded society.

Although the ethics of research is concerned mainly with the methods employed in that research (see Chapter 3), ethical and neutral social research is possible. However, the researcher must always be aware of the many ways in which the ideal of neutrality/objectivity can be influenced by outside values.

The role of research-funding institutions

Research is often expensive, and budgets in the developing world are small. Sadly, accurate information does not seem to be highly valued by decision-makers in Africa who would rather spend the scarce funds at their disposal on providing services, even when very little is known about the efficacy or cost-effectiveness of those services. The costs and harmful consequences of a poorly researched intervention done without a feasibility study or evaluation and monitoring data are enormous when compared with the cost of carefully designed social research.

Given the scarcity of resources available to social researchers, the people who control funds have a powerful influence on the kind of research that is done. Often different topics become fashionable at different times in conjunction with the prevailing and changing concerns of donor agencies. Examples of this include research on women during the United Nation's Women's Decade and research on handicapped people during the Year of the Disabled. Societies experiencing social stress, racial tension or industrial unrest may allocate funds to find solutions to these problems, but these investigations will in all likelihood be done within a certain political framework. As a result, the research will be based on certain premises, and the findings are likely to reflect those premises, ideologies and expectations.

Although a very broad range of structures use the services of social science researchers to address specific problems and queries on a contract basis, the list of agencies that will embark on research of a broader nature designed to improve society is short. These agencies fall into a number of different categories, including:

- Agencies attached to the governments of particular countries. The Zambia Institute for Policy Analysis and Research (ZIPAR) provides research-based policy advice for the government, the private sector and civil society. The Economic and Social Research Foundation (ESRF) is the research think tank in Tanzania that focuses on five themes: inclusive growth and wealth creation, social services, social protection and quality of life, natural resources and environment management, governance and accountability, and globalisation and regional integration.
- International donors, such as those associated with the United Nations and the African Union. These include the United Nations Children's Fund (UNICEF) and many others.
- Independent philanthropic organisations (sometimes multinational), usually based in countries in Europe and North America. Examples of these include the Carnegie and Ford Foundations based in the United States of America and the Bernard van Leer Foundation based in the Netherlands. International development Agencies, such as NORAD (Norway), SIDA (Sweden), CIDA (Canada), DANIDA (Denmark) to name only few, use need assessment and evaluation research to ground their work in Africa.
- Corporate donors, such as large businesses, which allocate resources to social research as part of their social responsibility policies. An example of this might be Shell International, which funds a range of different projects.

Every donor organisation specifies criteria for funding. These criteria may relate to the research topic with only a relatively narrow range of topics being considered, or may relate to the nature of the research methods, or the characteristics of the researchers. Although in the past many donors have used their financial power to dictate research topics and methodologies to researchers, the current trend is to allow much more flexibility. At the beginning of the 21st century, most donors have become extremely sensitive to the problems of dictating research agendas from outside of the developing world and so are much more likely to let local experts and researchers guide their work.

Nevertheless, the prospects for independent, unbiased research in countries that must rely on external funding are rather bleak unless social scientists are cautious. The situation can be improved if researchers are conscious of these dangers and confront them. They can be helped in this task by a clear awareness of the real expressed needs

CHAPTER 17 Research management

of their countries and by a determination to undertake research that promotes genuine development in those countries.

It is the researcher's responsibility to find donors who are interested in the kind of research being proposed and to convince them of the usefulness of a project. For this reason, the **research proposal** is a crucial document that seeks first to convince readers (including donors) of the value of the research, as well as the expertise and experience of the researchers, and then to demonstrate the feasibility of the project plan.

Planning and managing a research project

Conducting research is a daunting task that often involves sleepless nights and frustration resulting from the myriad stakeholders and the bureaucracy that one often comes across. If social scientists hope to produce quality research, they must manage research projects effectively, which demands a range of skills and attributes. Developing and writing a research proposal in order to have research approved and funded can be done much more thoroughly once the planning and management aspects of the research have been addressed. That being said, the detailed management of the research process is an ongoing activity, which has to remain flexible and adjustable to changing circumstances.

In order to manage research well, the planning and execution of the research project is essential and must include the considerations outlined below.

Defining the scope of the project

Research projects differ in size and scope. Projects may be too big to be handled by an individual alone, or too small to involve multidisciplinary expertise. Whatever the size of the project, planning is essential. The researcher must be able to envisage the end point of the project at its inception, so that all tasks, in particular those that consume time and funds, are adequately planned for.

Research problem

This entails a brief statement embedded in literature about what it is that the researcher wishes to investigate. A well-presented research problem satisfies the '5 Ws': What is the problem? Where is it located? When does it occur? What aspects are of primary concern? Why is investigating this problem important?

Literature study

The extent of the literature review and the available libraries, archives and other information sources needs to be assessed. Time and money must be factored in for this process.

379

Methodology

1. *Approach:* It is important to show whether the approach is quantitative, qualitative or mixed-method.

2. *Design:* The demands of the research question determine the entire design of the study, as studies may be exploratory, descriptive, correlational or explanatory.

3. *Population and sample:* This should include a definition of the target population, sampling procedures and, where appropriate, of sample size.

4. *Data collection and analysis:* The development of the instrument requires expertise and time, and a pilot survey to test the quality of the data collection tools might be necessary. Planning and management of the actual data collection may involve processes regarding mailed or self-administered questionnaires, interviews, focus group discussions or other methods of data collection. Funds must be set aside for all this, as well as for the transcription and coding of qualitative data, statistical analysis of quantitative data, etc. Depending on the size of the project, the researcher may need to use research assistants for the data collection, transcription and coding, as well as other research activities.

Research outputs

All research projects almost invariably require reports to funders and interested stakeholders which take time and may incur some costs (see Chapter 16). Most often, a wide dissemination of the findings is desirable, involving oral presentation and discussions as well as written reports and articles.

Setting up a team

For a big multidisciplinary research project, it may be necessary to identify expertise and experience and set up a team on that basis. A team would be made up of people with expertise in various fields and include subject experts, statisticians, research assistants, etc. It is important that each person is able to add value to the project.

Selecting the research leader or principal investigator (PI)

In a multidisciplinary research project, the team has to have a project leader. The team leader, or principal investigator, is ultimately responsible for driving the project, in particular and for the quality of the research, all ethical provisions and the financial management. This includes also liaising with funders and other stakeholders, as well as coordinating and motivating the team to accomplish the project's milestones on stipulated deadlines. Clearly, the PI needs experience, knowledge, people skills, and an ability to work, and make others work, under pressure.

CHAPTER 17 Research management

Allocating roles and responsibilities

Project milestones are inextricably intertwined with each team member's roles and responsibilities, sometimes called deliverables. The process of allocating roles and responsibilities should be based on the expertise of each team member. This promotes task ownership and accountability, while encouraging a sense of group solidarity and spirit, with each member of the team feeling a sense of ownership towards the project.

Setting up a communication nerve centre

Any project requires clear communication between participants. In the case of a large multidisciplinary project, it may be essential to set up an office to coordinate and support the project. The purpose of this office is to provide both material and non-material support to the team. Team members may be scattered around a specific geographic area in the field and may need to get in touch with one another for any number of reasons, and may often need someone to untie knots in the project. The communication centre needs to be able to respond to the project's operational challenges promptly and effectively if the deadlines are to be met.

Setting up time frames

Research projects, like any other projects, are time-bound. They should have well-defined starting and end points. The time frames for contracted or funded research are normally stipulated by the commissioning organisation, but may be adjusted by the researcher as required. This is part of the importance of thorough planning: to have solid arguments for setting suitable time frames. In the academic world, for example, anyone enrolled for a Masters degree by research needs to set aside about 24 months to complete the project, whereas a PhD might be completed in anything from three to six years.

Setting the project milestones

A leader may involve the team in setting up the project's milestones that are time-bound. Such milestones are central to project planning and management.

Risk assessment plans

The team needs to embark on a serious risk assessment exercise that involves anticipating hurdles and project bottlenecks, and developing contingency plans to deal with them. For instance, research conducted in a politically unstable country must take into consideration constraints and delays that may arise from that situation. An exploratory study might be affected by a lack of preliminary information on the set-up. A qualitative study of some minority group, such as women who have aborted illegally,

381

might be strongly handicapped in the search for participants. Risk assessment plans are vital to every project regardless of its magnitude.

Financial resources

These are the lifeline for any research project, and investigators need to be competent in financial management if the project is to be successfully completed. Funding organisations always demand a budget as part of any proposal. Equally, individual researchers would be well advised to develop a budget for projects of their own. Budget items are likely to include:

- *Salaries:* The time of researchers, research assistants and support staff needs to be allowed for. When staff is already employed these funds might go directly to their institution. However, contract researchers make their living by selling their time and expertise. Only students conducting research for their own academic development are not compensated for their time and skills.
- *Library expenses:* Literature search and study entails the use of facilities such as access to electronic journals, interlibrary loans, as well as photocopies of articles in journals.
- *Computer consumables:* The research team may need to budget for computers with appropriate software, as well as printers and related consumables.
- *Stationery:* Research can consume a great deal of stationary and it is best to be well stocked.
- *Communication:* Mobile phones are the most popular and effective means of communication over much of the African continent. Large research projects depend on good communication, and money must be set aside for telephonic and internet-based communications.
- *Travel and accommodation:* When data collection takes place at a distance from the research office, researchers and possibly research participants will need to travel and perhaps be accommodated, which often involves significant expenses. Costs incurred in travelling to conferences and meetings to disseminate the research findings should also be included in the budget.
- *Data collection equipment:* This category might include digital recorders, tape recorders, specialist measuring equipment, and so on.
- *Training:* Training of research assistants may include familiarising them with research tools such as data collection instruments and the concepts behind them. It may also include training in data capturing, transcription and coding of interviews.

CHAPTER 17 Research management

Administrative processes

At the proposal writing stage, the researcher may need to make contact with authorities in charge of institutions, organisations and state departments. The aim of this contact is not only to get permission to access participants, but also to receive clearance from the ethics committee of that institution. Making this early contact serves to explore whether such a project might be supported or not, and whether permission will be granted timeously. A personal contact initiated by the project leader should be followed up by an official letter from the researcher and, in case of a supervised project such as those undertaken by master's and doctoral students, by the supervisor as well. This process may take longer than the researcher anticipated.

Getting a proposal approved

Planning invariably ends up in the development of a research proposal. Different institutions and funding organisations have different formats for developing research proposals, but producing a complete and systematic proposal is greatly simplified if a detailed planning and preliminary management of the research has been done. All the elements required for the specific funding proposal are then ready to be condensed and presented in the format required.

Writing a proposal is one thing, getting it approved is something else. Different organisations and universities handle this issue in different ways. In some universities, the process of proposal approval happens entirely within a particular department or school. In other instances, proposals go through a maze of bureaucracy that may sap the energy of the student. Researchers must set time aside for this process.

Conclusion: Highest quality research

The most fundamental of all the ethical guidelines to which the social scientist must attend is that of producing research of the highest quality. When social research is conducted without a proper understanding of the underlying principles of scientific enquiry, the results may be misleading and damaging to the very society it is intended to benefit. All social scientists have a responsibility to apply the methods of social science correctly and without compromise, so that society can be assured of the validity of any findings that might emerge (refer to Chapter 13). Whenever biased research is conducted and published, the credibility of all social researchers is damaged.

Highest quality research depends upon several factors. Firstly, social scientists must ensure that they do their job to the best of their ability at all times. Secondly, they must be adequately trained so that they have the expertise to do their jobs properly. Finally, research must be made available for peer review, most commonly through publication (see Chapter 16). This requires full reporting of methods (including mistakes and biases when they occur) so that each study can be realistically reviewed by other social scientists.

Only by the rigorous application of these principles can researchers ensure that the reputation and value of social research continues to grow in the developing world, and that the potential contribution to society that researchers have to make is acknowledged.

Key points

1. Conducting research is always subject to various pressures by society, as well as research and funding institutions.
2. Planning and managing a research project entails many steps, including methodology, implementation and finance.
3. Submitting a proposal to a client, a funding agency or an academic institution requires thorough planning of the research and how it will be managed in advance.
4. The moral responsibility for high quality research rests with the researcher!

Checklist

Keywords:

Check whether the meaning of these concepts introduced in this chapter is clear to you.

research proposal; multidisciplinary research; research funding institutions; peer review; research project management; project milestones; risk assessment plans; contingency plans; budgeting.

Your research:
Assess your readiness to start your research project by checking all the steps mentioned under 'Planning and managing a research project'.

Exercises

1. Make a list of the major organisations that produce research in your country.
2. The municipality in your city awarded you a tender to investigate the effect of marijuana smoking on road fatalities. How would you go about planning this project as an individual?
3. The Department of Roads and Transport in your country wants to introduce a ban on smoking while driving. This is a national project, and you have been funded to produce evidence that shows the relationship between smoking while driving and accidents. How would you go about doing this?

Additional resources

Litzman, P R & Krajewski, L J. 2003. *Foundations of operations management.* New Jersey: Prentice Hall.

Bibliography

Action research, a peer reviewed journal available at http://arj.sagepub.com/

American Psychological Association. 1982. *Ethical principles in the conduct of research with human participants*. Washington, DC: American Psychological Association.

Artz, L & Themba Lesizwe 2005. *Ethics relating to social science research with victims of violence and other vulnerable groups*. South Africa: Themba Lesizwe.

Babbie, E R & Rubin, A. 2010. *Research methods in social work*, 7th ed. Belmont, CA: Brooks/Cole.

Babbie, E R. 2004. *The practice of Social Research*, 10th ed. Belmont, CA: Wadsworth.

Babbie, E R. 2010. *The basics of social research*, 5th ed. Belmont, CA: Wadsworth.

Babbie, E R. 2010. *The practice of social research*, 12th ed. Belmont, CA: Thomson Wadsworth.

Babbie, E R. 2012. *The practice of social research*, 13th ed. Belmont, CA: Wadsworth.

Barlow, D, Hayes, S & Nelson, R. 1984. *The scientist practitioner: Research and accountability in clinical and educational settings*. New York: Pergamon.

Barnett, V. 1991. *Sample survey: Principles and methods*. London: Edward Arnold.

Beach, D. 1996. *The responsible conduct of research*. New York: VCH.

Blalock, H M & Blalock A B. (eds) 1986. *Methodology in social research*. New York: McGraw-Hill.

Bless, C & Kathuria, R. 1993. Fundamentals of Social Statistics: An African Perspective. Cape Town: Juta & Co.

Brown, L D & Tandon, R. 1983. 'Ideology and political economy in enquiry: Action research and participatory research'. *Journal of Applied Behavioural Science*, 19(3), 177–194.

Bryman, A. 2012. *Social research methods*, 4th ed. Oxford: Oxford University Press.

Bunge, M. 2003. 'The pseudoscience con-cept, dispensable in professional practice, is required to evaluate research projects: A reply to Richard McNally'. *The Scientific Review of Mental Health Practice*, 2, 111–114.

Campbell, D T & Stanley, J C. 1963. *Exper-imental and quasi-experimental designs for research*. Chicago, IL: Rand-McNally.

Campbell, D T. 1988. *Methodology and epistemology for social science: Selected papers*. Chicago: University of Chicago Press.

Carmines, E G & Zeller, R A. 1979. *Relia-bility and validity assessment*. Beverly Hills, CA: Sage.

Casley, D. & Lury, D. 1981. *Data Collection in Developing Countries*. Oxford: Claren-don Press/Oxford University Press.

Checking for plagiarism: https://www.writecheck.com

Collins, K. 1999. *Participatory research: A primer*. Cape Town: Prentice Hall.

Cook, T D & Campbell, D T. 1979. *Quasi-experimentation: Design and analysis issues for field settings*. Chicago: Rand McNally.

Creswell, J W & Plano-Clark, V L. 2007. *Designing and conducting mixed methods research*. Thousand Oaks, CA: Sage.

Dawson, C. n.d. *How to construct questionnaires*, downloaded from www.howto.co.uk/business/research-methods/how_to_construct_questionnaires/Accessed on 30 November 2012.

De Vos, A S, Strydom, H, Fouche, C B & Delport, L S L. 2007. Research

Denzin, N K & Lincoln, Y S. (eds) 2011. *The Sage handbook of qualitative research*, 4th ed. Thousand Oaks, CA: Sage.

Evans-Pritchard, E E. 1962. Social Anthropology and other essays. New York: The Free Press.

Ferrinho et al. *Human resources for health* 2011, http://www.human-resources-health.com/content/9/1/30

Fielding, N, Lee, R M & Blank, D. (eds) 2008. *The Sage handbook of online research methods*. Los Angeles, CA: Sage.

Frank, A G. 1992. World system in crisis, in Contending Approaches to World Analysis by W R. Thomson (ed.) Beverly Hills: Sage.

Freire, Paulo. 1970. *Pedagogy of the oppressed*. Boulder: CO, Paradigm.

Gay, L R. 1981. *Educational research: Com-petencies for analysis and application*. New York: Merrill.

Golafshani, N. 2003. 'Understanding Reliability and Validity in Qualitative Research', *The Qualitative report*, 4, 597–607.

Goode-Halt, D. 1984. *Methods in social research*. New York: McGraw-Hill.

Greenwood, D J, Whyte, W R & Harkavy, I. 1993. 'Participatory action research as a process and as a goal'. *Human Relations*, 46, 175–192.

Gudda, P. 2011. *A guide to project monitoring and evaluation*. Bloomington, IL: AuthorHouse.

Haney, C, Banks, W C, & Zimbardo, P G. 1973. Interpersonal dynamics in a simulated prison. *International Journal of Criminology and Penology*. 1, 69–97.

Haslam, S A & McGarty, C. 1998. *Doing psychology: An introduction to research methodology and statistics*. London: Sage.

How2stats blogspot at http://how2stats.blogspot.com/p/home.html

Institute of Education. n.d. *The Research Ethics Guidebook: A resource for social scientists*. University of London, www.ethicsguidebook.ac.uk

International Development Evaluation Association (IDEAS) – www.ideas-int.org

Kaplan, R. 2001. The Aversion Project – Psychiatric Abuses in the South African Defense Force during the Apartheid Era, *South African Medical Journal*, 91(3), 16–17.

Koch, T & Kralik, D. 2006. *Participatory action research in health care*. Oxford: Blackwell.

Kpedekpo, G & Arya, P. 1981. *Social and economic statistics for Africa*. London: George Allen & Unwin.

Krueger, R A. n.d. Focus group onterviewing, downloaded from www.tc.umn.edu/~krueger/focus.html. Accessed on 30 November 2012.

Kuzek, J Z & Rist, R C. 2004. *Ten steps to a results-based monitoring and evaluation system: A handbook for development practitioners*. Washington, DC: The World Bank.

Lang, G & Heiss, G D. 1994. *A practical guide to research methods*, 5th ed. Lanham, MA: University Press of America.

Lazarus, S. 1985. 'Action research in an edu-cational setting'. *South African Journal of Psychology*, 15, 112–118.

Bibliography

Leedy, P D & Ormrod, J E. 2012. *Practical research planning and design*, 10th ed. Boston, Mass: Addison Wesley.

Leedy, P D. 1989. *Practical research: Plan-ning and design*, 4th ed. New York, NY: Macmillan.

Lincoln, Y S & Guba, E G. 1985. *Natural-istic inquiry*. Beverly Hills, CA: Sage.

Lindlof, T R & Taylor, B C. 2011. *Qualitative communication research methods*, 3rd ed. Thousand Oaks, CA: Sage.

Little J H & Pillai, V. 2008. *Systematic reviews and meta-analysis. Pocket guides to social work research methods*. Oxford: Oxford University Press.

Litzman, P R & Krajewski, L J. 2003. *Foundations of operations management*. New Jersey: Prentice Hall.

Maslow, A H. 1954. *Motivation and personality*. New York: Harper.

Milgram, S. 1974. *Obedience to Authority*. New York: Harper & Row.

Miller, D C. 1991. *Handbook of research design and social measurement*. 5th ed. Newbury Park, CA: Sage.

Mintz, A. 1951. 'Non-adaptive group behaviour'. *Journal of Abnormal and Social Psychology*, 46, 150–159.

Neuman, W L. 2009. *Social research methods: Qualitative and quantitative methods*, 7th ed. Boston, MA: Allyn & Bacon.

O'Donohue, W S, Curtis, D & Fisher, J E. 1985. 'Use of research in the practice of community mental health: A case study'. *Professional psychology: Research and practice*, 16, 710–718.

Olsen, W K. 2004. Triangulation in Social Research: Quantitative and Qualitative Methods Can Really Be Mixed, in M. Holborn and Haralambos (Eds) *Developments in Sociology*, London: Causeway Press.

Online writing guide: http://owl.english.purdue.edu/owl/

Online writing support: http://www.eseo.cl/eng

Onu, J I. 2002. *Report of Social Capital Household Survey Pilot in Adamawa State, Nigeria*, downloaded from http://siteresources.worldbank.org/INTSOCIALCAPITAL/Resources/Social-Capital-Integrated-Questionnaire/AdamawaStatePilotRptShortVersionAug02.pdf. Accessed on 1 December 2012

Patton, M Q. 2001. *Qualitative Research and Evaluation Methods*. Thousand Oaks, CA: Sage.

Peil, M. 1982. *Social science research meth-ods: An African handbook*. London: Hodder & Stoughton.

Phillips, R & Pittman, R H. (eds) 2009. *An introduction to community development*. New York: Routledge.

Posavac, E J & Carey, R G. 1989. *Program evaluation: Methods and case studies*. 3rd ed. Englewood Cliffs, NJ: Pren-tice Hall.

Prewitt, K. 1980. *Introducing research meth-odology: East African application*. Nairobi: Institute for Development Studies.

Qualitative Health Research: http://qhr.sagepub.com/

Qualitative Inquiry: http://qix.sagepub.com/

Reason, P & Blackbury, H. 2008 (eds). *The Sage handbook of action research: Participative inquiry and practice*, 2nd ed. Los Angeles, CA: Sage.

Reverby, S M. 2009. *Examining Tuskegee: The Infamous Syphilis Study and its Legacy*. Chapel Hill, NC: University of North Carolina Press.

Richter, L, Norris, S, Pettifor, J, Yach, D & Cameron, N. 2007. 'Cohort profile: Mandela's children: The 1990 Birth to Twenty Study in South Africa'. *International Journal of Epidemiology*, 36(3), 504–511.

Royse, D. 2011. *Research methods in social work*. 3rd ed. Belmont, CA: Brooks/Cole.

Scheuren, F. 2004. *What is a survey?*, downloaded from www.whatisasurvey.info/downloads/pamphlet-current.pdf. Accessed on 30 November 2012.

Sheafor, B W & Horejsi, C R. 2011. *Techniques and guidelines for social work practice*, 9th ed. London: Allyn & Bacon.

Sideris, T. 2003. War, gender and culture: Mozambican women refugess. *Social Science and Medicine*, 56 (4), 713–724.

Social Research Association. 2003. *Ethical Guidelines*.

Solso, R L & Johnson, H H. 1994. *Experi-mental psychology: A case approach*. 5th ed. New York: HarperCollins.

South African Monitoring and Evaluation Association (SAMEA) – www.samea.org.za

Strobel, N. 2010. *Astronomy Notes*, Columbus, OH: McGraw-Hill. Available at www.astronomynotes.com/scimethd/56.htm.Accessed 22 November 2012.

Susskind, E C & Klein, D C. (eds) 1985. *Community research: Methods, paradigms, and application*. New York: Praeger.

Tashakkori, A & Teddlie, C. (eds) 2010. *Handbook of mixed methods in social and behavioral research*. 2nd ed. Thousand Oaks, CA: Sage.

Taylor, S T & Bogdan, R. 1984. *Introduc-tion to qualitative research methods: The search for meanings*. 2nd ed. New York: Wiley.

Tolan, P, Keys, C, Chertok, F & Jason, L. (eds) 1990. *Researching community psychology: Issues of theory and methods*. Washington, DC: American Psychological Association.

Unicef, ChildInfo. *Monitoring the situation of women and children*, downloaded from www.childinfo.org.

Van der Stoep, S W & Johnston, D D. 2009. *Research methods for everyday life: Blending qualitative and quantitative approaches*. San Francisco, CA: Jossey-Bass.

Van Zyl, M, de Gruchy, J, Lapinsky, S, Lewin, S and Reid, G. 1999. *The Aversion Project: Human rights abuses of gays and lesbians in the SADF by health workers during the Apartheid Era*, unpublished research report. Cape Town: Simply Said and Done.

Wilcox, R R. 2011. *Modern statistics for the social and behavioral sciences: a practical introduction*. Boca Raton, FL: Taylor and Francis.

Winter, R. 1987. *Action-research and the nature of social inquiry: Professional innovation and educational work*. Aldershot: Avebury.

World Bank. *Instruments of the Social Capital Assessment Tool*, downloaded from http://siteresources.worldbank.org/INTSOCIALCAPITAL/Resources/Social-Capital-Assessment-Tool--SOCAT-/annex1.pdf . Accessed on 1 December 2012.

Glossary

The aim of this glossary is to provide the reader with a general understanding of a concept or term used in this textbook, rather than to present a precise, sophisticated definition. In order to grasp a concept in its complexity, the reader should refer to the chapter in which this concept is studied.

Abstract: A brief summary of a study, including research questions, methodology, results and conclusions, found at the beginning of journal articles and other kinds of reports.

Action research: A form of participatory research which combines social action and research to resolve a specific problem facing a community and to increase human understanding of similar problems and their solutions.

Anonymity: The assurance that the identity of research participants remains unknown.

Antecedent variable: That variable which influences the independent variable and in that way indirectly affects the relationship between the independent and dependent variable.

Applied social research: Social research that has the primary aim of finding solutions to specific concerns or problems facing particular groups of people, by applying models or theories developed through basic social research.

Autonomy: Participants in a research study should decide to participate in the study of their own accord. Under no circumstances should they be coerced or pressured to participate. Thus, their decisions should be made autonomously.

Basic social research: Social research which has the primary aim of contributing to the development of human knowledge and understanding of a specific aspect of social reality.

Beneficence: The principle that social research should contribute to the improvement of people's lives.

Causal relationship: A relationship where change in one variable (the dependent variable) is shown to result from change in another (the independent variable), and where the direction of such change can be predicted.

Central tendency of a set of data: Some value that provides a general description of the bulk of the data, an idea of the general location of all the scores. The main measures of central tendency are the mode, the median and the mean.

Coding: The process whereby a qualitative researcher sorts fragments of text or transcribed speech into various thematic categories.

389

Cohort: A group of participants who take part in a particular piece of research at the same time.

Cohort study: A study that compares multiple cohorts.

Conceptual definition: The definition of a concept in terms of other concepts.

Constant: An empirical property that does not vary.

Content analysis: An approach to qualitative analysis which focuses on the themes or topics addressed by a respondent.

Control group: The group that is not exposed to the event or treatment in an experimental design, and is compared with the experimental group. Note that, because the control and experimental groups result from the use of randomisation or matching, they are equivalent before the event or treatment.

Control variable: That variable which is controlled (eliminated or neutralised) by the researcher, to avoid it influencing the relationship between the independent and dependent variables.

Conventional wisdom: A term used to describe certain ideas or explanations that are generally accepted as true by members of a community. There are many cases of conventional wisdom that have been proved wrong by scientific research.

Correlational relationship: The relationship between two variables where change in one variable is accompanied by predictable change in another variable. The variables are said to 'covary'. Correlational relationships are not necessarily causal relationships.

Correlational research: Social research with the primary aim of establishing correlational relationships between variables.

Cross-sectional design: A research design where all data is collected at a single point in time. Since this term does not relate to a specific design, it is also referred to as a 'cross-sectional study'.

Deception: Withholding of information from research participants in such a way that they remain unaware of the true objectives of the research.

Dependent variable: The variable that is observed and measured to determine the effect on it of the independent variable. It is that factor which varies as the researcher manipulates the independent variable.

Descriptive research: Social research with the primary aim of describing (rather than explaining) a particular phenomenon.

Descriptive statistics: Procedures for summarising information about a set of data or measurements.

Diagnostic evaluation: Research designed to increase the effectiveness of interventions by identifying neglected areas of need, target groups and unresolved problem areas.

Directional hypothesis: A hypothesis which specifies in what way (direction) the dependent variable will vary in response to a determined variation of the independent variable.

Glossary

Discontinuance: The decision of a research participant to withdraw from a study.

Discourse analysis: An approach to qualitative analysis that emphasises the choice of words and style that respondents use in expressing themselves.

Dummy table: A table of results constructed before the data are collected to assist the researcher in designing appropriate measuring instruments for the research.

Epidemiology: The study of how diseases occur and spread in society. Related to the word 'epidemic', the field of epidemiology is useful in planning and evaluating strategies to prevent diseases and in managing patients in whom diseases have developed.

Epistemology: The study of the different ways in which human beings develop and validate knowledge about themselves and the world.

Ethnography: A set of research methods and an approach to qualitative analysis for the investigation of respondents' cultural lives.

Evaluation research: Social research designed to investigate whether a particular project or intervention has met its stated objectives and how the effectiveness of that project might be improved.

Experimental design: The most rigorous type of research design which depends upon randomisation or matching for the construction of equivalent groups.

Experimental group: The group that is exposed to the event or treatment in an experimental design, and is compared with the control group.

Explanatory research: Social research with the primary aim of establishing causal relationships between variables.

Exploratory research: Social research that explores a certain phenomenon with the primary aim of formulating more specific research questions or hypotheses relating to that phenomenon.

External validity: A measure of the extent to which research findings can be generalised to a broader population.

Extraneous variable: That variable which, if not controlled, will obscure (confound) the observed relationship between the independent and dependent variables. It is thus sometimes called a 'spurious' or 'confounding' variable.

Feasibility study: A study designed to determine whether a particular strategy or intervention is likely to reach its stated objectives.

Field experiment: An experiment conducted in everyday social reality where the artificiality of a constructed setting is reduced at the expense of a loss of control of extraneous variables.

Focus group: A semi-structured group interview conducted by a skilled facilitator.

Formative evaluation: Research designed to find solutions to any problems that emerge during a particular intervention.

Frequency distribution: The different values or scores and the number of times each occurs in a set of data or sample.

391

Grounded theory: An approach to data analysis which builds theory from empirical data, avoiding preconceived theories or assumptions.

Hypothesis: A tentative, concrete and testable explanation or solution to a research question.

Immersion: The process whereby a qualitative researcher repeatedly reads through the data to deepen his or her awareness of the content and underlying themes contained therein.

Independent variable: That variable which is measured, manipulated or selected by the researcher to determine its relationship to an observed phenomenon, the dependent variable.

Indicators: Variables that are measured regularly in order to monitor the progress and impact of a project or intervention.

Inference: The process of generalising findings from a sample to the broader population from which the sample was drawn.

Inferential statistics: Mathematical techniques, or statistical tests, which allow the researcher to make statements about populations based on data derived from samples.

Informed consent: The ethical principle that research participants should be told enough about a piece of research to be able to make a decision about whether to participate in it.

Inter-coder reliability: A measure of the similarity in the coding performed by two or more coders.

Internal validity: The extent to which a particular research design excludes all alternate explanations for the research findings, or, in simple terms, whether the independent variable is really the cause of the variation of the dependent variable.

Interval scale: A scale of measurement characterised by regular units of measurement but no absolute zero, on the basis of which units are classified by quantitative value.

Intervening variable: That variable which is determined by the independent variable but influences the dependent variable, and is often difficult to manipulate or measure.

Interview: A data collection technique based on a series of questions relating to the research topic to be answered by research participants.

Laboratory experiment: An experiment conducted under artificial conditions which allows the researcher to control many extraneous variables, but which may not be typical of everyday social reality.

Literature review: An integrated summary of all available literature relevant to a particular research question.

Longitudinal design: Research designs where the data collection is spaced over a period of time. Since this term does not relate to a specific design, it is also referred to as a 'longitudinal study'.

Matching: The process of creating equivalent groups by balancing the effects of variables other than the independent and dependent ones. This is often achieved by identifying matched pairs of units and distributing them between the control and experimental groups. Note that groups constructed in this way are called 'dependent groups'.

Measures of variability: A type of statistics that summarises a distribution by indicating how variable or spread the data are. The measures of variability presented here are the range, standard deviation and variance (also called measures of dispersion).

Moderator variable: That variable which is measured or manipulated by the researcher to determine the manner in which it affects the relationship between the independent and dependent variable.

Multidisciplinary research: Complex research involving a team of researchers from different disciplines that cooperate on a single research question.

Narrative analysis: An approach to qualitative analysis that emphasises the stories that respondents construct about themselves and their world.

Nominal scale: A scale of measurement where units are classified in terms of two or more qualitatively different categories.

Non-directional hypothesis: A hypothesis which states that the dependent variable will change in relation to changes in the independent variable. However, the way (direction) of this variation is not specified.

Non-maleficence: The principle of doing no harm to research participants.

Non-probability sampling: Sampling techniques where the probability of each element of the population being included in the sample is not known.

Observation: A data-collection technique based on the direct observation of participants' behaviour.

Operational definition: The definition of a concept in terms of the way that concept is to be measured or observed. This form of definition is based on the observable characteristics of a concept and indicates what to do or what to observe in order to identify those characteristics.

Ordinal scale: A scale of measurement where units are classified in terms of rank-ordered categories.

Parsimony of ideas: If a set of observations may be accounted for by a complex theory and by a simple theory, then the simple theory is scientifically more acceptable. Scientists should thus not make any more assumptions than are absolutely necessary when making a scientific claim.

Participatory research: Research based on the principle of an ideal complementary and equal relationship between researchers and the community.

Peer review: A process by which other scientists anonymously check that research proposals and articles intended for scientific publication meet the minimum standards of scientific enquiry.

Phenomenological analysis: An approach to qualitative analysis which emphasises the personal, lived experience of the respondent.

Pilot project: A community intervention that is limited in scale and duration, and that is used to evaluate effectiveness before a broader intervention is implemented.

Pilot study: A small study conducted prior to a larger piece of research to determine whether the methodology, sampling, instruments and analysis are adequate and appropriate.

Population: The complete set of events, people or things to which the research findings are to be applied.

Population parameter: A numerical value that summarises some characteristic of the population.

Pre-experimental designs: A set of research designs characterised by very few requirements, but which do not approach the rigour of experimental and quasi-experimental designs.

Primary data: Data collected with the primary aim of answering the research question posed by the researcher.

Probabilistic explanations: Explanations of social reality expressed as statements of likelihood (probability), rather than certainty.

Probability (random) sampling: Sampling techniques where the probability of each element of the population being included in the sample can be determined.

Qualitative research: Research conducted using a range of methods which use qualifying words and descriptions to record and investigate aspects of social reality.

Quantitative research: Research conducted using a range of methods which use measurement to record and investigate aspects of social reality.

Quasi-experimental designs: A set of designs of similar rigour to experimental designs but with less rigid requirements which are more easily met by the social researcher.

Questionnaire: An instrument of data collection consisting of a standardised series of questions relating to the research topic to be answered in writing by participants.

Randomisation: The process of creating equivalent groups by ensuring that each unit of the study is distributed by chance (randomly) to a certain group (experimental or control).

Random (probability) sampling: Sampling techniques where the probability of each element of the population being included in the sample can be determined.

Ratio scale: A scale of measurement characterised by regular units of measurement and an absolute zero, beyond which the scale is meaningless.

Reductionism: The research method of considering only the essential necessary properties, variables or aspects of a problem.

Reliability: An estimate of the accuracy and internal consistency of a measurement instrument.

Glossary

Research design: The set of procedures that guide the researcher in the process of verifying a particular hypothesis and excluding all other possible hypotheses or explanations. It allows the researcher to draw conclusions about the relationship between variables.

Sample: The group of elements drawn from the population that is considered to be representative of the population, and which is studied in order to acquire some knowledge about the entire population.

Sampling: The technique by which a sample is drawn from the population.

Sampling error: Margin of error in the way the sample represents the population due to inadequate or inappropriate sampling.

Scales of measurement: Different systems used to measure or classify units, enabling comparison.

Secondary data: Data used in a specific study, although collected by a different researcher for the purpose of addressing a different research problem.

Statistic: A numerical value that summarises some characteristic of the sample.

Summative evaluation: Research designed to determine the extent to which a particular intervention has met its stated objectives.

Theory of change: A description of all the steps that must be completed in order to achieve a certain project goal or outcome.

Unit of analysis: The person, object or event from which data is collected and about which conclusions may be drawn.

Validity: The degree to which a study actually measures what it purports to measure.

Variable: An empirical property that is observed to change by taking more than one value or being of more than one kind.

Vulnerable population: Groups of people who are particularly vulnerable to being manipulated by a researcher to the extent that they are disadvantaged by participation in research. Typically they are not able to evaluate the consequences of participation or their social circumstances make it easy for a researcher to abuse power in a research context. Such groups may include children, mentally ill persons and people living in poverty.

Index

Compiled by J de Wet

This is a subject index arranged in word-by-word order, for example, causal is filed before causality. Indexed figures, tables and illustrations are indicated in *Italics, and see* and *see also* references guide the reader to the access terms used. Glossary definitions are indicated in bold font.

A

abstract/s 41, 50, 372, **389**

accountability gap 92, 99

action research 56, 89, 90-91, 92-94, 95, 97-98, 119, 201, **389**

    see also research

    aims 94

    community problems 98

    contract 93, 93

    implementation 95

    planning 94

    social context 98

actions 132

Africa 68, 89, 101, 110

African societies 2, 48

alternative hypothesis 274, 291

    see also hypotheses

analogy 18, 19

analysis of variance *see* ANOVA

anonymity 33, **389**

ANOVA distribution 290-292

antecedent variable *see* variables

applied research 43, 56, 59, **389**

appropriate referral

    for counseling 33

    for social work 33

    for medical treatment 33

articles 21, 41, 50, 51, 364, 365, 366, 369, 380, 382

association 63, 64

assumptions 5, 8, 9, 10, 15, 34, 108, 109, 110, 111, 112, 279, 281, 282, 288, 296, 316, 326, 327, 348, 352, 353, 356, 357

attrition 140, 159

autonomy 30, 37, **389**

availability sampling see sampling

averaging means 257

    see also means

axioms 3

B

background information 41, 53-54, 71, 97

bar charts 251-252, 252

    multiple 252, 252

    simple 251-252

baseline 139

basic research *see* research

behaviour observation *see* reactive effects

beneficence 29, 37, **389**

bias 9, 42, 98, 123, 130, 140, 144, 154-157, 159, 190, 200, 257, 356, 372

    sources 159, 359-360

    solutions 360-361

bibliographies 50

bimodal distribution 255

bivariate analysis 283

budgeting 384

C

case studies 16, 20, 61, 138

Index

causal
  explanation 64
  hypothesis 64-65
  relationships 62, 65-66, **389**
  proof 66
  variable 65
causality 63, 69, 70, 135
causation 7
census data 57
central tendency of a set of data 254, 258, **389**
charts 251
chi-square test 296-297, 298
circular reasoning 70
citation indexes 50
classification errors 357
code of ethics 25
  see also ethics
codes of good practice 28
coding *see* data coding
coefficient
  of determination 309, 312, 321
  of variation 263
cohort
  designs 143
  studies 136, **390**
combined mean 257
combining groups 315
common
  sense statements 6
  wisdom 6
communication 80-81, 99
communities 59
community 90-91, 92-94, 97, 98, 99, 101-103,
  107, 109, 110, 120, 124, 126-127, 128
  development 101-102, 110, 111, 113
  needs assessment 56, 101, 102-104, 106-107,
    110-111
  problems 92, 102, 105, 107, 120, 123
  projects 60, 92, 101-102, 107-110, 113, 128
  see also pilot projects
competence 29
concepts 71, 72, 80, 81-82, 86

conceptual definitions 80-81, 86, 87, **390**
conclusions 18, 21, 22, 36
conditions 132
conferences 364
confidence intervals 275
confidentiality 32
confirmability 220, 236, 237, 238, 242, 243
conjecture 6
constant/s 72, 73, **390**
  errors 357, 372
content analysis 338, 352, 354, **390**
contingency
  plans 110, 121, 381, 384
  table 247-248, 297-299, 300
contract research 43
contrasted group design 142-143, 143, 159
control
  group 147,148, **390**
  variables *see* variables
conventional wisdom 3, **390**
correct reasoning 3
correlation 309-311, 327
  coefficient 314
  multiple 316
  partial 316
  rank-order 316
  perfect positive *310*, 311
correlational
  relationship 137, 362, **390**
  research 56, 57, 60, 61-62, 66-67, 68, 69, 70,
    135, **390**
counterfactual condition 140, 159
co-variance 69, 70
credibility *see* validity
critical mass 47, 55
cross-sectional design 135-136, 159, **390**
cultural relativism 50

D

data 35, 183-184, 196, 218, 255, 342
  analysis 4, 21, 22, 23, 56, 58, 136, 174, 245,
    338, 347

primary 56
secondary 56
availability 61
class-intervals 248-249
coding 342-346, 348-350, 351-352, **389**
  preliminary 342, 343, 348, 354
collection 4, 16, 20, 21, 22, 32, 36, 42, 46,
  47, 54, 58, 61, 63, 69, 71, 94, 120, 130,
  131, 133, 136, 183, 184-185, 190, 201,
  202-212, 216-217, 219, 238
  concepts 183
  feasibility 46
  instruments 21, 47
  laboratory experiment 191
  methods 184, 187-195, 217
  techniques 183, 216-217
  tools 183
distortions 3
falsification 35
graphical representation 249
non-numerical 184
numerical 184
qualitative 184, 338
quality 183, 201, 220, 242, 243
quantitative 16, 22, 184, 339-341
representation 245, 246-247
saturation 180, 239
unstructured 341-342
databases 51
deception 34, 37, **390**
  debriefing 34
  safeguards 34
decision errors 277-278
  type I 278
  type II 278
decision rules 279, 280, 281, 284, 285, 288, 290,
  293, 298, 299, 303, 305, 306
definitions 49-50
degree of association 310
dependability 220, 236, 237, 238, 242, 243, 346
dependant groups 148

descriptive
  research 46, 56, 57, 60, 61, 68, 69, 70, **390**
  statistics 245, 264, 327, **390**
developed world 48
developing countries 27, 46, 51, 97, 99
diagnostic evaluation *see* evaluation
diaries 61
digital divide 68
directional
  hypothesis 277, **390**
  see also hypotheses
  tests 276-277
direct observation 54
  see also observation
disability 31
discontinuance 33
discourse analysis 353, 354
discrimination 30
dissemination of results 21, 22, 369-370, 372
distribution-free tests 282, 295, 296, 327
distributions 264, 301, 327
  see also normal distributions
drawing conclusions 362
dummy table 203, **391**

E
ecological fallacy 134
effectiveness studies 158
efficacy studies 158
email 51, 69
empirical 8, 10
  approach 4
  method 3, 4, 10
  observation 3
  reality 46
  testability 47, 55
empiricism 3, 10
environment 13
epidemiology 1, **391**
epistemological approaches 1
epistemology 1, **391**

equivalent
    form reliability 225-226
    groups 146-147, 154
errors *see* sampling errors
estimation 67, 270, 285, 307, 325, 357
ethical
    codes 31
    concerns 31-32
    evaluation 28
    framework 92
    guidelines 25, 31, 37
    issues 28, 92
    principles 25
    problems 34
    reasons 13
    research 25, 29
    review 31-32, 37
    rules 28
    standards 28-29, 36
ethics 25, 27, 28, 29, 36, 54, 383
    in analysis 35
    committees 36
    guidelines 29
    in reporting 35
ethnography 353, 354, **391**
evaluation *see* project evaluation
evaluation research 119-120, 127-128, 129,
    136, **391**
    aims 113, 124, 127-128
    diagnostic 113, 120-121, 122, 127, 128,
        129, **390**
    formative 113, 120, 122-123, 125, 127, 128,
        129, **391**
    summative 113, 120, 123, 124, 125-126,
        127, 128, 129, **395**
evaluators 127-128
events 4
evidence 6, 18
experimental
    designs 137, 146, 158, **391**
    factorial design 137
    post-test-only control group design 137

pre-test/post-test control group design 137
    group 147, **391**
    method 190, 191, 218
    mortality 156, 159
experiments 13
explanations 4, 5, 10, 12
explanatory research 20, 56, 57, 60, 62, 66, 67,
    68, 69, 70
exploratory research 46, 56, 57, 60, 68, 69, 70,
    83, 130, 131, 133
external validity *see* validity
extraneous variables *see* variables
extrapolation 323-324
extreme
    groups 315
    values 257

F
face validity *see* validity
factorial designs 151-153, 152, 159
facts 3, 12, 13, 18, 19, 23, 48, 183, 218
    classification 15
    conceptualisation 15
    meaningful 14
    selective 14
factual hypotheses 61
    see also hypotheses
falsifiable 9, 65
    observations 10
feasibility 47, 55
    studies 27, 101, 102, 109-110, 111
        assumptions 110
fidelity 31, 37
field
    experiment 191-192, **391**
    of investigation 3
findings *see* dissemination of results
focus group/s 17, 90, 138, 139, 200, 201-202,
    215, 219, **391**
    advantages 200
    bias 201

discussions 17, 21, 23, 201, 215
group selection 215
method 201, 218
structured 200
unstructured 200
formative evaluation *see* evaluation
freedom of choice 30
frequency 297
distribution 245, 249, 255, **391**
expected 297, 298, 299, 301
histograms 250
observed 297, 301
polygons 249, 250-251
Friedman test 308
F-test 291-293, 293
see also variance

G
gatekeepers 35, 103, 111
gender 30
general knowledge 2
generalisability of results 30
generalisation 7, 176
geometry 12
goodness of fit test 301
graphical representation of data *see* data
graphs 250
grounded theory 352, 354, **392**
group dynamics 202
groups of people 135
see also units of analysis

H
Hawthorne effect 147
Hippocratic Oath 28
histogram 250-251, 251
history 140, 144, 154, 159, 224
homosexuality 26
honesty 37
human
behaviour 18
reasoning 10

rights 27, 28, 31, 37
senses 4
hypotheses 6, 18, 19, 20, 21, 61, 71, 79, 82-83,
85, 87, 130, 138, 174, 282, **392**
characteristics 83
disconfirmation 84-85, 87
evaluation 85
formulation 84
directional 84, 87
non-directional 84, 87
replication *see* principle of replication
testable 20, 83
testing 84, 86, 130, 272-273, 278-280, 284,
327
example 280-281
verification 18

I
immersion 342, 348, 349, 354, **392**
impact studies 149
income level 30
independent
samples 283
variable *see* variables
index 186
indexing system 50
indicators 113, 114, 115, 116, 117, 118, 129,
165, **392**
individuals 29
see also units of analysis
inference 18, 162, **392**
inferential statistics 125, 264, 326, **392**
see also statistics
information 13, 27, 41, 50, 54, 61, 82, 94, 101,
110, 161, 190, 196, 264
see also background information
gathering 95, 161, 190
sources 50-51, 82
informed consent 30, 32, 33, 34, 37, 39, 361, **392**
form 32, 39-40
institutions 35-36
instrumentation 140, 155, 159

Index

instruments
    of investigation 6, 83
    of measurement 125, 155
intact group comparison design 141-142, *141*
    see also pre-experimental designs
intellectual processes 3
inter-coder reliability 346, 350, 354, **392**
    see also data coding
internal
    consistency see reliability
    validity see validity
internet 56, 68
    cellular phone technology 68
    growth 69
    online resources 69
    search 243, 371
        engines 51
    use 69
    users 69
interpolation 323
interpretation of results 21, 22, 347
interval
    estimation 270-271, *271*
    limits 249
    midpoint 249
    scales 186, **392**
    see also scales of measurement
intervening variable *see* variables
intervention 4
    research 158
    strategies 102
interviewers 197-198, 199
interviews 21, 23, 61, 90, 125, 127, 193-195, 197-198, 204, **392**
    guide 21
    focused 215
    follow-up 215
    non-scheduled 193, 194, 218
        semistructured 218
        structured 194, 195, 218
        unstructured 195
    open-ended questions 214

questions 205
    scheduled structured 194
    semi-structured 197, 218
    schedules 183
    structured 198, 218, 225
    unstructured 197, 198
intuitive
    method 2, 3
    reasoning 2

J
journal/s 51
    article 8, 21, 22
    peer reviewed 51
justice 30, 37

K
key concepts 46
knowing 4
knowledge 1, 3, 6, 10, 15, 16, 18, 56, 59, 84, 89-90, 99
    advancement 48, 84
    accumulation 6
    acquisition 1, 2, 5, 13, 19, 59
        sources 1
    building 18
    generation 48. 89-90, 113
Kruskal-Wallis H-test 303-305

L
laboratory experiment 191, 392
language 58
laws 4, 5, 8, 12, 13, 15, 23, 31, 40, 299, 319
    natural 4, 5, 10, 12, 15
    social 4, 5, 10, 13, 220
learning process 12
legal rights 31
Likert scale 186, 218
linear
    equation 319, 320
    regression 316, 319
    see also regression

literacy 199

literature 46, 231

    review 20, 21, 41, 48, 49-54, 71, 131, 366, 392

        findings 52

        purpose 49, 52

        research design 52

        sampling 52

        sources 49, 50-51

        techniques 49, 52

    study 54

logical thought 14

longitudinal

    designs 136, 159, **392**

    study 46

M

magnitude of skewness 259

management 12

Mann-Whitney U-test 301-303

mass media 364

matching 147-148, **393**

maturation 140, 144, 159, 224

maturity 159

mean 256-257, 258, 286-287

meaning 80

measurement 183, 220-221, 226, 231, 235, 243, 246

    accuracy 222

    errors 357

    instruments 220, 231, 246

    reliability 220, 221-222, 224-225

    validity 220, 221-222

    variability 222

    variance 222

    verification strategies 220

measures

    of central tendency 254, 259, 260, 266, 268, **389**

    of variability 260, 264, 393

measuring devices 82

mechanics 12

median 255-256, 258

    test 297, 300-301

meta-analysis 41, 52, 53, 55

    see also systematic review

method of authority 1, 2

methodological verification 239, 240

missing data 324

    see also data

mistake 372

mixed methods research 12, 15, 16, 22, 58, 73, 132, 220, 240-242

    evaluation 220, 240-241

mode 254-255, 258

model-building 18, 19

models 18-19

moderator variable see variables

monitoring

    see project monitoring

    and evaluation studies 57

moral

    issues 28

    judgements 45

mortality 140

multidisciplinary research 375, **393**

multivariate analysis 283

mystical

    explanations 2

    method 2

N

narrative analysis 353, 354, **393**

natural

    causes 5, 10

    laws *see* laws

    phenomena 5, 10, 12, 23

    sciences 3, 12

nature 12

needs 12

    assessments 27, 102-105

        surveys 103-104

        see also community needs

negotiation 92

Index

new knowledge 14

  see also knowledge

nominal scale 185, 186, 187, 251, 258, 282, 295, 296, **393**

non-directional hypothesis 87, 88, 276, **393**

non-maleficence 29, 37, **393**

non-parametric tests 281, 282-283, 295-296, 301, 305, 326-327

non-probability sampling *see* sampling

normal distribution 259, 264, 265-266, 301

  subdivisions 265-267, 266

normality 282

normal scores 267-268

novice researchers 46

null hypothesis 85-86, 87, 274, 288, 289, 291, 326

  see also hypotheses

numbers 58

O

object 4, 19

  accurately depicted 4

objectivity 3, 6

observable characteristics 81, 124-125

observations 1, 3, 4, 6, 7, 8, 12, 14, 16, 23, 42, 90, 125, 184, 188-189, 218, **393**

  control 189

  error 189-190

  interpretation 3

  laboratory 188

  limitations 189

  non-scientific 6

  record 189

  simple and participant 183, 188, 218

  unobtrusive 189

one-shot case study 61, 137, 138, 138, 139, 143, 159, 160

  see also pre-experimental design; case studies

open-ended interviews 16

  see also interviews

operational definitions 21, 81-82, 83, 84, 86, 87, **393**

ordinal scales see scales of measurement

orientations 132

organisations 35-36

  see also units of analysis

P

parameters *see also* population; sampling

parametric tests 281-282, 283-289, 326-327

parsimony 5

  of ideas 5, **393**

participants 29, 32, 35, 90

  dignity 31

  basic rights 29, 31

  observations 61

    see also observations

  report back 35

  risk 29, 35

  self-respect 31

  well-being 29

participatory

  action research (PAR) 90, 95 , 99, 113

  research 56, 89, 90, 103-104, 113, **393**

  see also research; action research

Pearson's

  coefficient of skewness 259

  correlation coefficient 311-314, 318

peer review 27, 31, 372, 383, **393**

perceptual 13

period of time see units of analysis

personal

  information 32

  interest 43

phenomena 16, 19

phenomenological analysis 353, 354, 355, **394**

philosophy 3

  of human rights 28

physical harm 29

pictogram 253-254, 253

pie charts 252, 253

pilot
projects 101, 102, 107-108, 109, 111, **394**
study 109, 218, **394**
placebo control group 147
placebos 29
plagiarism 36, 37, 371
plausible rival explanation 63
elimination 64
point estimation 270, 285
population 16, 27, 49, 161, 162, 164, 173, 179, 180, 284, **394**
characteristics 174
diversity 174
elements 164, 165
list 168
parameters 162, 163, 164, 180, 268, 269, 283, 313, **394**
strata 168, 170, 173
subgroups 174
post-test-only
cohort design 137, 159, 160
control group design 150-151, 159
post-test scores 147
practical
concerns 42-43
value 48
predicted value 319
prediction 7, 8, 10, 323
of future events 4
pre-experimental design 137, 138, 158, 159, **394**
intact group comparison design 137
one-shot case study 137
pre-test/post-test design 137
preliminary coding see coding
premises 7
presentations 363
pre-test/post-test cohort design 144, 159
see also cohort designs
pre-test/post-test design 139, 139, 148, 159
see also pre-experimental design
previous research 42
primary

data 184, **394**
see also data
research 57, 70
see also research
principle
of reciprocity 28
of replication 84
privacy 29
probabilistic
explanations 7, 10, 394
reasoning 130
probability 7, 174, 272, 273
(random) sampling 133, **394**
see also sampling
statements 7, 13, 15, 163
value p 276, 279, 280, 284, 285, 288, 290, 293, 298
problem/s 18, 19, 46
conception 41
define relationships 46
enhance understanding
fill research gaps 46
permit generalisation 46
practical 46
relate to wider populations 46
statement 49
timely 46
wider implications 46
project
assumptions 111
broad aims 121
evaluation 113, 114, 119, 121, 128
indicators 113, 114-115, 117, 128, 129
measuring 117
managers 113
monitoring 113, 117, 118-119, 128
framework 118
objectives 118-119, 121
promulgation of results 28
proof 14
psychological
harm 29

research 26

publication 36, 383

    style requirements 372

Q

qualitative

    analysis 338-339, 347-348, 353-354

    data *see* data

    research 4, 12, 15, 16, 17-18, 23, 54, 56, 58,
        60, 72-73, 79, 83, 130, 133, 136-137,
        138, 139, 158, 162, 184, 217, 220, 236,
        242, 338-339, 352, **394**

        confirmability 220, 237-238

        credibility 220, 236-237

        dependability 220, 237

        methods 8, 123

        transferability 220, 237

        triangulation 220

        trustworthiness 220, 236, 238-240

quality

    of life 16

    social research 27

quantitative

    data *see* data

        analysis 16, 245

    research 4, 10, 12, 15, 16, 17-18, 20, 23, 54,
        56, 58, 72-73, 79, 83, 130, 136, 138,
        139, 141, 158, 162, 217, 220, 242, **394**

        measurement validity 220

        methods 8, 245

        reliability 220

quasi-experimental designs 137, 142, 146, 156,
    158, 159, **394**

    contrasted groups design 137, 142-143

    post-test-only cohort design 137, 144

    pre-test/post-test cohort design 137, 144

    time-series design 137, 144-146

questionnaires 8, 16, 58, 69, 90, 125, 183, 193,
    194-195, 217, 218, 246, **394**

    accuracy 213

    completeness 213

    construction 202-204, 205

    design 207

    editing 213-214

    emailed 69, 195, 199, 200

    filter 206

    focus groups 195

    funnel 205-206

    internet-based 200

    mailed 195, 199

    quality 212-213

    response

        rate 199-200

        set 206

    self-administered 194, 196, 199, 204

    structure 205-206

    uniformity 213

questions 18, 199, 200, 205-207, 217, 218

    contingency 211, 218

    direct 209

    factual 208, 218

    fill-in 211, 218

    multiple choice 210

    open-ended 209-210, 211-212, 218

    opinion 208-209, 218

    ranking 210-211, 218

    statements 209

    structured 210, 211

    types 207

quotations 239, 240

R

race 30

random

    assignment 146, 156

    error 372

    sampling (probability) 133, **394**

    selection 146

randomisation 146, 148, 156, **394**

range 261, 314-315

    properties 261-262

rank-order correlation coefficient 316-317

rational

    knowledge 13-14

    thought 3

rationalism principles 10
rationalistic method 3, 4, 10
ratio scale 186, 187, 218, 282, **394**
raw data 246, 249
reactive effects 156, 159
reactivity 225-226
real
    lower limit 249, 250, 261
    upper limit 249, 250, 261
reality 3, 4, 8, 9, 13, 14, 42, 157
reasoning 1, 3. 10
    deductive 1
    probabilistic 1
    process 4
recommendations 21, 22
record method 184, 189, 190, 218
reductionism 1, 9, 135, **394**
reductive 8, 10
regression 309, 318-319, 320-321, 327
    see also linear regression
    analysis 319
    line 309, 310, 311, 312, 314, 319, 321, 324, 335, 336
    towards the mean 140, 141, 144, 154-155, 159
regularities
    of opinions 223
    of perception 223
relationships 3, 14, 67
relevance 27-28, 46
reliability 222, 223, 224, 226-229, 235, 240, 242, **394**
    see also validity
    equivalent form 223, 243
    internal consistency of measures 223, 226, 243
    inter-rater 223, 226
    item analysis 228-229
    split-halves 227-228, 243
    test-retest 222, 223-224, 243
replicable 8, 10, 52, 242
    conclusions 2

replication 87
reporting back 125
reports 8, 363
representation 18, 99
reputability study 123, 129
research 5, 8, 9, 10, 12, 30, 36, 48, 56, 80, 89-90, 95, 95, 101, 220, 242, 383-384
    abuses 28
    aims 4, 56, 61, 63, 69, 76, 81
    applied 56, 69, 70
    assumptions 108
    basic 43, 56, 59, 69, 70, **389**
    benefits 35
    classification 56
        see mixed-methods research; quantitative research; qualitative research
    data *see* data
    descriptive *see* descriptive research
    design 66, 67, 71, 126, 130-131, 136-137, 138, 153-154, 158-159, **395**
    dissemination 356, 363
    errors 356, 357, 358-359
    ethics *see* ethics
    evaluation *see* evaluation research
    exploratory *see* exploratory research
    feedback 36
    financial resources 382, 384
    findings 28, 356, 362
    focus 132, 158
    framework 49, 54
    funding 27, 377-379
        institutions 384
    leader 380
    management 130, 374, 379
    methods 20, 21, 50, 56, 59, 242, 379
    mixed methods *see* mixed methods research
    object 63
    outputs 380
    participants 25, 28
        rights 25
    plan 20
    planning 130, 131, 379

Index

primary *see* primary research

principal investigator 380-381

problem 20, 41, 45, 48, 54, 55, 56, 379
   see also problem/s
   formulation 20, 21
   identification 43

process 9, 12, 20, 23, 25, 48, 54, 90, 361, 372, 374-375

project 41, 130, 136, 217, 374, 379
   management 128, 384
   milestones 381, 384

properties 8, 10

proposal 36, 37, 374, 379, 383, 384, 393

questions 3, 20, 41, 44-45, 54, 64, 67-68, 71-72, 79, 86, 87, 131
   simple 45
   sub-questions 44-45

recommendations 363

reports 21, 71, 364, 365
   structure 365-368

role allocation 381

results 36, 49, 368, 372

risk assessment plans 381, 384

suggestions 363

theoretical value 48, 54

time frames 381

topics 42, 46, 50, 54, 55, 67, 72, 86, 87

type 56, 63, 71

value to science 35

researchers' 25, 84, 85-86, 103-104, 135
   interest 47-48
   motivation 47
   qualifications 29
   role 242

respondent/s 8, 69, 196-197
   validation 239, 240, 253

results 13, 22, 71, 349

reviews see systematic reviews

risks 30, 32, 34, 35, 39
   see also participant risk

S

sample/s 16, 71, 73, 162, 164, 165, 180, 238, 284, 286, 287 **395**
   dependent 173-174, 288-289
   independent 173, 287
   representative 165, 175
   size 161, 174, 179
   statistics 162, 180

sampling 30, 161, 175, 179, 238, **395**
   accidental 172, 176, 180, 181
   advantages 163
   biases 161, 175, 179, 184
   combination 178
   concepts 163
   convenience 180
   costs 163, 170, 171
   critical case 177
   data collection 163, 171
   difficulties 161
   distributions 268-269, 270
   errors 161, 163, 175, 179, 180 **395**
      bias in selection 175, 179, 180
      chance factors 175, 180
      non-response error 175, 179, 180
   extreme case 177, 180
   frame 165, 174, 180
   issues 30
   margin of error 163
   maximum variations 178, 180
   methods 20, 161, 163
   multistage 170, 171, 180, 181
   non-probability 161, 166, 172, 175, 179, 180, 181, **393**
      cluster 167, 173, 180
      convenience 166, 172, 176, 180
      purposive 166, 172, 176, 177, 180
      quota 167, 172-173, 176, 178
   probability 161, 163, 166, 167, 170, 175, 179, 180, 181
      interval 166, 167-168, 180

simple random 166, 167, 168, 169, 170, 180

stratified random 166, 168, 169, 170-171, 180

process 179

qualitative 179

quality 179

quantitative 165, 179

to redundancy 179, 180

representative 162

snowball 176-177, 180

strategy 178

strengths 161

systematic 170

techniques 170-171, 179

theory 162, 163

time 163, 171

types 161

weaknesses 161

well-defined population 163, 164

scales of measurement 183, 185-187, 218, **395**

absolute zero 185

ceiling effects 187

equal intervals 185

floor effects 187

interval 185, 186, 187, 218

magnitude 185

nominal 185, 218

ordinal 185-186, 218, **393**

ratio 185, 186-187, 218

scaling up 109, 110

scatter graphs 309

science 5, 6, 12

content 5

scientific

approach 1

claims 6, 9

enquiry 383

explanations 2

journals 364

knowledge 12

method 1, 3, 4, 5, 6-7, 12, 22

properties 4

observation 6, 10

see also observation

research *see* research

statements 6

theory 9

secondary

data 184, **395**

research 57, 70

see also research

secular trend 322, 323

selection bias 156-157, 159

self-reports 192-193

advantages 193

disadvantages 193

seminars 363

senses 6, 10, 13

sexual reassignment 26

significance levels 275, 276

significant difference 273

skewness of distribution 259

negatively 259

positively 259

SMART indicators 113, 115, 128, 129

see also project indicators

accurate 115, 116

measurable 115

realistic 115, 116

specific 115

time-bound 116

social

affairs 12

artifacts *see* units of analysis

change 90

conditions 43

development 48

interventions 119

issues 13, 27, 190

laws *see* laws

needs 99

network sites 51

Index

phenomena 6, 13, 14, 23

problems 27

processes 13

reality 1, 12, 13, 122, 123, 135, 137, 191

relevance 46, 48

research 1, 7, 27, 30, 69, 101, 113, 119, 125, 132, 191, 384

responsibility 27

sciences 3,12-13, 16, 57, 76, 135, 375

scientists 25, 51, 135, 375

society 1, 5,12,13, 27, 28, 29, 46, 48, 99, 295, 368, 376, 377, 383, 384

spuriousness 64

standard

deviation 261, 262

properties 262

error 269

of the mean 269-270

statistics 58, 326, **395**

abuse of 324-326

descriptive 58

inferential 58

use 324-326

statistical

analysis 16, 20, 327

inference 163

methods 53

tests 283, 308, *308*

power 174

structured questionnaires 16

see also questionnaires

Student t-test 284, 290, 292, 301, 303, 305, 308

study object 4

subjectivity 3

summative evaluation

see evaluation

surveys 16, 61

syphilis 26

systematic 8, 10

observation 6

rational thought 1

reviews 41, 52-53, 55

T

target audience 369, 372

tautology 64

temporal order 63

testable hypotheses *see* hypotheses

test effect 140, 155, 159

testing procedure 130

theology 3

theory 3, 12, 13, 14, 18, 19, 23, 42, 48, 61, 80, 86

of change 101, 107-108, 108, 109, 111, 114, 115, 116, 129, **395**

formulation 14

reformulation 14

time 135

time-series design 144-146, 145, 156, 322-323

topic choice 43, 44, 47-48

tracer studies 136

transcription 354

transferability 157, 229, 236, 237, 238, 242, 243

transmittable 8, 10

triangulation 178, 220, 238-239, 241, 242, 243

trustworthiness see qualitative research

truth 15

typology concept 186, 218

U

unethical studies 26

unit of analysis 131, 133-135, 158, **395**

groups 134

individuals 133

macro level 133

mezzo level 133

micro level 133

organisations 134

period of time 134

selection 133

social artifacts 134

unit of observation 309, 310

univariate analysis 283

Universal Declaration of Human Rights 28

V

validity 6, 130, 140, 158, 159, 229-230, 235, 242, 383, **395**
    concurrent 232
    construct 233, 343
    content 230-231, 243
    convergent 234, 243
    criterion-related 231-232
    external 130, 149, 157, **391**
    face 234
    internal 130, 131, 142, 149, 157, **392**
    predictive 232
value judgements 45
values 27, 376-377
variability 260-261, 264
    measures 260, 264
variables 6, 8, 9, 20, 44, 49, 56, 57, 61, 62, 63, 64-65, 67, 71, 72-73, 74-75, 78, 79-80, 84, 86, 87, 136, 137, 140, 148, 174, **395**
    antecedent 77-78, 86, 87, **389**
    control 76, 83, 86, 87, **390**
    co-vary 62
    dependent (DV) 73-74, 75, 76, 77, 78, 86, 87, 124, 131, 137, 138, 139, 140, 142, 158
    extraneous 78, 86, 87, 97, 131, 277, 359, **391**, 392
    independent (IV) 73-74, 75, 76, 77, 78, 86, 87, 125, 131, 137, 142, 158, 392
    intervening 77-78, 79, 86, 87, **392**
    moderator 75, 76, 78, 79, 80, 83, 86, 87, 126, **393**
    relationships 62, 66, 67, 73-74, 136-137
    secondary independent 75, 76
variance 263, 282, 290
    analysis of 290-292, 294-295
variation/s
    cyclical 323
    group
        between 291, 292
        within 273, 291, 292
    irregular 323

    random 323
    seasonal 323
    total 292
verbatim quotations 239, 240, 353
voluntary participation 30, 32, 37
volunteer effect 30
vulnerable populations 33-34, 37, **395**
    asylum seekers 33
    children 33, 34
    disabled persons 33
    mentally ill 33
    refugees 33, 357
    unemployed 33

W

weighted means 257
Wilcoxon test 305-307
words 80
writing guidelines 369-371, 372

X

Y

Z